CW00923817

THE STORY OF MANIC STREET PREACHERS

NAILED TO HISTORY

THE STORY OF MANIC STREET PREACHERS

NA RY

OMNIBUS PRESS
London / New York / Paris / Sydney / Copenhagen / Berlin / Madrid / Tokyo

Cover designed by Fresh Lemon
Picture research by Jacqui Black

ISBN: 978.184938.175.8
Order No: OP53185

Exclusive Distributors
Music Sales Limited,
14/15 Berners Street,
London, W1T 3LJ.

Music Sales Corporation,
257 Park Avenue South,
New York, NY 10010, USA.

Macmillan Distribution Services,
56 Parkwest Drive
Derrimut, Vic 3030,
Australia.

Every effort has been made to trace the copyright holders of the photographs in this book but one or two were unreachable. We would be grateful if the photographers concerned would contact us.

Typeset by: Phoenix Photosetting, Chatham, Kent
Printed in the EU

A catalogue record for this book is available from the British Library.

Visit Omnibus Press on the web at www.omnibuspress.com

Contents

Chapter One

When We Were Happy

"Children find everything in nothing. Men find nothing in everything."
Giacomo Leopardi, *Zibaldone Scelto*

Being children and knowing no better, they loved it at first. Then, as they grew, they came to understand its limitations and began to resent it. That resentment led to boredom, crushing boredom, and the need to escape its confines became overpowering. And with the advent of adulthood, escape they did. When asked questions by others, they were quick to pick at its every fault, bury it in insults, even disown it. But as time went by, they became more forgiving, and their words became kinder. One of their number, if not quite the prodigal son, soon returned to live beside it and might berate you for speaking badly of it at all.

The 'It' in question is Blackwood, South Wales, and Blackwood gave birth to the Manic Street Preachers as much as their parents ever did.

Perched on a hillside at the edge of the Sirhowy Valley, Blackwood lies just far enough from major roads to enjoy some clean air, though not quite the 'pure stuff' that city types form hiking groups to breathe. A busy road cutting right through the high street makes sure of that. Since 1996, it has been a part of the county borough of Caerphilly, though before Wales began unifying its local authorities, Blackwood fell within the auspices of Islwyn and Gwent County Council.

At its centre lies the Miners' Institute, or 'The 'Stute'. Originally built in 1925 as a snooker hall for local colliery workers, the Institute fell into disrepair during the Eighties, its fate mirroring that of the ailing mining industry. Re-opened as a multi-entertainment centre in 1992, Blackwood Miners' Institute now serves the local community for comedy, music and drama, its name a gentle reminder of harder times. Approximately 14 miles from the city of Newport and a little further to Cardiff, Blackwood – or Coed Duon, as it is known in Welsh – is a small town, the total population tipping 20,000 or so. That number has grown rapidly in recent years with local regeneration projects, new bridges and better link roads to bigger places putting Blackwood up there with other commuter-friendly locations in the area. However, it wasn't always that way.

The records have it that Blackwood started life as a model village founded by local colliery owner John Hodder Moggridge in the early 1800s. An enlightened man for his time, Moggridge was concerned by the poor living conditions available to his mine workers and built a series of small, but surprisingly sturdy cottages with accompanying allotments that he duly leased back to them – at a modest profit, of course. The Blackwood experiment proved such a success that he repeated the formula in nearby Ynysddu and 'The Ranks', some four or so miles away. By the 1830s, the village had extended its boundaries and even found a political voice, with one of its residents, Zephaniah Williams, a major activist within the growing nationwide Chartist movement. Now regarded as the first real example of the working class banding together to effect political reform, Chartists represented fair wages, a better standard of living and a vote for all men over the age of 21, regardless of origin or social position.

To that end, Williams and local Chartist leader John Frost planned what became known as 'The Newport Rising' at Blackwood's Coach & Horses pub in November 1839. The idea was noble enough: lead a march of protesters to the nearby town, bring attention to the cause and simultaneously set free their fellow activists thought to be jailed at Newport's Westgate Hotel. Sadly, their efforts to storm the Westgate armed only with pikes was soundly rebuffed by a small, but well armed military presence. When hostilities ceased, at least 20 protesters lay dead, with a further 200 men – including Frost, Williams and a number of

Blackwood natives – sentenced to be hung, drawn and quartered for high treason.

Relative mercy was shown: the sentence was commuted from death to transportation to Tasmania. If the plan itself failed, it at least showed that the men of Blackwood had some iron in their blood, this fact eventually commemorated by the building of the Chartist Bridge: a futuristic structure unveiled just outside the town in 2005, it links the east and west sides of the Sirhowy Valley, providing quicker routes for business and an end to the traffic tailbacks that marred Blackwood's high street for many a decade. The statue of a Chartist that guards the bridge, pike in hand, body turned towards Newport remains a less practical, but perhaps stronger memento of the town's involvement with that cause.

As the 19th century turned, Blackwood left behind its village origins, and showed the first real signs of the town it would eventually become: a long wide street, with trams moving its citizens back and forth, a parade of shops, a bank and more pubs than one might describe as strictly healthy for its size. In line with the Welsh religious revival of 1905, God also moved into Blackwood, with Methodist, Baptist, Pentecostal and Catholic churches soon arriving to offer alternative routes to salvation. When the Titanic was sinking near Newfoundland in 1912, a local man named Artie Moore was one of the first to hear its cries of distress through the hiss and crackle of his amateur radio set. Sadly, the authorities paid no attention to him at the time. Moore was later given a job with the Marconi Wireless Telegraph Company, whose radio system was installed on the Titanic when Moore tuned in that night. Some seven decades later, Blackwood would become home to some of the very electronics and communications businesses that Marconi paved the way for, though their arrival in the area would be a distinctly mixed blessing.

During World War Two, children from England's South Eastern counties were evacuated to Blackwood's surrounding areas, finding the hills – some peppered with cherry trees – a curious, but safe alternative to the blitz conditions plaguing their parents some 150 miles away. Not that Blackwood and its men didn't play a part in both World Wars, the names of those locals lost in battle now etched upon the town's cenotaph. By the early Seventies, Blackwood was more or less fully formed. Still on the hillside, still equally close to God, alcohol and the mining industry, it remained a place that traffic passed through when journeying to bigger conurbations such as Pontypool, Newbrigde and Ystrad Mynach. Many of its residents would also follow that traffic in search of their weekly wages, or the more earthly delights of Cardiff or Newport: "In the Seventies," said one resident, "Blackwood was a typical Welsh town. Still is, to a point. Good and bad habits, a bit of an in-betweener. Most people saw it from the window of a car."

Of course, the young Nicholas Allen Jones – or Nicky for short – didn't care about any of that. At least, not at first. All he really wanted to do was play. Born on January 20, 1969, Nicky Jones's abiding love – then as now – was sport. Cricket, golf, athletics, boxing, Nicky loved the lot. However, he particularly excelled at soccer, following his team of choice, Tottenham Hotspur, avidly as a child. Inevitably, Jones was keen to transfer the skills he witnessed on *The Big Match* to the pitch, or in Blackwood's case, a large unruly playing field owned by the local Gossard factory. As workers produced corsets and girdles inside, Nicky and his teammates were kicking a ball a hundred or so yards away. The dedication paid off: as a teenager, Jones would captain Wales' schoolboy team, his skills as an attacking midfielder eventually leading to a trial with Tottenham's arch north London rivals, Arsenal. Sadly, genetic predisposition in the form of a weak back curtailed Jones' football aspirations for good. That said, this wasn't yet a factor as he tore around the Gossard field trying to emulate Spurs' Steve Perryman and Glenn Hoddle.

Nicky's love of sport was inherited from his father, Alan, who after a spell in the army and time spent in the local collieries, eventually settled as a builder for hire. Alongside wife Irene, Alan bought a modest home in Woodfieldside, just outside central Blackwood, and set about the business of raising a family. Nicky Jones was not the first boy of the household. That honour fell instead to his brother Patrick, who, born in 1965, was four years Nicky's senior and his unofficial football and cricket coach. A "traditional lower middle class" brood, then, but not one following any of the usual clichés: "It's not a very rock 'n' roll thing to say," Jones later confirmed, "but I had a fantastic childhood. I hate those working class caricatures of chips and beans. It wasn't like that. My mum and dad actively encouraged me in everything I did. My dad was a hard worker with an anarchic streak, which definitely came through. Physically, I was more like my mum... more feminine."

The bond between mother and child was especially strong as Nicky – though naturally sporting – fell prey to a succession of childhood illnesses that often saw him home from school: "I'd spend hours on my mother's bed," he said, "watching her do her hair and all that stuff. I was just fascinated with that. I've always seen my mother as the most gentle, fantastic human being." Though he would later indulge the feminine side of his nature with some style, the young Jones was then content to give his all for silverware – albeit of a rather unique variety: "The major league was (our) Woodfield side against Pontllanfraith," Nicky later told *Q*, "and we used to play for a trophy my dad found in a rubbish tip. It was a Crown Green Bowls cup but we ran down the street with it when we won anyway. One day, Sean brought James to play for Pont."

The boys Jones referred to were Sean Moore and James Dean Bradfield, two local acquaintances living in Pontllanfraith, a mile or so away from Nicky's Woodfieldside home. For James, Nicky Jones was already something of a Blackwood 'face': "I remember seeing Nick first when I was about five years old. He stuck out because he was the tallest in the class." Unlike Jones, who would soon acquire the nickname 'The Wire' due to his impressive height, James Dean Bradfield was not a tall child: "fucking short, actually". Worse still, he was born with a lazy eye, or to give its proper medical term, amblyopia. To correct the condition, Bradfield had to wear large correcting glasses that earned him the unfortunate monikers 'Joe 90' and 'Beaker' from schoolmates. However, despite being named for a bespectacled puppet and Muppet, James was seldom bullied – there was a little too much fire in the eyes behind the lens for that.

Born in Newport, Gwent on February 21, 1969, James was similar in stature to his carpenter father, Monty: "My dad was a hard working, trade union, 15 cups of tea council man," James later told the *BBC*, "a good man and true." As stated, Monty Bradfield and his wife, Sue, who worked in a betting shop, had bought a house in Pontllanfraith, or 'Pont', for short. Moments away from Blackwood town centre, Pont was notable for being home to a number of miners plying their trade in local pits such as Oakdale and Penallta. Their post-work activities either took place at the nearby

Institute or within the walls of The Penllwyn, a large imposing pub at the heart of Pont's housing estate. An only child, Bradfield's unusual forenames were a gift from his father. Quite the fan of thrillers and westerns, Monty had originally wanted to call his son 'Clint Eastwood' up to the day of his christening, but sanity and his wife's objections prevailed. 'Clint' duly became 'James Dean' in honour of Hollywood's original teenage rebel. In light of later efforts, the name remains reasonably apt.

Like Nicky, Bradfield loved football, following the fortunes of Brian Clough's then "Can do no wrong" Nottingham Forest. He was also a keen rugby player with an additional gift for long distance running – one that would see him complete his first marathon by the age of 16: "It was me versus the hills, there was no choice," he later said. Thankfully, James' brief dalliance with the steeplechase was abandoned due to height issues: "Nick and I had this dream of me bringing glamour to the steeplechase... but I was five feet five tall. I was never going to win the steeplechase, was I?" Bespectacled, short but athletic with it, Bradfield had another more sensitive gift: for several years, he was a member of his school choir, "It was all right," his considered, yet curt response when once questioned on the subject.

Bradfield's spell as sole occupant of his bedroom came to an abrupt end in 1978, when his cousin, the Liverpool supporting Sean Moore moved in. Born on July 30, 1968, and a year older than James, Moore's arrival at the Bradfield house was due to his parents' recent divorce. With few alternatives available to her at the time, Sean's mother, Jenny, turned to her sister for help with living arrangements for the young boy. Subsequently, a bunk bed was purchased – Sean taking the lower rung, James clinging defiantly to the top. Over time, this temporary measure became a permanent solution. And though Sean would always remain close to his mother – a regular fixture at the Bradfield home – his father became a ghost, only re-appearing again in later years when his son found success. Learning of his father's re-emergence, Moore took a pool cue to his surroundings with inevitable results: "From the age of 10," he later said, "I became isolated as an individual, entirely self-sufficient. I live from day to day."

That self-sufficiency soon took physical manifestation, giving Moore a detached, almost sullen demeanour. This was certainly a factor at school, when if he felt a teacher's question to be stupid or irrelevant, he simply refused to answer – behaviour that eventually led him to being dropped from the top stream of his class. On the home front, things were also challenging, Sean having to adjust to a new household (replete with outside toilet), and the youthful presence of James Dean Bradfield in the top bunk. As with all such relationships, a period of adjustment was necessary: "It was a pretty normal childhood, really," James later confirmed, "we just used to fight all the time. Sean thought he'd take the role of older brother, and he beat me up a few times. The only thing that sort of hurt me was that he'd ignore me at school. I'd walk up to him and say 'Hello Sean, are we walking home later?', and he'd pretend he didn't know who I was. He just didn't want to be seen with his nerdy, young cousin. But things changed. With the benefit of hindsight, Sean moving into our house was serendipity." Over time, the arrangement began to work, Moore and Bradfield establishing a bond and simpatico more akin to brothers than cousins. Sean even developed an impressive patience with the younger boy, looking simply bemused when James – fresh with ideas of joining the army amid coverage of the Falklands War of 1982 – began a nightly weight training programme in preparation for the call-up.

If Nicky Jones could have picked a second brother for himself, it would surely have been Richard James Edwards, better known as 'Richey'. Another of the Gossard playing field boys, Edwards was a "decent right winger" who lived just up the road from Moore's family, albeit in a "slightly better house" on Church View in Woodfieldside. The property in question had been in the Edwards family for some nine generations, though they would later sell it to move to a modern bungalow near Blackwood town centre. Born on December 22, 1967, Richey was the son of Graham and Sherry Edwards, well known throughout Blackwood as hairdressers who owned the high street salon. Like Nicky's dad, Alan, Graham Edwards was in the armed forces before taking up the barber's trade, serving four years with a parachute regiment in a concerted effort to avoid following his own father's footsteps into the mines. Richey was soon joined by a sister, Rachel, some two years younger, with whom he shared his pale colouring. The siblings would grow especially close, though Rachel would always call her brother by his given name, 'Richard'.

Edwards' playmates had other ideas, and as appeared statutory throughout Blackwood's childhood ranks, Richey was given a nickname – two, in fact: "(I called him) Teddy Edwards," Nicky later remembered, "Because he looked like the TV teddy bear, a cuddly little fellow." Others were less affectionate, christening him "Titch" in honour of his diminutive size. According to his father, Richey was a quiet boy, happy enough walking in the surrounding hills or kicking a football with friends: "He was studious and thoughtful," Graham later said, "not the rebellious type at all." Central to the Edwards' family life was their commitment to the nearby Methodist church, where they attended services on Sunday mornings.

A clear alternative to the distant Protestantism offered by the Church of England, whose message was understandably lost to communities such as Blackwood, the Methodists had gained a strong foothold throughout Wales. Embracing the poor, downtrodden and – bold for the time – criminal classes, Welsh Methodists advocated reason, service and equality, with strict study of the Old and New Testaments fundamental to their faith. There was also a distinct Calvinistic flavour to Welsh Methodism, its notions of predestination and God's sovereignty over man's fate the subject of many a sermon. Richey attended both services and Sunday school, but his later remembrances point toward a young mind wrestling with the blind acceptance of what he heard there: "I never saw the point of organised religion," he said in 1993, "probably because I had to go to church so much when I was younger. I went to a tin-shack chapel when I was seven. There was some fat old cunt on a stage, screaming at you, naming you, humiliating you..." Though he could spout scripture parrot fashion with the best of them by his early teens, Edwards permanently terminated his association with the church at the same time, only returning to the subject of religion on his own terms a decade or so later.

Outside of the "tin shack chapel", the young Richey Edwards appeared otherwise at peace, a child largely unaware of the limitations of his birthplace, its essential smallness or the all-pervading melancholia it would soon activate within him. "As a child, you put your head on the pillow and fall asleep with no worries," he later told *Melody Maker*. "From being a teenager onwards, it's pretty rare that you don't end up staying awake half the night thinking about bullshit." For the moment such thoughts were entirely absent, Richey enjoying time spent with his grandmother while his parents worked nearby: "She was a beautiful person, a very contented person," he later confirmed. "Whenever the news came on, she'd say 'I've seen it all before'. I think a lot of old people are very wise." Even the local education system couldn't derail Edwards' innate sense of happiness, the time he spent with the others at recently opened Pontllanfraith Junior School flying by without major incident: "School's nothing," he once said, "you go there, come back and play football in the fields."

If Jones, Bradfield, Moore and Edwards were not quite the Famous Five – though Richey would soon own his beloved dog, Snoopy – they were each able to report a reasonable start to life. Not perfect by any means, but better than some. Of course, things change: "Maybe that's what fucked us up," Nicky would later say, "not the fact that we had bad childhoods, but that our childhoods were *too good*. That sense of freedom... reading books, watching films... building dams and messing around in dirt. Looking back, things like that seemed so worthwhile." Or maybe they simply came to understand that while Blackwood was heaven for a child, it could be hell for a teenager.

Chapter Two

The Bonds Of Boredom

Being the older two boys, Edwards and Moore were the first to experience the cleansing fires of secondary education, enrolling at Oakdale Comprehensive School in the autumn of 1979. Within a year, they were joined by Jones and Bradfield, and Moore's true work in ignoring his younger cousin at lunchtime began. "Sean was totally scary back then," Edwards remembered. Unknown to him at the time, James had similar feelings towards Richey: "Actually, I was slightly reticent to talk with Richey at first," Bradfield later admitted, "he seemed a bit cooler than the rest." Curiously, despite his rocketing height, nobody was particularly afraid of Nicky Jones: "He was just funny, Nick, quick with his mouth and good at sport. Likeable," a former classmate revealed.

Built on an elevated ridge overlooking Blackwood, and then home to over 500 students, Oakdale Comprehensive School first opened its doors in 1968, its new motto, 'Endeavour', neatly encapsulating what was expected from its pupils. In line with its charter, Oakdale would offer 'Praise', 'Encouragement' and 'Acknowledgement' in return. A mixed school, girls wore green skirts, boys wore black trousers and both wore regulation ties, all available at Lamberts (The Tailors) on Blackwood High Street. Registration was called at 8.30 a.m. and from 15.00 p.m. or so, your time (subject to homework requirements) was your own. A standard Comprehensive set-up then, where with luck or natural brightness, a modicum of real effort might be rewarded with a reasonable start to adult life.

Each of the boys took to their new surroundings in subtly different ways. As stated, Sean could appear intermittently shy or surly with teachers. However, they couldn't deny his gift for music, which first manifested itself through the boy's trumpet playing. In fact Moore was so talented, he was accepted by the South Wales Youth Orchestra as their youngest ever entrant. James, though still a quiet presence was also finding his way, showing an interest in both drama and English while avoiding the twin rigours of physics and chemistry. Nicky, always bright and keen to let everyone know it, divided his time between his love of the sports field and the second floor history department. And Richey, by all accounts a modest, but determined presence, excelled in most subjects, showing a particular flair for literature and politics. George Orwell's prescient novel *1984*, which fused these two subjects with great dystopian style, proved an early favourite with him.

For all intents and purposes, the four appeared at ease with student life, each finding a particular niche within Oakdale's educational structure to call their own. Yet, behind the scenes, they detested every minute of it: "Comprehensive school was the most depressing time for all of us," Richey told *NME* in 1992. "They either write you off or fit you in. If you're not academically gifted, it's 'Fuck you'. If you are, it's 'The banks are coming next week for a talk, and we think you should go.'" Nicky was quick to express the same sentiments: "Terrible, simply terrible..." Sadly, such disappointments were not only reserved for school, but also their surroundings. Now adolescents, the childhood mysteries Blackwood once presented had been quickly superseded by the realities of living stuck halfway up a hillside in an extremely quiet part of a then unfashionable country. In short, they felt trapped, bored and, worse, still far too young to do anything about it. The once model town suffered some serious verbal bombardment as a result: "If you built a museum to represent Blackwood," Edwards famously said years later, "all you could put in it would be shit. Rubble and shit." James Dean Bradfield also captured the frustrations of teenage life in the town: "A long terraced street. Steps down into the valley. A football field. A big disused slag heap with trees growing on it. Everything happened there. Bonfire night, Halloween, people even lost their virginity there. If there was a fight between Pont and Springfield, it happened on that slag heap."

Some 50 years before, a blooming cherry tree orchard marked the beginnings of a large watered area known as Pen-y-fan, where local teens would congregate. However, the orchard was long gone by the time Edwards and the others became familiar with the area: "We used to meet by the opening of Pen-y-fan. It was built when the mines (in that area) closed down, but the waters turned green and slimy. They put 2,000 fish in it, but they died. There's a whirlpool in the middle where about two people die a year." To compound their misery, Blackwood's premium attraction, a cinema built in the Twenties – which used to give free oranges to local children following Saturday matinees – had also closed down when the boys were eight. With only a 24 hour garage, alleged killer whirlpool and a slag heap you had to book in advance for fear of disturbing young lovers, entertainment options were few and far between. "Blackwood," Edwards concluded, "was a museum, a museum living in the fucking past." Sadly, the present was about to come knocking with some force.

In June 1983, Margaret Thatcher began her second term in office as Prime Minister of the United Kingdom, leading a landslide victory that saw the Conservatives come to power with over 42% of the public vote. The Premier's previous four years in power were not without incident though, her philosophy of de-regulation, privatisation of state industry and championing of free market economics failing to stem the mini-recession of 1981-82. However, fiscal recovery, general support for the Falklands War and insipid Labour opposition saw Mrs. Thatcher re-enter 10 Downing Street with a vastly increased approval rating. Her power now fully confirmed, 'The Iron Lady' as she had come to be known, announced in 1984 that 20 coal pits across the UK – including parts of South Wales – were to be closed. A measure taken to save her government the cost of subsidising the coal industry while potentially paving the way for alternative modes of energy, these closures would result in the loss of at least 20,000 jobs. For many, her decision was also a way of directly confronting an industry heavily aligned with the overall Trade Union movement, which she felt had gained a stranglehold over general working practices and were restricting free market economy. Inevitably, the National Union of Mineworkers (NUM) rejected the proposed closures and in March 1984, the vast majority of miners downed tools. So began one of the most bitter and protracted national strikes in UK history.

With benefit of hindsight, the miners were always destined to fail. Having learned lessons from previous confrontations with them in 1974 and 1981, the Conservative government ensured that power stations stockpiled enough coal reserves to keep energy running should industrial action take place. A shrewd move, it ensured power supplies to British homes were maintained during the winter of '84, when the strike was eight months old and at a crucial stage. Equally, a reported change in legislation banned the dependants of those striking from making state claims for 'Urgent Needs' payments, while also reducing other benefits they might be eligible for. From an observer's perspective, it was almost as if the Prime Minister saw the miners and their Union not as battling for their livelihoods, but rather, as enemies to future progress: "We had to fight the enemy without in the Falklands," Mrs Thatcher said at the time. "We always have to be aware of the enemy within, which is much more difficult to fight and more dangerous to liberty." Such rhetoric seemed curiously distant from the speech she gave when first taking power in 1979: "Where there is discord, may we bring harmony. Where there is error, may we bring truth. Where there is doubt, may we bring faith. And where there is despair, may we bring hope."

Indeed.

The miners' strike played out not as high drama, but harsh reality for Jones, Moore, Bradfield and Edwards as they saw their neighbourhood and its surrounding areas slowly succumb to the consequences of sustained industrial action: "I remember coming home from school (at the start of the strike)," James later told *NME*, "and my mum and dad would be in front of the television. There were a lot of furrowed brows. It seemed that everything was at stake." As events progressed the cost of the strike took a greater toll, daily demonstrations falling away to be replaced by charity food parcels and house evictions: "It was politics," Nicky said, "right there on our doorstep." By March 3, 1985, it was also all over. Though the miners' actions had initially gained support from the general public, the legality of the strike, sometimes questionable agendas of its leaders and the increasingly violent skirmishes between picketers and police across the UK slowly began to erode goodwill. This was further compounded by a terrible incident in November, 1984 that saw minicab driver David Wilkie killed when a concrete block was dropped by two striking miners on his car from a bridge some 27 feet above. Wilkie had been part of a police escort taking a non-striking miner to work at the Merthyr Vale mine, only 10 or so miles from Blackwood itself.

Ultimately though, it was depleted finances that finally brought the strike to an end. In short, miners – and the union that represented them – simply didn't have enough money to continue the fight. With 11,200 men and women arrested on picket lines and at least five deaths over the course of the year, it seemed more like the end of war than a sustained protest against the terror of change. Little wonder then, that at several pit gates across the UK, miners' wives distributed carnations to returning workers while brass bands played them in.

As was the case in Yorkshire, Nottingham, Kent and parts of Scotland, South Wales would soon see the effects of pit closures, with 12 shut down near Blackwood and Oakdale alone. Unemployment, previously at 8% now rose to a reported 80%, with miners handing back the tools of their trade in exchange for dole cheques. Having held the line for so long (almost 98% of Welsh miners observed the strike from beginning to end), it must have been the bitterest pill to swallow: "The Welsh miners were the last to give in," Nicky remembered, "but when they lost, our heads dropped. We were defeated." Sean, who played in the local Celeyn Miners' Brass Band, concurred: "Proud upright men being reduced to shells of their former selves."

For Richey, Welsh melancholia and the taste of defeat were entangled together, producing all too predictable results: "Depression was just our natural mood, where we came from, there's a natural melancholy in the air. Everybody... felt pretty much defeated... the ruins of heavy industry all around you, (seeing) your parents' generation all out of work with nothing to do and being forced into the indignity of going on 'course of relevance'". For those lucky enough to get employment, it was provided by electronics firms such as Toshiba and Sony, who, seizing an opportunity, now set up factories in the area. However, to maximise profits and stave off the costs of employee benefits or redundancy payouts, workers were hired only on three month rolling contracts. Pure capitalism had arrived in Blackwood and the rout was complete.

Inevitably, there was deep, abiding anger within the town. Yet, that anger was not only directed at those perceived to have caused the chaos, but also the notions of martyrdom it produced in some of the casualties. "We grew to despise the environment in which we lived," James told *Melody Maker*, "Many of the miners were self-convinced martyrs. They saw something romantic in the starving and suffering. It was part of being their social class and they were proud of it. Absolute crap. Everyone deserved better. My generation started to rebel... boredom was life, we were stuck in a vacuum and decided to be honest about it." His diatribe continued: "By that point, we hated words like 'Security', 'Passion', 'Ideology', 'Belief'. We wanted to turn those words into something else. We didn't want to be on our knees. Fuck that. We wanted to be intelligent, so we'd never be beaten."

For the teenagers, the strike also galvanised what would become a lifelong and abiding interest in, and commitment to, strong left wing politics. Traditionally a staunch Labour stronghold, Blackwood and south Wales as a whole had felt let down by their party of choice. That ill feeling was made markedly worse by a perception that Labour's newly appointed leader and fellow Welshman, Neil Kinnock, hadn't showed necessary solidarity to the miners' cause: "Everything Kinnock stood for," Richey later said, "is everything my grandfather would have spat at. A desperate craving for power at any cost... Labour were told by the right wing press they had to move towards the centre, but they should have gone more extreme." To make matters worse, Kinnock's constituency house was only moments away from James and Sean's front door. For Nicky, there was only one choice left: "When I was old enough to understand it, I went into Marxism." In this pursuit, he was guided by older brother, Patrick, whose strong interest in politics and major distaste for Conservatism were beginning to inform the content of his own short stories and verse.

Over time, Blackwood and its surrounding areas would prove Darwin right and begin adapting to the changes foisted upon them. When

Oakdale's last pit was closed in 1989, subsequent government support saw more businesses slowly but surely arrive – a nationwide need for microchips, fast food, communications systems and carpets all helping partially re-invigorate the local economy and get people back to work. Even the notorious Pen-y-fan was cleaned up, given a tourist shine and its own webpage. However, in 1985, the general feeling was that the Devil and her hordes had come to visit, giving Blackwood its own personal taste of hell. "Some people just fell away and didn't come back," said one resident. The terse, sometimes despairing struggle that was the miners' strike had a profound effect on Jones, Bradfield, Moore and Edwards, its destabilisation of their community only reinforcing a sense of being trapped in a town with no real future: "With the unemployment and the rain, there was a feeling of no hope in Blackwood," Patrick Jones confirmed, "a lot of younger people felt that." The reaction of the four was to close ranks, turn their backs on their surroundings and plan for better days. Or as Nicky would have it: "I don't think we could have done (anything) if we hadn't grown up in a shithole where the only way to escape was to create your own reality."

The first fruits of that reality manifested itself on a scrap of paper handed from one friend to another in a school playground.

Chapter Three

Convergences

Feeling disgusted by recent events, and bored beyond comprehension by what passed for Saturday night in town, Nicky Jones and his cohorts began searching for a base of operations from which they could plan their escape. They found it close to home in the shape of James and Sean's shared room. Here, they gathered, first to talk, then to argue, but always to plan. And like all planners, copious amounts of research had to be undertaken before they were ready to unveil any grand scheme to the world. In the case of Jones, Edwards, Moore and Bradfield, the research material used were films, politics, literature, art, philosophy and of course, music. Ultimately, as it all came from the same source, it was all grist for the mill.

First, the books, and there were many. Drawing their list from a variety of philosophies and pretty much every age, the Blackwood Reading Club was not precious or particularly abstract in its members' taste. Instead, they were just seeking quality. Hence, American poet Emily Dickinson's fragile meditations on death and the hereafter fought for shelf space with French Absurdist Albert Camus' godless musings on freedom. Nicky would bring the glum, but pithy works of Philip Larkin to bear, the Coventry born poet's fascination with human emotions reminiscent of William Shakespeare, another Jones favourite. Richey found time for them all, though he was particularly given to the work of celebrated French poet and ceaseless libertine, Arthur Rimbaud, whose drug-fuelled, hallucinogenic work, *A Season In Hell*, he loved. From free-wheeling 'Beat' authors such as Jack Kerouac, Allen Ginsberg and William Burroughs to classical thinkers such as Socrates, Plato, Mao and Marx – if you had ideas, then you were studied. Sylvia Plath's doom laden *The Bell Jar*. Hart Crane's kaleidoscopic *Four Quartets*. Divine comedies, serious plays, they read the lot – then argued about it: "We'd argue about anything," Richey confirmed to *NME*. "That's part of where we come from, of having fuck all to do and saying things to each other to create arguments. It got us through the day."

Films, art and television also had a special place at the table, and again, it didn't matter if the director or artist was a shameless populist or wilfully obscure. As long as the work bore scrutiny and genuinely excited its audience of four critics, then it passed muster. Hence, Francis Ford Coppola's operatic study of the Vietnam war, *Apocalypse Now*, fought for screen time with Ken Loach's small, but no less affecting, *Kes*. Similarly, Powell and Pressburger's fantastical *A Matter Of Life And Death* nudged Martin Scorsese's grim-faced *Taxi Driver* out of the video recorder. The group's approach to art was no different. Photographs of Francis Bacon's muddy figures were cut from magazines and stuck on their walls alongside Andy Warhol's Factory pop prints. Primal screams from Munch, Picasso's blue bombing of Guernica, Richey, Nicky, Sean and James puzzled over them at leisure.

There was also plenty of room for the simpler, but no less effective pleasures of terrestrial TV: from *Pebble Mill At One*, *Bullseye* and *The Krypton Factor* to *Ever Decreasing Circles*, *The Young Ones*, *Auf Weidersehen, Pet* and *Minder*, it all helped stave off the boredom. And if the four wanted for sport at weekends, ITV provided wrestling and football while the BBC covered golf and cricket. Plays and poetry, cinema and TV. High art, low art and all points in between. Basically, anything and everything to create a barrier between them and Blackwood.

Holding it all together somewhere in the middle was music, or more specifically, pop and rock music. After all, it offered such a delicious symbiosis of it all: the glamour of film and sports stars, the lyricism of poets, the opportunity to express an idea with bold, strident images and the sheer visceral thrill of making a hell of a racket while doing so. Though Sean was already committed to learning an instrument, the others too had already engaged with the wonders of music, buying their first singles as children. Again, Moore was first out of the traps here, nudging the money from his mother's purse to purchase a copy of Queen's cod-delicious 'We Are The Champions' when he was nine years old. Richey was next, buying Child's 'It's Only Make Believe' in 1979. Previously a hit for country stars Conway Twitty and Glen Campbell, Child's 'teen doo wop' treatment of 'It's Only Make Believe' sat well with Edwards' parents, who by all accounts enjoyed listening to their fellow rock 'n' roll revivalists, Showaddywaddy: "All we listened to at home when I was a child was the radio," Richey once remembered, "and all they played on that was Showaddywaddy's 'The Moon Of Love'".

Nicky was up next, choosing to part with his money for the grinding pleasures of Black Sabbath's 'Neon Knights', some three or so minutes of growling machismo, chugging guitars and, it has to be said, glorious thump. Among Blackwood's metal community, which numbered many at the time, Jones had made a wise purchase: "I just remember at school discos, where they'd have a 'heavy metal half hour'," Richey told *Kerrang*, "and all the girls would be pushed to the side and all the boys would have their fingers in their waistbands with their heads down. It was just like watching animals erupting across the school halls." Sadly, Edwards failed to mention whether Jones was among the wild beasts. Elsewhere, Bradfield also made the acquaintance of the town's rockers when he bought his first single in September 1980, though that purchase, Diana Ross' 'My Old Piano', could not be described as either heavy, or indeed metal. Sadly for James, he was caught leaving Woolworths with the record by a local metal luminary – "Dids... a really cruel bastard" – who proceeded to tell everyone he could in Blackwood of James' taste for jaunty disco ditties.

As they grew older their tastes changed, with Diana Ross and Child being jettisoned in favour of perhaps more serious fare. In Richey's case, he found real succour in the angst-ridden music of Macclesfield post-punk group Joy Division, whose hollow eyed, baritone singer, Ian Curtis, fascinated Edwards. Richey wasn't alone here: a troubled soul suffering from the twin demons of epilepsy and a failing marriage, Curtis' lyrics

– full of social dislocation and urban decay – struck a chord with many teenagers facing an uncertain future in Eighties Britain. When the 23-year-old Curtis took his own life in 1980, his legend was forever secured. "Ian Curtis was the only musician whose death I was saddened by," Edwards later remembered. Pouring over the words that Curtis left behind, Richey found disturbing images of mourning, isolation and on the song 'Atrocity Exhibition', real dread and apprehension in lyrics that spoke of 'the horrors of a faraway place' and 'mass murder on a scale you've never seen'. Suffice to say, Ian Curtis' lyrical preoccupations would have a lasting influence on the work Richey Edwards produced in later years.

The others too, were amassing their share of vinyl in true hunter/gatherer style with a plethora of musical tastes finding their way on to the turntable. Some early favourites included guitar driven, new wave pioneers such as The Skids, Simple Minds and Echo & The Bunnymen, while their newfound political ideologies were assuaged by the left leaning likes of Billy Bragg and The Gang Of Four. To mix things up, classic recordings by Frank Sinatra and guitar picker turned country legend Glenn Campbell were also aired, 'Wichita Lineman' in rotation alongside Magazine's equally forlorn but tad more aggressive 'Shot By Both Sides'. Predictably, band of the moment The Smiths were also explored, though the lyrics of their front man, Morrissey, were ultimately rejected by Edwards as too self-pitying for his taste. Having seen some of Blackwood's miners fall away to a similar malady, being "the son and heir to a shyness that is criminally vulgar" simply wasn't on Richey's priority list. Nicky Jones, however, held on a while longer, occasionally traipsing to school with a bunch of daffodils hanging out of his back pocket, in honour of Morrissey's affectation of the time. Thankfully, the mock beatings he received from school mates ceased when Nicky put the flowers back on his mother's table: "People always ask, 'Were you outsiders at school, were you really weird?'", Richey later told *Melody Maker*. "The answer was 'No'. We just stayed in our bedrooms and watched TV. We never had anything else to do. We made no effort to make friends because we felt so happy with each other." Jones concurred: "We were never particularly victimised for being weird because nobody ever saw us." But they do remember the daffodils.

When the four weren't fighting over the merits of The Smiths, there was room for the odd spot of hirsute glam rock, duly provided by Finnish hopefuls, Hanoi Rocks. Part New York Dolls, part Aerosmith with a liberal dash of punk spirit thrown in to sour the taste, Hanoi Rocks were all feather boas, leather pants and low slung guitars. Crucially, they were also regular visitors to hundreds of clubs up and down the UK in the early to mid-Eighties, gathering a firm following in South Wales. Jones and the others were duly caught up in Hanoi's appeal, their glam-heavy image and mutated Seventies rock 'n' roll crucially pointing the way to those who pioneered the original sound and look. As a consequence, The Rolling Stones' *Exile On Main Street* soon found its way into Bradfield and Moore's eager clutches. After that, it was only a matter of time before they discovered The Who, Pete Townshend's more questioning approach to lyric and song on works such as *Tommy, Who's Next* and *Quadrophenia* resonating deeply with the four teens.

Of course, when searching for the true essence of rock'n'roll, there was always going to be a disappointment or two. For Nicky it came with his first ever gig, spent in the company of Welsh heroes The Alarm at St. David's Hall in Cardiff. All soaring choruses and chiming, acoustic guitars, The Alarm's retro-revolutionary stance (as evidenced on their hit '68 Guns') was sadly neither as thrilling nor authentic as the 1968 Jones had in mind – a time when the Stones' 'Street Fighting Man' had called for "marching feet... and palace revolutions", following the Paris riots of the same year: "They were too nice and too positive," he later remembered, "but to give them their due, they had it ten times harder when they started, simply being Welsh."

Richey too, was less than enamoured by his formative live experiences, finding Mancunian newcomers James and the festival environment they were performing in a chastening experience: "When I think of James, I think of lying in a field at WOMAD, 1983. Vegetarian burgers, pissing rain, being sick, watching the worst live band I'd ever seen, realising that I was never going to a festival again. Biggest piece of shit I've ever heard." Still, Edwards could always look back with fondness to his first concert some months before, when he, James and Sean headed to Cardiff University to witness the mighty Echo & The Bunnymen. Many more visits to Cardiff and even further afield took place, with Jones joining the trio to watch the likes of The Waterboys (a particular Bradfield obsession), Spear Of Destiny and Sonic Youth. They would even see future 'Madchester' stars The Stone Roses in the intimate surroundings of the city's Square Club, the group then plying their wares to no more than a few dozen people. Sometimes the travelling, missed buses and enforced overnight stays in Cardiff were justified, though more often not: "Bands were written about in the music press as if they would change your life, and there would be 20 people there and the bands would be fucking shit," Richey later told *Select*. "Every song, total and utter rubbish."

As Edwards stated, the four were swayed to attend such gigs by their then bible of choice, *New Musical Express*, or *NME* as it was more popularly known. Officially classified as a music paper, though its remit was in truth far wider, *NME* served to influence thousands each week in their listening and viewing tastes – the publication's writers championing new bands, books and films, while also exploring the influences and culture behind them. Crucial in bringing punk to the masses in the Seventies, then providing credible alternatives when that movement fell away, *NME* and its rival publications (the now sadly defunct *Melody Maker* and *Sounds*) were at the forefront of setting youth trends and, when enough time had passed, destroying them in equal measure. Cutting edge journalism then, written for the young by the young. In Blackwood it was all manna from heaven, informing the friends' choice of reading, movies and bands – from Sartre and Scorsese to Rimbaud and Richards: "We lived for Wednesdays and the arrival of the music papers," Richey later confirmed. "We devoured them. When *NME* said things like Eddie Cochran (was) an anarchist, we went 'Yeah'. We fell for that because our lives were really boring."

Some 20 odd years later, their devotion to the music press may seem twee, naive, or worse still, sadly parochial. But for four teenagers living in a then depressed and fairly isolated area, the likes of *NME* and *Melody Maker* represented lifelines to a different, far more interesting, place: "Being stuck in the middle of nowhere when we were growing up, *NME* was our antenna to the outside," Nicky told the publication in 2001, "it opened up a new world." James, then as now, was more direct in his assessment: "Half the time they guided you to uncomfortable truths, the rest of the time, it was bullshit. But that'll do for me." And if those 'truths' or the accompanying 'bullshit' caused debates, arguments or full blown wars between them, all the better: "Everything we discovered," Nicky later said, "from *Betty Blue* to Malcolm Lowry came fast to us. We were a microcosm...bored so easily that we put into three years everything that took the Rolling Stones 20 (to achieve). It's just the way we are." The intense study referred to by Jones was all connected at the time to the growing idea they could put together a band of their very own. .

The signs this would happen had been percolating for a while, though there were several fits and starts before any vague plan took more serious shape. As a child, Nicky had briefly taken guitar lessons but abandoned the instrument, only to have it replaced by an inexpensive Bontempi keyboard his parents bought him for his 14th birthday. He abandoned this too, the demands of learning scales and chord sequences a source of real irritation rather than ceaseless wonder (Jones' mother subsequently donated the keyboard to charity in 2008). However, Nicky was an extremely interested observer when James got his first guitar at the age of 15, even offering to show him what he'd learned as a child. Ultimately, his help wasn't required, as Bradfield quickly knuckled down to teach himself: "I stayed in for three days, over a weekend, teaching myself chords," he remembered. "It was the first thing I thought I really could do. I had no fear of it."

Within a year James was proficient enough on the instrument to play along with 'Jessica' by The Allman Brothers, a song Monty Bradfield better knew as the theme tune to BBC 2's snooker coverage: "My dad nagged me not to play guitar, so I did it to show him I could do it properly. He wanted to hear The Shadows' 'Apache' as proof, but the snooker theme did fine." Duane Allman's country rock style was of little lasting interest to Bradfield Jnr., however, who would soon find himself drawn to the post-punk guitar work of The Skids' Stuart Adamson, Sex Pistols' Steve Jones, The Chameleons' Reggie Smithies and Dave Fielding and Simple Minds' redoubtable Charlie Burchill: "Charlie never gets a name check as a great guitarist," James later said. "When you say Simple Minds, people think 'Alive And Kicking' – but his work on the early LPs like *Real To Real Cacophony* and *Empires And Dance* was great, like a subplot to the melody. Listen to 'Sweat In Bullets' or 'The American', amazing records." A better known yet no less chance-taking guitarist, Fleetwood Mac's Lindsey Buckingham, was also a formative influence:

"I always loved the way he dips in and out of songs, spinning a little part and then dropping back into the song." No doubt Mr Bradfield was also treated to his son's rendition of Buckingham's howling guitar solo on 'The Chain', the Fleetwood Mac tune used as the theme for the BBC's motor racing programmes.

With Bradfield almost monk-like in his devotion to guitar, it wasn't long before Nicky Jones again began entertaining notions of returning to the instrument, eventually buying himself a scratchy Fender Telecaster copy: "To be honest, by the time I started learning again, James was ready to teach me. Really, I just wanted to look cool." If Jones lacked the discipline for true greatness on six strings, it was probably because he was more interested in the written word. Like older brother, Patrick, then studying Sociology and American Literature at the University of Wales, Nicky also had a talent for writing and was privately experimenting with both poetry and song lyrics. When he had finally captured something he was reasonably proud of, he passed the results to Bradfield during lunch break at school: "Nick's first lyric was called 'Aftermath'," James revealed. "As soon as he handed it to me, he ran away... Nick was being a bit shy about it."

'Aftermath', as it turned out, was Jones' personal take on the miners' strike, its subsequent effects on Blackwood and Margaret Thatcher's part in it. The line "This woman that fatefully sowed this seed," struck a particular chord with Bradfield: "It was a real doggerel diatribe against Thatcher," he later said. The next day, Nicky was back with two more efforts entitled 'Intellectual Monks' and 'Anti-social'. Though Jones hadn't been explicit about it, Bradfield knew he was expected to turn these words into songs. With 'Aftermath', he failed, but '... Monks' and 'Anti-social' were soon put to music: "These (lyrics) could be the next Morrissey/Marr," he subsequently told Nicky.

Teenage awkwardness now behind them, the decision to focus their efforts in a more productive manner came when Bradfield invited Jones to his parents' house on Saturday mornings for "rehearsals". At first, this practically meant James bashing out chord progressions as Nicky watched, trying to understand what the hell was going on. But over the coming weeks, they would find their measure, Jones putting words to Bradfield's musical ideas while strumming along where he could.

"Nothing will ever correlate with the mad idea that myself and Nicky had when we were 15 years old, and writing our first songs," James later said. "We had a preposterous, fucking big ready-made myth in our heads. I don't think anything we ever did (after that) will live up to that." However, two things were still missing: a backbeat and a singer. Sean Moore solved problem number one.

Aware of his cousin's rapid progress on guitar and the "Saturday show" going on in the front room, Moore had thus far kept an appropriate distance, sensing James wasn't quite ready to invite him to the party. "It was my thing," Bradfield later conceded, "and I didn't want Sean to barge into the band as I thought he'd take it over." In the end, Moore's involvement couldn't be halted: "I just got a biscuit tin and wooden spoon out of the kitchen and started banging away." While Bradfield remained reticent, Nicky was much more appreciative of his friend's talents. "Sean was already playing in a brass band, could read music and looked cool. He was in." The matter of appointing a singer was born of convenience, with James – the former choir boy – reluctantly taking on vocal duties: "We found out who could do what and who couldn't..." Bradfield later said, "I couldn't write lyrics to save my life (but) I was the only one who could sing, so I had to do it."

A firm direction in which to point their musical efforts was found one Friday night in early 1986 when Channel 4 screened a documentary celebrating the 10th anniversary of punk rock. Hosted by Factory Records supremo, writer, television presenter and self-confessed "Manchester gobshite", Tony Wilson, the documentary mined footage from Wilson's own Seventies TV show, *So It Goes*, and included performances by The Sex Pistols, The Damned and The Clash. To those watching in Blackwood, it was like something out of *The Book of Revelations*, James, Nicky, and Sean all transfixed by punk's descending angels. Twenty-three years later, Jones was still apostolic about the joy of it all: "The Sex Pistols' *Never Mind The Bollocks...* is the greatest album ever made," he told MTV. "The (album) so informed my life, from the graphic nature of the artwork, the statements of (cover) designer Jamie Reid to the overwhelming power of Steve Jones' guitar and the lacerating vocals of Johnny Rotten. When my children grow up, and need to be led towards a new form of living, I'll give them a copy of *Never Mind...*"

If Nicky had been suitably transported by the power of The Sex Pistols, he was also greatly taken by The Clash, whose vintage performances of 'Garageland' and 'What's My Name' fizzled with the band's trademark energy. Just as well, as sitting beside him, James had found new meaning to life: "I always wanted to be famous, like Napoleon," he later said. "Then I discovered The Clash... and my destiny was pre-determined." Infused with purpose, Bradfield began purchasing every Clash-related product available, while simultaneously learning their songs on guitar. His enthusiasm proved infectious: "The Clash's *London Calling* is probably my most played album of all time," Nicky said. "To us, they became icons, the sheer breadth of musical styles was huge. They could master punk, rockabilly, reggae, rock, hip hop. They were at the forefront of all those things. Basically, we wanted to fuse the misery of Joy Division with the excitement of The Clash."

Though they would continue to argue among themselves over the merits of the Stones and The Beatles, or which Joy Division LP was better (Nicky: "I loved *Unknown Pleasures*... it's a miserablist thing, living in Wales, lots of rain, etc..."), The Clash remained a constant, always pointing true north. This shameless infatuation would later cause them myriad problems with the music press, but at the time, it helped steal their resolve and focus their thoughts on the road ahead (if proof is needed of this, one only has to listen to the band's earliest, homemade recordings: those made in 1985 and early '86 confirm a heavy Smiths/indie influence, Bradfield's guitars circling around the melodies in a similar style to Johnny Marr. By late 1986, the chiming six-strings had all but disappeared, replaced by a distorted, buzz-saw-like sound. This is nowhere more apparent than on the song 'Whiskey Psychosis' where Bradfield seemed to be directly channelling Clash guitarist Mick Jones' penchant for choppy chording).

In a perfect world, Richey Edwards – always at the heart of every debate, always ready with another opinion – should have been a central part of the nascent group. But there were two essential drawbacks to his involvement: Edwards couldn't play an instrument nor showed any great wish to do so, and more, having recently graduated from nearby Crosskeys Tertiary College with 10 GCSEs and three Grade A 'A' levels, was due imminently at Swansea University to begin a degree in Political

History. The man chosen to take Richey's natural place in the order of things was Miles Woodward, AKA 'Flicker'. Another Blackwood face, Flicker certainly outperformed James, Nicky and Sean in terms of teen rebel chic, dressing like a second generation Kings Road punk while the others were still content to model sixth form casual wear, fops and flat-tops. The owner of a bass guitar (albeit with only two strings), Flicker was certainly no virtuoso, but the distressed Sex Pistols T-shirt, badge-adorned biker jacket and blond peroxide hair meant he at least looked the part. Deal done, Flicker joined the still nameless band at their new rehearsal venue, a shed at the bottom of the Jones family garden. Here, "three chord punk songs played on crap guitars with crap amps" were the order of the day, with Sean standing rockabilly-style at the back, hammering out the beat on just a snare and bass drum.

Despite the limitations of their surroundings, the lack of decent equipment and the fact The Clash had come to a highly embarrassing halt a year before with their last studio album, *Cut The Crap*, spirits remained high within the garden shed: "Our ambition," Nicky later reasoned, "was fucking psychotic, really. We had this evangelical desire to start a revolution and be absolutely massive. It didn't mean just getting a record deal. It was all conquering, psycho... egotistical." And if Jones was at the heart of all this righteous ambition, his friends weren't lagging that far behind: "We looked down on everyone else," Bradfield later admitted. "We felt that we could change things. Really, we came together around Nick. I was 'Baldrick' to his 'Blackadder'. More than anything, he talked about being great, being legends.... we started on the basis of those delusions of grandeur." Sean Moore was no less confident about their destiny: "Music was absolutely everything to me. My idea was about true, natural talent. We always knew the band was going to work and it was just down to us to make it happen." Yet, there was also a feeling of incompleteness, a break in the circle. Though Flicker was a part of proceedings, he was also not one of the original four architects of the escape plan: that seat was permanently reserved for Richey Edwards: "We were in a band before we even picked up guitars," Nicky later reasoned, "and even if we didn't know how... we knew Richey had to be a part of it." All good things come to those who wait.

Chapter Four

Education Is Never A Waste

By the autumn of 1986 Richey Edwards held a curious place among his circle of friends. In the preceding years, he had been in the midst of it all, arguing high and low art while simultaneously fighting for space in James and Sean's bunk bed palace. And when they occasionally ventured out to Dorothy's Cafe on Blackwood High Street for a change of scenery, he was there again, stealing window seats with Sean as Nicky and James ordered tea at the counter. Indeed, when Moore decided to incur the wrath of his in-laws by backcombing his hair in true Echo & The Bunnymen/Jesus & Mary Chain style, Richey was Ian McCulloch to Sean's Jim Reid, pouring coke and sugar on both their heads to fashion the desired spikes. Part philosopher, part trainee orator and a willing accomplice in Moore's follicular experiments, Edwards was also the first to officially break ranks by going to Swansea University. In truth, this was no great tragedy in anyone's life at the time. Though the 'Blackwood four' had grown close in recent years, they were by no means a symbiotic mechanism, each having their own lives, separate families, friends and individual interests. Richey was simply pursuing a path outside the immediate confines of town and into the wider world, even if said world was only some 30 miles up the road.

By all accounts, the years leading up to university had seen a subtle, yet defining change in the character of Richey Edwards. He had certainly found his childhood "almost perfect", but this ended promptly at age 13 when his family moved closer to town, and as a consequence, he saw less of his grandmother. The after effects of the miners' strike and "the cemetery" that was Blackwood only compounded his misery. As is so often the case with young men of his age, he was struck by a particularly bad case of acne, the spots on his face and neck making him shy with girls at the precise time his testosterone levels were soaring. He did briefly date a girl at Oakdale Comprehensive, though when the fledgling romance ended, he seemed only too content to return to his picture collection of current pixie du jour, Clare Grogan, the singer with Scots band Altered Images who starred in the hit movie *Gregory's Girl*.

When it came to anything stronger on the pictorial front, Richey baulked. Unlike the adolescent James, who allegedly visited a friend's house each day for a month to watch the same pornographic video, Edwards was physically ill when first confronted with images from a porn magazine: "One bloody great shock," he later remembered. "It wasn't the nudity as such, it was the deprivation. They were the saddest pictures I ever saw." The objection for Richey was in the "violence" of the imagery and the sad appetite of the men, if not the women, taking part. For some, this experience would have been a simple teenage rite of passage, an illicit glimpse into the adult world found beneath the bed of a mate's older brother. For Edwards, it appeared to be a break point from his still idealised notions of beauty, something that "affected me profoundly and will always haunt me". If this statement appears overtly dramatic, it's perhaps worth remembering that while there would be many a one night stand in his future, he would remain a virgin into his early twenties: "I think everybody's first love is themselves," Richey once said, "some more than others. Some can divide themselves and give themselves to another person... which I have never been able to do, because I've never trusted another person enough." As became clear, reconciling intimacy with the intricacy that accompanies it was a complex proposition Richey Edwards wrestled with throughout his adult life.

If, as Nicky Jones attests, "Richey hit a wall at age 16," he did a reasonably good job of keeping his bruises from public sight. Though

Edwards affected the standard 'doomed youth' combination of trench coat and spiked hair made fashionable by Bunnyman Ian McCulloch and Bad Seed Nick Cave, he was never bullied by Blackwood's more traditional alpha males: "Scared sometimes, but no, not bullied." Instead, Richey was seen as "a quiet type", seemingly modest, diminutive and a tad "bookish". but certainly no social pariah. This status was also maintained by the twin guns of Edwards' undoubted intellect and gift for the sly quip: "Richey was always mischievous," Nicky once confirmed, "great with a putdown, always a gleam in those eyes." As he entered his late teens and began making occasional visits to Blackwood pubs such as The Bierkeller and Red Lion, those 'eyes' got Edwards his fair share of attention from local girls but again, while he was content to flirt, nothing more really came of it. Getting out of Blackwood, not settling down within it, seemed everything to him.

Richey had achieved this ambition through relentless study, sometimes in spite of the educational system he found himself within. Like the others, Edwards had fought a private battle with comprehensive school, detesting its strictures and the apparent requirement that he immediately enter the world of banking on leaving its grounds. Yet, he was also aware that he had to engage with that system – and gain dominion over it – in order to manipulate a better future for himself. As his 'O' and 'A' level results proved, in this he had been extremely successful, negotiating the transfer from Oakdale to its 'feeder' college, Cross Keys, in model fashion. With precious few distractions offered by Blackwood, and a circle of friends as engaged by the written word as he was, Richey also had time to stray far and wide from his college curriculum, continuing his own studies into the work of Arthur Rimbaud and Jack Kerouac.

There were new favourites too: Joseph Conrad's *Heart Of Darkness*, J.D Salinger's *The Catcher On The Rye* and (courtesy of Ian Curtis) J.G Ballard's *The Atrocity Exhibition* all offered Edwards a taste of the blacker hues of the human condition. Equally, George Orwell's *Animal Farm* and Aldous Huxley's *Brave New World* provided satirical and futuristic alternatives to the political tomes he was expected to read in preparation for university. Serious books, serious attitude, serious boy. With a family both proud of their son and presumably expecting even more from him, there must have been a considerable weight on Edwards' shoulders when leaving for Swansea University. Nicky Jones, who was hoping to take the same road soon enough, saw the humour in it all: "It's very working class to want to better yourself. Me and Richey were attracted to being clever to prove we were better than the other... plebs."

Armed with high hopes, at least 40 cigarettes and vague ambitions to become a college lecturer, Richey Edwards arrived at Swansea to commence his Political History degree in September 1986. His temporary home was a dormitory room on the fourth floor of Mary Williams Hall, part of a 10 storey building housed neatly on the campus site. Bed, wash basin, cupboards and a writing desk were all provided, while shared kitchen and bathroom facilities were available down the hall. His floor was all male, though girls' dorms were both above and below. If he wanted for food, the cafeteria was near the building's exit on the left. Standard college accommodation, not worth more than a paragraph in a letter sent home to one's parents. It was now up to him to make what he could of his new circumstances.

Sadly, Edwards didn't make much of it at all. Like an intellectual puritan arriving on foreign shores, only to be greeted by friendly natives whose revels included sleeping late, copious amounts of alcohol and lashings of casual sex, Richey's initial inclination was to jump back on the boat and set sail for home: "I thought university would be full of people who wanted to sit round and talk about books, but it wasn't like that at all," he later told *NME*. "It was full of people who wanted... to do as little as possible. I never equated university with fun. I thought it was about reading and learning, but for most people, it was about getting laid."

Edwards' subsequent anecdotes about his early experiences as a student make for grim reading. Hating dorm life with a passion, where dozens of people milled up and down the halls at all hours, the high spirits and constant interruptions outside his room literally drove him to drink: "I used to get woken up constantly by pissed up students coming home thinking it would be funny to rampage up and down the corridors knocking on everyone's door (or) deciding to have a party in the kitchen at one in the morning." To counteract these sometimes nightly interruptions and get back to sleep, Richey succumbed to the inevitable: "I started drinking in my first term," he later admitted. "It was something I'd never allowed myself to do, but it was just a question of getting to sleep. It was so noisy, and I needed to get to sleep and wake at a certain time... drinking gave me that opportunity." Unlike the revellers he was keen to blot out, Edwards' drinking bouts were held alone – just him, a pack of cigarettes and a bottle of cheap vodka. Though he didn't know it then, the beloved "blank sleep" alcohol set up a pattern of behaviour initially beneficial to his work, but one that would also lead to more lasting difficulties.

Having found a workable though far from ideal solution to the night horrors, Richey fell into a well-established pattern of working hard on his education, while also penning occasional poems and short stories. While these 'distractions' were beginning to feel more valuable than his studies, no lectures were missed or text books unread. A semi-permanent presence in the university library, on the odd occasion he did stray into the student bar, the conversations Edwards had only confirmed his sour view of what passed for student life: "I despised those people who sat in the bar going 'I haven't been to one lecture this term, I'm so outrageous'. I think if you miss two or three lectures on the trot, you should be fucking thrown out. Or drowned." Seeing education itself as a pleasure and privilege, rather than the liberties one could take when circling its orbit, Edwards was out of synch with many of his peers. As a consequence, he made few close friends: "They'd have big... discos, but I was in bed after *Minder*." There was one real lapse from all the seriousness, however, when Richey broke character from the role of 'model student' and dressed up with his classmates as a sperm for rag week. Unfortunately, if his efforts were caught on camera, they have yet to surface.

A difficult year at Swansea University behind him, Edwards returned home to find his friends had taken some real strides forward, even departing the garden shed for the thrills of their local metropolis. Growing more confident of his abilities, James had begun busking in Cardiff City Centre, his repertoire consisting of acoustic versions of Clash and Pistols classics, alongside the likes of Primal Scream's 'Velocity Girl' and "something or another" by The June Brides: "'Velocity Girl' used to go down well," Bradfield said, "and when there was a rugby match at Cardiff Arms Park, I did 'La Bamba'. It was the biggest earner and (I) actually got pound coins." Occasionally, he was joined by Jones and Moore on these excursions, though the latter left his full drum kit at home, the one attempt made to get everything on the bus over before it even began: "We used to busk down in Cardiff," Sean remembered. "We'd buy a single fare from Blackwood and the object was to get enough for the fare home, buy a seven-inch from Spoilers and get a burger from McDonald's or Wimpy. Then I'd feel ill all the way home."

For James, however, it surely wasn't all about the experience or the money. Stories even have him throwing back coins to anyone kind enough to pay for his renditions of 'Garageland' or that old Welsh favourite, 'God Save The Queen'. Instead, these busking expeditions probably had much to do with the fact that – despite recent attempts to put himself out of a job – he was now the group's singer and had to get used to it. Always more keen to concentrate on his guitar playing than vocals, Bradfield had successfully persuaded Moore and Jones some months before that they might be best served with a proper lead vocalist, possibly female.

After all, it made some sense. South Wales band The Darling Buds, featuring 19-year-old singer Andrea Lewis, were building up an impressive live following, while neo-punks Transvision Vamp – with combustible frontwoman Wendy James – had just signed a deal with MCA Records. Willing to at least entertain the notion, the group approached local teen Jenny Watkins-Isnardi to see if she was interested. Her first audition, which consisted of singing down the phone to Nicky, passed muster and following a second face-to-face encounter with Jones, Watkins-Isnardi was permitted to join the band for rehearsals. However, it came to nothing, their potential new vocalist seeking different frontiers elsewhere during the summer of 1987. Jenny's departure put James back in the hot seat. Guitarist, singer, frontman, no more experiments.

In reality, Bradfield already had experience of this triple role when his band made their unofficial live debut supporting local legends Funeral In Berlin at the Crumlin Railway Hotel in nearby Newbridge. Formed by Steve Gatehouse, Nick Curtis and Craig Bruzas, and stealing their name from a 1966 spy film starring Michael Caine, Funeral In Berlin were already close to heroes among the Blackwood trench coat brigade. This was largely due to a remarkable appearance at Cross Keys Workingman's Institute, where the group ended 30 minutes of Jesus & Mary Chain-approved white noise with a rampant display of amp smashing. To attendees Nicky, James, Sean and Richey, it was the nearest they had personally come to the spirit of 1976. To the social secretary of the Institute, it was probably a good excuse to re-consider any future engagements. Whatever the case, Funeral's Steve Gatehouse was told by Jones after the gig that he and his friends were inspired by the performance and forming a band of their own. A friendship duly established, Gatehouse offered them a support slot when they were ready. That moment came at the Railway Hotel.

There is some dispute about the actual date of this first gig. Some put it as early as February 5, 1986, others later. Regardless of date, it remains certain that the group – Nicky Jones (now 'Wire'), James Dean Bradfield, Sean Moore and Flicker – performed a brief set in the basement of the Railway Hotel pub in support of Funeral In Berlin. By all accounts, their debut was a jolly affair that saw pint glasses flying through the air (with one glass improbably imbedding itself still unbroken in a wall), near riot conditions and an irate landlord berating the promoter. With sober witnesses few on the ground, such recollections might sound a little fanciful. That said, those who survived the onslaught do recall the group playing every song at breakneck speed, James' vocals being largely inaudible through the PA, and Nicky covered in make-up. Steve Gatehouse is also adamant that a pint glass did indeed imbed itself in the wall, though several subsequent attempts by the assembled crowd to replicate this little miracle proved unsuccessful.

The group's set that night was a varied mixture of covers and originals. The Undertones' classic 'Teenage Kicks' was given a brisk run out, as was The Jesus & Mary Chain's recent Top 50 hit, 'Just Like Honey' (always a good choice when inciting "a bit of the ultra violence"). Of their own material, virgin renditions of 'Love In A Make Up Bag' and Nicky's 'Anti-Social' were aired, though each of these songs would soon to be consigned to the dumper or cannibalised for use in later material. Playing to the gallery, the band were meant to have finished the show with a spirited version of The Sex Pistols' 'God Save The Queen' before descending from the stage in search of a bar now serving beer in plastic cups.

Richey Edwards was not present at his friends' inaugural performance in Newbridge, but he genuinely loved the band's new name, The Manic

Street Preachers: a flinty rallying call that combined punk edge with a bit of old fashioned oratorical fury. That it also sounded like the title of a Clash song title probably didn't hurt either. Yet, coming to rest on 'The Manic Street Preachers' had been a long and arduous process, with several hundred suggestions and a brief detour into art collectivism before the name was finally agreed by all. To explain, James Dean Bradfield was originally keen on not just creating a band, but an actual movement: "We called ourselves 'The Blue Generation' for a while because we felt destined for collective greatness." This idea was possibly inspired by their abiding love of Big Flame, the jazz-punk act who appeared on *C86* – a forward thinking cassette collection of new indie guitar groups given away free with *NME* in early 1986. More than just a band, Big Flame were successful club promoters, hosting a weekly 'Wilde Club' night at Man Alive in their native Manchester, while also arranging concerts for up-and-coming groups across the UK.

Given that Richey had penned a 24-page poem entitled 'Another Dead Eleven O'Clock' and stage play, 'Tearproof' (written in collaboration with Moore and Jones), there might be an opportunity to wrap band, poems and plays into one great 'art balloon'. In the end, the concept came to nought. Richey dropped the poem, and the play – about a shy gay man killed by a group of musicians – failed to win a drama competition when entered: "It was crap," Nicky's brother, Patrick, later admitted. But if 'The Blue Generation' fell away at the first hurdle, Bradfield, Edwards and the others remained faithful to the Big Flame ethos, if not the music itself: "The Eighties for us, was the biggest non-event ever, like (most of) *C86*," Richey once said. "All we really had was Big Flame. They were the most perfect band, but we couldn't play their records because they were too avant garde." Despite having problems with their sound, Edwards and the others wrote many a letter to Big Flame – who unlike many other bands they sent fan mail to, actually bothered to write back.

Another far less complicated name suggested for the group was 'Betty Blue', the English title given to the 1986 French movie *37°2 le matin* (*In The Morning*). Something of a cult hit at the time, due in part to its star Beatrice Dalle's willingness to appear naked in almost every shot, *Betty Blue* was all Gallic *amour fou* for undergraduates: comic, tragic, utterly bonkers, but nonetheless entertaining. Suffice to say, the film poster adorned many a serious-minded student's wall in the late Eighties. Thankfully, after due consideration, Betty Blue was dropped from the bank of possible names the group were toying with. The Manic Street Preachers, however, stuck. "We were never completely comfortable with the name," Bradfield later said, "and even tried to change it a few times, but we couldn't think of anything better." To this day, there has been no real explanation where such a curious phrase came from. One story has Bradfield being confronted by a senior citizen on one of his busking expeditions to Cardiff with the words: "What are you? Some sort of Manic Street Preacher?" Unlikely. Edwards maintained it was inspired by the title of a Jasmine Minks mini-album, *1234567, All Good Preachers Go To Heaven*. Better, but no-one else confirms this assertion. Another tale attributes the name to Sean's misreading of the lyrics to Dusty Springfield's immortal 'Son Of A Preacher Man'. Ridiculous. And James would have us all believe it came to him in a dream. Plausible, but possibly too romantic, given the source. Ultimately, the exact origin may be lost, but the name stuck – and there are far worse.

At last a gigging band, the Manic Street Preachers' progress was dealt a temporary blow when Nicky Jones set out on an occasionally wayward, but finally fruitful trip to higher education. Like Richey before him, Nicky had been an excellent scholar, gaining eight 'O' levels, with four at Grade 'A', before leaving Oakdale Comprehensive. He was even briefly considered for a place at Oxbridge, though his application was later turned down. By his 17th year, however, the wheels were starting to come off as Jones mixed weekly band rehearsals with weekend visits to Blackwood's Red Lion pub. His teenage high jinks culminated in a drunken effort to hot-wire a Ford Escort on the way home from a club: "Nicky tried joyriding once," Richey later told *Melody Maker*, "He stole a car when he was 17. He didn't drive it into a shop. He sort of rolled down the street (but) didn't get very far. He was a stunted joyrider. I think he fell asleep, drunk at the wheel." Jones received a conditional discharge for the prank.

By his finals, once high hopes had slipped to more moderate expectations. Tutors at Cross Keys Tertiary College were now predicting that Nicky's 'A' level grades would be no higher than three 'D's, a crushing blow to any dreams of university: "I never really tried with my mocks and stuff," he later said. Spurred on by his mother, Irene, Jones hit the books hard at Blackwood Library to avoid the embarrassment of real exam failure. In the meantime, he was offered a place at Portsmouth Polytechnic, which he grudgingly accepted. The cat was thrown among the pigeons when his results came in: "Three 'A' level passes, two at Grade 'A', one at 'B'. "Richey got three 'A's. The cunt." No hard feelings there. To make matters worse, Jones' opening two weeks at Portsmouth were an appalling experience, the student pursuing a "Club 18-30 holiday" agenda rather than actually attending any lectures: "I was having a thoroughly miserable time". Again, Nicky's mother came to the rescue, making a series of telephone calls to the University of Wales that culminated in her son being offered a place at Swansea University reading Politics.

He celebrated his good fortune by moving into shared accommodation with two fellow sportsmen and regularly visiting Richey, who had recently vacated Mary Williams Hall in favour of the nearby, but considerably quieter 'Uplands' block.

Nicky Jones would be the first to admit he was no perfect student, his attendance at Swansea University driven less by a voracious need to learn and more by a clinical desire to avoid the responsibilities of adulthood: "A lot of it was three more years of not having to decide what to do with your life," he confirmed to *NME*. Unlike Edwards, who took part-time gardening work in Blackwood during his first year break, Jones had never had a job and was keen to keep it that way: "I'd literally never done a day's work in my life, not even a paper round, so I just couldn't handle going to work in an office." There was also the matter of being a good son to consider: "I guess a lot of going to university is just to please your parents, and they'd always been pretty good to me." A self-confessed "outwardly nervous... nerdy casual" who wore Pringle sweaters, kept his distance from the Student Union and bombarded Edwards with (often successful) requests to play golf when he should have been in class, Jones was content to do his time until the weekends when he could return to Blackwood and his band.

While Jones and Edwards wrestled in their own distinct fashions with university life, Sean Moore and James Dean Bradfield pursued different agendas. Having studied music at school and gained his 'A' level, Sean had chosen to drop education and take a clerical job with the Civil Service. The benefits were threefold: it gave him a regular income, didn't overtly tax his brain and also allowed him time to concentrate on drumming. James too, had also ceased academic study, his interests in drama and philosophy not as compelling as the pleasures of guitar: "James just buried himself in guitar playing," Richey said. "He was more dedicated than all of us." Like Moore, Bradfield's obsession with music was total, resulting in an erratic attendance record at Cross Keys College, where he even turned up on the wrong day for his last class: "I got to the gates and they were locked. It was closed. Really fucking depressing."

Now on the dole though also working 'cash in hand' at a local bar, James was content to keep writing songs while immersing himself in his latest discovery, Guns N' Roses, whose debut LP, *Appetite For Destruction*, was released in the summer of 1987: "James learnt every note of that record," Nicky confirmed. "As a band, they looked and sounded perfect, and they weren't just heavy metal. They put the roll back into rock. The songs just engrained themselves in your memory." Citing the glam-sleaze of Hanoi Rocks, the "snap and fizz" of Aerosmith and the attitude of the Sex Pistols as major influences, Los Angeles-based urchins Guns N' Roses were a sharp breath of toxic air to the Eighties music scene, bringing back a sense of danger to rock'n'roll at a time when it seemed content to powder and preen itself into oblivion: "Guns...," said Jones, "showed you could be a real rock'n'roll band... when America was plagued with dodgy soft metal acts like Warrant and Poison." For Bradfield, Guns N' Roses' top hat wearing lead guitarist, Slash, was the key to it all, his fluid style and way with a riff providing him endless hours of entertainment: "A lot of 'romance' in the playing, sure," said James, "but fantastic all the same." As with The Clash, Guns N' Roses' attitude and musical firepower would also find their place in the Manics' eventual sound and style.

It wasn't all study, work, guitar playing and plans for world domination. As befitting their age, the friends had also discovered sex. Bradfield, for instance, was using his time as a barman to try and make the acquaintance of local girls, his virginity finally lost on the top of the bunk bed he still shared with Moore. Thankfully, Sean was absent at the time – his attentions now firmly locked on Rhian, a young woman for whom he had harboured a long time crush and would eventually settle down with. Nicky was also part of a couple, having hooked up with another local Blackwood teenager, Rachel. A classic 'on again, off again' relationship, he later described their mutual loss of 'V Plates' with excruciating honesty: "It was one of those slipped in, slipped out things that sort of happen."

Richey too, had developed crushes while at Swansea: in the first instance, he was hopelessly fixated on a petite blonde girl he'd seen around campus, even breaking his own code of ethics by attending the year end student ball in hopes of meeting her there. Edwards' hopes were dashed when she arrived in the company of her boyfriend, leaving him to spend the evening in the company of a vodka bottle. Another chance meeting weeks later at the local Cinderella's bar went slightly better, but again, nothing came of it. The next girl to command his attention was called 'Ceri' (short for Cerys), a fellow student, a little alternative, and again a 'cute blonde'. As before, Richey was disappointed, Ceri preferring the company of a fellow flaxen haired boy. In both cases, there is a suspicion that Edwards was still idealistic in his views of potential relationships at this point, the letters he wrote to friends confirming a distinctly romantic rather than simply predatory soul. Or perhaps, as is the case with almost all of us at one time or another, his longings were simply pointed in the wrong direction.

With Rachel in Blackwood and no suitable match as yet for Richey, Nicky saw a lot of his friend while at Swansea, the pair finally moving into a shared house on King Edward's Road during Jones' second year at University. When not studying, Wire's days were spent listening to The Beatles' *White Album* or the Sex Pistols before the demons came calling and he headed into town to feed his only real addiction – fruit machines: "I got to be a bit of an expert at it," he said. But not that much of an expert: "I was completely addicted and ended up £3,000 in debt because of it." Student finances under strain, much of Nicky's funding came from a barman 30 miles away: "James used to mail me fivers and tenners, which seemed like loads then."

By now, Edwards had abandoned his original idea of becoming a teacher in favour of doing "something" in the music industry. He had even spent a small chunk of his grant on a second-hand guitar, though there was always enough left for the alcohol needed to induce sleep: "I'd buy a bottle of wine, sit around and drink it. That would be the full extent of my expenses, well, maybe I'd buy a CD as well." Buying a guitar though, was an unusual move forward. Thus far, a fan of music rather than an active participant within it, Richey's real interests still centred on novels, movies, poetry and occasional song lyrics: "Everybody's got a corner of their heart you can't get into," James Dean Bradfield later confirmed to Q, "and Richey was always more into books and films than rock'n'roll. I think those art forms are much more idealised. I think they influenced the way he viewed his life and the way he thought it would be."

Of course, Edwards was completely uninterested in becoming a virtuoso. Bradfield would always be a far more proficient guitarist and he knew it. Yet, just having a guitar opened a passageway for him, representing possibilities and the chance to contribute to something he had so far not seriously considered. Until then, Richey Edwards had drawn a murky line between actively supporting his friends' musical aspirations, while not actually participating in them. The debt he felt to his parents and the sacrifices they had made for his education were always present in his mind, and equally, whatever else the future held it would be one devoid of hammer and claw: "I went to university to avoid manual work." But his continuing links to Blackwood, its alternative community and the friendships he had cultivated with the likes of Patrick Jones and Funeral In Berlin's Steve Gatehouse were all markers of involvement. An adult life lived in "blessed mediocrity" was simply not a consideration.

In the end, providence and circumstance were already playing their part in helping clarify Richey's next steps. Since Nicky and he had taken rooms together, the two had struck up quite the writing partnership, stockpiling lyrics for Jones' band. Works in progress included 'Ruthless', 'Sunglass Aesthetic', the imaginatively tilted 'Colt 45 Rusty James' and 'Motorcycle Emptiness', both penned in honour of Edwards' latest film discovery, *Rumble Fish* (more of this later). Even in these formative stages, they both took highly different approaches to the craft of lyric writing: Nicky was scathing in analysis, but lighter, even optimistic in his messages; Richey, on the other hand, was much more stylised yet far bleaker in outlook. If Jones was occasionally willing to open the curtains and let in the sun, Edwards was equally quick to move into the shadows it created. For a while at least, that contrast of light and shade proved a fine match: "At Swansea, I did Politics and Richey did Political History. That's where we nicked all our lyrics from, really," Nicky later joked.

Outside the walls of King Edward's Road, other events were conspiring to place Richey 'stage right' with the Manic Street Preachers. Since their debut supporting Funeral In Berlin at Newbridge's Railway Hotel, the band had sporadically gigged here and there, picking up the odd show mid-bill at Blackwood's Little Theatre or headlining at the nearby Pontypridd Rugby Club. The group had even made it as far as Cardiff, playing at TJs in front of the few local supporters fervent enough to follow them into the smoke. Another Cardiff gig, this time at the now defunct Red Square club was also notable, if only for the fact that two people attended – one of whom was Richey's sister, Rachel. The Manics' set at this time was still a confection of covers and originals, the likes of 'Anti-Love' and 'Eating Myself From The Inside' rubbing shoulders with Stiff Little Fingers' 'Alternative Ulster' and a warped run through of Blondie's 'Union City Blue'. Punk inspired, then, but not punk enough for bassist Flicker: "The others were also into indie, while I liked a lot of heavy metal and American punk. They were starting to go more pop. I just wanted to go more hardcore," he said. When James suggested that Flicker go from his preferred two string bass guitar approach to the more traditional four string set-up, it all proved too much: "He refused on principle, then left."

Following Flicker's departure, an immediate reshuffle took place in the Manics' ranks, with Nicky Wire abandoning rhythm guitar to take up bass playing duties instead. Now skirting six feet three inches tall, the bass' bigger size suited Wire far more than any diminutive Fender copy. It was also easier to play – a big plus point for the still faltering guitarist – and crucially, allowed him to emulate two more of his heroes, The Clash's Paul Simonon and Sex Pistol Sid Vicious: "Now I know that not many people are that fond of Sid," Wire later admitted, "but when you're 15 and want a poster on your wall, he was important. Sid looked great, held his bass low and I copied that." With a vacant position on rhythm guitar now available and Edwards the owner of same, his joining the band was only an awkward conversation away. After all, he was not only working as their co-lyricist and unofficial advisor, but also driving the band to gigs and even hauling their amps onstage: "He was the best looking roadie I've ever seen," one Blackwood native quipped.

For the time being though, Edwards remained preoccupied with his last year at university, which by the sounds of it, couldn't come quickly enough. Choosing Soviet-German inter-war relations as his thesis, he was, on the face of it, still courteous to his lecturers and diligent in his studies. Elsewhere however, there were problems. Richey's diet, for instance, consisted of Pot Noodle tubs liberated from Blackwood's Golden Wonder factory and a bizarre concoction of sweetcorn and rice tipped into a baked potato he christened 'White Noise'. As a consequence, his weight had dipped alarmingly, settling just under six stones: "That was the skinniest I ever got," he later said. In addition to the poor diet, Edwards' drinking had accelerated to binge levels at weekends, though he controlled it for 'blank sleep' purposes during week nights. A "30 a day and rising" cigarette habit was also causing a persistent cough. The most alarming development, however, was Richey's habit of making small cuts with a metal compass on his forearms: "When it came to my finals," he later told *NME*, "I suddenly realised 'I can't go into my exams pissed, so the way for me to gain control was cutting myself a little bit. Only with a compass, you know, vague little cuts. That way, I found I was really good during the day... I slept, I was feeling good about myself." Control mechanism or aid to concentration, the practice nonetheless gave James Dean Bradfield pause when he saw it in action on a brief visit to King Edward's Road in the run up to examination time.

Despite his best efforts, Edwards failed in his ultimate ambition of receiving a first class honours degree, missing the target by a mere two percentage points: "Richey was devastated," Nicky said. "He was just two percent away. God, he even used to go out to dinner with his tutors." Devastated perhaps, but a life lesson had also been learned: "I'm not stupid," Edwards later confirmed. "Sometimes, I might come across (that way)... but that's nothing to do with academic qualifications. I think there's a real difference between intelligence and knowledge. There are plenty of people with letters after their names who only know figures and dates. It's possible to know a lot of facts, but know nothing at all."

As Richey was coming to the end of his university experience, James, Sean and, after a fashion, Nicky, were recording their first single. Unlike previous homemade attempts such as 'Behave Yourself Baby' and 'England Is Still A Bitch', this session was professionally recorded at South Bank Studios in Cwmfelinfach, some five miles from Blackwood. Sitting in the producer's chair was Colin Powell, a jobbing musician who once jammed with Jimi Hendrix in New York, while engineering duties were ably covered by his assistant, Tony. Unable to afford much studio time, still amateur bassist Jones stepped aside, leaving Bradfield to overdub his parts. Some 40 minutes later two songs were on tape, and for an exceedingly small but vocal minority of Manic Street Preachers fans, the band would never improve on one of them.

In the case of the 'B' side, 'Tennessee (I Get Low)', there really wasn't much to write home about, the tune meandering and its subject matter – a sweary, cod-American ode to doomed romance – undistinguished. But the 'A' side was an altogether more intriguing proposition. Beginning with a screech of feedback, 'Suicide Alley' sped up like a distressed racehorse, flailing this way and that, before skidding across the finish line some two minutes and 30 seconds later. The drums were overly busy – flicking in and out of time as a result – and James' breathless delivery meant he choked some of the high notes, but those slashing guitars and the sheer ferocity of approach couldn't be denied. That 'Suicide Alley' sounded very much like The Clash circa 1976 was unfortunate. That the lyrics, supposedly inspired by the bouts of violence that ended many a night's drinking at Newbridge Rugby Club, were underwhelming was regrettable. That 'Suicide Alley' sounded genuinely excited, *genuinely exciting*, was much more important. There really was something there.

Funds ebbing away, the Manics were unable to buy a master tape of the songs from South Bank. Instead, they took a cheaper, much fuzzier 'reel to reel' with them to a local record pressing plant where 300 copies of the session were pressed, then promptly stored under Sean's bit of the bunk bed. Having already followed the 'Do It Yourself' punk ethos with commendable precision, Nicky drafted Richey in to take a photo of the band, later reproduced as an image on the first run of single sleeves, which they glued themselves (Edwards' photo underlines the band's Clash fixation to an almost comedic degree, the Manics dressed/posing in exactly the same manner as The Clash did for their debut LP).

The last part of the plan was making sure that copies of 'Suicide Alley' got to the right people, people sympathetic enough to advance their cause and aid, even abet their perfectly reasonable requests of 'world domination': "Yes, when we started, we did want to conquer the world, but that was just a young boy's dream... the myth of complete arrogance," said Wire. "You only get one time in your life, usually when you're young, before you realise what it takes." To use that time, they would need another tactician on board, one capable of manipulating the press and seducing the record companies while simultaneously retaining the love of their fans. Thankfully, they knew just the man for the job: 21 years old, seldom kissed, soon to be unemployed but bright as a proverbial button. Richey Edwards' time had come.

Chapter Five

Escape Velocity

Following a protracted but always loving courtship, Richey Edwards finally succumbed to the Manic Street Preachers' charms when he joined them onstage for a show at Swansea's University of Wales. Edwards only came on for the last song, a new tune entitled 'Sorrow 16', but it was enough to seal the deal – even if he 'officially' held out until his degree was concluded. Swiping at the guitar now and again, it was apparent to all present that Richey couldn't really play the instrument, but he looked cool, so it didn't matter. And that was essentially the way things would remain for the next five or so years.

Edwards didn't join the Manics because he wanted to 'play' rock'n'roll. The playing was perhaps the smallest part of it all. It was more what rock'n'roll represented: the glamour, the confusion, the poetry, the screams and sighs it teased from its disciples. And make no mistake: Richey had been an eager disciple of rock'n'roll, scrupulously following its progress in the music papers each and every week. No mere acolyte, he knew his rituals from his ceremonies, his saviours from his charlatans. But the decision to put aside an academic career in favour of one in music wasn't taken lightly. Unlike James and Sean, who were driven by a combination of blind confidence in their abilities and an uncertain future if they failed, Edwards had options: a good degree and the prospect of a bright career ahead of him. The decision led him to talks with tutors and fellow students about what a 'break year' might look like on his CV. Equally, he was privately concerned about the Manics' credibility, their retro punk leanings already leaving some fellow musicians in South Wales' alternative community distinctly cold. However, the commitment the band showed was total, their ambition psychotic, and their arguments for his involvement extremely persuasive. Even his parents understood there really wasn't a choice at all: "When Richey came out of university, I began to realise he wasn't looking for work and was more into rock 'n' roll," his father, Graham, remembered. "Some parents would have told him he was wasting his education, but as long as he was happy, I went along with it."

Already chauffeur, roadie, photographer and occasional lyricist, Edwards' accession to proper Manic Street Preacher also meant a new designation, 'Minister of Propaganda', the title a fitting description for the strengths he brought to the group: "Yes, Richey was our Minister of Propaganda," Sean later said. "He'd studied modern political history. In a way, he was our think tank." Edwards was well prepared for this post, already being quite the 'man of letters'. Hundreds of them, actually. A keen writer, he had been firing off missives to friends, family, and whatever band took his fancy for years: striking up correspondence with Big Flame and the Jasmine Minks, trading written asides with Funeral In Berlin's Steve Gatehouse, airing his views to specialist music fanzines and local press, even drumming up interest in the Manics before he was a member, Edwards was no stranger to paper and pen. But as a member of the group, he redoubled those efforts on behalf of his band, the copies of 'Suicide Alley' sent to music journalists and record companies being accompanied by stinging, hellishly long, post-modern versions of the traditional press release: "We are young beautiful scum... the suicide of the non generation," he intoned, "we are the only young kids in UK channel boredom to realise the future is in tight trousers... not the baggy loose attitude scum fuck retard zerodom of Madchester."

Using Edwards' abilities as a stunt-writer/propagandist was partly inspired by the Manics' then current love affair with Public Enemy. A politically charged, socially conscious rap collective hailing from Long Island, New York, Public Enemy had turned many a head with their

1987 debut album, *Yo! Bum Rush The Show*, and steel-tipped follow up, *It Takes A Nation Of Millions To Hold Us Back*. Led by vocalist Chuck D, PE (as they were known) were full of righteous anger at the treatment of the African American community, a fact evidenced on the likes of 'Black Steel In The Hour Of Chaos' and their later classic '911 Is A Joke': "Black people have far more genuine rage than any white man," Richey later reasoned. "White people feel repressed, black people are oppressed. (That creates) a real militancy. Public Enemy combined that militancy with being glamorous. They were like Aretha Franklin on smack." James who, with Moore, knew every word to every rap, took a slightly more grounded view of their appeal: "Public Enemy were saying things we couldn't identify with, but at least they sounded pissed off."

Another Public Enemy trait of great significance to the Manics' was how each group member was apportioned his own set of responsibilities within the collective. For instance, Chuck D wrote the majority of lyrics and fulfilled the role of frontman, while Terminator X and Flavor Flav spun decks and provided comic relief. Crucially, there was also a role for a 'Minister of Information', this post taken up by the sometimes controversial Professor Griff. To Nicky Wire, the idea was perfection itself: "Really, it all came down to our shared love of Public Enemy and the idea they used around the Marxist division of labour. If NWA were the Sex Pistols of the era, then Public Enemy were The Clash. Richey and I convinced James and Sean that though we were really bad musicians, we could do the talking, the writing and look good as well. Luckily, it worked."

Work, it did. Roles in place, Bradfield and Moore took care of the music while Edwards and Wire widened the sweep of their mail shots to music writers and publicists: "We realised that as individuals we were very limited, so we took a very academic approach at being a band. We were quite clinical... like magpies, collecting information, keeping dossiers on journalists and learning how to manipulate them." Such selective targeting cost money, however, and with Sean the only one in a proper job, they turned their collective charms upon the finance sector: "When we properly started, we used to go to NatWest, all the banks actually, and try and get a loan," Richey later said. "We'd tell them 'This country is dead musically, there's got to be room for an exciting rock band'. We'd show them copies of *NME*, saying 'Look at that, anything good in there? Now, look at us, we're really exciting. We basically told them we were going to be this really massive rock'n'roll band. They just couldn't see it."

Or as likely, the loan officers involved were simply confused by what was sitting in front of them. At a time when youth were in thrall to a Manchester music scene led by the baggy, loose fitting likes of The Stone Roses, Happy Mondays and Inspiral Carpets, the Manics were a four man pile up of teased hair, tight white jeans, box fresh plimsolls and girls' blouses fresh from *Top Shop*. Retro-chic or future past imperfect, the group's visual amalgam of Hanoi Rocks/New York Dolls 'twinkling' and Clash-like 'trimness' ran screaming from current trends. This was precisely the idea, of course, but still a hard sell to those lacking credentials to see past the eyeliner into a new golden age of glam/punk elegance. Whatever the truth of it, the band's new image was a long, long way from Nicky Wire's Pringle sweater-wearing past: "Yep, we used to get the piss ripped from us," he said. "I'd walk around dressed up like The New York Dolls and be called a poof, but I also didn't look at those people and think 'Worthless scum'. If they'd been working in a factory all week, they've got every right to get smashed out of their head and take the piss out of my haircut." Though James and Sean (who never really took to the cockatoo styling) were less extreme than Wire and Edwards in their choice of clothing and make-up, they were still fiercely loyal to their friends' right to wear it: "Richey and Nick used to get the piss taken out of them all the time," Bradfield told Q, "(comments like) 'Look at those fags over there! Go and suck each others' cocks in the corner, you faggots!' That kind of thing used to get my back up. We were just divorcing ourselves from our surroundings by the way we looked and dressed."

Their surroundings caught up with them in ugly fashion on December 22, 1989, when Bradfield and Edwards were set upon by a dozen or so youths at McDonald's restaurant in Newport City Centre. What led to the confrontation remains somewhat murky, though the gang taking exception to the duo's appearance seems a good bet. What actually set it off however, is a little less easy to confirm. According to one account, James and Richey were simply jumped. Another story has Bradfield fronting up to the group and maybe even throwing the first punch. Regardless of who did what and in what sequence, the skirmish resulted in Edwards being kicked to the ground and Bradfield getting a broken jaw. All in all, a grim end to Richey's 22nd birthday celebrations: "That was the end of our night," he later said, "a very thrilling birthday."

Years later, Edwards clarified his philosophy on such random violence: "If I was in a pub and someone attacked me, and I knew I done nothing wrong, I would happily take a beating without doing anything and feel really superior. I would never hit somebody back. If I'd done something wrong, then that's different. But if I was minding my own business, I could easily take a kicking. I'd think 'I don't give a fuck because you're scum. You're way down there and I'm above you because I can take it.' It's a bit biblical, 'turn the other cheek' and all that..." For James, who was unable to sing for the next six months due to his injury, the Newport incident just helped close the hatch tighter around the band: "We came to look down on anyone outside the circle of the four of us."

The temporary break in gigging caused by James' broken jaw meant more time to write songs, and in a perfect world, more time for Nicky to concentrate on his final year at University. Unlike Richey, the bassist's commitment to his studies was beginning to flag, a fact not helped by the dim view he took of his lecturers: "I enjoyed my 'A' levels," Wire later told *NME*, "because you had a certain freedom to write what you liked, and also you had teachers who wanted to teach you. At university, all the lecturers really want to do is write books. They don't have the first idea of how to teach and they don't care about making the subject interesting. They just indulge themselves." Uninspired by Swansea's tutorial squad, losing interest in his environment and with one foot firmly placed in the band, Nicky resorted to asking his friend for help: "Richey was obviously an academic, and I wasn't. I got him to do some of my essays (because) he finished a year before me, being a year older." Edwards' involvement must have helped, because despite Wire's final year of ennui, he still scraped a 2:2: "I was pleasantly surprised by that," he laughed.

Nicky's academic resolve must also have been tested to the limit when he learned some months before his finals that Richey's constant bombardment of the music press had hooked a fish – and a whopper at that. Steven Wells, then working as Singles Editor at *NME*, was one of those journalists targeted as potentially sympathetic to their cause. After several previous efforts, one of Edwards' tersely worded letter bombs finally piqued Well's interest: "We look like nothing else on earth. A car bomb kiss-off to the *Face*. Politics and adolescent cheap sex. Fuck the rotten edifice of Manchester... too boring. Too macho males afraid of themselves." That Edwards was still a virgin and Wire owned almost everything The Stone Roses had released was information Wells didn't have at hand. He did, however, have a copy of 'Suicide Alley' in front of him. Remarkably, he made it his 'Single of the Week', calling the band "retrogressive" but "inspired". Given the fact that parts of the Blackwood alternative community, and indeed, the surrounding valleys and towns of South Wales thought the Manics at best ordinary, or at worst "shit", this was progress on an unqualified scale. It was also a clear marker that their futures lay elsewhere. Again, that was always part of the plan: "We were very cynical people," Richey told *NME* in 1991. "We saw bands do all the pubs where we lived, do 200 gigs a year, get really big local followings, and they're all under the illusion that somebody from Sony Music will be driving through the middle of South Wales and say 'Hey, what a good band... sign here'. And of course, we knew that wouldn't happen. We knew we had to move to London."

Some eight gigs into their professional career, The Manic Street Preachers hit the M4 on September 22, 1989 in search of England's capital city. Three and half hours and some 150 miles later they found it. For some of the group, this was their first visit to London: "At the start," James quipped, "we didn't even know how to get across the Severn Bridge." The venue they were due to appear in was a pub on Great Portland Street called The Horse And Groom. No legendary Marquee, not even on a par with Hammersmith's Red Cow, but a decent enough place to start their campaign for superstardom – even if it didn't have a proper stage. The concert itself was organised by Kevin Pearce, Editor of *Hungry Beat* and *Esurient Communications*, two good 'glue and staples' fanzines Richey Edwards read and regularly contributed to: "I'd get a letter a week from Richey," Pearce confirmed. "He had enough energy to fuel the nation." Several acts were featured on the bill, to be headlined by proto mod-rockers The Claim. Two pounds to get in for punters, a free beer or two for the bands, but no dressing room provided. Given The Horse And Groom usually put on folk and jazz trios, the last point normally wasn't a concern. For the Manics though, it might mean taking over the gents' toilets for last minute make-up touches. Sensibly, they stayed hidden in their Ford Transit until show time.

At 9 p.m. or thereabouts, the band opened their set with a brand new song, 'New Art Riot'. Like their appearance at Newbridge's Railway Hotel, the Manics weren't given to anything but speed, hurtling through 'Dead Yankee Drawl', 'Destroy The Dance Floor', 'Faceless Sense Of Void' and several others before ending proceedings with 'Suicide Alley': "This is a single we released a bit ago," said James, "we've got a few to give away if you want." Bang, crash, wallop, all over. As with U2's earliest London gigs, thousands now claim to have attended the Manics' performance at The Horse And Groom. Given the room could only hold 150 people at a push, most of them are being economical with the truth. One person who was definitely there that night was *Melody Maker's* Bob Stanley, later to make his own musical mark in a more subtle, though no less effective, way with the slow-burning St. Etienne: "After the first number, James said something like 'Thanks, that's the most applause we've ever had. (After that), we were totally won over." Impressed by their attitude and relative tunefulness, Stanley gave the Manics front page coverage in his own fanzine, *Hopelessly Devoted*, their song 'UK Channel Boredom' (backed by The Laurens' 'I Don't Know What Trouble Is') appearing on a flexi-disc that came free with the magazine. The band were also featured in a similar way by another fanzine Editor, Mark Brennan, who obtained permission from the Manics to include both 'Suicide Alley' and 'Tennessee (I Get Low)' on a punk/skinhead compilation called *Underground Rockers Vol 2*.

Having gained the ear of *Melody Maker's* Bob Stanley and *NME*'s Steven Wells (who gave the Manics their first national interviews in April and August 1990), the group now truly closed doors on Blackwood and began playing venues across England. The decision wasn't hard. If they didn't capitalize on the ground they had gained it was all over before it began. This fact was made crystal clear by the news that Funeral In Berlin, who inspired their earliest efforts and provided them with several support slots, had recently broken up. "We knew we were lucky to find ourselves," Wire said, "and if you're lucky in life, you can find someone to build your life around." So began a life of late night motorway trips, small venues and pay-to-play shows at venues such as London's Rock Garden, a "tourist hole" smack in the middle of Covent Garden that record company types occasionally frequented. "It was straight to London," Richey confirmed, "scrounging money to get on the pay-to-play circuit. £50 for 15 minutes." The majority of funds for these trips came from the pocket of still practising civil servant Sean Moore: "Sean basically funded us when we were travelling about in Transit vans."

The band's letter writing campaign also continued, Edwards and Jones shameless in their efforts to attract attention by trying to drown every other successful group out there in streams of vitriol. Unfortunately, the Manics' innocence regarding some of the music journalists they admired was soon shattered. Expecting fearlessly objective critics on the trail of genuinely new music, the group was disappointed to find up-and-coming London bands often shared the same Camden Town watering holes as those who wrote about them. "Unbelievable," Edwards said, "five bands and loads of journalists all drinking at the same tables." Worse still, those self same writers seemed no better than "public school dropouts... who'd fucked up because they weren't that intelligent". The tactics soon employed by both camps to win ground over the other were in turns funny, irritating and occasionally downright hostile, but never less than entertaining to read.

A breakthrough of sorts finally occurred following another small-time London appearance, this time at Kentish Town's Bull And Gate pub. In the audience that night – as he had been months before at the Horse And Groom – was Ian Ballard, the man behind Damaged Goods. Beginning his company in 1988 by producing punk postcards and posters from a small office/living room in Walthamstow, East London, Ballard had grown Damaged Goods into a small, but credible alternative record label. Thus far, he had dealt exclusively with the re-release side of the market, re-issuing old punk albums by the like of Slaughter And The Dogs, Pork Dukes and the wonderfully named Snivelling Shits. All vintage 1977 product, all finding an audience with late-twentysomethings eager to re-capture the fire of their youth. However, Ballard was now keen to get involved with new bands and the Manics' high-energy set impressed him, as did their official spokesman: "Richey Edwards was very intelligent," Ballard later told *Select*. "He'd sit there quoting things and I'd nod thinking 'I don't know what you're talking about.'" On first meeting, Edwards and the others were unsure that Damaged Goods' ethos was right for them, but Ballard's honesty and integrity were impressive. A one-off single deal was duly agreed over a handshake. No contract required.

In mid-March 1990, the Manics began recording their second 'debut' single for Ballard at Workshop studios in Redditch. The results of the two day session, produced for a total cost of £186 by Mark Tempest, actually ran to four songs in all, making it an EP. Before it was released, the band were back on the road, picking up support slots with the likes of Mega City Four and Senseless Things, two upcoming pop-punk indie acts whose fan base could at least enjoy the Manics' 'Go Faster' antics. Devotees of the more mellifluous The Family Cat, whom the group also opened for around this time, were perhaps less giving. Their brief turn opening for The Levellers was better received, however, Nicky even spending the night before his university finals playing to an appreciative house of 'crusties'.

On June 22, the Manic Street Preachers finally released *New Art Riot*. The front cover design, entitled 'Collapsed European Stars' was essentially a warped version of the European Community flag (put together by Richey's college mate, Dan) while the back sleeve proclaimed the welcome/warning 'Made In Wales'. A further statement, "I am nothing and should be everything" from Karl Marx's early essay *A Contribution to the Critique of Hegel's 'Philosophy of Right'* also appeared on the artwork. With these wry nods to the founding father of Communism, the rights of the State vs. the private citizen, the pleasures of heritage and the sagging health of the EU, it was apparent to all the EP was not the work of Milli Vanilli.

Sadly, the music presented on *New Art Riot* wasn't quite as impressive as its eye-catching sleeve design. 'New Art Riot' itself was a distant cousin to The Clash's 'Tommy Gun', but distinctly lacking its sense of true dynamics. The second track, 'Strip It Down' was a tad more impressive, though yet again, it strongly recalled The Clash's use of stop/start rhythms. Next up was the lively 'Last Exit To Yesterday', which with its emotive chorus and chugging barre chords, gave the first real hints of the Manics' future musical direction. Finally, listeners were treated to 'Teenage 20/20', a tune that began with James channelling Chuck Berry's historic guitar riff on 'Johnny B. Goode' before cannibalising both The Stooges' 'No Fun' and Stiff Little Fingers' 'Alternative Ulster' for the next three, long minutes. On the plus side, the musicianship was getting stronger, Moore now in full command of his kit and James beginning to favour a more melodic approach to his guitar parts and vocals.

If the tunes present on *New Art Riot* lacked the overall naivety and directness of 'Suicide Alley', the lyrics at least, were a quantum leap forward. The title track for instance, literally declared war on old world order, the Manics' calling for the return of the guillotine to deal with aristocracy, while simultaneously bemoaning potential revolutions sold down the river for the sake of a pay rise: "Hospital closures kill more than car bombs ever will," being 'New Art Riot''s best line. Elsewhere, howls of protest ruled the roost. 'Strip It Down' derided rampant consumerism and the vapid lifestyles they inspired, while 'Last Exit...' and '... 20/20' drew blood on the subjects of love, emotional dependency and callow youth. Sloganeering in their attitude, nihilistic in their values, Edwards and Wire were taking a vintage 1976 broadsword to every UK band with baggy pants, a bowl haircut and a blissed out smile. "Hallelujah, clap your hands," indeed.

Given that the 300 copies of 'Suicide Alley' had either been sent directly to journalists, record companies or sold on across the counter at Dorothy's Cafe on Blackwood High St, *New Art Riot* was the first chance real music punters had to hear the Manics. While never threatening to trouble the charts, the EP still sold 4,500 copies on its initial run, a decent enough tally for an independent label release. It also won over the critics, with *Melody Maker* taking the opportunity to champion the band's old school punk leanings while simultaneously pouring cold water on the current 'Madchester' nu-hippie scene: "I'd rather the youth of today were taking their inspirations from the past," they said, "and thinking, challenging, acting, than this fucking 'hey-man-dash-let's-mellow-out-and-love-everybody-Manchester-vibe'... Single of the Week." *NME* was not to be outdone in terms of stirring rhetoric: "Amphetamine guitars skidding across jagged MC4 melodies, a late 70s up-against-it stance and a sloganeering sleeve." Truthfully, *New Art Riot* didn't deserve such praise, but sensing that the Manics might be on to *something* and the need to back a new trend always uppermost in their minds, the music papers weren't stupid enough to assassinate any potential front-cover stars. At least, not yet.

The business deal cut with Damaged Goods meant that, following the release of *New Art Riot*, the Manic Street Preachers were now free to pursue other record companies in search of a more substantial contract. For his efforts, Ian Ballard would retain rights to the EP, subsequently re-packaging it in an array of formats to a legion of new fans in the coming years. Bob Stanley too, also benefitted from the EP's title track, the Manics giving him the rights to a rough demo version of 'New Art Riot' (recorded in late 1989 at Colin Powell's South Bank Studios) in thanks for his early *Melody Maker* support. Stanley released the song, backed by an early demo of 'Repeat' under the catch-all title 'Feminine Is Beautiful', via his mail order label, Caff Records, in July, 1991. "For the Caff single," Bob remembered, "they pooled their giros and recorded two songs live the previous Christmas. They didn't buy the master tape and it was taped over. The vinyl had to be cut from a third generation cassette."

Backed by the music papers as 'ones to watch', and gaining a small, but increasingly devoted following through their gigging efforts, it was now essential that the Manics found a "manager of substance" to take up their cause. They had already dabbled with representation of sorts in the form of Mark Jones, an old friend from Blackwood responsible for booking their earliest gigs. But as Jones was allegedly as interested in building model rockets as he was with the Manics' progress, the association soon ended. Only the very best would now do. Again turning to music journalists as a source of potential support, Edwards and Wire contacted *NME*'s Steve Lamacq. A previous recipient of one of Richey's best "yellow A4" rants and an original copy of 'Suicide Alley', Lamacq recommended Phillip Hall as someone who might be interested in hearing what they had to say.

Born in the West London suburb of Ealing in 1959, Phillip Hall was music business through and through. A graduate of the London School of Printing, he used his journalism degree to break into the music press, writing for *Record Mirror* during a period when Duran Duran, Frankie Goes To Hollywood and Wham! all fought for cover stories. After time served, Hall took a job with EMI, before accepting the position of Head of Press at Dave Robinson's smaller, but highly influential Stiff Records. When the independent Stiff went the way of the dinosaur in 1985, Phillip took it as a sign to set up his own public relations company, Hall or Nothing, with younger brother, Martin. Their first real clients were punk-folk troubadours The Pogues, whom Hall worked with while at Stiff. Hall or Nothing's canny representation of Shane MacGowan's unruly bunch was rewarded with *Music Week*'s Les Perrin PR award. The client list quickly grew, with Phillip taking on additional publicity duties for The Stone Roses, whom he gently pushed from the triumphant chaos of their Spike Island appearance to genuine stardom. For this campaign, he was given another *Music Week* PR award in 1989. If these achievements were not enough, Hall had also re-bolstered the reputation of the annual Reading Festival, as well as given new life to the Irish-themed Fleadh, a yearly 'wig out' attended by thousands in North London's Finsbury Park. By 1990, he and his brother were busy launching their own record label, Sacred Heart, responsible for launching the career of 'New Cool Rock' darlings, Kingmaker. Relaxed, reliable and described by his peers as "one of the nicest men in music", Phillip Hall's reputation was impeccable.

When the Manics were first given Hall's address by Steve Lamacq, they were largely unaware of who he was, or indeed, his impressive history: "We really had no idea of what Phillip did, or how potentially helpful he could be to us," Nicky later admitted. Ignorance being bliss, Edwards sent a copy of *New Art Riot,* their latest set of publicity photos and another of his Manifesto/State of the Nation-type addresses, which concluded with the words: "Sign us up, help us escape or we'll die from boredom." Given that The Pogues were close to breaking up at the time, The Stone Roses were in a protracted legal battle with their then record company, Silvertone, and Hall's additional PR interests included The Waterboys, James and The Sundays, it remains a miracle that he even read Richey's plea. Even more of a miracle, if one factored in his recent marriage to wife, Terri. Yet, after phone calls to Lamacq and Damaged Goods' Ian Ballard to check their credentials, he wrote back to the group, promising to attend their next London concert. Greeted with the news that no future London dates had been booked, Hall and his brother took the unusual step of venturing to Newbridge Comprehensive School in South Wales to watch the Manics rehearse.

The auguries on the day of Phillip and Martin Hall's visit were not good. Prior to their arrival, Nicky had managed to whack a bass guitar into his nose, and was now a vision of eyeliner, foundation and congealed blood. Equally, the Manics were painfully embarrassed by their classroom surroundings, making them feel uncomfortable, unprofessional and shy all at once. It didn't matter. When the Halls finally met and heard the group – came to understand the sheer madness of the ambition – their interest was sufficiently piqued to discuss the possibility of representing them. "Within three months (of first meeting)," Wire later recalled, "Phillip Hall had officially become our manager." Hall's first real course of action was to move the Manics out of Blackwood to London, putting all four up in his Shepherds Bush house. Conditions were more than a little cramped, and Phillip's new bride was probably less than thrilled at the prospect of opening up the marital home to a group of strangers, but it saved on costs and he could work on getting them regular appearances on the capital's concert circuit. With Sean and James now 22 and 21 respectively and still sharing a bunk bed set-up, it was an invitation not to be missed.

The Manic Street Preachers proved themselves impeccable house guests for the six or so months they stayed with Phillip and Terri Hall. Unlike the majority of young men, they were gentle in their manners, and led by Nicky Wire, scrupulous in their cleaning. The group even went as far as suspending writing sessions each night in order to have meals prepared in time for the Halls' return from work. However, it wasn't all like an episode from *The Waltons*, as Terri became occasionally upset by the amount of effort her husband was devoting to his new charges. Wire also faced the harsh realities of Edwards' alcohol-assisted 'blank sleeps'. "I slept in the same bed as Richey," Nicky later told *The Face*, "and I'd wake up with the vodka seeping out of his skin." Another of Edwards' occasional habits – absent-mindedly cutting his forearms – was dealt with by a bout of group throat clearing until he became aware of his actions and stopped. To Hall, a former punk and witness to Shane MacGowan's bold experiments with the human constitution, this probably seemed mild behaviour, but behaviour to be carefully observed nonetheless.

To push the Manics to the next level, they would need serious funds for equipment and touring. Hall would solve some of the problem by plunging £45,000 of his own savings into the group, but a record deal was also needed. It came from Heaven, or more accurately, Heavenly Records. Described by its founder and former Creation Records press officer, Jeff Barrett, as "Less a record company, more a label of love", Heavenly Records was a marvellous, independent enterprise that took its ethos from punk but re-worked it for the 'Second Summer of Love' generation. To confirm the point, Heavenly's two major signings by 1990 were Flowered Up – the closest North London had yet come to producing a credible version of the Happy Mondays' 'Madchester' sound – and the gentle, yet self-aware bliss-pop of St. Etienne, led by soon to be former *Melody Maker* journalist, Bob Stanley. Like many music types, Barrett was already aware of the Manics through their letters, having been handed a copy of one of Richey's earliest epistles by *Hungry Beat* Editor Kevin Pearce: "(I was told), 'Read this'," Barrett said. "It was passionate... on fire; it wanted to change the world." Unfortunately, the accompanying demo didn't match the burning manifesto so Jeff passed on the band.

Fast forward 18 or so months and things had changed. The Manics were now brandishing two 'Single of the Week' nods from *NME* and *Melody Maker*, Hall Or Nothing were involved in their progress and Heavenly's own Bob Stanley was even singing the groups' praises. It was time for Jeff Barrett and colleague Martin Kelly to take a closer look. The pair got their chance when the Manics performed another showcase at London's Rock Garden: "They played the most amazing set," Kelly told *Record Collector*, "and we said, 'We've got a label, can we sign you?'" The initial response the duo received was a semi-serious "Fuck off," though when it became clear that they were legitimate in their offer, seats were pulled up and discussions commenced. If the group were concerned that Heavenly was too gentile, too blissful a home for their punk-leaning aesthetic, Barrett's philosophy for the label struck a real chord: "Two things mean a lot at Heavenly. Conviction and tunes – oh, and a complete disrespect for what's gone before." Conviction and disrespect the Manics had in spades, and they were now even working hard on the tunes. As with *Damaged Goods*, a singles deal was agreed with a handshake, no contract required.

Now a part of the Heavenly stable, the Manic Street Preachers found themselves on a short UK tour in support of label mates Flowered Up. That the headliners, led by 'orbiting' lead singer Liam Maher, were given to long and rambling musical jams that drew inspiration from acid house and psychedelia, was perhaps an ill omen. The fact their dancer, Barry Mooncult, gyrated bizarrely throughout the set dressed in a green Lycra bodysuit with a giant flower around his neck was surely a sign that the Manics should not take up the tour. Surprisingly, they were accorded a cordial enough welcome from Flowered Up's 'sky high baggie' following, even if the hundreds gathered each night were too loved up to understand what all the shouting was about: "Well, at least we actually got paid," being Bradfield's summation of events.

It's unlikely Flowered Up's core audience bought many copies of the Manics' new single, 'Motown Junk', when it was released on January 21, 1991. Too bad really, because musically, it was a little gem. Opening with a spiralling rally cry of 'Revolution!" sampled from Public Enemy, the song was awash with punk energy, though this time the Manics' Clash obsession remained more background reference than outright homage. Its title too commanded real attention, pouring scorn on the faux-soul posing of dinner party favourites such as Simply Red and Wet Wet Wet – then making an excellent living re-constituting the sound of Detroit for city bankers and barrow boys alike. However, 'Motown Junk''s most telling line, 'I laughed when Lennon got shot', was another thing altogether. While taking pot shots at rich, blue-eyed soul revivalists was hardly a matter for eyebrow-raising, chuckling at the assassination of a Beatle was venturing into territories even Johnny Rotten and Joe Strummer had failed to explore. Strangely, there wasn't much hoo-hah over the Manics' odd sense of humour at the time, James' snarling vocal delivery perhaps rendering the line largely incomprehensible. This fact was played upon by *NME*'s Steven Wells in his review of the band's first appearance at London's Marquee club that April: "Like the Manics say: 'Something grunt blah blah blah/blah blah we destroy rock un roll!". Bradfield's diction, however, didn't stop *NME* or fellow music paper

Sounds from proffering 'Motown Junk' as another 'Single of the Week', the latter stating: "(This is) viciously capable snot-core brat guitar rock."

The songs backing 'Motown Junk' were also flying flags of potential controversy. 'Sorrow 16', for instance, was all youthful dislocation, sleepless nights and blind obedience to a faceless enemy. And the anti-monarchist 'Corporate Rape Machine' had a title deemed so offensive by record plant employees, it had to be renamed 'We Her Majesty's Prisoners' before they would press it. For James, the final results were worth the hassle: "I felt a lot of pressure when we came to record 'Motown Junk'. We'd given it all this rhetoric, and then we had to walk it like we talked it. (But) it was the starting point for us... the first time we'd created a record we could live with." Housed in a sleeve featuring a photograph of a charred watch found at Hiroshima, its hands frozen at the exact moment America's nuclear strike destroyed the city, 'Motown Junk' gave the Manics their first chart entry: number 92 with a bullet. It also became their first real anthem, the song a staple of their concert set and excuse for their fans to "go fucking mental" to this day – though as the years progressed, James slowly but surely excised the Lennon reference from live performances.

Four 'Singles of the Week'. One chart entry. Managed by Hall Or Nothing. Signed to a hip independent label and not one of their number yet 24 years old. The escape plan hatched in a Blackwood bedroom, cultivated in a garden shed and fed regularly between lectures at Swansea University was at last beginning to bear fruit for the Manic Street Preachers. Logic now dictated they consolidate their position, foster diplomatic relations with those who could further aid their cause and reap the rewards of such prudence. Being "objectionable bastards", they chose instead to verbally firebomb their competition, goad the music press into a messy love/hate relationship and seemingly benefit from the results.

Guerrilla tactics from Generation Terrorists.

Chapter Six

Advancing Into Battle

As the Manic Street Preachers geared up for their second single release with Heavenly Records, it was becoming abundantly clear they occupied a singular position within the then current UK music scene. While almost every other young act was mindful of the stranglehold Manchester's 'Second Summer of Love' had over youth culture, and were either incorporating its influence to gain attention or wilfully silent in offering any criticism, the Manics were publicly deriding the movement to anyone willing to listen. "What I've got against bands like the Happy Mondays," Nicky Wire told *Melody Maker* at the time, "is they're too old and stuck in a working class cul-de-sac. They just don't offer any hope. Sure they may have excessive habits, but other people do exactly the same things every day." Edwards too, wasn't sparing the rod when it came to Shaun Ryder's 'Psychonauts', seemingly content to wish them out of existence: "Where we come from, the Manchester scene means nothing at all. The kids dream of LA beaches, the big US myth."

The bottles of piss and vinegar weren't solely reserved for Manchester. In fact, according to the Manics, the majority of bands vying for attention at the start of the Nineties were equally without merit, being too fat, too boring, too short, but curiously, not too tall. The list of faults was endless: "It's obscene fat people are allowed in bands. (Look at) The Bridewell

Taxis, The Paris Angels." Indie rock fared no better: "We want to destroy all these subcultures that had been around for so long," said Richey. "Gothic, Anarcho, the Wonderstuff, Stourbridge scene, Carter USM. It's all so terrible, so... unclean. I'd rather people killed themselves for us than Carter or Ned's Atomic Dustbin." The group were even happy to bag their own teenage heroes: "Electronic," said Wire, "are fat, bloated hideous bastards who deserve shooting. Johnny Marr trying to do windmills on a guitar when he's one foot tall and weighs 50 stones. It's as bad as Emerson, Lake & Palmer." From Slowdive ("I hate them more than Hitler") and Northside ("They look useless") to The Charlatans ("Their fans have moustaches") and Bowie ("Boring old cunt"), the Manic Street Preachers wanted to carpet bomb the lot.

Of course, music journalists were beside themselves with joy over such pronouncements, the Manics' deliberate lack of tact and diplomacy making their column inches fly by in a barrage of laughable putdowns, all the while being delivered with such grace and charm: "Their manners were impeccable," said one former *NME* scribe, "quietly sitting there, offering you cigarettes and being thoroughly pleasant while at the same time slagging absolutely everything off. It was always done with good humour, but I'm bloody sure they weren't really joking at times." Quite right. When one got behind the spotless manners and gentle delivery, the Manics were earnest in their disgust at the lack of glamour, the scarcity of intelligence and the paucity of true rock'n'roll spirit being paraded on the UK music scene. Or more simply, they felt that scene had let itself get fat around the hips, and they were there to get it back in shape. "We started out at a time when rock'n'roll was dead over here," Richey confirmed later. "The UK was in the grip of dance, rap and the acid house thing. All that Manchester stuff sounded so contrived, and the only real rock'n'roll was coming out of America. We were consciously reacting against all that. Our friends laughed, (saying) there was no audience for us. But we felt we had to bring back rock'n'roll." And, by all accounts, kill it: "Yeah, we wanted to be the *last* rock'n'roll band."

The Manics' version of rock'n'roll's last hurrah was a highly politicised, left leaning sex machine, smart as Lenin, pretty as Bardot. "We wanted to mix politics and sex," Edwards once said, "look brilliant on stage and say brilliant things." For Wire, the pennies dropped in exactly the same areas. "We had this... burning agenda. At the time, there was a gap for an intellectual working class band, the perfect mix of politics and beauty, making a noisy, intense racket." As ever, the patterns and the place that had formed the band were the very things that made it all tick. "We wanted something to believe in, but couldn't find anything to believe in. It was Culture, Alienation, Boredom and Despair," Wire admitted. "They were the tenant of our lives. It became overplayed... but at the start, that was our manifesto."

There was no doubting the sincerity of the Manics' ambition, nor the passion with which they were pursuing it. Yet, their penchant for slagging off all competition – regardless of how intelligent the comments or how entertaining they were in print – was also irritating some of rock's intelligentsia, even those secretly desperate to start an exciting new storm in the seas of UK rock. After all, the Manics were hardly above reproach themselves. With typical clarity, James Dean Bradfield later confirmed what some were thinking about his group at that time: "Yeah, we were four dickheads from Wales, (but) you know, no other dickheads from Wales were making music at that point. And yes, we were pretentious beyond belief and looked like complete and utter fucking pricks."

At the very start of the Manics' campaign, Richey Edwards' sharp use of sloganeering rhetoric and rock'n'roll symbolism when bombarding the music press had raised the eyebrow of many a recipient and actually impressed a few more. These reams of paper, with their talk of "destruction, sex and heroin" and "the suicide of... of young, beautiful scum" painted pictures of wasted youth stumbling out of doorways and unmade beds, looking for anything that might kill them before nightfall. Yet, in the flesh, the Manic Street Preachers appeared a very different proposition: polite to a fault, shy around women and worse still, harbouring a major Clash fixation, right down to the stencilled slogans that adorned their shirts and blouses: "The Manics," said The Fall's bassist, Steve Hanley, "looked like kids doing The Clash in a school play." Hanley was bang on the money. "When I look back now," Nicky Wire later admitted to *The Face*, "we tried so hard to copy The Clash. We had the same clothes, the tight jeans, the same guitars, the same hair colour. But to us, they were icons." At the time, however, such a straightforward admission would have been unthinkable. "The reason people and bands are repulsed by us is that we're a modern day interpretation of rock'n'roll," Wire said in 1991. "They think we want to be The Clash or the Stones, but we don't. We just know what rock'n'roll *could* be."

Deny it they might, but those stencilled shirts with their burning messages were telling a very different story to critics about whom the Manics were really indebted to. After all, such sloganeering was at the very heart of the original punk explosion, though one had to travel back a decade or so to the Situationist movement to unearth its proper origins. Formed in 1957 by a small group of "Marxist and artistic agitators", Situationist International (or SI) believed that if avant garde images, confrontational slogans and "disruptive events" were placed in everyday circumstances, they would 'jar' the observer's imagination and snap them "from casual spectacle into the living moment". Once truly awake, the next logical stage was to confront the actuality of existence and exert control of one's life – preferably by staging a Communist revolution. SI's French leader, Guy Debord, certainly thought this possible, daubing Paris' city walls with such abstract rallying cries as 'Demand The Impossible' during the student riots of 1968. Though SI eventually fell prey to internal squabbling, its influence lived on in the work of punk designers such as Jamie Reid and was taken up with gusto by The Clash in 1976, the group covering their clothing in combustible statements such as 'White Riot', 'Hate And War' and 'I Am A Prostitute'.

The Manics' own take on Situationism got off to a less than distinguished start in 1989 with the group daubing drab words like 'Teenage Beat' and 'TV Overdose' on their apparel. However, progress was rapid and by 1991, more striking declarations such as 'Lonesome Aesthetic', 'I'm Your Baby Doll', and 'London – Death Sentence Heritage' were covering their chests. There was no individual mastermind behind these antics, it being left to each group member to express their thoughts on clothing as they saw fit: hence, James gave birth to 'New Art Riot' and Nicky to 'Culture Slut', while Richey launched 'Kill Yourself' and Sean the marvellous 'Joe Bloggs Fuck Off'. These visual sound blasts, which often found their way into song titles and lyrics (and vice versa), soon numbered in the hundreds and would be copied by fans – even creating a small cult of their very own.

For the time being, however, they were judged by naysayers as yet another example of the Manics' love affair with past punk glories, or more sourly, a simplistic form of Hucksterism designed to gain maximum attention for the group. Bradfield was having neither: "We didn't feel a generation gap with those people older than us, we felt one with people of the same age. I think that's why we used sloganeering language a lot. We thought it was all they understood and deserved." To Edwards, who had studied Situationism with needle point intensity, and was greatly taken with the philosophies of Guy Debord, it was a device to both promote thought and provoke response: "You can ignore our songs, he said, "but when we walk down the street, and you see our song titles on our chest you've got to think something..."

If certain critics were sniffy about the Manics' "second hand sloganeering" and their not so hidden aspirations to emulate Joe Strummer and Mick Jones, they remained curiously quiet about the group's penchant for make-up and blouses. In a way, this would have been just as easy a target for them to pick on, the band's satirical debt to Hanoi Rocks, The New York Dolls and early Guns N' Roses as pronounced as their obligations to The Clash. More, the glam styling, the naive efforts at casual androgyny, were now dreadfully passé – relics hanging only on the slim shoulders of heavy metal guitarists and singers who really should have known better. Yet, despite the fact the Manics were covering the likes of Axl Rose's 'It's So Easy' in their live set, and had more than a sniff of Stones wannabes such as Dogs D'Amour about their apparel, music writers seemed content to leave it all alone. In Sean Moore's perfect world, the glad rags would have stayed on the racks of women's clothes shops where they belonged: "I just didn't feel comfortable in it," he later confessed. "I got though one tour with a Dorothy Perkins blouse, but it wasn't cut properly so I'd be drumming away, getting stuck to all this horrible crimpolene nylon stuff, which was chafing my arms." Moore eventually got his wish, the majority of the group dropping the glam look by 1992. That said, Nicky Wire's quest for getting in touch with his feminine side would take on ever more fantastical meanings as subsequent years went by.

Pretending to be the mighty Clash when they were musically more akin to second division punk bands such as 999, Sham 69 or, hands over ears, The Members. Only happy when pouring scorn on their contemporaries or kicking sacred cows, despite their own dearth of talent. Four sloganeering, preening intellectuals quoting Marx, T.S Eliot and Dostoevsky as if they were personally responsible for discovering them. Now they were even passing 'reading lists' of recommended books to journalists for publication in the weeklies. No respect for their elders, no respect for their contemporaries, no respect full stop. Actually, when the critics thought about it, this was nothing short of bloody marvellous. Of course, if there was irritation, even righteous anger, concerning the Manic Street Preachers' approach to self-publicity among music writers, it was far outweighed by the fact the band were also fresh, different, *against* everything else going on at the time. And if they really were university graduates simply playing with the concept of pop, or just playing with the people who wrote about it, so be it: they were doing so in a marvellously efficient, extremely entertaining manner. Love them. Hate them. In the end, it didn't matter. The Manics gave good interview.

Buoyed by the largely positive reaction to 'Motown Junk', the Manic Street Preachers were now making inroads into other potentially lucrative areas of publicity, grabbing their first television spots on BBC2's youth culture shows, *Rapido* and *Snub TV*. A Radio 1 session for DJ Mark Goodier also allowed them to hijack the airwaves. Hoping to steal *NME* and *Melody Maker*'s thunder, *Sounds* even gave the band their first front cover, a photographer capturing four fresh-faced young men peering out innocently beneath the slogan 'Generation Terrorists'.

To capitalize on all this hype, the Manics embarked on a short UK tour beginning at Hull's Adelphi club on February 1, 1991. However, several dates in, Nicky was rushed to hospital for surgery on a thyroid cyst in his neck. While the band made light of it, stating Wire's condition was the result of poor lifestyle choices such as "boredom... no sleep and a diet of coke and chips," gigs were still pulled in Reading, Coventry, Leicester and Southampton's Joiner's Arms. Given that this venue only held some 200 people, it was a telling reminder that while the Manics might have been talking domination of the masses to the press, the masses in question were still largely oblivious to their would-be masters.

This began to change ever so slowly with the band's second single for Heavenly, 'You Love Us', released on May 25, 1991. The best thing they had done thus far, 'You Love Us' was a knowing, two-fingered riposte to those journalists who had questioned the sheer majesty of the Manics' genius as well as their first successful experiment with hard rock dynamics. Again, the group chose a sample to open proceedings, though this time it was the chilling, scraped violins of Penderecki's classical lament, 'Threnody to the Victims of Hiroshima', rather than Public Enemy. The set-up worked, with Penderecki's atonal strings soon giving way to an excellent Guns N' Roses impersonation, one part 'Paradise City', one part 'You're Out To Get Me'. As the song rumbled towards its conclusion, another sample – this time liberating the drumbeat from Iggy Pop's self-defining 'Lust For Life' – helped bring the band home in some style.

Though neither Penderecki nor Pop complained about the use of their music on 'You Love Us', the Manics were threatened with several writs by those (alive and dead) whose image had appeared without permission on the single's cover. A wonderful montage, featuring among others *Betty Blue*'s Beatrice Dalle, mythic bluesman Robert Johnson, *Taxi Driver's* Robert De Niro, 'Great Beast' Aleister Crowley, reggae superstar Bob Marley, Hollywood icon Marilyn Monroe, Brit rock legends The Who and, cheekily, The Clash, the sleeve was a real attention grabber. It was just regrettable that *Heavenly* had allegedly forgotten to seek clearance from those actually appearing on it. Perhaps if the Manics had stuck to their original plan of using a picture of former world middleweight champion Chris Eubank on the cover ("because everyone hates him as well"), they might have avoided such hassle. Backed by a semi-comical promotional video that cast Richey as an ambisexual Elizabeth Taylor lookalike mincing around a catwalk and Nicky in full white-dressed, blonde-wigged Monroe regalia, 'You Love Us' reached a creditable number 62 in the UK charts. The law suits were later dropped.

With another single came another tour, though this time the venues were bigger, better attended and the Manics themselves were exhibiting the first real signs of prowess as a live act. Walking on stage to a backing tape of Beat poet Allen Ginsberg's controversial *Howl* – its opening line 'I saw the best minds of my generation destroyed by madness...' so loved by The Clash, they invited Ginsberg to guest on their 1982 LP, *Combat Rock* – the group were still a chaotic proposition, but one that now knew how to work a crowd. Covering double duty at centre stage, James Dean Bradfield was all flailing elbows, straining neck muscles and slow spins, his growing mastery of the guitar obscured by a complete inability to stand still. Nicky Wire too, was no slouch, his Cheshire cat grins to those in the front rows rapidly disappearing (as did James) when he attempted another star jump. Across the boards to Bradfield's right was Richey Edwards. A more controlled though by no means static presence, Edwards was either battling for supremacy with the three chord shapes James had taught him, or as likely, giving up the ruse in favour of simply looking like a rock star. And at the back was Sean Moore, trying to hold it all together while smiling occasionally at the punk rock circuit training taking place a few feet away.

With all the energy coming offstage, it was predictable that audiences might get a little worked up. In Scotland Bradfield took a punch to the nose while Nicky's hair was almost pulled out of his head. Brighton University proved no better in terms of gentility, the audience showering the band in beer cans throughout their set. With respect, the Manic Street Preachers were partially to blame for such behaviour, their reputation for casual guitar smashing and occasional bear-baiting crowd tactics leading to inevitable disruption on the dance floor. Equally, the group had a strict 'No Encores' policy, their failure to re-appear on stage sometimes leading to resentment and fresh can throwing.

The tendency for high spirits and sporadic violence at Manics gigs came to an early crescendo at the most unlikely of venues in May 1991, when the band agreed to perform at the Downing College Ball in Cambridge. With benefit of hindsight, the band shouldn't have taken the gig. Aware of their 'punk eccentricities', the Student Union had booked the Manics in the hope their appearance might enliven a predictably 'formal' event. Add a little drama, scare the cat, but nothing too serious. To this end, they offered the group a substantial fee for their services, a substantial fee for an hour or so's work. Still in debt due to their experiments in onstage destruction, the Manics took the bait.

The first clue that all might not be as it seemed came when they arrived at Downing to find several security guards gathered around a PA system owned by Criterion. Heavy manners, indeed. Things got worse when the group started their live set. Despite there being only two people in the hall at the time, a group of bouncers immediately encircled the stage. As the marquee filled up, it became apparent to both band and audience that Nicky Wire was in the advanced stages of drunkenness. During their second number, Wire tried to undo Bradfield's trousers, while jokingly offering him oral relief. James' measured response to Nicky's mock entreaties was telling him: "One step nearer and you're dead." Warned off, but still circling the airport, Wire turned his attentions to a mike stand instead, kicking it playfully for sport. Presumably trying to steady himself, the bassist then put a foot on a monitor. Already wound up by proceedings, and fearing for the life of their PA system, Criterion cut the power. Cue howls from the audience, Wire shouting at whoever would listen, band thrashing their equipment, student confronting James, James hitting said student, bouncers ejecting James and his colleagues from the stage, more angry words exchanged. The Manics hadn't even played four numbers.

Then, it livened up a bit. The local rugby team were drafted in to deal with the band. Bradfield, by now on a roll, successfully managed to take out the biggest of them with a couple of well-aimed punches. The venue's soundmen, angered by all the chaos, soon descended on the Manics' tour manager, but were talked out of further action by the music press, cameras hanging from their necks and ready for action. A skirmish then broke out between the band's road crew and security guards, as the former tried to extricate the band's belongings from a nearby dressing room. At some point, the police and their dogs arrived, finally escorting the Manic Street Preachers and their helpers from the premises. Because they had failed to complete a set, Downing College refused to pay the Manics for their services, though Phillip Hall kindly counter-offered to set right any costs for damages incurred. The incident got the Manics their first national press coverage, with the tabloids only too happy to have punk back in the headlines. For Richey Edwards, it was a storm in a tea cup: "They deserved Carter and Kingmaker," he quipped.

On the face of it, the Downing College May Ball had all the makings of a classic 'us against them' story: working class punks invading the sanctity of higher learning, frightened society women clutching their pearls as fine upstanding men fought to see off the musical equivalent of chimney sweeps. The clichés were potentially endless. In reality, a university graduate paid to entertain his equals got drunk, acted foolishly, then fell foul of an overcautious student union and PA company determined to protect their equipment by using 'heroic' measures. A tale for the pub then, the real truth of it all falling away to exaggeration and ever more colourful language as the drinks piled up. Nothing more than a storm in a beer glass, really.

What happened next, however, was a little bit of rock 'n' roll history.

Chapter Seven

Signs And Wonders

In his role as News Editor at *NME*, Steve Lamacq had been initially supportive of the Manic Street Preachers. An early recipient of one of Richey Edwards' numerous 'state of the nation' addresses to the music press, he had put the band in touch with their manager, Phillip Hall, and even namechecked them in *NME*'s 'Tips of the Year' for 1991. However, recent events had conspired to sour the milk between group and writer. Unlike the Manics, Lamacq was squarely behind the UK alternative rock scene of the time, giving regular coverage to the likes of Carter USM and The Senseless Things. Therefore, when Edwards and Wire began cutting such groups to the quick during interviews he took sides, picking on the Manics' own frailties during a live review of another up-and-coming band, Bleach. The Manics responded in kind at their next gig, dedicating the B-side of 'You Love Us' – the withering 'Starlover' – to Lamacq. This was no casual choice. Similar in scope to The Rolling Stones' notorious 'Star Star', which portrayed groupies as objects of scorn, 'Starlover' was a bitter attack on the critics, DJs and scene makers earning a living from the rock'n'roll machine. Subsequent slurs from each side did little to improve relations and handbags were drawn.

Perhaps wanting to capitalise on the spat between them for circulation purposes, *NME* sent Steve Lamacq and staff photographer Ed Sirrs to cover the Manic Street Preachers' appearance at Norwich Arts Centre on May 15, 1991. In Lamacq's mind, it was an opportunity to bring an objective eye to a band who thus far had received largely glowing praise from the music press, even if privately some journalists were dubious of their actual talents. "No-one was really taking them to task, so I thought I would," he later said.

The gig itself was a small affair with only 40 or so people in the audience. The Manics played their usual set, opening with recent single 'You Love Us' before rolling through a mix of the new – 'Spectators Of Suicide' – and already established 'Strip It Down'. Matters were brought to a close some 35 minutes later, and as was their habit, no encore was performed. Though Lamacq briefly chatted with the group at their hotel before show time, James Dean Bradfield had ignored him on the drive to the venue and then spent the pre-gig run-up watching a football match with Nicky. If an interview were to be conducted, it would have to be now. The group consented to talk, covering a plethora of subjects between cigarette breaks, though the main thrust of conversation centred on Lamacq's concerns regarding their credibility, image and motivations. The discussion broke up without any great resolution on either side: "30 minutes of friendly enough discussion and vitriol," he later wrote in *NME*, "for the most part agreeing to disagree." As Steve Lamacq packed up his belongings, Richey Edwards asked for a moment of his time to clarify some of the points raised before. The two adjourned alone behind a nearby barrier while the other Manics talked with fanzine writers.

In conversation, Lamacq and Edwards again spoke of the Manics' authenticity, the journalist re-iterating his doubts that the band were a credible proposition. "I said something like 'The way you portray yourselves, the slogans, the actions, the way you look doesn't really show off your depth. That might mislead people, and they may not think you're for real.'" Richey's response was sincere: "I know you don't like us, but we are for real. When I was a teenager, I never had a band who said anything about my life. That's why we're doing this. Where we came from, we had nothing... believe me, we are for real. We do mean what we do."

Lamacq became aware that while Edwards was talking, he had rolled up his shirt sleeve and was quickly cutting his forearm with a razor blade.

Richey made 16 incisions in all before he concluded business. The result of the cuts, the first of which was almost bone deep, read '4Real'.

The two continued to talk for at least three minutes following Edwards' actions: "People ask me 'Why didn't you stop him at the time?'" Lamacq later said, "But it was his presence, the tone of his voice was mesmeric. He just had a spellbinding face." When the spell was finally broken by the steady flow of blood from Richey's arm, Steve Lamacq tried to make light of it: "I finally said... 'Look, you're making a mess on the carpet." He then went in search of manager Phillip Hall to quietly inform him that "Richey was a bit shaken up." Within minutes, moves were afoot to take Edwards to hospital, but not before *NME* photographer Ed Sirrs had captured the wounds for posterity: "Richey actually said, 'Do you want to take a photograph of this?' So I... whipped out my camera. He then said 'I'd better take the bandages off'. They'd just been put on, so (the cuts) were mint."

The subsequent photo shows Edwards resplendent in a lilac shirt bearing the slogan 'Spectators of Suicide', his forearm heavily cut, his eyes remarkably clear. For Lamacq, who didn't see Sirrs' shot until the next day, it was the first opportunity to understand what Richey had carved into his arm during their conversation: "I don't know where the razor blade came from, because I just kept looking intently into his face. He didn't seem to be in pain... he could have been writing in Biro. And I didn't actually know what he'd written until I saw the photos... because his arm was obscured with blood."

The immediate aftermath of '4Real' saw Edwards being treated in the Accident & Emergency wing of Norwich General Hospital, where he received 17 stitches for his wounds. As model a patient as he had been a student, Richey refused treatment until all those without "a self-inflicted injury" were seen.

In the meantime, Steve Lamacq and Ed Sirrs had headed back to London, where the previous night's events were discussed at length with *NME*'s Editor, Danny Kelly, and (behind the scenes) with their legal team. The principal concern for the music paper was whether publication of Sirrs' photo would appear opportunistic, or worse, lead to 'copycatting' among Manics fans. As the debates raged, a now shaken Steve Lamacq headed to the local pub. When he arrived back at the news desk, there was a message waiting on his answer machine from Richey Edwards apologising for any upset caused by the method he'd chosen to make his point. A week later, Sirrs' photograph (now in black and white) ran in the news section of *NME* while Lamacq's review of the gig was printed at the back. Overall, it was a lukewarm assessment of the Manics' performance that night, though the journalist's final sentences were telling: "The fact is I'm not sure the Manics have everything under control at the moment. DON'T BE DAFT BASTARDS."

In the Manic Street Preachers camp, the incident was publicly treated with an unusual blend of artifice and sincerity, the band simultaneously making light of things while underscoring Edwards' actions with bold, supportive rhetoric: "It was the highlight of my year," Wire said soon after the incident, "... seeing Richey's blood was brilliant. (Besides), it was one of the most boring concerts of all time. There were only about 25 people there. The only bad point was we had to cancel the gig the next day because his arm was swollen."

Years later, Nicky was still confirming it all as high art: "I didn't actually see Richey do it, but when I saw him come out, I just thought it was such an amazing, fantastic statement. I thought 'O God', I wish I'd got to do that." Bradfield too, was keen to turns heads away from pure shock value towards something much more thoughtful: "You can trace self-mutilation in pop from Iggy Pop to Julian Cope, but they just wanted to be mad fucks, whereas Richey is the least violent person I know. What he did just showed that as soon as a person is willing to turn violence against themselves as a statement, people become totally shocked. But they can also go out and beat someone up and that's all right. It doesn't make any sense."

Privately, it was a different matter. The extent of Edwards' injuries to himself had genuinely shaken the band, their real feelings only coming to light five years on: "Richey's smoking and drinking were increasing by that point," Sean Moore later confirmed to the BBC, "and he'd started to put cigarettes out on his arm. But I don't think the cutting *really* started until we did that gig in Norwich. I wish Richey hadn't felt he needed to do that. I regret that it was the start, I feel, of a downward spiral in his life." For Bradfield, it was much the same: "There must have been a different ingredient inside of him."

And so to the man himself. If Richey Edwards internally acknowledged his actions were light years away from grazing his arms with a compass – that an occasional, albeit worrying habit had just escalated to something of greater psychological significance – he kept it to himself. Instead, a mixture of light humour, gentle sarcasm and justifications related to class, credibility and internalised anger were offered in service of truth: "If you'd spent a couple of hours talking to Steve Lamacq, you'd have done the same." When pressed, Richey offered more: "I was really fucked with Steve Lamacq," he said. "I didn't know what I could possibly say to make him understand. How easy and cheap would it have been for me to just hit him? I would never do that. I'd rather cut myself, because I can justify that, whereas I can't justify hitting him. I tried talking to him for an hour to explain ourselves. (But), he saw us as four hero-worshipping kids trying to replicate our favourite bands. There was no way I could change his mind. I didn't abuse him or insult him, I just cut myself: to show him that we were no gimmick, that we were pissed off, that we are for real. It was the only way to get through to a 24 year old who thinks like a 45 year old." "It's sad," Edwards later concluded, "that no-one seems to realise working class resentment is always turned upon itself."

Nearly two decades later, Richey Edwards' behaviour that night in Norwich still has some power to shock. Unlike The Sex Pistols turning working class guns on the monarchy, or John Lennon declaring The Beatles bigger than Jesus Christ, the world hasn't yet downgraded the image of a young man so persuaded by his cause he's willing to cut his arm to pieces in service of it to a redundant file marked 'So what?'. According to James Dean Bradfield, that might have been the intention all along: "Richey knew exactly what he was doing when he did that. He knew it was an iconic image in the making, he knew the mere actions were shocking in themselves."

Gesture, statement, great art, madness. To Nicky Wire, it was simply a sign of things to come: "Let's face it, you didn't need any clues for Richey," he told *Q* in 1996. "When he carved '4Real' on his arm, nothing could surprise you after that. Alcoholic, anorexic, drugs, self-mutilator... all your favourite things rolled into one."

A calling card, then.

Chapter Eight

The Fabulous Disaster

'4Real' had illustrated in a series of deep, dramatic cuts that the Manic Street Preachers took their art very seriously indeed, and in Richey Edwards' case, were even willing to bleed for it. Predictably to the band's fans, Steve Lamacq became 'Public Enemy Number One' for a time, while less involved souls looked on in with a mixture of piqued curiosity, silent wonder, or for those with a weak disposition, some queasiness. For the Manics themselves, the attendant publicity generated by Edwards didn't greatly hurt. After all, they signed a 10 album deal with Columbia Records – part of the Sony Empire – on May 21, 1991, six days after the incident.

The wheels at the record company were spinning some time before the events of Norwich Art Centre. Sony's Managing Director, Tim Bowen, had ventured to Surrey University in Guildford to see the band on February 17, and though it was allegedly a quiet night by Manics standards, he was still impressed by what he saw: "I thought they were the most exciting thing I'd seen since The Clash in 1977," Bowen later told *NME*. "I just thought they were amazing, refreshing, even for an old fart like me." As Tim Bowen was the man responsible for signing The Clash to the label some 15 years before, this was high praise indeed. Sony's MD drew however, the line at describing the Manics as outright revolutionaries: "They're no more anarchistic than anyone else their age... or mine, come to that."

Sony/Columbia was neither the first nor last of the major labels to court the Manic Street Preachers. In fact, three others had shown real interest, with one actually inviting the group to smash up their office furniture if it helped gain their signatures. The Manics graciously declined in the face of such outright vulgarity. After something of a Dutch auction, they finally agreed to put pen to paper with Tim Bowen's men for a £250,000 advance. The reasons behind the band settling there were myriad. The Manics had all been genuinely impressed by Bowen coming to Guildford from his ivory tower in the heart of London's West End. More, they trusted Sony/Columbia's A&R and marketing teams – led by Rob Shreeves and former Student Union Entertainment Secretary Rob Stringer – to raise, even explode their international profile. Equally, the Sony group was home to some of the largest artists in the world, their roster including Bob Dylan, Michael Jackson and Bruce Springsteen. And purely as fans, the company had also brought their beloved Clash to their Blackwood stereo systems, while currently representing the interests of their newest heroes, Public Enemy. "They just chased us big time," Bradfield later confirmed, "and the man that signed us was a massive fan. It's quite the mistake to think that music fans don't work at major record companies. Sometimes, you find some good people at corporates, among all the infidels."

Another strongly compelling reason to join Sony/Columbia was that it was a global brand, a corporate entity, a major concern. In short, a proper record company. For a band like the Manic Street Preachers, with a collective eye on true glory, aligning their long term futures to an independent label was never part of the plan: "The whole 'indie' mentality that grew up with punk," reasoned Edwards, "seemed like bullshit to us because the most subversive band in the world was Public Enemy and they were signed to Columbia. The level of corruption on an indie label is just on a smaller scale." Elsewhere, he went even further: "(Labels like) 4AD and Creation became spiritual homes and everyone forgot about Gracelands," Richey told *NME*. "The dumb shits never saw past Camden Town and missed out on the likes of Black Crowes, NWA, Ice T and Alice In Chains. Indie culture won."

Edwards' co-propagandist, Nicky Wire, held the Manics' party line, insisting this was no sell-out: "Signing to a major label record company is the price of an education. We don't care what they do to us. The credibility of indie labels is shit." Potentially, though, there was still fun to be had at Sony's expense: "Being on a major makes everything easier... you can use all their money... their resources, their marketing, tell them what to do and they do it like obedient servants." Out of public earshot, the Manics handed back £6,000 to Heavenly Records for any losses incurred by the independent label ("A really nice gesture," said Jeff Barrett) while spending their new riches on the following items: a modest holiday for Sean and partner, Rhian; a portable CD player, Gameboy and some new clothes for Richey; more clothes and an end to his student loan/fruit machine debts for Nicky; and last but not least, a brand new £800 Gibson Les Paul for James. Evidently, the Manic Street Preachers didn't do bling.

By signing to Sony/Columbia, the funds behind the Manics were now in place, with the road from Blackwood to potential stardom taking five years – or just two, if you started the group's clock running when Richey officially joined their ranks. To their head of propaganda, such quick progress was no different than working one's head around a tricky politics question: "It was easy. I always thought it would be." Signed, sealed and soon to be delivered, it was time for the Manics to announce their manifesto/masterplan for fans and critics alike. A marvellous piece of reductionism, it covered seven points in all, three less than the Communist Party managed when they published theirs in 1848. It was also breathtaking in its arrogance:

- Release a debut double album on a major label featuring at least 30 songs, songs so utterly perfect they will provide a template for all other bands to follow in perpetuity.
- Sell at least 20 million copies of the album in question.
- Take their live show to the stadiums of the world, while conquering the United States in the process.
- Through their music and statements, create revolution in the UK, bring about an end to monarchy and peerage and replace it with a form of Socialism in line with the principles of Marx, Lenin and Stalin.

- Condemn all other musical groups, thus establishing the Manic Street Preachers as the one true musical group.
- Achieve these objectives within one year, after which time the group will disband.
- Look splendid throughout.

As journalists marvelled, fans applauded and almost everyone else raised their eyes to heaven, the Manics kept their thousand yard stares intact. Behind the stony faces, however, there was some doubt they could achieve such lofty goals. "When we formed," Edwards later told *Melody Maker,* "we wanted to sign to the biggest label in the world, put out a debut album that would sell 20 million, then break up. Get massive, then throw it all away. But, by the time we were giving interviews and saying that to the press... we didn't really believe it. We knew we couldn't quite do it. But, if we had aimed any lower in the beginning, I don't think anyone would have paid as much attention to us." There was even some slight dissension in the ranks, with James Dean Bradfield privately battling over manifesto point number six: "Richey and Nicky were out there talking about selling 20 million albums, then splitting up. Splitting up? I was thinking 'Hmmm, I'm not sure I want to do that'."

For the moment they didn't have time to break up, as the Manics' first single for their new record company, 'Stay Beautiful', was released on July 29, 1991. An uptempo chugger redolent of, but not quite as distinguished as 'Motown Junk', 'Stay Beautiful' was a solid, dependable way for the band to open their big budget account. Bradfield's voice showed the benefit of some extra studio time, while the overall sound was crisp and professional. The song itself was originally called 'Generation Terrorists', but the Manics chose to keep that title 'in the trunk' for something bigger and better. With radio airplay in mind, they also chopped the last two words from 'Stay Beautiful''s pre-chorus line: "Why don't you just fuck off?" the group and their fans only too willing to re-instate the missing sentiments when it was sung live.

If the song's title and lyrics didn't stray too far from rock 'n' roll's familiar pre-occupations with remaining pure and unsullied in the face of everything, the B-sides were another matter entirely. 'R.P. McMurphy' took its inspiration from the tragicomic character of Ken Kesey's 1962 novel, *One Flew Over The Cuckoo's Nest*, later made into an Oscar-winning movie starring Jack Nicholson. In the tale of a rebel who feigns mental illness so he can be transferred from prison to a psychiatric institution, McMurphy is eventually brought low by an authoritarian nurse, the demonic Nurse Ratched. In the Manics' hands, the tone of both book and film was kept impressively intact, while they added a few chills of their own: "Straitjacket your own beauty, because it's only a breakdown away." 'Soul Contamination' too, was lyrically strong, full of warnings about mass control, evil cartels and weakening resolve. Promoted on the back of a mini-tour, which saw Sony-purchased balloons bearing the single's name fall from the ceiling at the conclusion of shows, 'Stay Beautiful' rose to number 40 on the UK charts. For an act committed to selling 20 copies of their debut album within 12 months, this was a slow start.

Seeing their single fail to crack the Top 30 did little to dampen the Manics' spirits. Master plan still achievable, the band pushed all doubts aside and descended on the leafy village of Ripley, Surrey to begin work on their first – and allegedly only – LP. Their destination was Black Barn Studios, a £1,000 per day recording complex exquisitely housed within a rambling Tudor cottage close to the parish church, cricket pitch and Anchor pub. The birthplace of guitarist Eric Clapton, and occasional stop-off point for touring cyclists, Ripley was sedate, gentrified and though miles away from the distractions of the city was easily accessible from London as it sat five minutes off the A3. A perfect place then, to create the masterpiece of masterpieces. The man chosen to guide the Manics to glory was producer Steve Brown. A seasoned hand who had previously helped ABC and Wham! to international success, Brown was not just interested in pop acts. In a career that stretched back to the early Seventies, he had engineered sessions for hard rockers Thin Lizzy, produced The Cult's stinging 'She Sells Sanctuary' and even worked on a short-lived Sex Pistols/Johnny Thunders side project. As James Dean Bradfield said: "Steve Brown had previous."

Given the working title 'Culture, Alienation, Boredom and Despair', sessions for the album began well enough, but urgent intentions soon fell prey to crippling delays – new and old songs being started, abandoned, then re-worked and re-worked again. As Bradfield and Moore grappled with the intricacies of transferring live blasts of energy to an unforgiving studio environment, Wire and Edwards mused over last minute changes to song lyrics. This 'equal division of labour' was typical of their working practices. But for James, who had to mould Edwards and Wire's complex wordplay into something that could actually be sung and played, it came with real challenges: "There's a 25 percent split on songwriting all the way down the line. I always thought that the way we write our songs and perform them was fairly unique because my position is quite voyeuristic," he said. "I'm completely singing someone else's sentiments and... they're hardly the 'old moral bystander' lyrics. I just set myself a rule (that) I've got to take the lyrics on to a level of understanding before I can actually write music to them. If I don't write the lyrics, therefore I must interpret them to the best of my ability. My rule is that I must understand it, but I don't necessarily have to accept it. I think people should do it more in pop music. Sometimes, it can give you a very detached point of view, which makes things a bit more interesting." In the end, it was all a matter of trust. "Yeah, there's a lot of trust between us. They trust me to never be blasé about interpreting the material and I never write a tune before the lyrics. Some people write music and the words come along and they say, 'Oh yeah, I've got something to fit that.' If that's the way people write songs, then I feel like you might as well just go to the supermarket."

As Brown, Bradfield, Moore, and to a lesser extent Wire, continued to work on songs Richey Edwards took no part at all in the musical process. While the few guitar chords he had mastered were useful as muted background noise on stage, his lack of skill on the instrument meant that once James was confident with the words, Edwards was superfluous to proceedings. More, he showed no great interest in learning the mechanics of the studio itself, seemingly bored by faders, compressors and reverb plates. His contributions therefore behind him, Richey was free to commandeer the Sony courtesy car and head in search of London's Soho district. Once there, he allegedly walked the streets before dipping into clip joints and strip clubs to while away his time. On the odd occasions he returned to Ripley, Richey would fill his day creating photo montages on the studio's wall or playing Sonic The Hedgehog for hours on end. His dedication paid off when he finally defeated the evil Dr. Robotnik: "Sonic," Edwards quipped, "ruled my life."

Of greater concern to the band was Richey's rapidly reducing food intake, his diet now centred on basic rations such as cheese and tomato sandwiches and numerous cups of tea. While his diet may have been diminishing, Edwards' drinking was slowly increasing, leading to occasional crises of confidence. Rumours persist that he broke down in tears several times during this period, telling James he would have nothing without the band: "I felt Richey was the oldest and yet the youngest of us all," Bradfield once said. "He'd only experience things by forcing himself into situations. He was quite immature in terms of what he'd experienced."

When the band finally finished their work at Ripley, Edwards was again visibly upset, ritually burning his studio wall photo montage. Sitting cross-legged, he watched Stalin and Elizabeth Taylor turning to ashes while simultaneously listening to old Hanoi Rocks tunes at high volume. All in all, it was a curious Valhalla.

By the time mixing of the Manics' debut disc concluded at London's Hit Factory, Richey Edwards more resembled his old self, though curiously there was now more to worry about. The cost of making the album had run seriously over budget, nearing £500,000 in total. Additionally, the planned eight-week stay at Black Barn Studios had stretched to nearly four months, pushing the record's release date back into the early spring of 1992. And there was still the matter of a cover sleeve to yet be negotiated between band and label. The Manic Street Preachers had three particular images in mind. The first, *Piss Christ* by New York artist Andres Serrano, was a sepia-tinged photograph of a crucifix submerged in a glass box of what was believed to be Serrano's own urine. Permission for its use was refused to the band, though the photographer later allowed heavy metal icons Metallica rights to two of his other works, *Blood And Semen* and *Piss And Blood*, for the covers of their *Load* and *ReLoad* albums.

The Manics then turned their attentions to Bert Stern's legendary photographic sessions with Marilyn Monroe for *Vogue* in June 1962, some six weeks before the actress' death. Of the 2,500 photos taken,

Monroe had famously scratched or splashed paint on the ones she disliked. It was these rejected images that the group wanted to use. On this occasion, progress was better, but too much money was asked for image copyright. Their last choice was Mark Quinn's *Self*, essentially a death mask parody fashioned from globules of the artist's own blood and frozen within a plastic representation of his own head by a small refrigerator. Sadly, Quinn had sold the work to Charles Saatchi, who was again asking too much in reproduction fees. At this point, the Manics' record company stepped in with their own unique idea: "Sony wanted us to have a giant missile coming through a theatre stage for the cover," Nicky laughed. "Priceless, really." They finally resolved the cover sleeve issue by the use of camera trickery, digitally altering a photograph of Richey Edwards' left arm tattoo from 'Useless Generation' to 'Generation Terrorists', the name decided upon for their debut album: "At the age of 10 or 12, everybody is full of some kind of optimism," Edwards later explained to *Melody Maker*. "In those five or so years, your life has been dramatically changed and pretty much destroyed. That's what the title means."

Before the world could hear and see the full results of the Manic Street Preachers' endeavours, two singles were released in rapid succession to stimulate interest in the forthcoming LP. The first of these was a double A-side, 'Repeat/Love's Sweet Exile', which arrived in shops on October 29, 1991. In Manics circles, 'Repeat' already had history to it, the song something of a concert favourite and a fine excuse for Bradfield to show off his lead guitar skills. On record however, the anti-monarchist rant, with its eight-line refrain circling around the phrase "Fuck Queen and country" sounded puerile and attention-seeking, or "Punk for imbeciles" as one critic kindly put it. 'Love's Sweet Exile' (originally titled 'Faceless Sense Of Void') was a little more interesting, though its flailing drums and heavy-handed instrumentation sounded more like the work of a prog-metal band than rock music's new self-appointed saviours. Backed by a chaotic live version of 'Stay Beautiful' and U2/Guns N' Roses composite 'Democracy Coma', 'Repeat/Love's Sweet Exile" actually did the trick of pushing the band into the UK Top 30, the single climbing to number 26 before rapidly disappearing again. The reasonable chart placing had no doubt been helped along by the

Manics' spirited appearance on Channel Four's live youth torture show, *The Word*, where they 'accidentally' performed the expletive-ridden 'Repeat' instead of the more sublime '... Sweet Exile'. Both the band and the show's then-producer, Jo Whiley, woke up to outraged headlines in the tabloids the next day, ultimately doing neither any harm at all. Additionally, the promotional video also caused a small stir, Nicky and Richey mock-cuddling up to each other like a pair of pandas dressed in S&M clothing. Truthfully, the only shock to be had from the clip was the sight of Sean Moore in a Batman mask.

By January 16, 1992, the Manics were at it again, this time with another 'new' single, a re-recorded version of 'You Love Us'. While the music papers cried foul at the band already trawling their back catalogue before their first album was even released, 'You Love Us' made sense. It was catchy, pithy, fleet of foot and crucially, might give them a real hit. Sony seemed to think so anyway, handing the Manics £38,000 to produce a video worthy of the song. To their credit, they gave it the good old college try – Edwards and Wire once again mincing it up in semi-comical fashion, as Bradfield and Moore showed admirable alpha-male restraint. Prefaced with the 1910 Futurist movement slogan: "Regard all art critics as useless and dangerous," and featuring the Manics' 'Glamour Twins' in a twin-necked shirt bearing the words 'Suicide Babies', the promo's artful gimmickry did the trick. The Manic Street Preachers got their first *Top Of The Pops* appearance and 'You Love Us' rose to number 16 in the charts. Richey celebrated by moonwalking on the beer glass-crowded table of a central London pub. World domination was now only a debut album away: "With the confidence we have in this album," Wire told *NME*, "we won't be happy unless it sold 16 million." Though the figure was already some four million down on the original number quoted in the Manics' master plan, it was still fighting talk.

Housed in a gatefold sleeve featuring Richey's bare torso, a crucifix hanging from his neck and altered rose tattoo proudly bearing the LP's title on his arm, *Generation Terrorists* arrived in shops on February 10, 1992. Slightly light on their promise of 30 songs, *Generation Terrorists* featured only 18 tracks in all, but among the lyric sheets, photo montages and plethora of themed quotes from Chuck D to Confucius, one hardly noticed. Of course, given the ceaseless proclamations and bold edicts, all anyone was really interested in was whether the Manics had delivered an album to end all albums or simply reneged on their pledge. In the end, *Generation Terrorists* was a bit of both – a paper moon shining brilliantly at times, though still fragile enough to catch fire in the flames of its own ambitions.

Things certainly started combustibly enough with 'Slash N' Burn', a propulsive little rocker that somehow melded the best bits of The Who, the Stones and Guns N' Roses while still sounding thoroughly modern. The lyrics too, were clever stuff, presenting the ancient 'chop down/ burn/re-fertilise' Third World farming method as a guide to survival in modern day living. However, the following tune 'Nat-West-Barclays-Midlands-Lloyds' was less inspiring, Edwards and Wire determined to present high street bank logos like the Iron Eagle and Black Horse as foul symbols of the Apocalypse. Possibly true, but clumsily executed nonetheless. Elsewhere, there were other musical misfires. 'Another Inverted Disease' (or A.I.D.S) had pretensions to be a proper Guns N' Roses song, when it more resembled the work of funk-metal specialists Extreme. 'So Dead' too, fell at the first hurdle, a tuneful but ultimately redundant exercise in power-pop dynamics. And with 'Methadone Pretty', James had kidnapped the lilting chorus of Blondie's 'Union City Blue' only to hold it prisoner within a bad song by shock-rockers Kiss. In Bradfield's defence, he had a hard job at times, cramming byzantine lines such as "Burning communion of the 20th Century" and "Soak mind control in christening water out of jail" into traditional rock melodies.

But when the Manic Street Preachers got it right, they did so with admirable confidence and real intensity. For one, 'Spectators Of Suicide' had made a fine transfer from concert stage to album, its 'lighters aloft, sway together' anthemic qualities all intact, even if the song's pessimistic chorus line sucked some of the romance away: "Democracy is an empty lie." 'Crucifix Kiss' was also a success, Richey's childhood issues with religion in general and the Methodist Church in particular aired in a succession of scathing putdowns over a stirring hard rock backbeat. And by handing over the master tapes of 'Repeat' to Public Enemy's engineers, Nicholas Sansano, Hank Shocklee, Dan Wood and Frank Rivaleau, the Manics had made a wise decision. Previously an entertaining, if old fashioned punk song, 'Repeat (Stars And Stripes)' was

A new breed of Generation Terrorists. The Manic Street Preachers outside the Moulin Rouge, Paris in March 1991. L-R: James Dean Bradfield, Richey Edwards, Nicky Wire and Sean Moore. *(Paul Slattery)*

The Manics at play while supporting Flowered Up at the Manchester International in November 1990. *(Paul Slattery)*

The Manics with Traci Lords (centre), who contributed vocals to their 1992 Top 30 single, 'Little Baby Nothing'. According to Richey, Traci was "female power" personified. *(Paul Slattery)*

The 'Glamour Twins'. Richey and Nicky at their panda-eyed, androgynous best. *(Paul Slattery)*

Weapons of mass destruction. L-R: Richey's Fender Telecaster, James' Gibson Les Paul and Nicky's Rickenbacker bass gu
ready for deployment at Brighton's Zap Club on August 6, 1991. *(Paul Slattery)*

The Manics onstage in Brighton. *(Paul Slattery)*

August 1991. The Manics indulge their gentler side among the stone circles in Avebury, Wiltshire. *(Paul Slattery)*

The Manics in rehearsal during the summer of 1991. Nicky Wire and Richey Edwards. *(Paul Slattery)*

"Revolutions are the locomotives of history." The Manics pay their respects at the tomb of German political theorist and founding father of modern Communism Karl Marx in London's Highgate Cemetery, 1991. *(Tom Sheehan)*

"Tight white jeans, leopard skin tops, punk rock attitude." *(Ian Tilton / www.iantilton.net)*

All work and no play... The Manic Street Preachers in party mood. *(Tom Sheehan)*

now awash with breakbeats and loops, James' corrosive lead guitar breaks integral rather than superfluous to the overall rhythm. "Originally, we wanted Public Enemy to produce the record," Nicky Wire remembered, "but they wouldn't do it. Actually, I'm really glad they wouldn't work with us... they're way above anything we could ever do." As Wire said, though Public Enemy declined the Manics' entreaties to produce them, they did consent to re-mix 'Repeat', providing four versions for the group to choose from – the best of which ended up on *Generation Terrorists*. Another moment of curious quality was the Manics' cover of 'Damn Dog', originally sung by Robin Johnson in the 1980 cult movie *Times Square*. Taking the song by the scruff of the neck, the band actually sounded as if they were having some fun among all the dead democracy, mind control and "Fuhrer Nazarenes".

That said, the Manic Street Preachers were at their best when in a serious mood, a fact confirmed by *Generation Terrorists*' stand-out moment, the bleak, yet beautiful 'Motorcycle Emptiness'. As touched on earlier, the song's lyric owed much in atmosphere to one of Richey Edwards' favourite films, Francis Ford Coppola's *Rumble Fish*, based on the S.E Hinton book of the same name. Originally condemned on its theatrical release as 'Camus for teenagers', the movie's plot was sparse and expressionistic: a young man hero worships his older brother and former gang-leader – the Motorcycle Boy – wishing to emulate his deeds on the neighbourhood's shoddy battlefields. However, the Motorcycle Boy has long grown tired of the fighting, and worse, seems to find his current existence without purpose or value. "He was born in the wrong era," one character states, "on the wrong side of the river, with the ability to do anything and finding nothing he wants to do."

Coppola's own favourite of his works, *Rumble Fish* didn't find much of an audience when released in 1983. But it was big news in Blackwood. In fact, Richey was so in love with the film and its sentiments, he briefly nicknamed himself 'Richey James' in honour of the Motorcycle Boy's younger, impressionable brother, Rusty James.

Set to music by Bradfield and Moore, 'Motorcycle Emptiness' was all swirling guitar figures, clever shifts between major and minor keys and chiming orchestration. Edwards and Wire's lyrics were also a kick in the teeth to America's hair metal bands of the time, inverting the clichés of 'endless highways', 'lonesome outlaws' and 'steel horses' used by the likes of Bon Jovi and Poison, and presenting something far less romantic in their place: "Each day living out a lie, life sold cheaply forever." This being the Manics, there were several political references to the counterfeit nature of society and perils of consumerism amid all the anti-hero angst, but pound for pound the song was their first real classic and they knew it: "Even when we were being dismissed as a tossy, two-chord version of The Lurkers, we knew we had 'Motorcycle Emptiness'," Edwards later told *Deadline*. "No matter how bad things got, we always knew we could write a song like that."

Rounded off by another would be teen anthem, 'Condemned To Rock 'N' Roll', *Generation Terrorists* was 73 minutes and 11 seconds of tantalising near misses and outright bullseyes. Ambitious, thought provoking, but occasionally much too clever for its own good, it would have made a fine single album, but in truth it floundered as a double set.

Critical reaction to *Generation Terrorists* at the time was either tepid or wildly enthusiastic, depending on which papers or magazines you read. Among the naysayers, there were complaints that the Manics' targeting of financial houses, government and monarchy was trite, old hat and redundant: "Punk tactics designed only to shock rather than call for real change," being one opinion. Others objected to the band's overuse of sloganeering language, accusing them of lacking subtlety and depth. There were also jibes that the Manics' lyrics were too recondite, too impenetrable to be understood, Edwards and Wire using verbal camouflage to disguise a lack of original ideas. Yet, others took their side, seeing the Manics' ambitions as worthy, their cause as brave: "The first thing to acknowledge is the band have done it, they've pulled it off (and) released the debut double album they'd set their black roll'n'roll hearts on all along," said *NME*'s Barbara Ellen. "It's a great, woolly rock mammoth aimed at the US market with the type of precision and determination lone assassins reserve for offing US Presidents... People who steer too close to the sun often get their wings melted. The great thing (is) the Manics dare to fly. 10/10."

Melody Maker was equally generous, future Manics biographer Simon Price capturing the essence of *Generation Terrorists*' soaring intent and occasional folly: "The first words (on the LP) are 'You need your stars'.

'There's nothing I want to see, there's nowhere I want to go' are the last. 18 tracks. No love songs. In terms of glamour, sex, style, revolution and anything else that really matters the Manics are the most necessary band in Britain. As… long players go, *Generation Terrorists* is neither a *Sign O' The Times* spectacular nor a *Sandinista* disaster. As a testament of (wasted) youth, it's a damaged diamond." *Q*'s Martin Aston rounded it all out rather nicely, focusing on a key strength missed by many: "What the detractors seemed to have ignored is their melodic approach, which aids a quest not to prolong their Clash-inspired thrashy origins." At their best, Aston concluded, the Manics could be as "poppy as George Michael".

For those in the blue corner then, the Manic Street Preachers were a vulgar throwback to the worst excesses of punk: anti-this, anti-that, all rant, no solution. Musically, there were also nothing new, taking their cues from The Clash and The Sex Pistols and mixing in a bit of Aerosmith, Hanoi Rocks and Guns N' Roses to give their sound a bit of spice. In the red corner, the Manics were rock'n'roll's saving grace, a well-read, fiercely intelligent alternative to "all that baggy nonsense" emanating from the North. However, while the group had been crafting *Generation Terrorists* in Ripley, there had been a change in the competition, 'Madchester' now bested by the more feral sounds of 'grunge'. In a lightning raid on the music scene, bands such as Alice In Chains, Soundgarden and Pearl Jam had taken a movement born in Seattle, USA and foisted it upon the world. Part classic rock, part punk, but also completely of itself, grunge was busy cleansing away hair-metal and baggy trousers and replacing them with rumbling down-tuned guitars, quiet verses, raging choruses and a hell of a lot of social complaint.

At the forefront of it all was Nirvana, a terribly gifted trio led by Kurt Cobain, a howling, out of control guitarist with personal issues and a fierce anti-commercial agenda. Like the Manics, Nirvana's roots were in punk, though they also acknowledged the knowing classicism of bands such as Led Zeppelin and Aerosmith. Lyrically too, there were similarities, themes of feminism, psychological dislocation and rebellion all regularly surfacing in Cobain's words. However, while the Manics hung on to the glamour and iconography of rock'n'roll, Nirvana had ditched it completely, presenting themselves as a dressed down, plaid wearing alternative to the worse excesses of all that had come before.

Critical darlings, the wave of the future, Nirvana had sold a million copies of their latest album, *Nevermind*, by early 1992, with eight million more soon to follow: "The first time I heard Nirvana," Nicky Wire said, "I was crushed because they were so good. There we were, dressed up like The New York Dolls, and they come along looking grungy and cool. It immediately made us feel out of date." Now threatened with appearing like yesterday's men before their careers had truly begun, the Manics came out fighting.

Literally.

Chapter Nine

Everything That Glitters

Late on delivery and grossly over budget, *Generation Terrorists* had cost Sony/Columbia a proverbial arm and leg. When one added video and promotional fees incurred in introducing the Manic Street Preachers to an international audience, the record company would have to sell at least two million copies of the LP to break even. To equal the boasts the Manics themselves had made for the album, it would have to sell ten times that many. *Generation Terrorists* did neither, entering the UK charts at number 13 on February 22, 1992. In sales terms, this was reasonable enough for a debut, but by no means an earth shattering success. To drive up performance, the band would have to do better and that meant more touring, more singles, more everything: "To be honest," Richey Edwards later said, "coming up to London thinking we could sell 16 million records within six months was absolutely fucking insane." Bold statements now resembled sickly albatrosses around their necks, but there was no alternative but to push on.

The Manics began a series of UK dates in support of *Generation Terrorists* at Warrington's Legends club on January 31 before zigzagging across the UK for further appearances in Newcastle, Leeds, Sheffield and Southampton. Now a well-oiled machine, the band had a promising new support act in The Wildhearts (whom Nicky Wire described as "the best new band in Britain") and their very own tour manager in ex-King Kurt drummer Rory Lyons. Lyons soon earned his keep at Cardiff University on February 17, breaking up any real trouble when Nicky got into an altercation with a bouncer. Not one to be kept down, Wire was at it again within three days, this time smashing his bass into a £20,000 camera being used by a Japanese TV station to film the Manics at London's Astoria.

Perhaps feeling left out of all the controversy, Richey wryly suggested in a *Smash Hits* interview of the time that the magazine's readers shouldn't try getting 'past the age of thirteen'. The magazine wisely chose to pass on printing the remark. The Manics fared better as guest reviewers for *NME*, James putting on a bravura performance as both critic and comedian, while awarding Teenage Fanclub 'Single Of The Week': "Good. They sound like Slade with Scott Walker on vocals." Unfortunately, he was less giving to former touring partners Mega City Four: "They sound too melancholy, like they're suffering from the vapours." The Four responded by sending *NME* Editor Danny Kelly a fawning letter they received from the Manics years before begging for a support slot.

After a short break, the band resumed their touring duties in mid-March, this time promoting a new single, 'Slash N' Burn', from *Generation Terrorists*. An obvious choice for release, the song was hardcore enough to please existing fans, yet melodic enough to make a few more. Backed by 'Motown Junk', 'Sorrow 16' and hidden gem 'Ain't Going Down', 'Slash N' Burn' peaked at number 20 in the charts. The Manics celebrated their good fortune by making oafs of themselves at the Irish Republic Music Awards in Dublin. Using his Pogues connections, Phillip Hall had secured the group a prestigious televised spot at the IRMAs, where they performed 'You Love Us' to a packed house of industry types. Sadly, several litres of Guinness were consumed before the group took the stage, resulting in amplifiers being overturned, Bradfield trying to crowd surf, and when he failed, shinning up the lighting rig instead. At the post-show dinner their drinking continued, eventually leading to a food fight at the table. Soon thrown out for their behaviour, Sean ended up in a night club while Nicky (presumably on a mission) was ejected from their hotel bar when one particularly observant waiter spotted he was wearing only boxer shorts. Hall duly made all the right apologies to all the right people while the band slept off their collective drunkenness.

The next step for the 'Generation Terrorists' was a hugely important one if they were to crack the magical '20 million sales mark': a short, but profile-raising tour of the USA. For the Manics, the States was key to their master plan and they were rightly nervous of engaging with American audiences. The band's sound was hard-hitting enough to appeal to a certain Stateside demographic and parts of *Generation Terrorists* had been deliberately recorded with this in mind, but they had already hit major snags with the album's US release. 'Nat West-Barclays-Midlands-Lloyds' for instance, was completely irrelevant to Americans saving their money with the likes of J.P Morgan, Chase and Citigroup, so it was quickly dropped from the LP's track listing. Worse, Sony's US arm wasn't keen on 'Condemned To Rock N' Roll', so that too was excised. Finding the original masters too anaemic for FM radio, 'Love's Sweet Exile', 'Stay Beautiful' and inexplicably 'You Love Us' also had to be remixed. The final insult, however, was reserved for the album's overall length. Seeing a double set as 'too difficult' to market, the decision was made to release *Generation Terrorists* as a single album. The Manics, now heavily in debt to their record company, took the news squarely on the chin. "We are owned by Sony," reasoned Edwards at the time, "pure Sony control. We're not doing anything daring, we know they completely own us. They can do anything they want with us... even drop us."

The group arrived stateside in April, 1992, for their first date at New York's cavernous Limelight Club. Essentially a showcase for Sony's American arm of the business and several assorted journalists, the Manics got off to a wobbly start by stepping on stage at two in the morning – a traditional enough time for headliners, but way past bedtime for most record company types. The band were hoping for more some days later when they fulfilled their dream of playing infamous punk watering hole CBGBs, the ramshackle venue that launched the live careers of the Ramones, Talking Heads and Blondie, among others. Learning their lessons from the Limelight debacle, the Manics appeared in the more 'exec' friendly timeslot of 9.30 p.m., delivering a brisk 30 minute set. Sadly, audience response remained muted. "The only good thing about New York," said an angered Nicky Wire, "is that it killed John Lennon."

Things didn't get much better on the West Coast, the Manics landing in Los Angeles shortly after the acquittal of four LAPD officers accused of severely beating African American Rodney King. Given the assault was clearly captured on video tape by a witness and subsequently aired on TV across the globe, the verdict enraged LA's already angry black community, leading to a series of riots in the city's South Central district. Attention rightly distracted elsewhere, local media coverage of the group's visit was sparse. However, their concert at the Whiskey was still well received, the Manics performing a strong set in front of rock dignitaries such as Jon Bon Jovi, Motley Crüe/Metallica producer Bob Rock and Guns N' Roses' very own Gilby Clarke. Another famous attendee, Red Hot Chilli Peppers bassist Flea, even telephoned his compliments to the group. Yet, the Whiskey show was a small victory among several larger defeats. As youths, the Manics had been hopelessly given to the mythology of American rock'n'roll, drawing inspiration from its portraiture, excited by its sounds. And if age had made them more suspicious of such things, they still held the likes of Guns N' Roses, Alice In Chains and The Black Crowes in high esteem, citing them as examples of how rock music *could* be. But the reality of the States and its 'hard sell' marketing culture was something else altogether, forcing the group to retreat rather than embrace their big adventure: "(We're) poxy white British kids in the heart of this grim nature of corporation," Wire told *NME's* Stuart Bailie.

While Sean and Nicky hid from sight in their hotel rooms between shows, and James made pained attempts to avoid all contact with "bullshit media types", Richey was exhibiting all too familiar behaviours. Bored, disappointed and seemingly contemptuous of the States, he was again drinking heavily, the alcohol sometimes causing an allergic reaction that made his '4Real' wounds swell up to twice their size. This did not dissuade him from further bouts of cutting through, Edwards even taking a steel paper clip to his arm during a TV interview. He was also shaken when the Manics' single 'Slash N' Burn' was tactlessly aired by LA 'college' station KROQ in observation of the city's recent riots: "Richey feels things so fucking intensely," Nicky later told *Melody Maker*. "He's always had a vision of purity, of perfection... a kind of childlike vision that became completely fucking obliterated. A misprint on a lyric sheet, or whatever, would just upset him so much." A trip to Disneyland provided partial respite, though once again, Edwards was looking for meaning among all the candyfloss. "Hollywood and Disneyland are the legacies of Europe's cultural imperialism," Nicky observed. "Tomorrow the riots will be forgotten, but Mickey Mouse will still be there."

The Manics' American road trip produced a few quick wins. 'Motorcycle Emptiness' had been picked up by metal radio stations, with some airplay seeping into mainstream AOR outlets too. But there was no big bang, no instant embrace from Uncle Sam or Donald Duck for that matter. Unless MTV ran the group's videos in endless rotation, or Guns N' Roses handed them their rock 'n' roll crown on *Oprah*, the Manics were unlikely to go ballistic in the US within their golden 12 months. Even Richey Edwards, once so vocal concerning the inevitability of their ascent, was now publicly doubting the master plan: "In terms of something explosive, I don't think it will happen. People just aren't that interested any more. They're too selfish." Ever the optimist, Nicky Wire remained defiant and just a little psychic: "Whatever happens, we'll always be... important."

Back home on British soil, there was more love to be had. Following 'Slash N' Burn''s Top 20 success, Sony Columbia released 'Motorcycle Emptiness', the jewel in *Generation Terrorists'* crown, as a single in early June. Backed by the gorgeous, acoustically driven 'Bored Out Of My Mind' and a faithful, if frantic cover of Alice Cooper's 'Under My Wheels', 'Motorcycle Emptiness' also benefitted from an excellent promotional video. Directed by the Manics and manager Phillip Hall, the clip was captured 'on the fly' at various locations in Japan while the band were there on tour some months before. Unable to obtain a permit from authorities, they were forced to set up, film, and then run in fear of the police while a hired interpreter "ran interference" from curious onlookers or angry local officials. In this way, the Manics managed to capture prime footage of their sad-faced travels through rush hour Tokyo, Yokohama Temple and Osaka's Tempozan Harbour, the home of the world's largest ferris wheel. Fresh, engaging and mercifully inexpensive to make, the video helped push 'Motorcycle Emptiness' into the UK charts for six weeks, peaking at number 17. Nicky's brother, Patrick, must have been pleased too, the song's key line "under neon loneliness", having been taken from his poem of the same name.

As Patrick Jones began a creditable ascent into the ranks of the literati, his younger sibling was still having trouble forming a sentence that didn't cause offence to someone or other. Sharp as a tack but possessing all the diplomatic skills of a rogue elephant, Wire was capable of gravitating between loveable scamp and complete liability within minutes. Of course, he seemed to enjoy every minute of it: "I never needed people to love me," the bassist said, "in fact, I revel in being hated. I just do... if people dislike me, it just gives me strength." On this occasion, it was the travelling community who were the butt of his comments in an *NME* interview. "As far as I'm concerned, I wouldn't care if they were rounded up and put on an island... you know this idea that the 'land is ours'? That's a very obscure and pathetic notion. We live in a twentieth century democracy where people buy land... what the fuck have they done to earn it? I think they deserve total hatred and contempt." Wire was subsequently made to look hideously uninformed as the music paper, reacting to streams of hate mail for the band, dragged out expert witnesses to debunk his theories. The best of the comebacks, from New Gypsy Council Chairman Charlie Smith, was nothing if not succinct: "People like this are not even worth entering into a conversation with... do they really need to say things like this to get publicity?"

If Wire was chastened by the pounding he took from *NME* readers, Shelter representatives and other homelessness experts over his comments, he did a fine job of hiding it. In fact, Nicky was in a welcoming mood for any abuse pointed in his direction. "Our audience has become far too reverent over the last two tours, so if we have an antagonistic section (present), it'll be a blessing." Seemingly unable to keep out of the spotlight, Wire's next appointment with the press occurred during the Manics' first appearance at Reading Festival. As their set came to a close, Nicky indulged in a bit of now traditional equipment smashing, ramming his bass into an amplifier before throwing it into the crowd. Unfortunately, the instrument got no further than the stage pit, striking two bouncers in the head and arm respectively. One received a concussion and eight stitches, the other a fractured bone. This time Wire was all apologies, though neither party threatened to sue over their injuries.

By August 1992, the Manic Street Preachers had released five singles in all from *Generation Terrorists*, just under a third of the album's 18 tracks. Yet, despite their ability to now sell out reasonable sized venues such as London's Town & Country Club and Nottingham's Rock City, the band had not cracked the UK Top 10. Given the small fortune Sony Columbia had so far spent, a genuine hit single was needed. It came via the group's lively, if ever fractious relationship with the music press. Eager to celebrate its 40th anniversary with a charity theme, *NME* was busy putting together *Ruby Trax*, a unique compilation featuring some of the UK's top music artists covering their favourite number one singles. Released in conjunction with Forty Records, all proceeds generated would go to The Spastics Society. In particular cases, these cover versions seemed wholly logical: Tears For Fears remaking David Bowie's 'Ashes To Ashes', Blur setting their sights on Rod Stewart's 'Maggie May'. Elsewhere, the choices were much more humorous, with Carter USM attempting to do justice to Pink Floyd's 'Another Brick In The Wall' while comedian Vic Reeves tried his hand at Ultravox's po-faced 'Vienna'.

Like St. Etienne, Suede, Boy George and a host of others, the Manics were asked to provide several cover suggestions in advance. Their potential list was nothing if not diverse with Dexy's Midnight Runners' 'Geno', Alice Cooper's 'Schools Out' and somewhat improbably, the Bay City Rollers' 'Bye Bye Baby' all given due consideration. They eventually settled on Nicky's inspired choice, 'Suicide Is Painless', better known as the 'Theme From M★A★S★H'. A 1970 Robert Altman film focusing on the lives of three US surgeons during the Korean War, *M★A★S★H* soon became a long-running television series, drawing worldwide acclaim for its mix of medical drama and pitch black comedy. It also had one of the oddest title tunes in TV history. Written by Johnny Mandel with lyrics provided by Altman's 14-year-old son, Mike, the song's famous refrain "Suicide is painless, it brings on many changes, but I can take or leave it if I please" was melancholic, morbid and life-affirming all at once. This combination of light and shade also made it a perfect candidate for the Manics treatment. "We chose it because it reminded us of a very gloomy time in our lives," Richey later said. "It was number one when there was a Musicians Union strike, and there was no *Top Of The Pops*, which meant there was eventually no music on TV at all."

Recorded in an eight hour blitz at Cardiff's Soundspace Studios for a total cost of £80, 'Suicide Is Painless' captured the band in the raw and they were all the better for it. Stripped of *Generation Terrorists'* mega-budget production values (though Steve Brown did oversee the session), the Manics sounded urgent and gritty, recalling the best of their work with Heavenly Records. A decision was subsequently made by *NME* to release the song as a double 'A' side single, backed by Fatima Mansions' surreal take on Bryan Adams' 'Everything I Do (I Do It For You)'. As a bonus, the CD and 12" version would also contain 'Sleeping With The NME', a sound excerpt recorded by *Radio Five* while they were making a documentary about the music paper at its Kings Reach Tower headquarters. So far, so dull. However, the tape in question was actually made on May 16, 1991, thereby catching *NME* editorial reaction the day after Richey Edwards carved '4Real' into his forearm at Norwich Arts Centre. If nothing else, 'Sleeping...' was a delightful snapshot of the pain and comedy involved in whether to publish Ed Sirrs' 'horrible' photographs: "Can we print the picture?" asked journalist Andrew Collins as the tapes rolled, "because it really is horrible. I find it extremely horrible. He's upset, people down there are upset, grown people are upset by this picture. It's a horrible picture." And so it went...

Released on September 7, 'Suicide Is Painless' finally saw the Manic Street Preachers into the UK Top 10, the single entering the charts at a highly respectable number nine before jumping again to number seven the week after the band appeared on *TOTP*. Not quite stardom then, but definitely a move in the right direction, even though the song was only a cover version – albeit for a charitable cause. If celebrations were due, they would have to take place on the road as the Manics were still on tour throughout the UK in the autumn of 1992. To capitalize on the group's new standing, Sony Columbia once again turned to *Generation Terrorists* for another hit, this time releasing 'Little Baby Nothing' on November 15. One of the LP's more emotive moments, the song focused on the enduring superiority of women over men, despite the fact they allowed themselves to be simultaneously objectified and abused by them: "To steal vacant love and to destroy, your beauty and virginity used like toys..."

'Little Baby Nothing' was also notable for featuring a vocal duet between James and former American porn star Traci Lords, who became temporarily notorious in 1986 when it was discovered she had appeared in at least 20 films before reaching the legal age of consent. The resulting furore and investigation into the scandal temporarily rocked the US pornography industry, resulting in several changes to the legislation governing it. Lords subsequently severed all ties with her past, going on to study acting at the prestigious Lee Strasberg Institute and then appearing with a young Johnny Depp in John Waters' cult favourite *Cry Baby*.

However, Traci Lords was not the Manics' first choice for 'Little Baby Nothing'. Instead, they had keenly pursued Kylie Minogue, only to learn the pop princess' manager was allegedly asking for more money that the band had to pay. At this point, their attentions shifted to Lords. "When we wrote the words to that song," Bradfield later explained, "it was obvious that it would be quite condescending for me to sing those lyrics. We needed somebody, a symbol, a person that could actually symbolize the lyrics and justify them to a certain degree. (When Kylie) fell through, we asked Traci to do it." The deal was struck after Lords met with the group backstage at a London gig. "She saw the lyrics and had an immediate affinity with them. It was definitely easy to incorporate her personality into the song. We just wanted a symbol for it and I think she was a great symbol."

Despite the circumstances surrounding her past life, the band had no reservations about working with the actress. "Because of her porn background, (people) obviously think 'dirty slut, really unintelligent', but we obviously knew it wouldn't be like that," Nicky said. "When we met her, she was probably the most intelligent American we've ever met in our lives and she was just perfect for the song." Richey too, was taken with the US actress, treating her to the highest of compliments: "Traci Lords is *female power*. Yes, we wanted her or Kylie... because both women were perceived as puppets. No-one could imagine that they might have their own vision on how they wanted to be sold."

Unfortunately, Traci Lords' keening vocal contribution to 'Little Baby Nothing' could not save the song from chart disappointment. Though backed by two little belters from the Manics' formative years ('Suicide Alley' and 'Dead Yankee Drawl') plus a new song, 'Never Want Again', the single stalled at number 29. Its sales certainly weren't helped by a promotional advert depicting a naked woman, her torso cut to apparently resemble a butcher's carcass. Underneath the figure blazed the words: 'Break the dull steak habit'. While the design was originally created in the Seventies by a group of US feminists, hundreds of complaints unsurprisingly rolled in from their Nineties UK counterparts. The Manics said the picture was there to illustrate the perils of sexism, not encourage them. In turn, Sony's lawyers pointed to the origin and history of the image. Nevertheless, the Advertising Standards Agency concluded it was offensive, asked for it to be withdrawn and the Manics had their lowest chart position since August 1991.

Realistically, the argument surrounding the single's promotion campaign had little to do with its lack of success. In sales terms, it might even have helped. The truth was that Sony Columbia had already mined the Manics' debut LP for five songs and 'Little Baby Nothing''s failure was a clear sign that *Generation Terrorists* was exhausted as a source of any further UK revenue. In the Far East, however, it was a different story. Following a mini-tour of Japan some months before, interest in the Manics was high and their debut LP had now entered the Top 20. Given the group's highly stylised image, youthful glamour and the fact that the video for 'Motorcycle Emptiness' was filmed in locations like Tokyo and Osaka, such attention was only to be expected.

Though on the road for much of 1992, the Manics resisted the temptation to simply vegetate in front of their TV and flew to Japan for several sold out dates. For Edwards, it was another opportunity to engage with a culture that genuinely interested him (Richey had recently added the works of Japanese nationalist author Yukio Mishima to his book collection). While for Nicky, now known among his bandmates as an increasingly serious hypochondriac, it was a brilliant excuse to enquire of others what constituted the symptoms of malaria. That said, Wire was also quite a fan of the country. "Japan is a culture we respect. There's no sex crime, children can go to school alone. But then again, women can be treated here as second class citizens." This was not a fate reserved for the Manics, who were treated like royalty for the duration of their stay. Pursued by enthusiastic, but terribly polite fans from hotel to gig – many of them brandishing homemade Nicky and Richey dolls – it was all a far cry from the flying glasses and stage invasions they had grown used to on the UK club circuit. Like so many pale-faced, panda-eyed musicians before them, Japan had fallen in love with the Western promise of the Manics' pretty boy rock 'n' roll: "Complete... fandemonium," Wire later remembered.

When the Manics finally returned from the Far East, it must have been a time of considerable reflection. In just 17 months, the band had released a debut album, an obscene number of singles and concluded their first world tour. They were now stars in Japan, curiosities in the US, and either loved or loathed on their home soil – depending, of course, on the quality and subject matter of Nicky's next outburst. Yet, the Manics were also making promises of future greatness during that time, talking up their future legend to all who would listen: "The most important thing we can get is massive and then throw it all way," Edwards had said. "We want to make one album, one double album, 30 songs and that'll be our statement. Then we'll split up. It's all we want to do... it's all we've aimed for all our lives." Thirty songs, multi-platinum sales, total domination, exit stage left, still looking majestic. A marvellous plan, a fantastic conceit, all delivered with acid wit and pinpoint clarity. No doubt about it, the Manics could talk the hind legs off a donkey. But the only thing they hadn't been absolutely clear about was what happened if the master plan failed to materialise...

Chapter Ten

Temporary Caesars

A good, though not truly great album, *Generation Terrorists* sold moderately well in the UK market during its first year of release, some 100,000 copies finding their way mostly into students' and teenagers' bedrooms. Worldwide, it had shifted another 150,000 or so, bringing the final tally to something approaching 300,000. Call it a third of a million, perhaps even 400,000 if one added the sales of singles and the like. However, no matter how the mathematics were cut, *Generation Terrorists'* performance was still at least 15 million short of the total sales Nicky Wire was predicting before its release.

To give them their due, the band had been dropping hints to journalists since the American leg of their 1992 tour that the master plan might be in jeopardy, talking of achieving "lasting importance" rather than multi-platinum success. They also spoke with pride of opening doors for other groups, allowing the likes of up and comers such as The Verve and Suede to act like "stars again", of bringing glamour and intelligence back to rock'n'roll. But when all the aesthetic posturing was stripped away, the reality of the Manics' situation was little different from many mid-table bands of their ilk: they were still heavily in debt to their record company, still playing to audiences nearer hundreds than thousands and still in need of music press support for the next headline. "We knew the hypocritical nature of that statement as soon as we made it," Edwards said of their multi-million sales prediction, "and any decent journalist knew it as well... no band would ever sell 16 million copies of their first record. It never happens, does it?" If the manifesto hadn't materialised, one still had to admire the audacity with which the Manics had advertised it. And if they were now exposed as just another band in pursuit of the proverbial cherry, then so be it. At least they would be entertaining on the way. Or in the case of Nicky Wire, just plain offensive.

In terms of publicity, 1992 had been a mixed year for the Manic Street Preachers bassist. On the one hand his sly quips, quick putdowns and clever revisionism of the band's original manifesto promises made for great reading, a gifted spin doctor always ready with one more killer line. On the other, when the mood took him, Wire could come across as mean-spirited or just plain clumsy, a fact underpinned by his needless remarks about Britain's travelling community and accidental felling of two bouncers at Reading Festival. However, he had usually drawn the line at outright stupidity, with at least some explanation or qualification for his outbursts. Sadly, during the Manics' Christmas concert at London's Kilburn National Ballroom on December 11, Nicky skidded over the line between verbal misdemeanour and full blown insult: "In the season of goodwill," he said between songs, "let's hope Michael Stipe goes the same way as Freddie Mercury pretty soon."

Wire's remark was sparked by a rumour then circulating within the music industry that R.E.M vocalist Michael Stipe was HIV positive. Though this was ill-informed gossip that later proved to be completely without foundation, Nicky's decision to share it – with some added venom of his own – seemed utterly senseless. Suffice to say, the music press had a field day with him, their letter pages filled with readers' righteous indignation, their editorial columns full of political fire and brimstone. "All that will be remembered of this," said *Melody Maker*, "is that Nicky portrays AIDS as a form of punitive justice." The Manics' fellow performers were also more than willing to hoist Wire by his own petard. "If suicide is painless," reasoned Boy George, "then why doesn't he just slit his throat and shut the fuck up?" When several neo-Nazis waded into the argument in support of Nicky, mistaking his comments as agreement with their own far right views, it was surely time for him to speak up.

But this time, the bass player was uncharacteristically still trying to find the right words. "I never want to hold back from making those impulsive statements," Wire said. "If we're not impulsive and we don't realise that we're fallible, we may as well just be the sort of boring band that are in Q. I want to be ostracised by certain parts of the community, because I detest what they stand for. But I don't detest R.E.M. or Michael Stipe, I was just trying to put across the point that there are so many diseases in the world. Everything gets misconstrued when you're on stage."

Behind the scenes, Wire knew his comments had caused genuine offence, and though the band were publicly supportive of him, they were also more than a little irritated at having to defend another gaffe from their resident giant. Even Sony/Columbia, which had previously ignored the Manics' displays of wilfulness for the sake of record sales were horrified by the bassist's apparent lapse of reason, asking whether his position in the group was tenable. Richey and James took to fire-fighting on their friend's behalf, stating his remarks were meant, however badly, to draw attention to the perceived godliness of rock stars and the hollow liberalism with which AIDS was treated. Neither argument really cut muster, and the fact that Nicky listened avidly to R.E.M.'s *Fables Of The Reconstruction* while at university thankfully went unmentioned.

Yet, as the time went by, it transpired that there was more on Wire's mind that night than just vicious sport at somebody's expense: "It was just a huge indestructible urge in me to vent something that came out horrendously," he admitted to *The Face* in 1997. "It was supposed to be a comment on rock martyrdom and David Bowie saying the Lord's Prayer (at the Freddie Mercury Tribute Concert), after he'd lived the most decadent life. But Phillip was incredibly ill at the time and it was just a disastrous thing." The news that their manager and close friend, Phillip Hall, had been diagnosed with cancer was given to the band shortly before their Kilburn National appearance, and the general mood in camp was black. While it was no excuse for Wire's subsequent insensitivity, it perhaps made his lashing out at the world easier to understand: "That's the one comment I could be pushed into showing a morsel of regret about," he later said, with considerable understatement. As for Michael Stipe himself, he maintained a dignified silence concerning the incident until 2001, when he was asked by Q whether he had forgiven Nicky for the slight. Stipe's reply was a dual edged sword: "Is that the one that's still alive? Of course..."

A real error in judgement on behalf of Wire that threatened to compromise the Manics' supposed standing as 'rock intellectuals', 'Nickygate' was also the first time the band had seriously fallen foul of the media. Thus far, they had enjoyed the benefits of largely positive press coverage, with even their detractors privately admiring of their media savvy. Always ready to clarify the lines of engagement, there was even a feeling that the band were guiding the hands of journalists while articles about them were written. Not any more. Picking on Emerson, Lake & Palmer or Slowdive was one thing, perhaps even worthy of sustained applause, but wishing a man dead was just vulgar. Knowing the knives were out, it was time for a temporary separation between writer and subject. "We'd become too close to the press," Wire later confirmed. "We needed to distance ourselves again."

The opportunity to do so came through making their second album. The man chosen to produce this time around was Dave Eringa. Long haired, blond and exceedingly thin, the Essex-born Eringa had first met the Manics nearly two years before, when he engineered and contributed keyboards to their Heavenly singles, 'Motown Junk' and 'You Love Us'. Similar in age and sharing the same self-deprecating sense of humour, band and engineer had kept in touch, resulting in Eringa being asked to oversee a series of demos cut in preparation for the LP during the summer of 1992. The Manics were impressed with the results and approached Sony about the possibility of the young engineer taking on full production duties: "I'm sure they had to fight for me, although they'd probably hate to admit it," he said. "We'd done some good work together on 'Motown Junk' and I suppose they don't like the idea of working with new people very much."

Though not yet officially in the producer's chair, Dave Eringa began work on a new set of demos with the group at Kent's Impact Studios in December 1992. From here, they moved to the more opulent surroundings of House In The Woods at Cobham in Surrey for further pre-production duties. Work was swift, with up to two tracks being cut per day, including early versions of what would eventually become 'Sleepflower' and 'Drug Drug Druggy'. At this point in proceedings,

Sony's Managing Director personally called Eringa to confirm he had the job: "Utter, utter... relief."

All hands in place, band and producer now decamped to Outside Studios, located within Hook End Manor, Reading. More residential pile than recording complex, Hook End Manor offered its guests a gym, swimming pool and two on-site caterers – available 24 hours a day. In addition to the impressive surroundings, the studio itself had a huge control space, stone room for drums and 'dry area' for vocals. To top it all, when one needed a breath of fresh air, the doors opened onto a massive courtyard located at the back of the Manor. A snip then, at £1,500 per day.

Recording began in earnest on January 25, 1993, with the Manics and Dave Eringa keen to capture the spirit present in their work of the previous summer: "Really," Eringa told *Melody Maker*, "it was a case of re-creating the vibe of the early demos we all loved so much." Though studio time was expensive, the band was willing to spend hours, if not days, in search of the perfect sound: 25 microphones were used on Sean's drum kit alone, while James tried various combinations of amps to capture the tone he heard in his head. Even Edwards, now capable of holding down several chords due to Bradfield's patient tutelage, got in on the act, nervously laying down a rhythm guitar part for the track 'La Tristesse Durera'. As always, Richey was more comfortable providing lyrics than musical ideas. "At the start of every album," James said, "I'd get a file from Richey with spare lyrics, bridges, things like that. It felt like I was being given homework, homework I really enjoyed."

In mid-February, the Manics had their first near disaster, when the song 'Drug Drug Druggy' was almost lost to a malfunctioning tape machine. "It was four o'clock in the morning," Dave Eringa remembered, "and I was almost in tears while James was sitting there being very calm and philosophical." By copying the last chorus on the song onto a new tape reel and transferring it back to the original recording via multi-tracking, thousands of pounds were saved. For potential single 'Roses In The Hospital', however, no expense was spared, the studio's doors being opened into the courtyard and ambient mikes placed outside to let Sean's drums "breathe". Unfortunately, a flock of ducks were 'taking the waters' nearby, and the sound of their cackling was picked up in Moore's headphones. Soon incensed with the noise, the drummer abandoned his kit, tore outside and shouted "Shut the fuck up!" at the birds, who promptly scarpered only to regroup moments later to start the whole thing off again.

During studio downtime, the Manics were able to indulge themselves in Hook Manor's luxuriant atmosphere, forming several bad habits in the process: "We were recording in a huge studio," Bradfield remembered, "spending £1,500 per day, four poster beds, swimming pools. We felt like we were buying into the whole record company 'stick', taking the cheque, eating the grapes in a big bath filled with milk like Julius fucking Caesar." Having been on the road for nigh on two years, such excesses were nonetheless understandable: "We'd been working so hard up until that point, and we were just beginning to reap some rewards money wise," said Nicky, "but we were also getting sucked into MTV land, and sometimes all we did was sit on our arses."

If Bradfield and Moore kept fairly regular hours working alongside Dave Eringa and Wire oversaw potential album artwork when not playing bass, Edwards again found himself at a loose end. Often, he filled the space with drink. Now downing somewhere near a bottle of Vodka per day, Richey was becoming increasingly concerned with his appearance, hating the puffiness and additional weight alcohol brought to his face and body. In an effort to counteract it, Edwards ate little but fruit and spent many hours at the in-house gym. While the drinking still continued, Edwards' overall physique did benefit from his frequent workouts, muscles hitherto invisible now making their first appearance.

By mid-March, studio sessions were nearing an end and several musicians were invited to sweeten the sound of the Manics' efforts. Ian Kewley, a former Q-Tip and then current member of vocalist Paul Young's backing band, added Hammond organ to another potential Manics single, 'Life Becoming A Landslide'. Veteran string arranger Nick Ingham also visited Hook Manor, providing lush orchestration on both '... Landslide' and future 45 'From Despair To Where'. Last but not least, M People's Shovel proved a welcome guest, bringing his percussion skills to much of the album while lightening the mood with endless jokes. Results on tape, Dave Eringa was joined by engineer Dave Bascombe at West London's Olympic Studios on April 1 to begin the mixing process.

Twenty days later, the Manics' second album, *Gold Against The Soul*, was complete. Despite a five month gestation process, it had come in ahead of time and under budget.

To provide a taster for the new Manics record, Sony Columbia released 'From Despair To Where' on June 1. The subject matter of the song was typical Manics territory, asking the question why Western culture seemed so inherently unhappy, despite all the material luxuries available to those living within it. The music, however, was all about new frontiers, emphasis now being firmly placed on melody rather than just sheet metal guitar riffing. James' voice was also an elevated presence throughout, carrying 'From Despair...'s tune and attendant sentiments with both clarity and passion. If there was a complaint to be had, it was in the production, the Manics losing their raw charm to a choir of multi-tracked vocals and swooping violins. Still, at least they no longer sounded like a Clash tribute band. Backed by the claustrophobic but gentle ballad 'Hibernation', a sour, if realistic take on the perils of marrying young and the Heavenly version of 'Spectators Of Suicide', the single stalled at a disappointing number 25. This lowly position might have had something to do with an accompanying video that had albino Alsatians roaming a country mansion while the band played with tin foil. Meant as a homage to Luis Buñuel's controversial 1960 film *The Exterminating Angel*, which featured sheep running riot in a locked room, the band ended up using dogs instead for fear of any Welsh/Ewe jokes.

Or any more Welsh jokes at all, really. Since leaving Blackwood to meet their press some four years before, the Manic Street Preachers had seen and heard every single Welsh-themed headline or variant thereof that journalists could fire their way: 'Into The Valley', 'Out Of The Valley', 'Cyrmu Feel The Noise', 'The Newport Dolls', 'It Takes A Nation Of Millions To Hold Us, Bach'. The list was endless. "Every single fucking Welsh cliché was used," Nicky later said. "Whether it was 'Taff' or 'Leek' or 'Daffodil', 'You Sexy Merthyr-Fuckers'. We're 10, 20 miles away from Merthyr. 'Meet Leek Manifesto' was another one. 'The Boys From Bangor'. Bangor is three hundred fucking miles away from us! We're closer to London than Bangor." In short, the Manics had no great wish to be associated with Wales any more than they did Blackwood. They hadn't learned the language at school, and on the face of it, showed absolutely no interest in promoting Welsh culture, history or values. "The Welsh fans think we're doing something good, something important for Wales," said James. "We've never said anything good about where we come from. All we've ever said is we actually come from Wales, from a town where's there's nothing to do. We've never felt a sense of pride in where we come from."

Regrettably, it wasn't quite that simple. At the time of the Manics' ascendancy, Wales was still the butt of many a cultural jibe – being seen as unfashionable, out of touch or worse still, relevant only to the people who lived there. And while the Welsh themselves hadn't quite suffered the overt racism of 'No blacks, no dogs, no Irish' in post-war England (they weren't immigrants, after all), there was enough historical baggage, enough casual racism between the Welsh and English to describe relations as "requiring improvement". Therefore, to Manics fans living in Wales, the band were now in a position to promote their country, fly the flag and show the rest of the world what Welsh groups could bring to the table. Thus far, the only lasting Welsh musical exports in the light entertainment field had been Tom Jones, Shirley Bassey, Mary Hopkins, Bonnie Tyler and Shakin' Stevens who were all more likely to appear on *Sunday Night At The London Palladium* than at the Reading Festival. And when a few rock bands such as Badfinger, Budgie and latterly The Alarm had threatened to upset rock's apparent embargo on Welshness, they had fallen away to tragedy, cult status or decreasing record sales. Surely, the argument ran, the Manics could challenge previous stereotypes and pave the way for more lasting Welsh-themed success.

The band were having none of it. If The Alarm wanted to release albums in their native tongue, or howl 'Welshness' from the rooftops, then more fool them: "We've never learned anything from other Welsh bands," said Edwards, "just never to be remotely like them. It's really patronising the way they suddenly learn to speak the Welsh language, when they'd written songs about the bright lights of Mersey or Liverpool about two years before. And the Welsh language was never important to us at all. I mean, what's the point in resurrecting something that's completely dead? Dead culture doesn't interest us." Nicky was equally disparaging: "The very fact that we're from Wales meant there was no point in trying to act cool... and we've had to fight against (the anti-Welsh) thing a lot. People assume that because we were from there, we'd be like The Alarm... shit and thick." The reality of the situation was that the Manic Street Preachers had taken all their references, their icons, from British and American culture. That was their starting point, and still their principal source of inspiration. Being Welsh really had nothing to do with it, even if the racism and lack of understanding they encountered from the music press occasionally stung. "It's cheap disdain because journalism comes from London," James said pointedly, "and London's a place where people lose touch with things that are important in other peoples' lives. The anger and concerns of a young band from the Welsh valleys isn't going to make much sense to those people."

Picking fights with journalists appeared far from the Manics' minds when they began their round of press interviews to promote *Gold Against The Soul*. Battered by the experiences of 'Nickygate' the previous Christmas, the band were on their best behaviour and unusually full of compliments. Suede, Alice In Chains, Nirvana and, curiously, Happy Mondays were all in their good books, while Californian agit-rockers Rage Against The Machine drew particular praise from the quartet. Any enquiries regarding Nicky's recent brush with infamy were in turn swept aside, the band more eager to promote their new material than past mistakes. Answers were also briefer, slanders avoided and jokes kept light rather than libellous. Tellingly, the band also looked different than before. James' hair was nearly tipping his shoulders, while Sean's was well on the way to his nipples. Richey had lost much of the make-up, now sporting shaped sideburns to further accentuate those ever-hollowing cheeks. Only Nicky seemed in touch with the glamour of the old days, his kohl eyes and foundation bringing back memories of when he wanted to be a New York Doll. The biggest leap forward was the removal of the sloganeering shirts and blouses. No more stencils, no more paint. The messages, it seemed, were being reserved for their songs.

Released on June 20, 1993, *Gold Against The Soul* was a much different beast to *Generation Terrorists*. In time, the Manics would come to almost disown the record, but a large part of the band they would subsequently become resides in its 10 songs, even if one has to pull back a curtain or two to make the discovery. Not as bad as they or many a critic would have it, nor as good as it needed to be, *Gold Against The Soul* nonetheless caught the group in transition between reasonable club act to something with far more potential. Captivating and frustrating, it's the lost child of the Manics' back catalogue and therefore deserving of some long due attention.

The first break from the group's 'tattoo-bearing shock tactics' past came with *Gold...'s* record sleeve. Designed by Mitch Ikeda, a Japanese photographer destined to become their 'official lensman', it presented a multiple-limbed upper torso, head obscured by three roses in full bloom. The sepia-toned, almost classical image was a direct nod to the Yukio Mishima and Eikoh Hosoe collaboration *Barakei (Killed By Roses)*, a book of photographs and prose much loved by Richey. Primo Levi's 1986 poem 'Song Of Those Who Died In Vain' in memory of those lost to war and conflict was re-printed on the inner jacket. A much more traditional choice of intellectual message from the band, its last line – "We'll drown you in our putrefaction" – could have been written by Edwards himself. And so it was with the music and lyrics of *Gold Against The Soul*, James and Sean pursuing a more professional, almost classic approach to the group's sound, while Richey and Nicky moulded their previous obsessions into harder, jagged more personal shapes. When the two gelled, they produced grand results. When they didn't, the band struggled to find its own identity.

On the instrumental side of things, there was no faulting the Manics' performance. James' multi layered guitars, Sean's pinpoint drumming and Nicky's new proficiency on bass guitar made for a tight little unit, the band light years away from the amateurish enthusiasm of their earliest recordings. And they had certainly taken advantage of all the toys Dave Eringa and Hook End Manor had to offer, the sound of *Gold Against The Soul* polished to crystal perfection. As far as the songs themselves were concerned, it was a straight 10 round fight between real, lasting quality and derivative heavy metal posturing. On the plus side, tracks like 'Sleepflower', 'Yourself' and 'Nostalgic Pushead' stayed the right side of metal mania, retaining a melodic sensibility that held all the raging guitars at bay.

Unfortunately, 'Symphony Of Tourette' and the album's title track were much less impressive – the former little more than a cold re-write of Guns N' Roses' 'You're Crazy', the latter an bizarre amalgam of Def Leppard and The Beta Band. Worse, at over five minutes long, 'Gold

Against The Soul' could have been the work of an energetic prog-rock band, surely anathema to the Manics' punk and rock'n'roll roots. 'Drug Drug Druggy' was slightly better, though its similarity to Jane's Addiction's 'Been Caught Stealing' was also a tad distracting.

The album's remaining songs saw the Manic Street Preachers backing away from all the bump and grind in favour of a new tunefulness that audiences would come to expect from them in future years. Previous single 'From Despair To Where' hit all the right buttons, Bradfield singing the melody rather than just shouting it. 'Life Becoming A Landslide' too, had a strong musical foundation, its chorus built for radio. And though one could easily hum the tune to David Bowie's 'Sound And Vision' over parts of 'Roses In The Hospital', the rest of the song's swaying, anthemic feel more than made up for the likeness.

If Manics fans were unnerved by the new metal sheen and melodic sophistication of *Gold Against The Soul's* sound, they could at least take heart in the lyrics that accompanied the tunes. Embracing a despondency that was sometimes uncomfortable to hear, Richey and Nicky had surrendered neither their anger nor questioning natures to trite couplets or blue sky thinking. They had, however, moved from overt politicisation to a more introverted stance, using personal experiences and feelings to inform much of the material on show. 'Sleepflower' for instance, took Edwards' quest for 'eight hours of oblivion' to new levels, asking why so many of us resort to artificial aids such as drugs, alcohol and exercise for a simple night's rest: "At least a beaten dog knows how to lie."

'Yourself' was dedicated to the lie of airbrushed perfection, magazines and fashion houses setting impossible standards of beauty for the average person to emulate. "Every day," Richey told *Melody Maker*, "you look in a bathroom mirror and try and convince yourself that you look OK so that you can carry on your daily routine, when you know that you're a flabby piece of shit. It's difficult to keep feeling good... when you see all these perfect, airbrushed images." Although Edwards was making a larger societal point here, it was also perfectly clear he was talking predominantly of himself.

'Life Becoming A Landslide' was still more bleak and personal. Richey had taken his own jarring experience with pornographic images as a child and crafted a lyric about reconciling the impact of that event on any potential adult relationships: "If you (see) pornography at an early age, it becomes difficult to reconcile that with the idea of love you're later presented with." On the face of it, 'Roses In The Hospital' offered a more optimistic world view, its words resting on the notion of finding beauty in the most unlikely places. Yet its references to self mutilation and burning oneself to "just feel something" again made for uneasy listening, the lyrics hinting at a certain frailty of mind absent from Edwards' previous work.

However, there were occasional bouts of satire and black humour. 'Nostalgic Pushead' focused on the tendency of the middle aged to disparage ideas exciting to the young, offering a 'Seen that, done that' response rather than embracing the joy of youthful discovery. 'Drug Drug Druggy' also had its moments, pointing a finger at those who viewed certain narcotics as fashionable, while simultaneously scorning alcohol – even if they produce similar, albeit equally debilitating effects. 'Symphony Of Tourette' was neither satirical nor funny, Richey concentrating on the terror Tourette's sufferers must feel when they publicly lose control to their condition: "It's a 20th century disease... there's just no cure for it." And on the title track, Wire and Edwards surpassed themselves in venting spleen at "apocalypse" Britain, burying Thatcherite politics, pit closures and the hypocrisy of the "caring Nineties" in a pile of nihilistic rubble: "People," Richey said at the time, "have just become so selfish." As stated, when lyric and tune collided in harmony, the Manic Street Preachers were potential stadium fillers. 'Sleepflower', 'From Despair...', 'Life Becoming A Landslide' and 'Roses In The Hospital' all showed both musical growth and an admirable retention of the band's gift for complaint and rock dynamics. Elsewhere, the Manics sounded at sixes and sevens, James forcing a dictionary of convoluted phrases into a miasma of fuzzed up guitars and chunky percussion. Yet, as with *Generation Terrorists*, they had again produced one genuine classic in the form of 'La Tristesse Durera (Scream To A Sigh)'.

A perfect marriage of word and melody, the song's title took its inspiration from a phrase in one of the last letters written by the artist Vincent Van Gogh to his brother, Theo: "The sadness goes on..." Running with Van Gogh's sentiment, Edwards crafted a sad, touching meditation on the indignity of old age, where the elderly – still full of wisdom and experience – are either ignored or removed from public sight. "It's a beautiful image when the war veterans turn out at the Cenotaph," Richey told *Melody Maker*, "and everyone pretends to care... but then they're shuffled off again and forgotten." Slow-burning and magisterial, with Bradfield switching from breathy falsetto to angered growl to convey the song's emotional drama, it was difficult to find any fault with 'La Tritesse Durera' at all.

Too slick and too 'American' for some. Too far a jump from their shouty, sweary punk roots for others, *Gold Against The Soul* certainly had faults, and many of them. An album specifically designed to put the Manics on an international stage – even break the States – its glossy veneer, 'just so' orchestration and carbonised rock guitars were all pointers that Sony wanted back on their investment. And from some fans' perspective, what made things worse was the fact the Manics were going along with it. "Yeah," Nicky Wire later admitted, "with *Gold Against The Soul*, we were looking for that big hit. We'd let ourselves get pampered, lost our anger, and as a consequence, lost our way." James Dean Bradfield also turned on the record, seeing it as a betrayal of their original ethos: "Too... smooth. *Gold...* was absolute dogshit." Perhaps Bradfield is being a little harsh. If there is enduring value in *Gold Against The Soul*, it's the fact that it allowed the Manics to unshackle themselves from the sheer naivety of their previous incarnation. By introducing more melody to their sonic palette, while retaining some of the harder edges to the sound, they gave themselves more room to manoeuvre and less chance to be cornered or pigeonholed. This would serve them well in coming years, when the need to change in accordance with their circumstances became crucial.

In July 1993, however, *Gold Against The Soul* had no such context or historical placement. It was simply the band's new record and a cause for confusion and occasional sneering among fans and critics alike: "Superficially competent... but scratch below the surface and you'll find few signs of life – just a vaguely expressed, bemused and bored dissatisfaction," said *Q*'s Peter Kane. "*Gold Against The Soul* is the sound of a band digging in for a long term career rather than knocking over a few of the statues. When will they ever learn?" Elsewhere, *Melody Maker's* Peter Paphides was more giving, but still not wholly convinced: "I'd be the last to deny that all the Manics' fatalism is occasionally hard to stomach. And once in a while, I think about all the textbook Nietzsche (the band) hurl at us, and I wonder if they truly understand a word of it. (However), any contradictions you throw at them are merely used as armour. The final twist, though, is that *Gold Against The Soul* can, in parts, be called great art. Don't laugh: it's true."

Both critics had their points. It was undoubtedly true the Manics had made a hell of a noise about selling 20 million albums of their debut disc, taking over the world, then splitting up to enjoy the spoils of a war well waged. Now here they were, betraying the terms of their original promise and returning, cap in hand, for another bite of the cherry. Conquering heroes reduced to mere careerists. Equally, so dense and abstract was their wordplay at times, it was sometimes difficult to understand what they were talking about, or if they even knew themselves. Still, the people who ultimately decided the Manics' fate were the record buyers, their judgement expressed across the counter of a shop. This time, the band did a little better with them, *Gold Against The Soul* entering the UK charts at a respectable number eight, and staying around for a further 10 weeks.

As ever, the Manics hit the road in support of their product, a warm-up gig at London's Marquee paving the way for another full blown jaunt across the UK and Europe. Eager to champion new and sometimes controversial talent, the band had picked two youthful acts to provide support for the tour. Credit To The Nation was a politically savvy hip hop group hailing from Walsall, led by teenage wunderkind Matty Hanson (otherwise known as MC Fusion). Scoring a well-deserved hit with 'Call It What You Want' (based around a cheeky sample stolen from Nirvana's 'Smells Like Teen Spirit') Credit... were frontrunners in a new UK rap scene. "The best thing about the Manics," Hanson said at the time, "is reading Richey's interviews. We were actually interviewed with him, and I don't know shit compared to him. It was a humbling experience." Also on the bill was Blaggers ITA, an uncompromising agit-rock collective whose 1991 album, *Fuck Fascism, Fuck Capitalism, Society's Fucked*, clearly demonstrated their support for revolutionary politics. Their lead singer/rapper was Matty Blagg, an ex-borstal boy who had fallen in with the British Movement as a youth, only to publicly decry its views in later life as a passionate anti-fascist.

The Manics' tour ran into trouble following their very first concert at Leeds' Town And Country Club on July 1. At the after show party, held at nearby Leeds Corn Exchange, an argument began between *Melody Maker* journalist Dave Simpson and Blaggers ITA. Simpson had recently written an article about the band in which he had referred to Matty's past associations with the British Movement. The Blaggers' vocalist took exception to the writer's remarks and the pair entered a heated discussion that lasted for several hours. At some point, things became physical, with Simpson sustaining a broken bone beneath his eye and haemorrhaging behind its retina. *Melody Maker* immediately ran news of the incident, which then escalated into a torrent of complaints and calls for the Blaggers to be dropped from the tour.

While fusion/techno specialists Fun-Da-Mental immediately cancelled their forthcoming dates with Blaggers ITA, the Manics held back in making the same snap decision, fearing it might turn the band into "sacrificial lambs". However, that didn't stop them from sharing their views on the incident with the press: "I just don't believe in bullying, full stop," James Dean Bradfield said at the time. "I don't agree with it as a means to an end. I told them the morning after it happened 'I disagree with what you do and I don't believe in bullying'. No matter what they think, it's just a different form of fascism." Nicky Wire was equally irritated by what happened: "There's nothing good or brave about violence. We use violence in our words, which is the best way." After much thought, the Manics made the decision to continue with the Blaggers as a support act, but their entourage were thrown off the tour. It wasn't the end of the band's troubles. Though Matty Blagg, the group and their record company, Parlophone, strenuously denied Dave Simpson's version of events, public opinion turned against them. Frozen out by the music press, and dropped from subsequent support tours and festival bills, Blaggers ITA subsequently lost their contract with Parlophone in 1994.

The rest of the Manics' UK dates continued without incident, inexorably leading the group towards several festival appearances during the summer period. In the past, they had been at best disparaging of such "cow in a field" events. Richey and James hated the idea of appearing in daylight (it destroyed the illusion of rock glamour), while Nicky just hated festivals – the idea, the locations, everything. More likely, in line with Edwards' WOMAD experiences of 1983, the Manics just preferred the inside of a concert hall to the threat of constant rain and overflowing toilets.

Their first date with destiny was at Long Marston's Phoenix Festival, a new enterprise set up by Mean Fiddler impresario Vince Power to rival the likes of Glastonbury and Reading. The inaugural event also featured Sonic Youth, Faith No More and Bradfield's beloved Black Crowes. The Manic Street Preachers did not distinguish themselves at Phoenix, fighting a losing battle with the PA system, some persistent hecklers and middling attendance numbers. Stripped of their now trademark 'Hammer and Sickle' backdrop (a sly nod to The New York Dolls, who used the same flag to court controversy in the Seventies), and exposed to the sun like rock'n'roll vampires, the band looked distinctly ill at ease with their surroundings. In fact, the only real highlight of their appearance was Nicky's striking new look, which matched thick-rimmed glasses with a headscarf, thick white tights and a lovely floral dress. He would continue to wear the outfit on and off for the rest of the Manics' remaining festival dates, including Eire's Fiele.

If things had gone badly for them at Phoenix, they got markedly worse in August when the quartet appeared at the Heineken Festival in Swansea's Singleton Park. A free, relatively small event, with the Manics headlining a bill that included new talent such as Lovecraft and Captain Scarlet, the band had agreed to appear as a 'thank you' to those locals who supported them in early days. Yet the gesture was lost upon a crowd using anyone on stage as a target to hone their throwing skills. As the group hurtled through their set, Nicky was struck on the head by an empty bottle of Liebfraumilch, instantly crumpling to the floor and bringing 'Drug Drug Druggy' to a premature end. At this point, a further salvo of cans flew their way, narrowly missing the Manics' road crew. Bradfield called time, shouting "One down, three to go, you brainless wankers!" as he herded his colleagues into the wings. When Wire rallied, the band made a brave return to the stage, though again, they were greeted with more flying objects. After James issued a final warning, the target practice ceased and they were allowed to conclude their set with some style – Richey marking the occasion by striking a crucifix pose from atop a speaker, before stage diving into the punters below.

Following their performance, Nicky began to feel nauseous and was taken to nearby Singleton hospital as a precautionary measure. It transpired that much of the trouble at the festival derived not from a hatred of music, but two rival football and rugby factions who had hi-jacked the event to settle old scores and get drunk. Edwards didn't see it as much of an excuse for their boorish behaviour. "Most bands look forward to their homecoming gig," he told *Melody Maker*, "and though I wasn't expecting roses and petals, the amount of abuse we get is non-stop. Anything from Welsh bands complaining about us betraying Wales to gangs of blokes pouring lager on me... Tom Jones doesn't get that."

Shortly before the Manics took on Singleton Park and fought it to a draw, Sony Columbia had released 'La Tristesse Durera' to the shops. The single was backed by the heavy metal thunder of 'Patrick Bateman', its title and lyrics drawing inspiration from the serial killing central character of Brett Easton Ellis' 1991 novel, *American Psycho*. Nearly as controversial as the book itself, the song raised several eyebrows and a complaint or two for the line: "I fucked God up the ass." Regrettably for the Manics, God returned the favour, as the potentially world-beating 'La Tristesse Durera' miraculously stalled at number 22 in the charts in late July, 1993.

The band's next move of note was to appear at Milton Keynes Bowl on 18/19 September in support of American rock gods Bon Jovi. The Manics' placement on a bill that also included metal-lite youngsters Little Angels and the vulgar, but entertaining charms of Billy Idol, seemed odd. That the headline act made their living from singing about "steel horses" and "loaded six strings" while also being wanted – dead or otherwise – made the Manics' participation for many early fans unconscionable. Bon Jovi was corporate rock, pure and simple, and Edwards, Wire and co. were now dancing with an immaculately styled devil. The truth of it was far less vulgar. The band had never hidden their stadium-filling aspirations, and was probably jealous they were not headlining the show themselves. Equally, their earliest punk associations were now in the rear view mirror, the group trying to forge ahead on less straightforward terms. Additionally, they had always attracted a small, but dedicated following among metal heads, now grown larger thanks to the sturm and drang present on *Gold Against The Soul*. All this, plus the fact at least one of them owned Bon Jovi's *Slippery When Wet* as a teenager.

A weird experience for both band and audience, the Manics played the 'reverse graveyard shift', coming on stage at three in the afternoon, when some punters were still drifting in from their train journeys. Again not taking at all well to the sunlight, their set was a muted affair combining minor hits, the occasional dip into the back catalogue and recent 'headbangers' from their second album. While Richey headed off to get drunk and watch Billy Idol, Nicky, James and Sean wondered if they might meet the headliners: "There wasn't much interaction, to be honest," Wire later recalled to Q, "and we played a terrible set. I remember Jon Bon Jovi coming on and thanking the bands. (He said) 'It's been a fantastic night and I'd like to thank everyone who's supported us, starting with The Maniacs!' That's how much they knew us."

If the Manic Street Preachers weren't perfect matches for a Bon Jovi audience, it didn't stop their record company trying to make some capital from it all. 'Roses In The Hospital' was released to coincide with their Milton Keynes appearances, backed by 'Us Against You' and the stirring 'Donkeys'. And to prove they were all friends now, there was even a faithful cover of the Happy Mondays' 'Wrote For Luck' to sweeten sales. "Oh come on, I always loved Sean Ryder," smiled Wire (based around a single chord, 'Wrote For Luck' was one of the few songs Richey Edwards felt really comfortable playing at Manics gigs). For the first time in nearly two years, the Manics broke into the Top 20, nestling at a comfortable number 15 in the UK charts.

'Roses In The Hospital''s success came as a slightly late wedding present for Nicky, who married his teenage sweetheart, Rachel, on September 25. An on/off relationship that had finally found lasting ground, the pair said their vows at a quiet ceremony in Blackwood. Sean too, was now fully committed to his partner, Rhian, with whom he had set up home in Bristol where she worked. Even Richey, so long the virgin – but no more if recent reports were believed – had taken to a mysterious young woman. Though he drew the line at calling her his girlfriend, she was seen in his company from time to time and seemed to make him laugh. Only James, whose two year relationship with his girlfriend had recently floundered, was officially calling himself a single man.

All in all, 1993 was a bizarre year for the Manic Street Preachers. It had seen them wrestling with their identity, expanding the perimeters of their sound, and shedding some old fans while also gaining new ones in the process. A Top 10 album and three Top 30 singles later, they had consolidated their position as an act with genuine potential, but were still suffering critical barbs regarding their authenticity and past declarations. The "young, beautiful scum" that promised to be "the biggest rock 'n' roll nightmare ever", and bring a "geometry of contempt" to the world stage were now supporting Bon Jovi in 'super parks' while also releasing suspiciously well crafted pop singles. "We always were a mass of contradictions," confessed Nicky Wire at the time. Their master plan in tatters, but still arrogant and talented enough to do something about it, the Manics would again have to re-think their position before taking any real forward steps.

Sadly, they would have to do it without their manager, Phillip Hall, who lost his battle with lung cancer on December 7, 1993. Though undergoing chemotherapy, Hall had continued to oversee his charges for much of the year, his brother Martin taking up the group's managerial reins when he was too ill to work. More a friend and mentor to the Manics than straightforward business associate, Phillip Hall had guided them cleverly and guarded them closely since 1990, and his loss was a profound blow: "Phillip was the first person who understood us," they told *Melody Maker*, "... and his input into the band was invaluable. Without his help, motivation and generosity, it is doubtful we would have carried on." Feeling it was "impossible to give a performance of real quality," the Manics cancelled their scheduled concert appearance at London's Brixton Academy on December 10.

There would be no real time for mourning. Having recently completed dates in Japan, Germany and Portugal, the Manics were due back on the road for another short UK tour booked in January, 1994. With further shows to follow in the Far East and Europe, the opportunity to reflect and remember would now have to take place in hotel rooms and on tour buses rather than at home. In fact, 1994 was scheduled to be one of the busiest years of the group's life, a pile up of concert halls, festivals, recording studios and TV appearances. It was also a year where their personal and professional resolve would be tested to breaking point and one of their number would begin taking his first steps into rock 'n' roll's house of mystery.

Chapter Eleven

A Spell Of Riot

The passing of Phillip Hall seemed to mark a turning point for the Manic Street Preachers. With *Gold Against The Soul*, they had allowed themselves to musically evolve, open up their sound, even make the acquaintance of real tunefulness. But the results felt hollow, overproduced and in opposition to their original values. In pursuit of 'the big hit', they had lost something of themselves in the process, leaving them feel unfocused and faintly soiled. For a group whose vaulting ambition had so often threatened to leap over itself, they were now in some danger of being classified as 'corporate rock sell outs', ordinary rather than legendary. A re-acquaintance with old principles was required.

The first real signs that the Manics were back in touch with their inner, screaming child came from the B-sides to 'Life Becoming A Landslide', the last single to be released from *Gold Against The Soul*. While 'Are Mothers Saints?' was another example of the band's more recent wistful, melodic leanings, the two remaining tracks pointed at old flames and future shocks. With 'Charles Windsor', the Manics returned to their mid Eighties obsessions, covering an old, monarchy-baiting McCarthy tune with some distinction. McCarthy were one of the groups discovered by the four via *NME's C86* cassette experiment, their combination of jangling indie pop and left-leaning political satire being a particular favourite with James. All jutting elbows, chopping guitars and breakneck pace, 'Charles Windsor' was a jolting alternative to 'Life Becoming A Landslide''s more stately considerations. But a bigger clue to what the Manics had in store for their public came with 'Comfort Comes'. An angular, jarring thing, its lyrics sourly recounting the end of an affair, the track more resembled a Nineties version of Magazine or The Pop Group than the sound of a Welsh Guns N' Roses. Stadium rock, this was not.

Despite being in possession of one of the strongest choruses the group had yet written, 'Life Becoming A Landslide' failed miserably in its mission to storm the charts in February, 1994. In fact, the single's placing at number 36 was the lowest position for a Manics single since their first Sony Columbia release, 'Stay Beautiful', some three years before. Though they were now a strong concert draw with a devoted fan base (their re-scheduled Brixton Academy appearance on January 28 had sold out in a matter of days), the quartet had not yet found that elusive crossover hit with which to prise open the purse strings of the average music punter. At the time, the Manics couldn't have cared less, being in hot pursuit of their original Mojo.

In an admirable display of returning to first principles, the group had left London in favour of Cardiff to work on new material. Their destination was Soundspace Studios, the £50 per day rehearsal/recording space where 'Suicide Is Painless', their only Top 10 hit thus far had been cut. Located in a grubby part of Cardiff's docklands area, the studio was in close proximity to kerb crawling routes and local prostitution. "Bleak, seedy, perfectly suited to us really," James later told *Volume*. "(No) decadent rock star rubbish."

Geographically, Soundspace was also a fine fit for the Manics. Richey had recently bought a quiet, third floor apartment in the more 'dignified' surroundings of Cardiff's Atlantic Harbour district, its wide bay windows overlooking the nearby waters. A trendy locale and part of the city's overall programme of rejuvenation, the harbour area was also only half a mile's walk to the studio. With Nicky now living with his wife, Rachel, close to Blackwood, the bassist was also within driving distance of Soundspace, though he still needed Edwards behind the wheel. For Sean, a resident of Bristol, his journey was a tad longer but he was typically stoical regarding the commute: "Regular work, drum till six, then go home. It was like a little office job." As for James, who had recently moved to London's Maida Vale district, things were much more tricky. But he was determined to make the best of the city's night time distractions while pursuing temporary accommodation: "Me and Richey would go out after (the studio)... have a really good drink, then go to the dodgy disco," he told *NME*. "A bit of pullage, try and get girls... really ordinary things." If all else failed, there was always the bunk bed in Blackwood.

The Manics' brief while at Soundspace was a simple one: wherever possible, stay away from record company advice, communicate openly and honestly with each other about the new material and thereby reconnect to their muse. While previous guiding hands Steve Brown and Dave Eringa would become lightly involved at a later stage, the group had made the bold decision to produce themselves, with Alex Silva acting as resident engineer. Agenda in place, recording sessions were run like clockwork, Richey scooping up band members in his car before depositing them all at the studio each morning.

As ever, Edwards had already provided Bradfield with a notebook full of lyrics, thus allowing him to rest up as his colleagues worked on songs. During breaks, Nicky might rouse him from the sofa for a brief sojourn around the shops, but otherwise, Richey was free either to crack open a bottle or recover from the effects of the previous night's carousal. For all intents and purposes, he seemed to be enjoying himself: his writing had been unusually prolific, his family was close by, and in the evenings, he was free to drink and try his luck on Cardiff's club scene – sometimes returning to his flat, sometimes not: order and disorder, hand in hand. If it wasn't quite healthy living, then at least it followed a schedule.

The Manics finally came up for air on March 2, 1994, appearing at London's Clapham's Grand theatre in aid of the Imperial Cancer Research fund. The concert honoured their late manager, Phillip Hall, and featured a rousing support slot from another of his great success stories, The Pogues. Little new material from the Manics' forthcoming album was aired on the night, though Suede guitarist Bernard Butler – who had recently lost his father to cancer – did join the band for two numbers: The Faces' 'Stay With Me' and a clattering version of 'Motorcycle Emptiness'. Roughly equal at the time in terms of popularity, Suede shared the Manics' love of rock 'n' roll glamour and strident lyricism, though Butler's group drew more on David Bowie than The Clash as a primary influence. That said, he and Bradfield's guitars meshed reasonably well, a friendship between bands was established and more importantly, £20,000 was raised for charity.

The Manics' next live engagement of note was a two night stopover at Bangkok's Mah Boonkrong Hall on April 22 & 23. Thanks to the support of DJ Wasana Wirachartplee (Thailand's female John Peel), 'Motorcycle Emptiness' had become a massive hit throughout the country, resulting in 50,000 sales of its parent album. As this figure constituted platinum status in Thailand, the Manics were now genuine stars, a fact underlined by the 3,000 fans who showed up to meet them at a pre-gig signing session. However, a moment of potential confusion for the group occurred later in the evening when Sony representatives awarded them their first platinum disc, making several gushing references to the King and Queen of Thailand as they went. Things became clearer when the Manics were reminded that Thailand was a fiercely royalist state, and that any displays of anti-monarchist rhetoric could be met with the severest measures. In short, try singing "Fuck Queen and Country" here, and you might be in for an interesting night.

In the end, the group's live appearance in Bangkok turned out to be a throwback of sorts to their debut British tour, with the unwelcome addition of armed police wielding cattle prods to control the unruly crowd. Though Mah Boonkrong Hall had a capacity limit of 2,000, there were nearer 3,000 present, causing a cramped and extremely sweaty environment. That said, Thailand's Manics contingent rose to the challenge, many fans arriving in homemade stencilled shirts, while others brandished copies of Ed Sirrs' '4Real' photograph above their heads. For the quartet, who had now left behind such overt sloganeering apparel, it was still a telling gesture of support. For the police, it was all just potential trouble, any efforts made by audience members to pogo or mosh being greeted with the threat of removal at the sharp end of an electric stick. Railing against such potentially heavy handed tactics, Nicky blurted "Long live the King, may he reign in Hell!" on mike, only to be greeted with a telling silence. Evidently, these were monarchist punks.

Despite Wire's brave/foolhardy remarks, the Manics and their supporters were allowed to meet again the next night, though the band were asked to consider turning the volume down on this occasion. Playing on the fourth floor of the Hall, cracks had appeared in the ceiling of a restaurant below, and officials were genuinely worried fans might fall through the roof. In the end, their concerns proved unfounded, the only real troubles starting backstage when Bradfield commenced a short solo acoustic set towards the end of the show. Clearly the most popular Manic with Thai fans, Richey had been bombarded with well-wishers and presents since his arrival in Bangkok. Two such gifts were waiting in the dressing room when he, Nicky and Sean left James to perform a faithful rendition of Burt Bacharach's timeless 'Raindrops Keep Falling On My Head'. One, a large Snoopy cuddly toy was a sweet gesture, evidently sent from someone who knew Edwards had a dog of the same name. The other, a set of small ceremonial knives, had been presented to him earlier that day by another fan. They came with a note he showed to Kevin Cummings, a press photographer there to cover the gig: "Richey passed me the note," Cummings told *Mojo*. "He'd been sent these swords which were like a table-top gift set. And this kid had said 'Would you slash yourself on stage for me?' Richey said to me, 'That's ridiculous, it's just exhibitionism'. Why would I do that?' So he cut himself backstage instead."

Taking one of the knives to hand, Edwards walked to a nearby toilet where he made several horizontal cuts to his bare chest. When he returned to the dressing room, he lit a cigarette and sat quietly alongside Sean and Nicky on the leather sofa until it was time to return to the stage. As Bradfield hit the cue to begin 'Motorcycle Emptiness', Wire walked into the spot light wearing his best floral dress, only to have it immediately ripped off by fans in the front row. He played the rest of the gig in his boxers. Richey, on the other hand, took his usual place in the line up, chest now covered in blood. He had made no effort to dress his "war wounds" and appeared in no obvious pain. The Manics finished the show with a rousing 'You Love Us' some 10 minutes later. Despite a now baying audience, the group stuck with their longstanding policy and performed no encore. On this occasion, they really didn't need to.

With journalists present to witness this latest display of self-harming and a photographer again there to capture the event, there were suspicions that Edwards was only mugging for the camera – albeit in a disturbing manner. Nicky, for one, appeared happy at the time to dismiss it as such, making light of his friends' actions where he could. Yet Sean, usually silent in such matters, felt the need to go a little further in support of his band mate: "The only people who are disturbed by Richey cutting himself are those who don't know him." If the Manics were keen to write off Edwards' actions as simply playing to the gallery, his next steps were more difficult to explain away. With a day or so left before their return home, the band and their crew killed time in the Pat Pong district of Bangkok, wandering around in the way that tourists do. Wire was absent from proceedings, his stomach having rejected the delights of Thai cuisine and forced him back to the hotel.

At some point in the evening Richey chose to break with the crowd, who were drinking in a local bar, and investigate Pat Pong's red light district by himself. Unlike Amsterdam, there were few police controls in the area, with hundreds of underage prostitutes of both sexes free to roam the streets. Edwards soon found himself in a local brothel where, after some discussion, he bought a hand job from one of the girls before re-joining the others. Barbara Ellen, in Bangkok to cover the Manics' appearances for *NME*, later heard of the trip and confronted Richey, asking how he reconciled his experiences with Manics lyrics decrying the West's exploitation of Third World countries. As ever, Richey was keen to be understood, though this time his response – though literate – was less than convincing: "All developing economies abuse their young. When Britain was a developing economy, we sent our children up chimneys and down coal mines, and out into the street to steal. This is just abuse on a wider scale."

Their discussion later widened into a more general disclosure on sex and relationships, Edwards confirming rumours surrounding his frequent liaisons with groupies while on the road and elsewhere. These encounters, he confirmed, were usually passionless affairs, little different from masturbation and more often than not, leaving him feeling grubby after the event. He also talked of his reticence in forming a real bond with someone, the potential terror of failure and subsequent hurt too prohibitive to contemplate. Again, intimacy without intricacy was where the line was drawn, and he was not stepping over it. But there were other, more idealistic notions at play when it came to real love: "Whenever I've got close to having any kind of relationship at all," Edwards said, "I know it's kind of fraudulent because I still find other people attractive. I think if I truly loved someone, that wouldn't be fair. *That's why* I've never had a fucking girlfriend."

Richey's rationalisation of emotional entanglements – his views of sexual longing and attendant gratification – and pure-hearted beliefs surrounding love might have confused those with a more pragmatic opinion of human relationships. They may have even been met with sighs of agreement from some high-minded romantic purists who shared his desire for gilt-edged perfection. And at lower altitudes, wily musicians looking to de-value temporary moments of backstage indiscretion to their partners may have found his words invaluable. But above all, Edwards' reasoning was easy to follow, and given his teenage experiences with sex, rang with truth. Like so many other things, while one might differ with his conclusions, the clarity of thought with which he had pursued them was admirable.

Yet, his self-laceration was different, a more extreme variant of personality, which was difficult to penetrate or immediately understand. To some, even those around him, it was also frightening. As always, he offered explanation: "When I cut myself, I just feel so much better. All the little things that might be annoying me suddenly seem so trivial because I'm concentrating on the pain. I'm not a person who can scream and shout, so this is my only outlet. It's all done very logically."

While Edwards remained convinced of the logic of his actions, there was mounting evidence to suggest that others were less sure. Even if his bandmates understood Richey's motivations, the rapid acceleration of self-abuse in different areas was becoming a cause of real concern. Having begun drinking in his first year at university to block the boisterous environment outside his door and take control of his circadian rhythms, Edwards was now on the wrong side of 'functioning alcoholic'. Driven by vanity months before, he had tried to right the harm drink was doing to his body, using weights and a punishing series of abdominal exercises to stem the quandary. "You could say I had an eating problem," he told *Melody Maker*, "because if I ate too much and I was drinking, I got all puffed up and blotchy. I'm too vain to be like that. I couldn't handle looking in a mirror. All is vanity. In the last year, I've been doing loads of exercise. I do about 1,500 sit-ups every day... weights as well. I take them on tour with me. I want a flat stomach, I want a six pack. I want a stomach like Brad Pitt. I'm incredibly vain."

By Thailand, the exercise regime had been largely abandoned, Richey getting his "flat stomach" through lack of food rather than sit-ups. The drinking, however, remained omnipresent, a night's sleep without it even more awful to contemplate than the difficulties of a relationship. "I don't think it's a big thing," he reasoned at the time. "I just want to get... I just want to forget about things when it starts getting dark. It's pretty impossible to sleep unless you've taken something. Otherwise, you just lie in your bed and think about everything and it just goes on and on and on." For James, who could match his band mate's passion for the hard stuff and also knew a thing or two about its narcotic effects, there might have been empathy for Edwards' dilemma. But make no mistake, they were pursuing markedly different agendas: "You know, I like a good fucking drink, and now and then, a little bit of a laugh with the girls... maybe I get pissed a little bit too much." As for Nicky, never the best of drunks and by now sensible enough to have begun curbing his own excesses, there was only wonderment at Richey's tolerance: "When we used to play 'From Despair To Where'," Wire later said, "there was a point at the start where Richey would have his whiskies lined up, and when James was doing the intro, he'd be kneeling down, going 'Boosh! Boosh! Boosh!' He'd just have a big smile on his face..."

That Edwards' drinking might have exacerbated his recent behaviours or intensified his pursuit of them was certainly possible. Yet, there were other factors that must have contributed to his state of mind in the spring of 1994. Shaken by the death of Phillip Hall, Richey had learned that Nigel, a close friend in college, had also committed suicide. "That threw him," Nicky said later. "It seemed to affect Richey an awful lot because he never made many friends and that was one of them." Things were further soured when it was announced that Kurt Cobain, the driving force behind Nirvana, had taken his own life on April 5. A great admirer of Cobain, whose pre-occupations with social liberation and the state of humanity mirrored some of the Manics' own work, Edwards had played Nirvana's last album *In Utero* constantly since its release in September 1993. But to cap it all, Richey's beloved dog Snoopy – now 17 years old – had recently lost the use of his hind legs and was now going blind. For Edwards, the animal was one of his few links to an uncomplicated, unsullied childhood and he took the news hard.

In subsequent years, the Manics' experiences in Bangkok and Richey's very public revelations about his private life have been construed by some as a darkening in the group's story, or at least a place where their compass was lost. Of course, if the Manic Street Preachers were a metal band, or something more akin to 'pure' rock'n'roll, these tales of tour excess, casual sex, habitual drinking and streaming blood might have been lauded. But the Manics hadn't promoted themselves as Bacchanalian foot soldiers marching to a 'Hammer of the Gods' style calling. Instead, their work had been based around a feminist supporting, politically engaged agenda, with sights set high on re-introducing a heady intellectual element to the music scene. Now, one of their number's actions seemed to speak otherwise. "In Thailand," Nicky conceded, "I just felt something was going out of control. Something... just snapped."

It is perhaps ironic or more likely telling, that at a time when Richey Edwards began to exhibit mounting signs of inner turmoil, the Manic Street Preachers chose to release their finest ever single, 'Faster'. Taking its cue from the sonic experimentation of recent B-side 'Comfort Comes', 'Faster' careered along at a skittering pace, its lean melody never explicit, yet omnipresent just the same. James' vocal delivery too was a thing of beauty, words being slowly dragged before doubling, even tripling in speed as verse acceded to bridge and then to chorus. This use of hypnotic patios created an almost jolting quality, as if one were being ordered to speed up in line with the song's title. If there were musical antecedents to 'Faster', those bands were not to be found playing in stadiums or enjoying multi-platinum sales. Rather, the track seemed to mine the post-punk explorations of groups such as The Chameleons, early Simple Minds and The Skids, James' screeching guitar also strongly recalling the work of Magazine and PIL's John McGeoch. "The trouble with most rock 'n' roll guitarists... is there's still a lot of romance in their playing," said James. "You can hear direct influences... an almost wistful nostalgia for what the guitar is. With John McGeoch, there was no romance. It was quite a brutal style. I loved the fact he defied definition and switched in and out of being a lead or rhythm player. Some Magazine songs, such as

'The Light Pours Out Of Me' were built around his guitar. He was quite brutal, but very lyrical as well. Sometimes, if you jettison all the romance, you can sound cold and academic, but he managed to do all that and still sound very rock'n'roll."

However marvellous the music of 'Faster' was, it was more than equalled by its lyricism, wherein wilful ambiguity, strident defiance and sad-eyed despair all fought for victory. Beginning with a vocal sample from the film version of George Orwell's *1984* placed over whistling, discordant feedback, actor John Hurt's weary voice set the tone for all else to follow: "I hate purity. I hate goodness. I don't want virtue to exist anywhere. I want everyone corrupt." After 30 seconds or so of more atonal rock dynamics came 'Faster''s now justly famous opening lines: "I am an architect, they call me a butcher. I am a pioneer, they call me primitive..." Later, the protagonist declares superiority over the likes of novelist Henry Miller, poet Sylvia Plath and the high IQ society, Mensa, before professing to believe in nothing, even if remains "My nothing". An ancient Chinese proverb: "If you stand up like a nail, then you will be knocked down" then closely follows, before the clashing messages dissipate into a chilling, final mantra: "Some damn easy to cave in, man kills everything."

In later years, Nicky Wire has stated the lyrics to 'Faster' were written by both he and Edwards, though he concedes that Richey contributed the line's share of ideas. With genuine humility, Wire also admits that neither party fully understood its final meaning, though he has offered some explanation for the song: "It's more a voyeuristic insight into how our generation has become obliterated with sensations," Nicky told *Melody Maker*. "We could deal with things but we prefer to blank them out so that virtually every atrocity doesn't have that much impact any more. I don't know if that's a bad thing, I don't even know if we're not on some kind of path to a 'super being' where all emotions are lost and everyone finally gets on perfectly because of that." According to Edwards at the time, 'Faster' was also a study of how everyday morality was simply a form of obedience to society's ruling class. Here, Richey was influenced by his studies of novelist/philosopher Yukio Mishima, who came to believe that Japan's latter day leaders had lost sight of the country's original moral values and were therefore unfit to rule. Fuelled by a desire to return Japan to its original pre-industrial structure, replete with samurai nobility and a re-instatement of the Emperor's powers, Mishima staged a bungled military coup in 1970. On its failure, he committed seppuku, ritual suicide by disembowelment.

When one reads the lyrics to 'Faster', references to sensory overload and moral hypocrisy do indeed present themselves. There are also several nods to the intractable nihilism present in Mishima's later novels and plays, with *Kyoto's House* and *The Harp Of Joy* both possible sources of inspiration. However, given Richey's then current state of mind and subsequent difficulties, it remains difficult to see 'Faster' as anything other than a series of barely concealed clues into Edwards' world view – declaration, justification and swansong all at once. After all, the lyrical ambiguities are there for all to see: the title itself is full of double meaning, capturing both the speed of modern life and a reference to wilfully abstaining from food to exert bodily control. The "pioneer/butcher" coupling too, could easily be perceived as Edwards' validation of his cutting. Notions of rampant narcissism battling with self-contempt and physical imperfection also run riot throughout the song, creating an uneasy juxtaposition. And finally, the first person declarations of triumph over lauded poets, novelists and would-be geniuses all confirm a psyche battling to exert its strength over doubt and inner uncertainty. War cry, rampant intellectual posturing or last will and testament, 'Faster' remains a beguiling insight into a fascinating mind, and still represents for many, Richey Edwards' and the Manic Street Preachers' defining moment.

Hitting the shops on June 6, 1994, 'Faster' was released as a double 'A' side single, sharing top billing with another fine track, 'P.C.P.', its lyrics a savage appraisal of society's mad pursuit of all things politically correct. "It's about the right to freedom of speech and freedom of the media," Nicky said at the time. "Once you know the state gets hold of that, you know everything's fucked. That's the one thing I think is really frightening about political correctness... the eradication of words. It's just so Orwellian, destroying words, changing dictionaries and changing the meaning of words." To further enhance sales, two more songs, the rip-roaringly fast 'Sculpture Of Man' and a live version of 'New Art Riot' – taken from the band's recent Clapham Grand charity show – were added to the CD and 12". As neither 'Faster' nor 'P.C.P.' could be construed as traditionally melodic, it remains a testament to the Great British public that the single reached a creditable number 16 in the charts.

That said, a notorious appearance on *Top Of The Pops* couldn't have hurt either. In a frankly surreal moment of television, Bradfield chose to perform 'Faster' with a balaclava masking his face. Though said balaclava had 'James' sewed on its front, thus rendering it closer to a child's mask than terrorist garb, the phone lines still lit up – the BBC receiving 17,500 complaints in all. "It wasn't meant as a pro-IRA statement," Bradfield confirmed to *Melody Maker*. "A balaclava is synonymous with all urban terrorist movements, you know. The more I appear in public, the more I realise that I've got to accommodate other peoples' beliefs to a scary degree."

Originally Nicky Wire's idea, James' subsequent agreement to completely camouflage his features had more ramifications than intended. "I asked James to put it on for a (pre-show) photo session," Wire said, "and when *TOTP* came along, it just seemed the right thing to do. We were supposed to appear again... but we ended up 'overlooked', shall we say." Yet, Ric Blaxill, the show's producer at the time, defended Bradfield's decision to don the offending item: "The Manics' record company weren't sure about it, but I wanted them to do it. I feel pop has a duty to be emotionally engaging and kids need to be provoked on an emotional level. It looked brilliant and they created controversy when it was necessary to do so." As the years went by, the group's views on the balaclava incident began to subtly change: "Hmm," said James, "we had this dream of performing self-immolation on *TOTP*, but we didn't get round to that either." Wire too, had his doubts: "Actually, we were just being stupid."

Following a well-received set in support of anti-Nazi causes at Brixton's Brockwell Park on May 28, the Manics tried to put aside their enduring dislike of all things 'festival' by appearing at the biggest one of the lot: Glastonbury. Taking the stage in the early evening of June 24, the band could hardly have been more out of place among all the hippy peaceniks. By now, the Manics more resembled extras in a war movie than cartoon punks, Richey's renewed obsession with the film *Apocalypse Now* demonstrating itself in his uniform of choice – combat fatigues and military boots. Nicky too, was all military angles, camouflage paint on his face, camouflage gear on his body. Sticking with the forces theme, James had taken the Russian sailor suit he wore in Bangkok back from the dry cleaners for a run out on stage. And not to be left out at the back, Sean was resplendent in a blue UN Peacekeeper beret, cheekily cocked to the side of his head: from 'Generation Terrorists' to 'Military Masquerade' in one sweeping gesture. Truthfully, given the fact that The Clash pursued a similar theme in their *Sandinista* and *Combat Rock* days only re-inflamed old, unflattering comparisons the Manics could have done without. But it has to be said, they did look dapper.

Performing a set of old favourites and a surprising number of new songs from their forthcoming record, the group were in splendid form throughout, their energy ably captured by Channel Four, which was there to film the event. For the majority of the gig, one would not have remembered the Manics' aversion to festival appearances, or Wire's earlier baiting of the travelling community who often frequented such events. In fact The Levellers, conquering heroes to what Nicky called 'The Jeremies' (or 'Crusties'), were playing on a stage nearby. However, old habits die hard, and Wire wasn't about to let their Glastonbury slot go by without marking it with his trademark enthusiasm for fields. "Somebody," he cried, "please build a bypass over this shithole." The crowd were so shocked by the remark, most of them forgot to boo. Though their show was one of the highlights of the weekend, the Manics themselves remained unconvinced, Bradfield even comparing it to a "cabaret for post-grad students". Nicky was a little more philosophical, pointing toward the fact that the quartet was now a thrilling live proposition: "There's something timeless about playing live. You control it, no-one else controls it. It's pure... the best thing about being in a band."

For those who saw Richey propping up the backstage bar post show, they would have noted an extremely thin, gaunt-faced man, his long fringe falling into tired, huge eyes. But apart from the weight loss, there was precious little visible evidence to suggest that Edwards was unwell, or worse, unstable. The smile was still there, his gift for irony and pathos undiminished. Yet, some weeks before he had given an interview at *NME*'s Brat Awards, which gave clearer indication of what was really going on inside: "The older you get, the more your life becomes miserable. The people you're brought up with die. Your grandparents and parents die.

Your dog dies. Your energy diminishes. There are fewer books to read, no more groups to discover. You end up a barren wasteland trying to find something new that never occurs. The sad thing," he concluded, "is there's nothing worth doing, there's nothing you truly enjoy and there's no purpose to your life."

This was not fighting talk.

Chapter Twelve

Ever Decreasing Circles

In late June of 1994, the Manic Street Preachers returned to Portugal for a series of shows. They had no great memories of the country, having been on tour there when Phillip Hall died some seven months before. This trip was to be even worse.

From their arrival, it became clear than Richey was no longer himself. For some time, he had been given to making curious statements, but they always had the poetry of intellect to them: "The only perfect circle on the human body is the eye," he had said. "When a baby is born it's so perfect. But when it opens its eyes, it's just blinded by corruption and everything else is a downward spiral." However, as evidenced, his recent proclamations had become more despondent, sometimes containing no obvious hope at all. As the tour progressed, Edwards' spirits only worsened. Seemingly incapable of sustaining a conversation, his cyclical thoughts and disconnected statements became a cause of real concern to Wire, Bradfield and Moore. He also appeared genuinely upset much of the time, breaking down in tears on several occasions. Though unqualified to judge the seriousness of the situation, his bandmates nevertheless tried to help, even putting him to bed after one particularly teary outburst in a car. Hours after the event, Nicky was woken by a phone call from his friend, eager to talk though it was by now 3.30am. They briefly watched TV together before Wire gave up from tiredness and returned to bed. The next day, Edwards made no reference to the event other than enquire how the bassist was, before handing him a Mars bar. Regrettably, these late night calls were now not uncommon: "Four, five thirty, five times a week," Nicky remembered, "asking me whether Colonel Kurtz in *Apocalypse Now* was telling the truth. I mean, you know something's wrong..."

Things reached a crescendo on the Manics' return from Portugal. On a temporary break, the band members went their separate ways, with Richey heading home to his Cardiff harbour flat. Wire, still worried by his friend's behaviour, soon received a phone call from Edwards in which he again began talking in bizarre sentences. This time however, there were several disturbing images amid the ramblings, and Nicky was unnerved enough to place a call to Richey's parents. When both parties tried to ring him the next day and received no reply, the alarm was sounded. Graham and Sherry Edwards arrived at their son's flat to find it in a state of complete disarray, while Richey himself was drunk, largely incoherent and covered in deep, self-inflicted cuts. "I couldn't tell you what actually happened," Wire said later. "I just saw the results. It was pretty frightening. Everyone was scared. I mean, there was a difference between carving '4Real' into his arm and the point he got to. He just didn't feel in control." There was now no alternative but to seek professional help.

In the first instance, Edwards was admitted to Whitchurch Hospital in north Cardiff. An NHS psychiatric hospital founded in 1904, Whitchurch's specialities included addiction/counselling services, and therefore seemed a logical place to begin Richey's recovery process. Yet, there were problems for the start. Sharing a ward with 12 other patients, privacy was not a premium and Edwards unsurprisingly felt at sea in his new, crowded surroundings. Moreover, to combat the effects of alcohol withdrawal and insomnia, he was prescribed high doses of Librium. Though this allowed him to sleep, it had other, less pleasant side effects. "James will tell you," he later revealed, "I couldn't even talk, I was just stuttering." Indeed, after visiting their friend several times, the Manics all came to the same conclusion as to Whitchurch's suitability for Edwards' needs. "I was actually shaken," Moore told the BBC. "Him, sitting on a chair, a little smile saying 'Oh, hello Sean, thanks for coming to visit me. I just thought 'This is not the place, he's got to get out of here'." Richey was the first to agree: "The Cardiff hospital was no good for me. After eight days in there, I just didn't know what the fuck was going on."

A decision was promptly made to transfer Edwards from the Whitchurch to The Priory in Roehampton, South London. An independent hospital housing only 92 beds at the time, The Priory was then establishing itself the 'go to' place for celebrities seeking cures from a variety of illnesses such as drug addiction and eating disorders. Elton John, Shaun Ryder and footballer Paul Merson had all passed through its doors. Yet, while it was written up by the media as little more than a "drying out clinic for stars", the hospital had a formidable reputation for success, its range of care covering everything from anxiety disorders such as depression to full blown psychotic episodes. "The Priory is not for the worried well," said head psychiatrist, Dr. Desmond Kelly, at the time. "The people here are seriously ill." The Priory was also extremely expensive, charging up to £300 per day for services rendered. Though the Manics themselves would have to foot the bill, they considered it money well spent.

As Richey began to exhibit some mild progress, discussions between him and his friends were held regarding his future role in the band. At first, Edwards appeared keen to relinquish his onstage duties and take a more consultative role – providing lyrics, overseeing artwork, things of that nature. However, as his self-confidence began to return, he changed his mind. For Phillip Hall's widow, Terri, who had taken up the Manics' PR reigns following her husband's death, a break from the road – temporary or more permanent – might have done much good. "Richey didn't like touring," she said. "The thought of doing it for the fourth or the fifth time was too much really. He'd never have admitted that, though. His life was the Manics, and he wouldn't drop out, even if it was making him ill, making him unhappy."

To the surprise of some of his friends, Edwards enrolled in the famous 12 Steps Recovery Programme while staying at the hospital. Essentially a set of principles designed to aid recovery from addictions or compulsive behaviours, the 12-step was originally devised by

Alcoholics Anonymous as a method of conquering alcoholism. Among its main points were admitting a lack of control over one's dependency, learning to live with a new code of behaviour and recognising a greater power that can provide strength at difficult times. Not given to the idea of 'greater power', this step was a particular problem for Richey, who struggled to find an appropriate figure. In the end, he settled on 'nature', though later conceded: "But then, nature can be very cruel."

Wrestling with problems of self-image, depression, possible anorexia and alcoholism, Edwards' time in The Priory must have been hellish. Yet, there were also occasional moments of levity to be had, these ably provided by the high-profile musicians sharing his accommodation at the time. "Sinead O'Connor being there was almost like a bit of solace for him," Bradfield later told *Hot Press*, "because he said there were a couple of incidents – and he wouldn't go into them – (where) it was good to see someone else from a musical background who was absolutely telling everybody to fuck off, (saying) 'How dare you analyse what's wrong with me in such a simplistic manner?' And that was Richey's point... they're always trying to find a simple way into the problem, which doesn't exist." Wire was as impressed by O'Connor's actions before she entered treatment for depression as he was while she was a guest of the hospital. "It's great she came back from the abyss. The old 'tearing up a picture of the Pope' thing, it's just so Manics-esque. It was so deeply admirable when she did that. We'd have thought about it, but not have the balls. It was simply fucking unbelievable." But perhaps not as unbelievable as an alleged invitation to Richey from visiting guitar god Eric Clapton to join him in a jam. "Richey said he was nice and all of that, but there was a terrible moment when Eric knocked on his door and said 'I hear you're in a band, how would you feel if I brought my guitar in... and we jammed in the room?'" Bradfield laughed. "And of course, that nearly put Richey back two weeks in his therapy because basically, he couldn't play guitar, and he didn't have the guts to say to him 'You're fucking me up, go away! Go away!'"

As Edwards struggled to bring order back to his life while simultaneously avoiding the attention of roving guitar heroes, Wire, Bradfield and Moore met with the music press to discuss their friend's condition and prospects. Always open about the band's affairs – even if it had occasionally cost them dear in the past – the Manics again chose honesty as the best way forward. Thankfully, having watched Richey's troubles grow in recent times, journalists were respectful of his dilemma and allowed the group space to update fans on cause, effect and cautious improvement. "You know," Wire told *NME*, "it was obvious that he had to go into hospital. There was no other option. He realised it. We realised it. His parents realised it. He's just really ill in a lot of ways at the moment. I think he feels deep down that it would have come to this whether he'd been a teacher or a bank clerk, but I personally think being in a band accelerated it."

Bradfield too, was keen to draw on the fact that while lifestyle was a contributing factor to Edwards' woes, there was a bigger picture to be considered. "It's not just about rock 'n' roll," he confirmed. "Richey's actually a very 'Richard Briers' person, very cardigan, pipe and slippers. But I think if he'd gone on to become a university lecturer, which he might well have done, the same thing could have happened... though in a more private way." James was also correct in isolating where some of the real problems lay. "It's strange. Richey's never had as many setbacks as me. He's more acutely intelligent than me, he's more beautiful than me and yet he's had more problems. But he has a very acute perception of things, and you can't lose that perception. It's just a matter of how you channel it."

Despite the Manics gaining grace and favour from the music papers, there was a wider sweep of speculation being generated from the dailies that all but announced Edwards was leaving the group. Manager Martin Hall was left with little alternative but to step into the fray with a few choice words: "Speculation that Richey is leaving the band is completely unfounded. Even from the clinic, he is still very much involved with the artwork design and other marketing aspects of the forthcoming album." As for more salacious rumours, such as Edwards trying to commit suicide while at The Priory, Hall was having none of it: "Richey is still very active... and is getting better. However, he (remains) very ill... and has decided to seek out professional psychiatric help to help deal with what is basically a sickness."

A fearfully honest approach was also taken by Hall in dealing with enquiries into Edwards' self-laceration, conceding that while his brother Phillip's death may have been one trigger, they were many others floating in the background: "Richey said he would have ended up the same way regardless. He doesn't see anything wrong with cutting himself. It makes him feel better. It's his way of releasing pain and his argument is he doesn't harm anyone else in the process. It's like a badge to show he's emotionally strong enough to deal with his problems. (But), he was at a point where no-one, including himself, knew how far he would go. If he had carried on without help, he might have ended up killing himself."

Richey Edwards' plight sparked a fine show of support from fans, writers and casual onlookers alike. The rock weeklies' mail bags bulged with sympathetic letters and several articles were written exploring the myths and realities behind self-harming and anorexia. Whether he liked, loathed or was even in a state to greatly care about any of it, Richey's recent travails had consolidated, even enhanced, his cult status. Yet, that status hadn't quite translated into huge sales, a fact underlined by the Manics' next single, 'Revol', released while he was still receiving treatment. Another lyric written in the main by Richey, 'Revol' seemed at first glance little more than a listing of past leaders, despots and revolutionaries, with each assigned their own particular emotional or sexual foible. Read as such, the song had some satirical value, the Russians – according to Edwards – quite a kinky, if dysfunctional lot. But as ever, there were serious points to be made, with Nicky Wire revealing some of Richey's thinking around the subject: "Some of it's beyond my head, (though I think) it's trying to say that relationships in politics, and relationships in general, are failures... probably because all his relationships have failed!"

Regardless of its hidden depths, 'Revol' really wasn't much to get excited about. To begin, Bradfield was again having trouble cramming Edwards' florid wordplay into the song's verse and choruses. Additionally, the tune itself wasn't up to much, its central melody bashed about the head by busy percussion and even busier guitars. Worse still, an angry bee appeared to be trapped somewhere in the mix, giving the track a distinctly queasy quality. Of much more interest was the 'B' side, 'Too Cold Here', a spare acoustic ballad that had James whistling his way through some bleakly affecting lyrics: "It's easier to make love to a stranger, than ask a friend to call..." Released as a separate two-CD package, featuring live versions of 'Love's Sweet Exile' (from Bangkok) and three numbers liberated from the Manics' recent Glastonbury show, 'Revol' only got as far as number 22 in mid-August. "'Revol' was an awful fucking song," James later confessed, "and I thought it could be a massive fucking hit. It's just deplorable, a piece of dogshit."

There was, however, a certain poignancy in the single's promotional video. In a return to the obvious sloganeering of their earliest incarnation, the clip was full of unsubtle, yet biting messages such as "violence exists, we did not create it" and "poetry comes out of the barrel of a gun". And as the promo was filmed before he entered The Priory, Richey was also there for all to see: stage right, guitar slung low, but painfully, painfully thin. "Scarred, starved beauty," *Melody Maker*'s Stud Brothers said at the time, "hopeless hopes, wild ambitions and bitter cravings."

As 'Revol''s video revealed, Richey Edwards was obviously in terrible health and required as much help as the doctors could give him. But that help didn't come cheap and the Manics were funding The Priory's costs from their own pockets. To ensure Edwards' continued progress, the band had no alternative but to contemplate fulfilling several live engagements, including T in the Park and the Reading Festival, without him. Aside from a *TOTP* appearance where Nicky was absent on honeymoon – his place taken by road manager Rory Lyons, wearing a Mickey Mouse mask – no group member had ever been marked absent from a gig. Of course, the Manics had latterly added *Gold Against The Soul* producer Dave Eringa to their line-up for live keyboard cover, and it was no great secret that Edwards had trouble carrying a tune. But the thought of actually replacing him, albeit temporarily, made them distinctly uncomfortable. Unsure of exactly how to proceed, they turned to the man himself. "We were thinking about cancelling everything," Wire said at the time, "but I talked to Richey about it and we felt it would be a bit of a cop out.. .Richey's not going to (appear). He just doesn't want to do it. We don't particularly want to do it either, but so many tickets have been sold and there are just so many contractual obligations. So we'll do it and get it over with." Decision made, the band would perform as a trio: no additions, no substitutes.

To their credit, the Manic Street Preachers' appearance at Glasgow's T in the Park on July 30 went well enough. And if truth be told, there was little difference to their overall sound, the crowd bouncing along to the likes of 'From Despair To Where' and 'Motorcycle Emptiness' in traditional fashion. Dressed in now familiar combat gear, camouflage nets hung behind them to further provoke a military theme, the band also looked sharp and full of purpose. Yet, without Edwards on stage, they genuinely hated every minute of it. "When we played Glasgow without him, it was horrendous," Wire later confirmed. "It just felt like a massive fucking spiritual betrayal." The group's spot at the Reading Festival on August 28 went much better, despite the fact that the show fell on the late Phillip Hall's birthday. But when Nicky and James were quizzed by the press about absent friends before the concert, they looked uneasy, if not dejected: "Richey's reached a zenith of shitness," reasoned Wire. "His lifestyle and his drinking reached a peak of ugliness and it had to stop. It's a mad vanity with Richey, it's damaged him and he's got to do something about it." On this point, Bradfield was equally clear: "Basically, it just went beyond any notion... where he was even perpetuating his own myth."

As for the inevitable questions regarding Edwards' future with the Manics, both Nicky and James tried to find a balance between blind optimism and harsh reality. "If he doesn't think he can come back," reasoned Bradfield, "then I'd have to seriously entertain whether I could carry on with the group. And I haven't made any concrete decisions. The basic, bottom line is that I'm sure he will be coming back. And the most important thing is his well-being as my friend." Nicky was also loyal to a fault, but also careful to ensure that Edwards' plight not be seen as anything other than deadly serious. "I would never want him to kill himself over something like a band. We could say that we'll never continue without Richey, but if we did get the urge again, people will only throw it back in our faces. I would never feel like doing anything without Richey, that's all I will say. You know, the worst thing about it," he also confessed, "would be if people think this is one of those things we're categorised for, as a hype or an image. I can categorically say that's not it at all. I wish that it was."

The brutal reality of Edwards' mindset and his apparent lack of regard for either hype or image came with the release of the Manic Street Preachers' third album, *The Holy Bible*. A bleak, yet beautiful offering, capable of bestowing the same concurrent sense of joy and sorrow that only the most gifted bluesmen can provide, *The Holy Bible* still needed to be approached with caution to obtain best results. For while the record's gifts were many, there was also a sense of real dread and apprehension to negotiate before one could truly get to grips with the sheer achievement of it all. At the heart of *The Holy Bible* were the lyrics of Richey Edwards, who by allowing his personal demons and private obsessions freedom to roam, had produced by far his finest work: a series of searing meditations on the nature of suffering, despair, political tomfoolery and the dangers of power without a conscience to guide it. Through their best efforts, Bradfield, Moore and Wire had provided a riveting musical backdrop to complement these images, although one had to concede it wasn't always easy listening. In short, *The Holy Bible* was uncompromising, inflexible and difficult to love, but worth pursuing just the same. "Well," said Sean with some understatement, "we knew from the moment we started work on it, it wasn't going to be played at parties..."

The first clue given to potential buyers that *The Holy Bible* might be a work of some originality came with the striking triptych that graced its cover. Entitled *Strategy (South Face/Front Face/North Face)*, the painting illustrated a monumentally obese woman from three angles, her body stripped to its underwear, her face stripped of all vanity. *Strategy...* was the work of Jenny Saville, then only 23 years old, but making quite a name for herself as a young British artist given to capturing unconventional notions of feminine beauty. Previously, Wire and Edwards had come across *Strategy...* in *The Independent On Sunday*, thought it perfect as potential artwork for their new album and given Saville a call. Unlike others in the past, she didn't ask the earth in image reproduction costs and was happy for the band to use her work. "It was a marriage made in heaven," said Nicky. A further hint as to what lay ahead could be found on the record's back cover sleeve with a quotation from Octave Mirbeau's controversial novel *The Torture Garden*. A satirical attack on the French government, written in 1899, Mirbeau's tome was famous for its graphic descriptions of flailing, crucifixion and its withering dedication: "To the priests, the soldiers, the judges, to those people who educate, instruct and govern men, I dedicate these pages of murder and blood." The book was also a particular favourite with Richey Edwards.

When one got past the packaging to the music of *The Holy Bible*, further surprises awaited. Unlike the glossy sheen that wrapped itself around *Gold Against The Soul*, the production of the Manics' latest album was spare, instruments crammed together, James' guitar, Sean's drums and Nicky's bass all fighting for space in the mix. There was also a marked absence of traditional harmony, the band more content to explore the use of flattened fifths, chromatics, dissonance and atonality than classic three chord structures. To further unnerve listeners, *The Holy Bible* was riddled with sound effects – whistles, echo, feedback and vocal samples creating an atmosphere of uneasiness. There were moments where real tunefulness broke free from this air of general discord, opening track, 'Yes', 'This Is Yesterday' and 'She Is Suffering' all displaying sad, but strong melodies. But such moments were few. *The Holy Bible* was almost militant in its demands upon the ear and one was expected to work in exchange for any pleasures granted. "At times," Bradfield later said, "I actually resented putting vocals over the music..."

The bands that influenced *The Holy Bible*'s sound and style mostly came from the fringes of rock and pop, being more content to conduct sonic tests with rhythms and scales than actively court mainstream success. Hence, a strong echo of John Lydon's pioneering experimentalists PIL resounded throughout *Bible* tracks such as 'The Intense Humming Of Evil' and 'Archives Of Pain'. John McGeoch's scratchy guitar work with Magazine and Siouxsie & The Banshees could also be heard in James' approach to 'P.C.P.', 'Faster' and 'Revol'. Elsewhere, the Manics were indebted to the machine-like terror of Killing Joke, 'Mausoleum', 'Ifwhiteamericatoldthetruthforonedayitsworldwouldfallapart' and 'Of Walking Abortion' all recalling Jaz Coleman's industrial pioneers. From the blunt instrument trauma of American groups Alice In Chains and Nine Inch Nails to post-punk groundbreakers like Joy Division, Wire, Gang Of Four and The Skids, *The Holy Bible* doffed its proverbial cap to the lot.

That said, the Manics hadn't callously stolen their musical ideas. Instead, they had used their influences well – mining from the source, perhaps, but only to craft new shapes to suit their needs. And by choosing such a spiky bunch to draw inspiration from, it allowed Bradfield and his colleagues to concentrate their attack, sounding raw and urgent all over again. In this respect, they were light years away from the well crafted, but glib professionalism of their last record. "I felt we'd really let ourselves down with *Gold Against The Soul*," James told *Melody Maker*, "we'd inhabited too many personae. *The Holy Bible*'s... more stripped down. We wanted to get away from that 'decadent rock star rubbish' and communicate more honestly. To do that, we sat down, gave ourselves headings and structures, so each song was an essay. We just rejected our past in a lot of ways."

The music of *The Holy Bible* also had to act in concert with the words and ideas Richey Edwards had provided. And as the song titles suggested, almost all topics he had covered were not for the faint of heart. Responsible for over 70% of lyrics on the album, Edwards had taken an almost Manichean stance with his subject matter – his conclusions black or white, but mostly black. Yet, if one could get past the themes of morbidity, desolation and anguish, there was a brilliance to it all that was hard to deny.

With 'Yes', the spotlight shone on cultural judgements of prostitution, Richey pointing out that the majority of would-be accusers were happy enough to whore their own skills for personal gain. As the Manics had made great profit from their self-declared status as 'Media Sluts', this was an opportunity not only to acknowledge the hypocrisy but also decry the hollowness behind it. "The majority of your time," Edwards later told fans, "is spent doing something you hate to get something you don't need." With its furious images of pimps arguing prices with clients and movie stars snapped to death by paparazzi (each photo stealing a little more of their soul), 'Yes' was a fine way to open *The Holy Bible*'s account. 'Ifwhiteamerica...' was again top draw lyricism, Richey and Nicky compiling a long and damning list of the USA's transgressions against its own people and abroad, while also taking a hacksaw to the country's lax gun control laws. 'Of Walking Abortion' was another in a long line of anti-fascist swipes from Edwards, his scorn this time being poured on Miklós Horthy, the Hungarian leader whose pre-war alliance with Nazi Germany brought disaster to his country. Horthy's fellow fascists were also not above Richey's gift for prosecution, or his plea for society to remain vigilant in avoiding their ideas: "Mussolini hangs from a butcher's hook, Hitler reprised in the worm of your soul."

A beautiful, swirling song and one of the undoubted highlights of *The Holy Bible*, 'She Is Suffering' dealt with almost Buddhist ideas of shedding desire in exchange for purity. Borrowing a line or two from one of Edwards' favourite novels, Fyodor Dostoyevsky's *The Brothers Karamazov*, 'She Is Suffering' also carried the phrase "Nature's lukewarm pleasure", his favourite description of sex. Backed by the now forgotten gem 'Love Torn Us Under', 'She Is Suffering' was released as a single in October, 1994, reaching number 25 in the UK charts. The track that followed it on *The Holy Bible* was 'Archives Of Pain', a pure Nicky/Richey collaboration, where pen and paper were furiously swapped between the two before they were satisfied with the results. Taking its name from a chapter in the book *Discipline And Punish* by French philosopher Michel Foucault, 'Archives Of Pain' was a vivid negation of the public's abiding interest in murderers. "It was written as a reaction to the glorification of serial killers," Wire told *Melody Maker*, "... everyone gets a self destructive urge to kill, but I don't particularly like the glorification of it. The song isn't a right-wing statement, it's just against this fascination with people who kill."

Following the battering ram assault of 'Revol' came Richey Edwards' most profoundly moving lyric, '4st 7lb'. Casting himself in the body and mind of a teenage girl suffering from anorexia, Edwards invited us into a world where an innocent takes pride and delight from the ebbing away of flesh, her goal to reach the horrifying target weight of the song's title, "I want to walk in the snow and not leave a footprint" being one of its more affecting lines. Alongside 'Faster', '4st 7lb' stands as a testament to Edwards' skills as a poet, his wordplay a near flawless insight into a disorder that demands a terrible control and can exact the highest price. Given the pinpoint clarity Richey brought to his subject matter, and the causes behind his own admission to The Priory, it is also hard to see it as anything other than thinly veiled autobiography: "Vanity/innocence/anorexia: true or false?" he later said.

Edwards and Wire again drew on personal experience for 'The Intense Humming Of Evil' and 'Mausoleum'. Having visited the Nazi concentration camps Dachau and Belsen, and Hiroshima's Peace Museum the year before, their reflections on the butchery and violence of men was ably reflected in these "brother/sister" songs. "Dachau is such an evil, quiet place," Wire said. "There's no grass, (no) worms, let alone any birds. All you hear is the humming of nothing." Richey had been genuinely shaken when visiting the camps, subsequently becoming depressed by the revisionism taking place around the Holocaust, with historians stupidly arguing about the exact number of Jewish deaths rather than addressing the crime itself.

If there was a moment of relative calm on *The Holy Bible*, it came with 'This Is Yesterday', its lyric written from the standpoint of a pensioner wallowing in youthful remembrances. Richey referred to the song as "Memory more comforting than future", which covered its sentiments perfectly. But 'This Is Yesterday' provided only temporary respite, as the track that followed it, 'Die In The Summertime', was surely *The Holy Bible*'s darkest moment. With words so utterly bleak that Nicky Wire came away disturbed after reading them, Edwards had returned to old age to provide a storyline, though this time his protagonist only craved death: "Scratch my leg with a rusty nail, sadly it heals." With these images of self-harming and further reference made to the comforts of childhood, it seemed foolish to imagine Richey was talking about anyone other than himself. "It was pretty obviously about his state of mind," Nicky later confessed, "which I didn't quite realise at the time. (But) if you're close to someone, you always try to deny a thought like that."

An austere, disturbing and sometimes draining work, *The Holy Bible* was also the closest the Manic Street Preachers had come to fashioning their very own masterpiece. "With that record," Wire observed, "we all had our roles to play and we all had trust in each other. There was a strong work ethic, telepathy and a discipline to it." For Bradfield, the experience of making *The Holy Bible* had allowed him and the band to take ownership of their influences and create something new from them: "The album is our most honest and kind of sounds like an exclusive language. My early influences were bands like The Clash,

Sex Pistols and Magazine. And for once, I think I've actually reflected those influences and assimilated them. I've never really achieved that before."

By taking such an approach, the Manics had also put their temporary flirtation with corporate rock behind them. "*Gold Against The Soul* was too smooth," Edwards later said. "Everything had clean surfaces, everything was antiseptic. We'd signed to a major label and were being babied. That had to stop, I think. And it did stop."

Though the musicianship and song writing evidenced on *The Holy Bible* were inspiring, and Bradfield's guitar work often superlative, the lion's share of credit for making the record what it was went to Richey Edwards. "The velocity of his intelligence then was scary," James remembered, "and the velocity of his commitment was astonishing." Wire also confirmed Edwards' commitment to the project: "He was just incredibly prolific at that point, always writing lyrics, always writing lists. It was 'Let's do this, let's do that'. He just couldn't switch off. At the start of it all," Nicky told journalist Niall Doherty, "we were all obsessed with chart hits and we wanted to be huge. But by the time of *The Holy Bible*, Richey was becoming far less convinced by that, and he wasn't writing lyrics to get hits."

With Richey Edwards' highly personal, often autobiographical lyricism running rife throughout *The Holy Bible*, the record has sometimes been described as 'confessional' in nature. This is surely wrong. After all, confession implies penitence and Edwards was not on his knees here. Instead, he was simply stating his own version of truth. And if that felt uncomfortable or pulled the listener closer to the fragility of human existence than they wished to be, so be it. Richey was not compelling anyone to listen, but simply compelled to say what he thought: "I don't want to force my opinions down anyone's throats. We write our lyrics and you take what you want from them." Nonetheless, at times during *The Holy Bible*, it appeared that Edwards had followed Yukio Mishima's advice in capturing the essence of suffering far too closely for his own good. "The special quality of Hell," Mishima once wrote, "is to describe everything down to its last detail."

Unlike *Gold Against The Soul*, which drew distinctly mixed reviews, *The Holy Bible* was lavished with praise from critics, the Manics' bravery reaping them rich rewards: "*The Holy Bible*, then," reasoned *Melody Maker*'s Simon Price, "(has) biceps of tungsten, veins ready to burst, its metal under unendurable torque. It's about everything... it's Richey's album." *Q*'s Tom Doyle also found much to admire in *The Holy Bible*'s uncompromising stance, dwelling on the band's ability to surprise and occasionally confound: "The emphasis here is on intensity and energy with shock lyrical tactics being employed by pen-chewing worksmith duo Nicky Wire and Richey Edwards... *The Holy Bible* proves the Manics to be a band that can subtly re-invent themselves at every turn." But it was perhaps *Mojo*'s Richard Lowe who best captured the thoughts of those who had previously written the group off as little more than punk rock imposters: "A funny thing has happened to the Manics. They find themselves being acclaimed as a really good rock band with something worthwhile to say. We get wired, edgy, powerful guitar rock... sometimes ugly, often thrilling (and) lyrically, it's mind boggling. Every ounce of angst, hate, despair, paranoia, disgust, fury and self-loathing they've ever felt, every idea they've ever had has been poured into these dense, impenetrable songs."

With its striking cover image, excellent reviews and the sheer quality of the material present, *The Holy Bible* gave the Manics their highest ever chart position, the record debuting at number six in the UK on September 10, 1994. But unlike its predecessor *Gold Against The Soul*, which had stuck around the charts for almost three months, *The Holy Bible*'s initial shelf life was brief. Three weeks after it had entered the Top 10, it completely disappeared again. Further, the band had hoped the album might be strongly promoted in the States, and a more radio friendly US remix was worked upon. Yet again, there were difficulties with Sony's American business arm, their executives downright cagey about offering major support for the record. This hesitance was no doubt driven by several key factors: the album's cover could be misconstrued as a negative comment on obesity, a problem – then and now – in the United States; equally, the uncompromising nature of the songs and highly 'British' influences that had inspired them might confuse or underwhelm a stateside audience. But most likely, in a country known for its own particular brand of religious fundamentalism, *The Holy Bible*'s title would surely cause offence.

In fact, this was true elsewhere in Europe and the UK, where the Manics had already encountered some negativity around the album's name. "In every hotel, in every part of the world, the only constant is The Holy Bible," Richey later said by way of explanation. "And the album's called that because for me, whether you choose to believe or not – believe in religion, Christianity, whatever – or whether you're agnostic or an atheist, the simple fact is that religion has shaped world history and still does. Even if people deny that, it's still an important factor in world events right now." For Edwards, it was about facing reality more than anything else: "The holy book in any religion is supposed to be about the truth, and I think the way most religions choose to speak that truth to the public is always in a way (that) beats them down and keeps them in their proper place... In most European countries, the very fact that women priests might be ordained offends a lot of religions. They're trying to say that women are second class and inferior, which is basically what they mean. It's those types of people who have been offended by the title *The Holy Bible*. (But), if the Holy Bible is true, it should be about the way the world is, and I think that's what my lyrics are about... they speak about the world as it actually is, don't ignore things, don't pretend things don't exist. I don't think that's any way to live your life, really."

Eventually, a deal with Sony America was struck. The Manics' new record would be released stateside in the spring of 1995, backed by a well-targeted promotional campaign and 36-date tour. Given the recent success of other 'difficult to market' product such as Nine Inch Nails' *The Downward Spiral* and Nirvana's impenetrable *In Utero*, there remained hope that *The Holy Bible* might yet crack the US. And if wishes were fishes...

In the autumn of 1994, such concerns were of minor importance as the Manics wrestled with other, more pressing concerns: not least the fact that Richey Edwards, having now completed his treatment at The Priory, had just reported back for active duties with the group. With a round of French shows alongside Northern Irish punk/metal battlers Therapy and further European and UK dates to follow, it would be a stern test for Edwards. But it also offered an opportunity to place recent events behind him, regain his equilibrium, perhaps even plan for the future. For all concerned, friends, family, fans, this was the hope and even Richey himself seemed optimistic. "I've learned all the songs for the French dates," he said. "I went back up to the hospital... and that was all good (so) I'm quite looking forward to it. I think it will be good." Sadly, it wasn't.

Chapter Thirteen

Intermission

Richey Edwards' return to the ranks of the Manic Street Preachers was always going to be met with a combination of real joy and trepidation by his fellow band members. As his closest friends, they had been privy to the alarming change in character displayed in recent months, and remained concerned that too much stress might again be Edwards' undoing. But there had been real signs of improvement since he had been admitted to The Priory, and publicly at least, Wire appeared reasonably hopeful regarding Richey's next steps. "Obviously, he's better than he was," Nicky said before the Manics' appearance at Reading Festival, "but we still don't know if he'll be well enough in time for the tour. I think it looks quite promising (and) it's still six, seven weeks away, so there is time for him to get better."

Edwards had used the Manics' autumn dates as a prime motivator for his recovery at The Priory. Always imbued with a strong work ethic, he felt that it would be "cheating" not to join them on the road, even if he took no great pleasure from touring: "It's the thing that makes it feel like a job." But more than that, the Manics had been – were still – the most important thing in his life and he would not give that up easily. Therefore, following his discharge from hospital, Richey joined his colleagues at Blue Stone Studios in Pembrokeshire, South Wales for pre-show rehearsals. Judging from photos taken at the time, he appeared in slightly better health, having gained some weight during his time away. However, there was some evidence of fresh scarring on his upper arms, and his eyes looked cloudy – no doubt a result of the prescription drugs he was taking to manage his condition.

Though Edwards was more keen to promote the Manics' latest album and their forthcoming tour than himself, he nevertheless consented to discuss his recent experiences with *NME's* Stuart Bailie, a consistent champion of the group. "It just went wrong," he said. "I just wasn't coping very well and I thought my body was probably stronger than it actually was. My mind was quite strong, and I pushed my body further than it was meant to go. For the first time, I was a bit scared, because I always thought I could handle it." Richey was also eager to stress that his troubles were not linked to the nature of his profession. "It's very romantic to think 'I'm a troubled writer', but mental institutions are not full of people in bands. They're full of people with so called 'normal' jobs. Or were full. 68,000 beds have been closed down in the last couple of years, which I wouldn't have been aware of, unless I was actually in one." As to the one question that had to be asked, Edward's response was empathic: "In terms of the 'S' word, that does not enter my mind. And it never has done, in terms of an attempt. Because I am stronger than that. I might be weak, but I can take pain." All in all, Richey's re-engagement with the music press went well enough, his honesty winning, his negation of suicidal thoughts a relief to all. Yet, *NME*'s Bailie later described Edwards as possessing "the stare of a war veteran, abstracted, out of reach".

There were other noticeable differences in Edwards' character following his treatment at The Priory. On leaving the hospital, he was still adhering to the 12 Steps programme for recovering addicts, and would occasionally read self-help literature aloud, much to the general embarrassment of the band. In fact, Wire thought they "sounded like prayers". More used to hearing their friend quote Ballard, Mirbeau and Mishima than Ernest Larson's *Believing In Myself*, there was a general suspicion that not everything he had recently learned was of value. "We all think The Priory filled him up with a lot of shit," Nicky later said. "All the things The Priory stood for, in one way or another, Richey had ridiculed viciously in the past... deep down, he knew it was just crap. It's pseudo-religion anyway. If he'd become a born again Christian, I think it would be better." For James, simply the experience of entering such a place, let alone a protracted stay within its walls, would be life-changing. "Whatever happens, I do think you come back a completely different person," he told the BBC. "They destroy your 'self', so to speak. They just want you to be another person... that's their job."

Whatever one thought of the methods used to help Richey Edwards, they ultimately proved unsuccessful. While the Manics' dates with Therapy went by without major incident, by the time the band returned to the UK, Richey was again showing signs of major imbalance. On leaving hospital, he had taken to writing 'Love' on his knuckles, a harmless, if odd affectation that Bradfield dismissed as 'Priory bollocks". He also asked his bandmates to address his as 'Richard' rather than his more familiar designation. Bemused, they simply ignored the request, nicknaming him 'Android' instead. But there were other, more troubling quirks: for instance, Edwards had begun to identify heavily with Dennis Hopper's demented photojournalist in *Apocalypse Now*, even purchasing the same camera used by the actor in the film. He wore it about his neck constantly. Moreover, he returned to a previous obsession with Def Leppard's ill-fated guitarist, Steve Clark. A gifted musician but chronic alcoholic, Clark had reacted badly to the pressures of fame, succumbing to chronic stage fright and threatening to break his fingers rather than perform. An early hero to Edwards, he had lambasted the *NME* in 1991 for giving over pages of copy to 'useless acts' while devoting only a paragraph to Clark's death from an accidental overdose. Worryingly, Richey now talked of taking a knife to his own fingers so he too could avoid concert duties. Some reports even had him buying a meat cleaver, though it was allegedly soon thrown away by the band's road crew.

Another concern for the Manics was Edwards' continued weight loss. Only a month or so since leaving treatment, he was now back to old ways, eating squares of chocolate rather than regular meals. Noticeably gaunt, he nevertheless seemed to enjoy watching the pounds leave his body. "It's a well known fact that anorexics try to cover up their condition with baggy clothes all the time," Wire later remembered. "But on the first day of the British tour, Richey walks in and he's wearing the tightest pair of girls' leggings I've ever seen in my life. He still wanted the rest of the world to know he was fucked up. Everyone knew already. I said 'Why are you doing that? You haven't got to prove that you are whatever you are'." To further reduce his almost concave stomach, Richey had even re-ignited his daily sit-up routine.

There were more changes to his physique but this time they were done with ink. Two new circular tattoos appeared on Edwards' shoulders, their exact meaning a matter of some conjecture, but seemingly drawing inspiration from Dante's *Inferno*, another of his favourite books. One design appeared to be a representation of God's Universe as it was thought to be in Dante's time, with Earth, Hell, Purgatory and Paradise existing within a kind of celestial 'hemisphere': Heaven above, Jerusalem at the centre of the Earth, the inferno beneath. The second marking concentrated on Dante's 'Ninth Circle of Hell' alone. This was part of the abyss reserved for 'Betrayers', and its geography consisted of four subsections or 'Rounds': Caina, Antenora, Ptolomaea, and Judecca. Richey's tattoo bore the approximate phrase 'Traitors to their kindred, Traitors to their Country, Traitors to their Guests, Traitors to their Benefactors', each salutation corresponding to these particular areas of eternal pain. Arcane and obscure messages, the tattoos suggested that Richey's fascination with religion had been strongly re-activated while at The Priory. One last phrase, "I'll surf this beach" had also been tattooed upon his arm. A snatch of dialogue taken from *Apocalypse Now,* it was yet another confirmation of Edwards' current mindset.

If the Manics harboured concerns regarding Edwards' marking of his body with needle and ink, they paled into insignificance against greater fears as to what he might do with far sharper tools. Regrettably, when the Manics flew to Europe to begin a co-headlining tour with Suede, those fears were realised. Following a disappointing appearance at Amsterdam's Paradiso club on November 24, spirits backstage were low except in Richey's case, who appeared exultant. Puzzled by his behaviour, Nicky played a hunch and pulled back Edward's shirt only to reveal a deep vertical cut to his stomach. As James ran interference with visiting journalists, Richey was taken from the venue to hospital where he reportedly received a number of stitches for his wound. Only a week later, he was back in the wars, this time striking his head repeatedly against the wall of a Hamburg hotel. When Wire was called by staff to investigate, he found his friend covered in blood with several cuts to his face. Horrified, the band took to examining him each night before bed to ensure there were no further mutilations. "It had become this tragic, grotesque, downward spiral," Sean later said. "It was hard to understand where he was coming from. He'd got pretty confused." Wire also felt powerless to help his friend: "It felt like Richey was drifting away. I'd just lost him. Couldn't talk about rugby or cricket or football. He'd call you up at strange times about some documentary he'd just seen or something he'd tracked down. It was hard work, baffling at times."

After 23 shows with Suede throughout Europe, the Manics returned home for a three-night stop-off at the West End's Astoria Theatre on December 19-21. A Christmas treat for London fans and their first opportunity to see Edwards in action since his spell in The Priory, public expectations were high. Equally, the band had done a magnificent job of shielding their colleague's recent behaviour from the press, so the chance to simply enjoy the gigs rather than worry about rampant media intrusion was a genuine bonus to them. And if all else failed, they were at least back on home soil, or near as damn it. With a strong supporting line up that included Strangelove, Whiteout, the Dust Brothers, should-have-beens Marion and DJ Andy Weatherall providing inter-set entertainment, the first two shows went exceedingly well. Curiously, problems with the venue's PA ended up causing the band constant nosebleeds – sound waves seemingly interfering with sinuses – but it didn't affect their concert activities. In fact, the Manics' recent addition of Nirvana's 'Pennyroyal Tea' to their set was indicative of a new-found confidence, the group now willing to cover just about any song that took their fancy.

The third night at the Astoria proved especially memorable. Appearing relaxed, self-assured and tour-hardened, the Manic Street Preachers provided a set of real authority and no little humour. James, now a consummate showman even went as far as donning a Santa hat to accompany his solo rendition of Wham's camptastic 'Last Christmas'. 'Faster', 'New Art Riot', 'La Tristesse Durera', 'Roses In The Hospital' '4st 7lb'. Old and new songs, loved and less so, were all dispatched with considerable power and energy. Following a fine set, they offered one last gift to the crowd, reducing their on-stage equipment to splinters and shards. "When we smashed eight grand's worth of gear and lights, they were five of the best minutes I've ever had in my life," Nicky later told *NME*. "It was just brilliant... it meant more than any of the songs. It felt like something was finished." At the heart of the destruction was Richey Edwards. Combat rock clothes, classic Bowie *The Man Who Fell To Earth* haircut. Thin as a rake, pale as a cloud, diving headlong into Sean's kit, broken guitar trailing behind him. For anyone lucky enough to be there that night, "the beautiful boy" looked almost happy among the chaos and destruction, like a child again. An indelible image, really. And just as well, because it was his last performance with the band.

Chapter Fourteen

A Beckoning Silence

Arthur Rimbaud wrote about a season in Hell. 1994 had seen the Manic Street Preachers experience almost a year long spell in roughly the same vicinity. "From Thailand to the smashing up of the Astoria," Nicky Wire confirmed, "it was hospitalisation, no money, drudgery, hateful, miserable... just awful." It wasn't just Wire who had felt the burn. To escape the rigours of touring and pressures surrounding Richey Edwards' continued traumas, James Dean Bradfield had been drinking alcohol as an emotional prop and useful narcotic – his body and mind dog-tired as a result. Sean Moore, though still a poster boy for stoicism, had also felt the stress of recent events, trying wherever possible to balance his workload with keeping an ever-watchful eye on the comings and goings of his oldest friend.

As for Richey himself, 1994 had been a journey without maps. Having provided the Manics with the best writing of his career and the template upon which *The Holy Bible* was built, Edwards had spiralled out of control: the cuts had grown deeper, the behaviours more difficult to understand, the weight of it all too much for a time. Then, following the false dawn of The Priory, he again appeared to falter, the Manics' European tour marked by heartbreaking episodes of self-harming and mounting inner disorder. There had been small wins, though. Since leaving hospital, Richey had fought and largely won his battle with drink, exchanging his litre a day vodka and whiskey habit for copious amounts of caffeine. Equally, his guitar playing had greatly improved, even if he never quite mastered Nirvana's 'Come As You Are', despite countless attempts from James and Sean to teach him.

But for every seeming victory, there was a comparable defeat. Though he needed to stay clear of alcohol to maximise the benefits of the Prozac he had been prescribed, Edwards greatly missed its effects. "I can't do anything I want to any more," he complained to Nicky. There was also the matter of gleaning any satisfaction at all from touring. While the band felt their co-headlining tour with Suede had brought out some of the better performances of their career, Richey was less convinced. "It was the first time I thought we weren't all reading from the same page," James later told *NME*. "Richey had taken to 'marking' gigs then, and not a lot of them got very good marks. We were enjoying them, and he was giving them shit marks. I thought 'This just ain't making him happy'."

Of that, there was little doubt. In addition to actually marking concert appearances, Edwards was also scoring the quality of his days from nought to 10 while on tour. Some days, such as when he visited Paris' L'Empire de la Morte – a series of extended catacombs/tunnels running beneath France's capital city, filled with old skulls and bones – were awarded a 'nine'. Others, including his time spent in Amsterdam and Hamburg, were awarded considerably less. Most days though, he seemed content to pass in his own company. "Richey just lived in his bunk the whole time on the tour bus," Nicky said. "It was like a rabbit hutch. He was on 60 cigarettes a day, 20 cups of coffee, and then he'd complain that he couldn't sleep. He'd just stand under this vent on the bus, puffing away." On stage too, there seemed a magnificent absence to Edwards. Part Brian Jones before the end of his tenure with The Rolling Stones, part Lucifer Morningstar – all he needed were the burnt wings, and he would be perfectly cast as a fallen angel – Richey looked distracted, diverted and detached.

But then came a partial improvement in his mood, coinciding with that fine set of shows at London's Astoria theatre. Driving home to Wales for the Christmas break with Sean Moore, Edwards was quiet, but not withdrawn, seemingly content to exchange small talk while puffing away on an endless procession of cigarettes. This lifting of spirits continued throughout the festive season, which Richey spent with his family in Blackwood. While there, he swapped gifts, visited Nicky at his house in nearby Wattsville, but mainly rested – though as ever sleep was hard to find. "It was quiet and calm," said Moore. "We all had a nice Christmas." When the Manics reconvened in early January at House In The Woods studios in Cobham to explore ideas for a new album and prepare for their forthcoming US tour, Edwards again appeared much improved. An enthusiastic presence throughout, he also seemed genuinely pleased with the prospect than the Manics might contribute a song to Danny Cannon's forthcoming film version of Judge Dredd, starring Sylvester Stallone. A long time fan of the comic *2000AD,* in which the granite-jawed Judge first appeared, Richey was eager to write a set of lyrics that truly captured the spirit of the character. Five days later, when the first sessions ended, as usual, he provided his bandmates with gifts: keeping with tradition, Nicky received a Mars bar, though this time it was accompanied by a copy of *The Daily Telegraph.*

When later asked about Edwards' mindset during rehearsals, Wire was adamant that his friend was approaching something akin to his former self. The jokes were more sarcastic, the work ethic stronger and the recent oddities of character mainly held in check. Moreover, Richey had previously given Nicky a journal of written material he had been working on, containing themes for songs, some completed lyrics, drawings and other ephemera. The journal was subsequently photocopied, then distributed among the band. Again, this was standard practice for Edwards, the sharing of his thoughts always a catalyst to the shaping of any new musical material. However, by the time Nicky and his wife, Rachel, returned from a short holiday break in Barcelona, Richey had succumbed to bad news. On January 14, his dog Snoopy had finally passed away, and Edwards went missing for two days. On his return, he said that his pet's death had shaken him and he had gone to nearby Swansea to be alone for a while. Despite sporting a newly shaved head, Richey did not appear to be unstable. "He was upset," Wire later confirmed to *Melody Maker,* "(but) he cried naturally. It was nothing to do with The Priory, it was just that his dog had died."

A week or so later, Edwards was visited at his Cardiff harbour flat by Midori Tsukagoshi, a journalist with the Japanese rock magazine *Music Life*. He found Richey to be a genial host, a little distracted perhaps, but perfectly willing to provide his thoughts for interview. At times during their conversation, Richey sounded – if not happy in the traditional sense of the word – at least wistful, his responses polite and considered. Asked why he had shaved his hair, Edwards spoke of boredom, the shedding of vanity, and curiously, how the act of cutting away his locks had helped him sleep. Later, he also attributed it as a mark of respect for his dead dog. This theme of shedding or abandoning old things also returned when Richey admitted to throwing 80% of his recent writings in the river, because they "just weren't good". His bandmates subsequently disputed the claim, adamant that he had thrown nothing away. When questioned regarding the events of the previous summer, Edwards re-iterated the fact that his body and spirit had simply betrayed him, too much alcohol weakening his constitution until he was simply unable to rise from bed. He also confirmed the presence of cyclic, persistent thoughts in his mind, "thinking about the smallest things over and over". But having dispensed with drink he now found his days longer, his ability to write extended because of it – even if he still worried that the results could sometimes be "rubbish".

Again, he spoke of his admiration for Yukio Mishima, sounding in awe of the compassion and gentility inherent in the author/philosopher's work. However, Richey also poured water on the supposed 'sensitivity' of many indie bands, concluding that most of their shoe-gazing antics were "just pretence". In this respect, he sounded very much like his old self. Elsewhere, he professed to miss his virginity, but claimed to regret nothing: "Regrets are meaningless. You can't change yesterday or tomorrow. You can change only this present moment." Edwards also talked of his romantic feelings, confirming that for years he had been "involved with one girl", though had as yet done nothing about it: "I've never told her I love her... I've only kissed her once, twice. That's all. How can I explain? When I love someone, I feel trapped." Finally, he spoke with pride of his band, and the fact that he had found better ways to express himself: "I don't think I've changed what I say, but maybe I'm saying it in a different way."

With the interview concluded, Richey posed for photographs. He was wearing a set of pyjamas, oddly reminiscent of the uniform worn by concentration camp prisoners in Dachau and Auschwitz. On his feet were a pair of black Converse trainers, the same brand Nirvana's Kurt Cobain was wearing the day he shot himself. On his knuckles were written the word 'Love', as ever in black ink. For the pictures, he sat in front of an *Apocalypse Now* film poster, his shaven head eerily blending into Marlon Brando's own bald pate above him. As Brando had played Colonel Kurtz in the movie, a military man driven insane by the atrocities of war, the image was a tad unfortunate, even a little vulgar. Perhaps Richey wanted it that way. Without hair to frame his face, he looked subtly different – still good looking, but more nondescript. The eyes, however, remained huge: a little red from want of sleep or medication, but huge nonetheless. Their business concluded, Tsukagoshi shook the rock star's hand, and left. "The last time I spoke to him, he seemed very positive," the journalist said. "As usual, he was a very artistic person." Though Midori Tsukagoshi didn't know it at the time, he had just conducted Edwards' final press interview.

Eight days later, on January 31, James and Richey checked into the Embassy Hotel on Bayswater Road. A typical 'overnighter' used by businessmen visiting London, the Embassy was close to Hyde Park and Notting Hill and almost on top of Queensway, a busy cosmopolitan street littered with shops, restaurants and the odd pub. It was also convenient for major link roads to Heathrow Airport, from which Edwards and Bradfield were due to travel the next day. Their destination was the States, where the two were promoting advance interest in the Manics' first major US tour, scheduled to begin at the DPC in Tucson, Arizona on February 22. In a way, they were working backwards. Though *The Holy Bible* had not yet been released in America, the band were already demoing new material for another record, having spent the previous evening in a London studio. Early indications were that the material would be considerably more melodic than their last release, the general mood much more contemplative. For Edwards, who had recently passed Bradfield a note reading 'Idea for next album: Nine Inch Nails meets Pantera meets *Screamadelica*', this softening of the Manics' sound could have been a problem. Yet, he seemed content and good-humoured during the sessions, raising few obvious objections to Bradfield and Moore's ideas.

Ever the voracious reader, Richey had recently finished *Novel With Cocaine*, by M. Ageyev. Best described as '*Catcher In The Rye* with added drugs', the book was a harrowing yet brilliantly descriptive account of a young man's growing addiction to cocaine. The novel was actually written under a pseudonym, its journey to public light almost as mysterious as the real name of its author. Originally passed to a Parisian literary journal specializing in Russian texts, the manuscript was later published to considerable acclaim in France, before being translated into English by Michael Henry Heim. When *Novel With Cocaine* then received international success, critics expected 'Ageyev' to step forward from the shadows to take his or her bow. But the writer, who had allegedly been a patient in a mental hospital for a time, chose to avoid all recognition. Though the book was often attributed to Nabokov, it was later believed to be the work of Marc Levi, an obscure Russian novelist who died in 1973. Regardless of its origin, Edwards had loved *Novel...* and gave it to a female friend to read before heading off with Bradfield. Strangely, he also asked her to pay particular attention to the introduction. She later learned *Novel With Cocaine* actually had two introductions, though he never specified which one was of enduring interest. A little mystery, then as now.

When James and Richey booked into the Embassy Hotel, they were given adjoining rooms. Being the quicker of the two to freshen up, Bradfield knocked on Edwards' door and enquired whether he wanted to venture out onto Queensway to see a film or do a little shopping. Richey asked for half an hour's grace. When the Manics' frontman again knocked for his friend, Edwards confessed to having changed his mind and now wanted to stay in. "He said he'd see me in the morning," James recalled. "He was smiling, running the bath. He was in a good mood." Already suited and booted for the evening, James went out with another acquaintance at 8.30 p.m., returning to his room just before midnight. His earlier conversation with Richey, though brief, had been entirely pleasant. In fact, nothing out of the ordinary. Bradfield would never see him again.

At seven in the morning on February 1, 1995, Richey Edwards left the Embassy Hotel. Though seen passing through reception by several staff, he did not actually check out. Instead he went directly to his car, a silver 'L' registration Vauxhall Cavalier, and drove away. Left behind in Room 516 was a small, carefully wrapped box of presents for the girl Richey had talked of to Midori Tsukagoshi only a week before. Inside, he had placed some books and two video cassettes: the first was Sidney Lumet's 1977 movie, *Equus*, the second, Mike Leigh's 1993 film, *Naked*. Along with several small quotes written on the outside of the box, there was also a note. It simply read: "I love you". Other items in the room included a full suitcase, assorted toiletries and a bottle of Prozac. The bed remained unmade. Several hours later, Richey arrived at his flat in Anson Court, overlooking Cardiff harbour. Here, he left his credit cards, another bottle of Prozac, his passport, a motorway toll receipt for £2.70 and 30p in change. He then returned to his car and again drove away. Given later police reports, these details would seem fairly certain and are unlikely to be challenged. Beyond that, all bets are off.

The flags went up almost immediately at the Embassy Hotel when Edwards did not respond to morning wake-up calls from the Manics' manager, Martin Hall. With a flight to America booked later that afternoon, and given his charge's recent troubles, Hall took no chances and asked that the door to Richey's room be unlocked (Bradfield had suggested breaking it down). On entry, the box of presents and other items were found. Gillian Porter, the band's press officer, was there at the time. "The box was wrapped and there were little quotes at the side, but that was what he used to do," she told *Vox*. "We opened the box to see whether there was anything inside that might lead us to him, or offer any clues." Both the box and its contents were later passed on to the girl they were intended for.

With no sign of Edwards, and nothing in the box or room giving an indication of his whereabouts, Hall and Porter began ringing friends and family for information. Graham and Sherry Edwards, who had last seen Richey only a week before, confirmed their son had telephoned them the previous evening, but aside from saying that he wasn't particularly looking forward to the US trip, seemed reasonably well. James Dean Bradfield was also adamant that Edwards was in good spirits.

Having exhausted his own set of potential leads, Martin Hall visited Harrow Road police station on February 2 to inform authorities that Richey was missing. On the subsequent report, 'Station Copy Form 584

(C)', there were references to Edwards' various tattoos in the 'Marks, scars...' section and confirmation that he smoked under 'Habits/other characteristics'. There was also one particular line captured within 'Circumstances' that undermined both Richey's own account of his recent troubles and how far things might have gone some months before: "Subject has made previous suicide attempt and is taking anti-depressants." Report logged, Hall then drove to Cardiff where he met with Graham, Sherry and Rachel Edwards, who let themselves into Richey's flat. The various effects and a newspaper he left behind proved that Edwards had come home, but again, there were no real clues as to where he might be. In response, Richey's father took out a personal ad in his local paper stating "Richard, please make contact, love Mum, Dad, Rachel," which ran for three days. Hall, on the other hand, brought in a firm of private detectives to begin searching for Edwards. He also cancelled the Manics' promotional tour of the States and two European gigs lined up in Prague and Vienna, giving the excuse that Richey had contracted an ear infection.

For the next two weeks, both police and investigators pursued various avenues in their search for Edwards. It transpired that he had taken out £200 per day from a variety of cash machines in the time leading up to his disappearance, but no further monies had been withdrawn since. For some, this might have been a sign of forward planning on Richey's part, but without a passport or credit cards and at most £2,000 in his pocket, it remained unlikely that he had enough funds to venture far. In the meantime, his family and fellow Manics waited for news: "Wherever Richey has been in the world," his mother Sherry said, "he's always got in touch. Whether it was a quick telephone call or a postcard, we always knew how he was doing." James Dean Bradfield remained bewildered, but hopeful. "There was no instruction manual to follow," he later revealed, "I just thought he'd done a 'Strummer runner'". Bradfield was no doubt referring to an incident that occurred in April, 1982, when The Clash's frontman temporarily disappeared to Paris with then girlfriend Gaby Salter, three weeks before the release of the band's fifth album, *Combat Rock*. Depending on one's source, Strummer's dereliction of duty was either a clever publicity stunt drummed up by he and Clash manager Bernie Rhodes to draw attention to the band's new record, or Joe taking revenge on Bernie for even suggesting such a ruse.

By February 15, all such theories regarding Edwards' actions and whereabouts had been abandoned and had been replaced with genuine worry. It was time to go public. South Wales police issued a statement confirming Richey was missing, while Graham Edwards recorded an interview with BBC Radio One: "Being in the rock 'n' roll business," he said, "(the band) are always under a lot of emotional stress, and I think this might have had something to do with it. This is completely out of character and everyone's very worried about him. If he needs time to be on his own, then that's OK. If he has any problems that we can help him with, I hope he remembers he's always had strong support from his family and the lads in the band." Across the Atlantic, 'Little Baby Nothing' chanteuse Traci Lords was one of the first people to have worked with Edwards to offer their thoughts: "Richey seemed to be the one with the strongest opinions, but also quite insecure as well, so I do identify with him. I don't know about all his problems but I just hope he's OK."

With the music press, Fleet Street and just about everyone else chasing the band for details, Hall Or Nothing issued a short, but telling statement: "Richey's family, the band and their management are unavailable for comment, and we would like to ask you to respect their privacy, and for your help and sensitivity regarding this matter." Inevitably, the request wasn't enough to stave off interest, so Nicky Wire stepped forward on behalf of the Manics: "If Richey doesn't want to come back," he said at the time, "then that's fine. We just want him to give us a call. We are genuinely worried. He has never disappeared like this before." Nicky's words were well chosen. Though Edwards had never absconded for such a long period, there were precedents. Aside from his recent withdrawal following the death of his dog, Snoopy, he had also gone missing for a time after the band's 1994 Glastonbury show, only to emerge a day or so later. They could only hope this was another, albeit longer, such disappearance.

The first dividends of going the 'public' route came on February 16, when police announced they had found Edwards' car abandoned at Severn View Service Station. The Cavalier had actually been discovered days before, its battery completely flat. This pointed to the possibility that Richey might have been sleeping in the vehicle for a time, running the heater or perhaps listening to tapes. Tom Cassidy, the station manager who had alerted police to the car, could confirm only that its doors were locked, and there was no suitcase or note inside. Though the discovery was useful news, it was also frightening. The service station was but moments away from the Severn Bridge, a 1,600 metre long structure that spanned the River Severn below and acted as the primary link between England and Wales. The bridge also crossed Aust Cliff, its red mudstone and black shale facade overlooking nearby Bristol Channel. Both bridge and cliff were well-known spots for suicide attempts. Inevitably, Edwards' family and bandmates soon received notification that the police and coastguard were sweeping the Severn Estuary and nearby shores for a body. That said, South Wales Constabulary were not about to give up hope, stating that Richey could simply have hitched a lift onto the motorway when he left his car behind.

In the meantime, supposed sightings of Edwards began to surface, first in dribs in drabs, then in the dozens. A Mrs. Williams from Guildford, Surrey was first out of the traps on February 20, having seen a man with a guitar case trying to get a ride eastbound at Delamere services. Though roughly matching Richey in height and build, Williams put the man at about 40 years old, and the lead was later dropped. Truthfully, the presence of a guitar case should have been clue enough for it not to have been Edwards. In Germany, long time Manics supporter Monica Pommer then stepped forward, claiming to have received a postcard from Richey postmarked 'London, 3 February'. Yet, when police asked to have sight of it, Pommer claimed the written message to be "too personal", and would only provide a previous card from Edwards – sent from Cardiff on December 13, 1994. In her covering letter, Pommer stated that if Richey had not returned by August 20, she would "go to Cardiff to say goodbye by throwing flowers into the sea". Her husband, Gregor, also wrote to the authorities, listing 12 reasons why Edwards might have taken his own life.

Such devotion was mirrored in the case of Sally Allen, a 16 year old who failed to return from school to her parents' home in Skipton, West Yorkshire, a fortnight after Richey went missing. Described by her mother as a "huge fan" of Edwards who "hadn't been right" since he had gone, Allen had allegedly cut off all her hair before disappearing. Equally worryingly, Mrs. Allen said her daughter was "virtually anorexic". Treated as a 'copycat' incident by police, an investigation was launched, but Sally Allen arrived back in Skipton three weeks to the day that she left. When questioned, Allen confirmed she had been on a 'Richey pilgrimage' to London, Bristol and Cardiff, but had grown homesick when confronted with the sight of Mother's Day cards in stores. A sad story, it only served to underline that for a certain type of Manics devotee, the news of Edwards' vanishing from sight was provoking genuine emotional disturbance.

Of other sightings or incidents reported, two seemed to have some authenticity. On Sunday, February 5, David Cross from Rhigos, Mid-Glamorgan, claimed to have seen and spoken with Richey outside Newport bus station. Having just got off a bus himself, Cross was on his way to the newsagents when he noticed Edwards (wearing a dark blue jacket) standing alone near a silver grey car. As Cross was a friend of Lori Fidler, another Manic acolyte who lived in New York and had set up the American branch of their fan club and fanzine *Scream Tour Sigh*, he couldn't let the opportunity to speak with Richey pass. "Although I didn't know him," Cross revealed in his statement to police, "I said to him: 'Hello Richey, I'm a friend of Lori's'. He said: 'How is she, how is she doing?'" When Cross confirmed Fidler was indeed well, Edwards said "I'll see you later," and headed away. Given the man's apparent recognition of Lori Fidler's name, the location of the incident and the fact that a silver grey car was close, police took Cross' testimony seriously when he reported it on February 21. As theories and allegations became progressively wilder, Lori Fidler would re-enter the Edwards story in the coming months.

Another sighting that commanded attention came from Anthony Hatherhall, a cab driver who said he had picked up a slim, gaunt-faced man from the Kings Hotel in Newport High Street at 7 a.m. on February 7, 1995. In his long and involved account to police, Hatherhall stated that the man had asked to be driven around the Gwent valleys, including Uplands, Risca and Pontypool before reaching his final destination at Severn View Services. "He requested that we go via the scenic route," Hatherhall told police, "and not along the motorway because he said he was always driving along the motorway." Of particular interest was the fact that this man appeared to putting on a cockney accent, though every now and then a more pronounced Welsh burr would break through.

Equally, he claimed to be looking for his boss whose lorry had broken down, though said boss was never located. Appearing distracted throughout the journey, Hatherhall's passenger also requested at one point that he was brought to the nearest train station. When the man was informed there was no line at Risca, and then driven to Blackwood bus depot instead, he became agitated, saying "This is not the place," before asking to go onto Pontypool. Unnerved by his experience, Hatherhall was relieved when he finally deposited his fare at the service station, £68 the richer. An intriguing tale that ticks some boxes if not others, Hatherhall stated in his account that the man he ferried about that morning was tall and long haired. At five feet eight inches (if that), Richey simply didn't match that part of the description, and unless he had recently purchased a wig, his shaven head also ruled him out of the running. Wire later poured cold water on the story, stating whoever the passenger in Hatherhall's taxi was, it certainly wasn't Edwards.

As weeks turned to months, the full implications of Richey's disappearance began to take its toll on his friends, family and bandmates. Nicky's brother Patrick Jones, who had set up the Blackwood Young Writers' Group in 1993 and was soon to publish his first book, *The Guerrilla Tapestry*, seemed genuinely shaken by recent events. "It's pretty sad," he said. "It makes you realise how fragile life is. Think about what it is to be famous: you really want it, but when you're there, you can't cope." Byron Harris, another of Edwards' close confidants, also struggled to understand what had happened. "Richey would never do anything without a reason," he told *Vox*. "He's a very intelligent man, and wouldn't disappear like this under normal circumstances." For Edwards' parents and sister, the situation must have been near intolerable at times, the lack of any firm news one way or another allowing neither solace nor closure. "We are like any other parents in this situation, trying to cope as best we can from day to day." his father said. "... I have racked my brains trying to think of something that will bring Richard back to us and I can't." In the case of the Manics themselves, any hope of Richey's return was beginning to dwindle. "The longer it went," Wire later told the BBC, "I thought 'He's not coming back'. It was a terrible two, three months. You felt every phone call, every knock at the door was related to the disappearance." For James Dean Bradfield, initial optimism was also falling away to serious doubt. "At first, I thought there'd be a happy outcome, that he'd show up after two weeks. Then I started to think 'He's taking this very seriously'. Then came the numbness."

Of course, tantalising stories and possible leads were still arriving at regular intervals. *The Sunday Times* published an article claiming that Richey had surfaced in New York and was keeping company with Lori Fidler. To illustrate their scoop, the paper ran a photo of the two together. However, Fidler strenuously denied any involvement with the piece, stating that a friend had betrayed her trust and provided the broadsheet with the (old) photograph they had used. Though Lori acknowledged that she and Edwards were close, she rejected any claims that they had been lovers. Further, when it was put to Fidler that Richey's box of presents was meant for her, she immediately rebuffed the idea, pointing instead to a girl called 'Jo', who followed a band named Faith In Me and had previously spurned Edwards' romantic advances. Strangely, no one at the time raised the point that if Richey had wanted to head stateside, then he could have simply boarded his scheduled flight to the USA and disappeared upon arrival.

Despite her attempts to extricate herself from such gossip, Fidler was pulled back into the Edwards story once again when police were contacted by a man in Irvine, Scotland, who claimed to have recently seen Edwards at Lori's Manhattan apartment. While this also came to nothing, Fidler did admit that Richey may have phoned her on the day he went missing. Unfortunately, she was not there to take the call herself, but a girlfriend confirmed that a "beep beep on the line" meant it came from overseas. "The man on the other end just said 'Hi Lori', and then hung up. I think," Fidler said, "it was him." Like most Manics devotees, Lori Fidler refused to believe that Richey Edwards was dead. Instead, she was sure that he was alive, living in England and "probably not far from home". In comparison with some theories, Lori Fidler's viewpoint was a model of restraint. Spurred on by Edwards' love of J.D. Salinger's *Catcher In The Rye*, a number of fans hypothesised that like the famous American author – who turned his back on fame in 1965 to live like a recluse in the New Hampshire backwoods – Richey had entered a monastic retreat. This premise was inflamed further when Cardiff police were tipped off that Edwards was residing at Henlow Grange, a secluded health farm in Bedfordshire. When investigated, it turned out to be another false dawn.

Sinead O' Connor, Richey's old acquaintance from his Priory days, also offered a possible lead when she informed authorities that Edwards may have visited a fan of hers living in Hereford. O'Connor had previously spoken with Richey about the man, a schizophrenic, who spent much of his time writing her letters. Allegedly, Edwards had arrived at his home seeking refuge. Again, following a police check, O'Connor's claim came to nothing. One of the more elaborate theories concerning Richey came from Oxford undergraduate Anna Bowles, who posited that he had gone to Germany on a 'Visitors' Passport' to observe the 50th anniversary of the Holocaust. As Richey had studied the subject at University, already been to both Dachau and Auschwitz, and had written with venom about Nazi war crimes on *The Holy Bible*, there was some logic to Bowles' idea. Yet again, subsequent enquiries proved fruitless.

The longer Edwards remained absent from view, the more plausible theories fell away to wild conjecture. But, as mentioned above, one central idea always refused to bow easily in the face of reason: that Richey Edwards might have committed 'pseudocide'. By faking his own disappearance, the argument ran, Richey had little to lose and much to gain. He could shed himself of his previous life, his responsibilities and troubles, and seek new horizons elsewhere. In short, leave behind a fame that had brought few rewards and pursue a new, calmer existence. This argument was given real credence when it came to light that in the months before Edwards vanished, he had been voraciously reading books on staging the perfect disappearance and creating a new identity. Even by leaving his car so close to the Severn Bridge, Richey was fulfilling another cardinal rule of faked suicides – deaths through drowning often end with the absence of a body. An extremely intelligent man, there was no doubt he had the intellectual capacity to pull off such a trick. But several factors ran against this conclusion.

In the first instance, Richey Edwards' psychiatric history pointed towards a troubled, often conflicted man who had recently struggled to overcome his emotional difficulties – sometimes with success, more often not. Having already abandoned his prescription medication, whether he had the personal strength or presence of mind to stage, then perpetuate his disappearance remained, at best, uncertain. Moreover, unless Edwards had made arrangements for a false passport and future funding, his travelling and financial options would be severely limited. There was also the matter of Richey's fame to consider: it would be difficult for the most ordinary and nondescript of us to pull off a vanishing act and prosper afterwards, but with an army of police and legion of fans seeking him out at every turn, that difficulty might prove insurmountable.

Additionally, Edwards' actions on February 1, 1995 had a certain finality to them. The emptying of pockets and personal effects, the placing of presents on his bed and, above all, the simplicity of the note he left behind rang with symbolism rather than artifice. It really did seem that Richey was saying his goodbyes. Last but not least, there was also the fact that in addition to books about disappearing, Richey Edwards had a strong interest in famous suicide notes and often committed them to memory. If there was a particular favourite among them, it had to be comedian Tony Hancock's parting shot: "Things just went wrong too many times." For Richey, "it was one of the most beautiful things" he had ever read.

Yet, without conclusive evidence to prove otherwise, and a strong need for many not to let go, theories continued to abound regarding Richey's possible whereabouts throughout the spring and summer of 1995. Many were touching, others simply bizarre: Arthur Rimbaud, author of Edwards' beloved *A Season In Hell*, had given up writing at 21 and enlisted in the army. Therefore, Richey must have joined the Foreign Legion. Edwards was an admirer of Yukio Mishima. Perhaps he had ventured to Japan and joined a secretive samurai order. Monasteries and missions, secret hideaways and desert islands. All were given due consideration. All were better than nothing. However, when the Manics themselves were drawn into the debate, some even suggesting they were in collusion with Edwards to keep him from public view, Sean confirmed that they were as in the dark as everyone else: "From the day he left us we've known nothing. Absolute zero. We're just waiting for the next clue to come along."

A terrifying reminder of the realities surrounding Richey's situation came when a tattooed man's body was washed up on the shore near

Beachy Head on July 21. Michael Davey at Eastbourne Coroner's Office immediately telexed Harrow Road Police Station (who retained overall responsibility for the investigation) with the message: "This might be Richey Edwards." Asking for sensitivity on the matter due to expected press interest, Davey and his colleagues set to work on confirming the unfortunate man's identity. In the end, it wasn't Edwards.

Inevitably, the sightings continued. Liverpool, London, Shropshire, Skipton, Swansea and a few other places besides. Richey, it seemed, was everywhere. Over a year and a half after he vanished, Edwards was allegedly spotted in India. This sighting, which occurred in November 1996, was genuinely intriguing. A Media Studies lecturer at South Wales' Neath College by the name of Vyvyan Morris had been "sitting, having a coke" while at Anjuna market in Goa when he thought someone close by looked extremely familiar. "I asked a bloke (who he was)," Morris later confirmed, "and he said 'That's Rick'." Appearing a "little worse for wear", the man in question was dressed in jeans and a kaftan top, with longish, matted hair. Morris was also told that 'Rick' had arrived in India some 18 months earlier. "I can't be 100 per cent certain," the lecturer concluded, "but I'm sure it was him." Morris' experience was of interest because Richey's sister, Rachel, had also heard that he might be living in Goa. As with all such credible reports, the police interviewed Vyvyan Morris, but unless Edwards had travelled under false papers, it remained difficult to see how he might have got to India.

Richey Edwards' vanishing on February 1, 1995 has subsequently become the worst of all things: an unsolved disappearance. Without a concrete trail to follow after Richey drove away from his Cardiff flat and finally abandoned his car at Severn View Service Station, it is difficult to know or even speculate what happened during this time. Equally, no body has ever been discovered, though given that the currents beneath the Severn Bridge are strong, there is room for the worst kind of speculation here. Detective Sergeant Stephen Morey, who had responsibility for investigating Edwards' case, conceded in January, 1996 that it might have been possible for Richey to have vanished without trace: good quality forged papers, a deal struck with a boat captain willing to deposit him at an unknown port, then the right kind of luck. Difficult to achieve, hard to maintain, yet it could be done. But DC Morey also raised the issue of how hard it would be to stay out of the spotlight, to avoid attention, to 'keep low' for life. This was the price Edwards had paid for his fame. When asked by *Vox*'s Andy Richardson what he thought had happened, the police officer was dutifully honest: "Personally, and this is my view and not the view of the Metropolitan Police Service, I believe that Richard Edwards may no longer be with us."

Of course, even 15 years on, Richey's actions continue to beguile. The lack of video or surveillance evidence either from Cardiff, the Severn View Service Station or elsewhere is perplexing. The various sightings and theories, credible or otherwise, also remain a tasty morsel for those seeking vicarious thrills or simple consolation in the face of what may have occurred. For statisticians and psychologists, the fact that Edwards was 27 – the precise age when most emotionally troubled men choose to end their lives – speaks volumes. And for rock'n'roll types, '27' surely refers to 'The 27 Club', an exclusive society of performers including Jimi Hendrix, Jim Morrison, Brian Jones and Janis Joplin, whose lives ended at precisely that age. If Richey Edwards is among them, then he's in distinguished company.

Others point to the very 'British' nature of Richey's disappearance rather than dwelling on any obvious notions of rock iconography. In this they're probably correct. After all, Edwards did not leave behind a fire-red Lamborghini or sleek, blue Rolls Royce next to the Severn Bridge. Instead, he walked away from a silver grey Cavalier: a family car, not a penis substitute. Nicky Wire, for one, subscribes to the Reginald Perrin aspect of it all, recalling the marvellous Seventies TV show where a middle-aged executive faked his own death and struck out on the road for new adventures. "People see it as a rock'n'roll mystery," Wire told *The Face*, "but he was driving a Vauxhall Cavalier. It's much more like Reggie Perrin. Richey had the intelligence to disappear and become a sewage worker with a big beard in a tiny bedsit."

They say that "satisfaction is the death of desire". In the case of Richey Edwards, the desire to know what exactly happened is still strong. As *Mojo*'s Stuart Bailie pointed out, unlike his suicidal heroes Yukio Mishima, Ian Curtis, Sylvia Plath and Kurt Cobain, Edwards made no "grand gesture (or) summation... he just walked off the page". This action, though heartbreaking for his parents and friends, also hermetically sealed Richey's place as one of rock music's more complex, curious and fascinating propositions. But for the band he left behind, there were much more human consequences to face than the building of a rock'n'roll legend. "When people talk about all the wounding and the blood," Nicky Wire later confessed, "the only real tragedy is that you lose someone kinetically, someone you've known since five, (someone) you've done all those things with... you feel you can't communicate. That was terrible. But in the last three weeks, there was a serene calmness to Richey. He was laughing more, the irony and pathos were back. Maybe that's because he'd reached certain conclusions and he felt some inner peace. We'd done a recording session and come up with some great tracks... I just saw it as 'Things are going to be OK.' Which maybe in his mind, that's what it was. But there are different meanings of 'OK', I guess."

For years, Richey Edwards had coveted sleep. Fought for it, chased it, even tried to seduce it with drink and prescription drugs. Maybe when he left the Embassy Hotel at seven in the morning on February 1, 1995, he'd had another sleepless night and was just plain tired; tired of dealing with insomnia, tired of thinking too much, maybe even tired of being Richey Edwards. Maybe he just decided not to be tired any more. But maybe not.

Everyone has their theories. No one really knows.

Chapter Fifteen

In Absentia

In his role as the Manic Street Preachers' 'Minister of Information', Richey Edwards had been a prolific letter writer, firing off a near endless procession of advertisements, justifications and manifestos in support of his band. These missives, mainly directed to journalists, editors and fanzine writers captured his gift as an orator, his skills as a critic and his unswerving dedication in promoting the cause of his band. Dozens of letters, thousands of words, one central idea: the Manics would change everything. Of course, they didn't. But they did make enough of an impact to create and sustain one of the more enduring and dedicated fan bases within the British rock scene. Not the biggest. Maybe not even the best. But surely one of the most passionate to have ever attached themselves to a group. In a nutshell, the Manics, and in particular Richey Edwards, spoke for these people. Now it was time for them to return the favour.

In the weeks and months following Edwards' disappearance, both the music press and broadsheets were bombarded with letters from Manic Street Preachers fans. Some old, some new, but all of them willing to offer their thoughts, condolences, sympathies and theories. An overwhelming response and outpouring of grief that frankly dwarfed public reaction to Kurt Cobain's tragic suicide only a year before, editors were genuinely shocked by the sheer volume of mail received. Of greater concern, however, was the tone of some of this correspondence and the images that accompanied it. Many fans seemed not only to be identifying with Edwards' problems, but actually emulating or enduring them. Despatches from anorexics, self-harmers and other sensitive souls became almost commonplace in the 'in box' of rock weeklies. Worse, photographs of cuts, bruises, wounds and much blood were also sent in the post. The majority of these letters were from teenage girls, more often than not the likeliest to fall prey to conditions such as eating disorders and self-mutilation. Responding to and identifying with Edwards' plight, these young women had found something within Richey that mirrored their own problems and concerns. It also highlighted the highly feminine appeal of the Manics, a band that had flirted with androgyny, championed women's causes, and in Edwards' case, even written first hand from the viewpoint of a starving, yet spiritually transported teenage girl. Unlike many of their ilk, the band had not been afraid to expose the female side of their nature. "I think," reasoned Nicky, "(women) see us raging on their side."

Though grunge had really ended with the death of Kurt Cobain, its themes of psychological dislocation and emotional trauma still hung heavily in the air in early 1995. Now, with the events surrounding Richey Edwards and the response his disappearance had provoked, there was talk among rock writers of a 'Culture of Despair' forming within the young. To address it and, one cynically suspects, sell a few copies of their newspaper, *Melody Maker* set up a panel of bands and readers to discuss and probe such issues. Hence, The Boo Radleys, Sleeper and Pulp joined a group of music fans to debate teen suicide, mental breakdowns and what might be done to curb it. The resulting front cover feature, excruciatingly titled 'From Despair To Where?' was published on April 8, 1995 and immediately picked up the interest of the nationals, BBC and Samaritans, who launched their own UK campaign to tackle the problem. R.E.M.'s 'Everybody Hurts' was used to promote the initiative, a fact that must have brought tears of joy to Nicky Wire.

Though such efforts were undoubtedly commendable, and hopefully provided succour to those who required it most, they was also an attendant fear that by further publicising Edwards' plight, it might lead to other, less positive results by creating 'The Cult of Richey'. This fact was not lost on James Dean Bradfield at the time. "Oh yeah," he said, "the Richey myth is now up and running." For Nicky, there were two real dangers to such press coverage. In the first instance, fans might turn Edwards into a tortured genius and 'saint to self harmers and anorexics all at once'. Secondly, they might also expect him to now assume the role of his missing friend. Wire was having neither, pointing towards Richey's own assessment of such behaviour. "We had so much poetry off anorexics and a lot of it was so shit even Richey was getting fed up," he told *NME*. "I said 'Look, I'm going to have to write a song taking the piss out of their poetry'. And he was laughing. He said 'Yeah'." On the matter of taking up Edwards' mantle, Nicky was equally dismissive: "It's (now) the 'Cult of Richey', isn't it? To be honest, some of those fans and their letters and fanzines have upset me, really. They seem to expect us to do the same thing. I'm not going to chop myself up and become an alcoholic."

The difficulty the Manic Street Preachers faced in the spring of 1995 had little to do any cults, factions or sects springing up around Richey Edwards. As a rock band, they were essentially powerless to stop such action, and lacking medical qualifications, wholly unable to offer help to those facing legitimate psychiatric problems. Instead, their dilemma revolved around one simple sentence: carry on or not. Having run through their own curve of disbelief, rejection and anger, they now had to either accept their situation as real and move forward together or hand in their cards and return to Blackwood. Yet, Richey Edwards still cast a long shadow over the making of that decision. "We didn't really know what to do," Sean Moore later confessed. "Richey was the spokesman… the frontman, (and) we just didn't know if the group was going to carry on."

When the Manics first formulated their master plan in Blackwood, its progress and ultimate fruition depended on a clear division of labour: James and Sean would take care of the music and Nicky and Richey would attend to lyrics, public speaking and "looking good". The band later referred to this as their "perfect symmetry", four people committed to the cause, each bringing a particular skill or talent with them to make it work. And when it worked, it worked extremely well, the Manics having written some fine songs, produced an excellent album, while simultaneously beguiling, bothering and bewildering both their critics. Of late, however, the Manics had run the risk of becoming a one-man show, Richey's problems always the main focus of attention, his disappearance threatening to overshadow both the band and its work. As Nicky said: "Things had got out of control." With Edwards, the Manics had access to a prodigious intellect, an acerbic orator and a gifted, sometimes superb lyricist. Now it seemed, they were also saddled with a lost spokesman for his generation. These were large shoes to fill.

On the other hand, while Richey had given much to the band, they were technically able to absorb his loss. Of course, Edwards had contributed ideas to the sound of the group, but only in the abstract. He had never actually written a note of music, and his guitar amp was often turned down to minimum volume so no-one could hear the limitations of his ability. This was of no real consequence as both Bradfield and Moore were excellent players, and Nicky despite his self-deprecation on the subject, had become a more than proficient bassist. Wire too, was also capable of producing fine lyrics, his contributions sometimes lost in the milieu as rock writers and fans fought to understand the meaning behind Edwards' latest outpourings. Observational and mildly optimistic where Richey was dark and wilfully oblique, the contrast had worked well. But given recent circumstances, it was reassuring to know that Nicky could carry the lyrical load.

As for actually 'fronting' the band, this was a more complex matter, but again there were possible solutions. In practical terms, James Dean Bradfield led the band onstage, his pit bull energy, impressive guitar work and strong voice focusing the audience and providing necessary theatrics. Wire was also a useful foil to Bradfield, the Cheshire cat grin, amateur gymnastic routines and occasional vocal outbursts creating entertainment for all concerned. With Sean content to hold down the back beat, and they would be truly lost without him, all future concert appearances were now assured of quality control.

However, the practical sticking point was Richey Edwards' previously formidable command of how the band were perceived and understood. In this respect, he had always been treated by both press and fans as the Manics' 'spiritual leader', a position now only strengthened through his continuing absence. Obviously, Nicky Wire – button bright, quick of quip – was the natural choice to step forward and take Edwards' place in the spotlight. Yet, there were some difficulties to negotiate. A man infinitely capable of swinging between enlightened thinker, loveable buffoon and social pariah within the space of three sentences, Wire's history with the music papers was chequered to say the least. Travellers hated him, R.E.M. fans hated him, and worse still, Nicky didn't seem to greatly care. That said, there was a charm, an eccentricity and essential likeability to Wire that was hard not to warm to and that could win different battles. If the more pragmatic Bradfield and Moore joined him at the front, or at least in front of the microphone, there was a real possibility the war could be won.

Ultimately, it was less a fear of what shape the future might take and more a need to escape their present tiredness that finally forced the Manics into action. "We made the decision to carry on in April," Nicky later said. "There'd been two months of waiting by the phone, feeling ill, exhausted. We'd been paralysed and unable to do anything. It was sad to think that perhaps he didn't like you any more." The band and manager, Martin Hall, subsequently met with Edwards' family to discuss the situation. The proposition was simple: they wanted to carry on, but would not do so without their blessing. Richey would not be replaced. A trust fund would be set up so that all due royalties would be banked in his name. "We wanted everything to be proper," Wire confirmed. For Graham Edwards, there were no issues to negotiate. In fact, he wanted the Manics back in the spotlight as soon as possible as it "might flush his son out". Though sorting out the legal side of things was a depressing experience for all, it was better than succumbing to torpor and continuing worry. "Carrying on," reasoned Nicky, "was more easy than just staying in and waiting."

The decision made and blessings granted, the Manic Street Preachers were now a trio again. In many ways, it was back to the drawing board, their 'newest' incarnation recalling the band's very first rehearsals in the front room of the Bradfield family home in 1985. Having committed to a life without Richey Edwards, the division of labour would have to be juggled, James and Sean taking on more press duties (whether they wanted to or not) and Nicky providing 100% of the lyrical output. But the biggest question was what direction the music would take. Bradfield and Moore had previously written songs to suit the thrust of Edwards' lyrics, the extremities of sound evidenced on *The Holy Bible* an able match for his pitch-black preoccupations of the time. However, the possibility of moving further down that road had given James pause for thought, the guitarist seeing potential trouble ahead if Richey really wanted to take it to the next level: "I was getting worried that I couldn't actually write music that would please him. I think that after *The Holy Bible*, he musically might have wanted to go to an even more extreme place, and that would have created an impasse in the band for the first time. Imagine," Bradfield concluded, "what *The New Testament* would have been like..." The question would remain forever unresolved as the Manics cut ties with their recent atonal experimentation, and instead went in search of melody.

Chapter Sixteen

Chosen

Since February 1, 1995, the Manic Street Preachers had been in stasis, the actions of Richey Edwards rendering them incapable of forward momentum until his disappearance was resolved. Each band member reacted to the situation in his own particular way. Nicky became fused to the TV in his Wattsville living room, content to watch sport, but scared to answer the phone for fear of bad news. Sean too, was suddenly a ship without an anchor. His routine suspended, days were spent sipping tea or shopping for gadgets, while nights were whiled away in the company of friends – getting drunk, working on his beer gut, things of that nature. James was also rudderless or, in his own words, "frozen". Unsure whether to forge ahead or simply give up, Bradfield chose neither in the end, opting instead to test the limits of his alcoholic endurance in a succession of heroic pub crawls. No one could blame them. Without news – good or bad – there was little to do but swim in uncertainty or take measures to numb the numbness. After three months of positive inaction and playing a "horrible waiting game", the Manics could wait no more. Seeking, then gaining the blessing of Richey's family, the band took their first steps forward as a trio, determined to do something rather than nothing.

The process of recovering lost ground began in early May when the band entered Soundspace Studios in Cardiff for rehearsals. Temporarily parking any old songs, the onus was on shaping the new material they had begun working on in London and Cardiff the previous January. As with sessions for *The Holy Bible*, the Manics stuck rigidly to a disciplined schedule while at Soundscape: arrive by a reasonable hour in the morning, work through until lunch, back for a few hours in the afternoon, and then home. There were to be no announcements to the press regarding their future. Instead, they would 'test the model for faults', and if none were found, then it would be time to go public.

As the sessions slowly began to yield positive results, the Manics invited producer Mike Hedges to join them at Soundscape. A veteran of the studio wars, Hedges was regarded within the music industry as a steady hand, having guided the likes of The Cure, Siouxsie & The Banshees, Texas and The Beautiful South to major chart success. In fact, his overseeing of Wah's 1982 hit 'Story Of The Blues' was justly lauded as one of the finest production jobs of its time. Hedges' most recent project, *The Sound Of McAlmont And Butler*, was another small triumph, melding now ex-Suede guitarist Bernard Butler's sharp-stringed attack to the buttery voice of soul vocalist David McAlmont with real style. The record also invoked memories of Phil Spector's Sixties 'Wall of Sound', where layers of instruments were stacked upon each other to produce a dense, symphonic effect. The Manics had heard the McAlmont/Butler album, fallen in love with it and as a result invited Hedges along to Cardiff to get his opinion of their latest songs.

The track they first elected to play him was an entirely new composition that the band felt was potentially something special. Unlike anything they had attempted before, 'A Design For Life' was a sparse, melancholic thing that cycled around a gentle guitar progression before hitting its stride in the chorus. Space had been left for a possible orchestral section to be added in the middle of the song, but otherwise, it was complete. "The first time I saw them," Mike Hedges later recalled, "was in a small rehearsal room. I was standing three feet away from them and they were incredibly loud. But I remember hearing 'A Design For Life' like it was yesterday." Suitably impressed, Hedges advised the Manics how he might approach the track. "Mike heard it and said 'I think it should sound like a jukebox record,'" James told *Mojo*. "I hadn't a bloody clue what he was on about, but I liked the sound of it, so he got the gig."

New producer in place, the group announced a cautious return to the newspapers on August 26: "The last six months have been very difficult for us, but we feel ready to start recording," read the press release. "We're just going to go into the studio and see how things go. There's no rush."

Some three weeks later, the group felt brave enough to release their first song without Richey Edwards in the line up. A cover of the old Burt Bacharach classic that Bradfield had made his own on stage, 'Raindrops Keep Falling On My Head' appeared on *NME*'s *The Help Album*. This all star compilation, featuring such names as Paul McCartney, Paul Weller and Sinead O'Connor, was released in aid of War Child, a charity bringing much needed relief to conflict zones in Bosnia and Herzegovina. In the Manics' hands, 'Raindrops...' stuck faithfully to Bacharach's original, even down to a lilting trumpet solo provided by Sean Moore, the first time he had played the instrument of his youth on record. But when James sang the line: "I'm free, nothing's bothering me," it was nigh on impossible not to think of absent friends.

'Raindrops Keep Falling On My Head' was the first result of the Manics' collaboration with Mike Hedges, the track cut at the producer's own studio, nestled within Château de la Rouge Motte in Normandy, France. Though Hedges' recording facilities were cosy, the abode that surrounded them was nothing of the sort: an old stone building with 10 bedrooms, good natural light, big trees and a huge garden, Château de la Rouge was an idyllic spot to make an album, but precisely the type of place that got the band into trouble when recording *Gold Against The Soul*. Given recent difficulties, however, the Manics felt they deserved their time in the sun. "We just wanted to get away from the memories," Wire confessed, "to get away from fucking everything." Building on the sharp focus of their Soundspace rehearsals, the group ploughed through recording sessions in France, grimly determined to put the past behind them and create a record of enduring value. In this ambition, they were ably assisted by Hedges, who always kept their efforts on point. "We couldn't have made the album without Mike," Wire later said. "He was an emotional blanket for us: encouraging, not trying to change anything. Just a magical person, really."

In the space of a month, basic tracks and even some completed mixes were on tape, so band and producer flew to Real World Studios in Bath for "clean ups". While there, they also cut a new song, 'The Girl Who Wanted To Be God' and worked on another stray number 'No Surface, All Feeling' – originally recorded at Big Noise Studios in Cardiff while Richey was still with the band. Almost there, the Manics and Hedges then headed to London's legendary Abbey Road Studios to add orchestration (courtesy of the wonderfully named Venomettes) to four songs, including 'A Design For Life'. By early 1996, the band's new album was complete. A time of genuine musical growth and no little enjoyment, the only depressing moment came towards the end of mixing, when papers detailing future arrangements for Richey's trust fund arrived needing to be signed. "It was the most... final thing," James later told *Mojo*. "Really depressing, all that legal shit. It just made him feel like a number."

During this period of frenetic, if bittersweet activity, the Manic Street Preachers also made their return to the stage, providing support to the Stone Roses at Wembley Arena on December 29, 1995. On paper, it was a curious coupling. The Roses, having lost their drummer Reni only months before, were known to be in meltdown: the group's second album, 1995's *Second Coming*, though years in the making had impressed few and their talismanic guitarist, John Squire, was now secretly planning his own escape. Whether they were in any shape to face each other, let alone a crowd of over 10,000 was a matter of some debate. Equally, the Manics – though recovering well enough behind the scenes – were still an unknown proposition without the presence of Richey Edwards. There was also the fact that Stone Roses fans were a far cry from their own core audience, preferring 'Fools Gold' to 'Gold Against The Soul'. In short, it had all the makings of a freak show. The Manics were fully aware of such risks, but felt that headlining their own 'comeback' concert in front of "the devoted" was a step too far at this stage of the game. "To be honest," Wire told *NME,* "we didn't want to face our own fans that early. (Deal with) the emotion of that. We just wanted to see if we could still do it."

Following a short set from reggae band Bad Man Wagon the world, or more specifically Wembley Arena, was given its first taste of the Manics without Richey Edwards. Arriving on stage to a surprise standing ovation, they looked genuinely humbled, the prolonged applause forcing Nicky to address those gathered in the hall before the group had even played a note. "What's up?" he laughed. "It's only us." Evidently, even if the Manics weren't quite ready to seek the company of their own supporters, a goodly number of the group's devotees had found a way of seeking them out instead. When things eventually settled the Manics launched into a set that, as a mark of respect to Richey, drew nothing at all from *The Holy Bible*, but focused instead on either old favourites or brand new material. Hence, 'A Design For Life', 'Australia' and 'Everything Must Go' were all given their first public airings. To provide necessary orchestration on these tracks, the group had drafted in the services of keyboard player John Green, his wide string sounds adding a certain majesty to their overall sound. And majesty, it seemed, was very much in evidence throughout the Manics' performance: no 'Tourette's'-like outbursts from Wire, no smashing of equipment at the end of the set. Just the steady hum of seasoned musicians providing a mature and optimistic performance. The Manics, for the moment at least, were in no mood for any more drama.

For those expecting Richey Edwards to emerge 'Christ'-like from the wings, all wounds healed, guitar slung low, his T-shirt reading 'Ever get the feeling you've been cheated?', the Manics' appearance at Wembley Arena must have been a profound disappointment. But to others, it was the first public sign that the band were up for the challenge of reclaiming their musical career, and putting past events behind them. And as for those who dwelled on Edwards' absence from shows, past, present, or indeed future, Nicky had the following message: "Richey will always be with us on stage. Whether he's actually there in body, well, I don't give a shit." At other times, however, Wire's spirited defiance just downright failed him. When Richey's sister, Rachel, appeared on LWT's *Missing At Christmas* TV programme on December 22 – the date of her brother's 28th birthday – seeking information about his whereabouts, Wire allegedly broke down in tears. Having slept next to, written with, and tended the wounds of his best friend, he was still having trouble dealing with the realities of it all: "A lot of the signs do point to the possibility that he's dead," Nicky later told *NME*. "And I'm not denying that. I've been to my doctor and he said 'You've got to face the fact that he's dead. You should go to bereavement counselling.' But it's impossible to do that without a body. How can you go to bereavement counselling when you don't even know someone's dead?"

Nearly four months on from their appearance at Wembley, the Manic Street Preachers finally broke their musical silence with their first single since Richey Edwards vanished. Beautifully understated, both melodically astute and emotionally intelligent, 'A Design For Life' was clear proof that the Manics' future as a premier league rock band was assured. Production wise, Mike Hedges had done a marvellous job, replacing the group's previously tight, compressed and overdriven sound with a sense of space and economy. In Hedges' hands, the Manics soothed as much as they overwhelmed, though 'Design''s chorus still carried an almighty wallop. The principle beneficiary of this more spacious approach was James Dean Bradfield, whose voice was now allowed to breathe out words rather than just attack them. In this he was surely aided by Nicky Wire, who unlike his absent friend, favoured shorter, simpler phrases when it came to lyric writing.

Part celebration of the working classes, part elegy to their weaknesses in the face of the bourgeoisie, 'A Design For Life' had been inspired by Wire's re-activation of interest in the work of George Orwell: "At the time I was reading a lot of Orwell," he confirmed, "and my wife was working in the libraries of Newport. I think at Pwll library, there's a plaque over the door that says 'Knowledge is power' and it was just a question of putting the two together." The "putting together" Nicky referred to became 'Design''s memorable opening line: "Libraries gave us power, then work came and made us free..." However, there was considerably more to come from Wire before he had finished, his final efforts taking up several pages of A4 and separated into two distinct poems: 'A Design' and 'Pure Motive'. These were handed in turn to Bradfield who then compressed them into one set of lyrics: "When I starting writing the music," James later said, "I could hear strings. It would have been a complete denial of that song to make it sound small." He was right. When orchestration was added to 'A Design For Life', the song took on a whole new character, imbuing Nicky's lyrical observations with a soaring, bittersweet edge.

According to Bradfield, 'A Design For Life' had been a genuine turning point for the Manics: "I think that song gave us the strength to carry on. It showed us we could be a different band, a different version of what we were. It allowed us to move forward." Moore was also happy with the result of their endeavours and genuinely impressed by Nicky's ability to capture the group's collective viewpoint: "'A Design For Life' encapsulated our view of the lifestyle of the working class and it also had a great sense of what this country's supposedly built on." Wire, for his sins, just wanted to get it on the radio: "I just thought it was a great song that deserved to be heard."

The Great British public heartily agreed and bought the CD in droves when it was released on April 15, 1996. Selling 92, 640 copies in the first week, 'A Design For Life' debuted in the UK charts at number two, only missing out on the top spot due to overwhelming demand for Mark Morrison's self-defining soul hit, 'Return Of The Mack'. For the Manics, 'Design''s success represented blessed relief from an uncertainty that had plagued them for over a year and each band member reacted to the news in subtly different ways: James, privately fearful that the single might bomb, took to his sofa and continued watching sport, though inside he admitted to feeling "relaxed and gorgeous"; Sean, ever the rationalist, simply called his friends to confirm that they knew the record was a hit; and Nicky went round to his mother's house for tea. He was mowing the lawn of his house when told of 'Design's impressive chart placing, so he abandoned the lawnmower and immediately called Richey's parents, who were thrilled for the group.

'A Design For Life' would go on to sell over 300,000 units by the end of 1996, more than the combined sales of all previous Manics single releases. By changing mood and tempo, and trimming back on the excesses of their former incarnation, the group had reaped considerable rewards and laid steel foundations for their forthcoming album. Yet, one wondered whether this might have been possible if Richey Edwards had remained with the band. As Bradfield had confirmed, the next chapter of the Manics' story might have read more like a horror novel (albeit a brilliant one) than a pithy dissection of working class triumphs and tribulations. Wire, perhaps more than anyone, understood the difference between he and Edwards when it came to matters of the page. "My lyrics are so different from Richey's," he later said. "And to be really honest, I don't think he could have written 'A Design For Life'. It would have been so complicated, so packed with references. Maybe it wouldn't even have been a hit." Alongside 'Motorcycle Emptiness', 'A Design For Life' was destined to become the Manics' official anthem. It also opened up a whole new audience for the group – in all probability, the very people that Nicky had been addressing with his lyrics. And if 'Design' was less coruscating, less startling in its imagery than Edwards' finest moment, 'Faster', it nevertheless contained an essential humanity that pulled at the heartstrings in a way only the very best songs can.

Sony wasted little time capitalising on the success of 'A Design For Life', firing its parent album, *Everything Must Go*, into shops in the last week of May. From the sleeve alone, it was apparent that all had changed. Designed by Mark Farrow, the cover presented three small portraits of three very ordinary looking men, the type one might find sitting around the table in a local pub. No makeup, no slogans, just clean shirts and clean shaven faces. This abandonment of the band's previous love of 'glamour' was quite deliberate. "Our new non-image is a bit like when Joy Division became New Order," Nicky told *The Face* at the time. "We've gone from punk to glam to *Apocalypse Now* and I couldn't really think of anything else to do. Especially without Richey. I'm not going to crucify myself and stub cigarettes out on my arm and become an anorexic or drug addict just to please people."

Wire's Joy Division/New Order analogy was apt. Following the suicide of Ian Curtis in 1980, Joy Division had struggled with how to proceed. Robbed of their singer, and beset with fans threatening to emulate his actions, the group stumbled for direction before deciding to change their name and distance themselves from their previously doom-laden image. The result, New Order, returned to active service with a new single, 'Ceremony', and album, *Movement,* a year or so after Curtis died. With a nondescript look and more commercial sound, the band went on to enjoy higher sales than in their previous incarnation. Again, all those years of studying the subtleties of rock history in their Blackwood bedrooms had served the Manics well.

If, unlike New Order, the Manic Street Preachers had baulked at actually changing their name, they seemed content to change just about everything else. As the album's title suggested, the band had conducted a 'clear out' sale of its past. Gone were the pile-driving guitars, compressed drums and thick-skinned bass sounds. In came space between instruments, and as a result, more room for tunes. In fact, Mike Hedges had given *Everything Must Go* an almost 'Sixties' sheen, with reverb, echo and swooping string arrangements recalling early Motown releases. In this atmosphere, it was at last clear to all what his fellow musicians had known for years: that Sean Moore was an extremely gifted drummer. Liberated by Hedges' production, Moore was a model of unfussy economy, unafraid to use rhythmic pauses and even silence as part of his percussive toolkit.

Of the songs on show throughout *Everything Must Go*, several deserved particular praise. 'Australia' for one, was another anthem in the making, bobbling along on the back of Moore's brisk stick work before reaching its sly, radio-friendly chorus. Wire's lyric here was dedicated to escape, the desire to get away from absolutely everything when life threatened to overwhelm his key driver. Obviously, the parallels between Nicky's recent experiences and lines such as "I want to fly and run until it hurts, sleep for a while and speak no words" required little explanation. "Australia always seemed like Mars to me," he later said. "You know, it's far away, somewhere you could escape to. There were certain times in our career where we've just wanted to escape somewhere. But Australia has always been somewhere I'm too scared to go to because I don't like flying."

The record's title track was also a marvellous pop rock moment, major and minor chords crashing into a sea of reverb-drenched drums and orchestral swells, its ending the sound of Bradfield's guitar slowly falling into oblivion. Lyrically, 'Everything Must Go' was as much a declaration of intent as 'You Love Us' had been some five years before. But instead of sticking two fingers up to the critics, this time Wire was actually seeking absolution from his own fans. "I just hope you can forgive us," ran the chorus, "but everything must go..." A message to Manics devotees that the group had to put aside the past in order to face the future, 'Everything...' was both sad-eyed lament to simpler times and raised glass to new hopes. "It's a plea for understanding," Wire told *Vox*. "We've got all this music to make and all these words to write, and it'd be a shame just to bottle all those up."

'Elona/Alone' was full of gentle melancholia, its words inspired by a time when Nicky was leafing through his wedding photographs and found a shot of himself standing in between Richey Edwards and Phillip Hall. All three were smiling: two were now no longer around. And though they had vowed to never do it, 'Further Away' was the Manics' first 'official' love song, Wire shyly recounting how much he missed his wife, Rachel, while on the road. For years, the band had avoided all such displays of overt sentimentality, even making a point to journalists early in their career that they would never stoop so low as to write "emotional drivel". This hard line was again reactivated during recording sessions for *Everything Must Go*, when Bradfield initially resisted using Nicky's lyrics. "When I first heard it," he said, "I thought 'I can't put that on the album'. Then I realised I was simply trying to win brownie points, holding the old party line." That said, James did his very best to chip away at too much overindulgence, littering the track with hard rocking guitar sounds and an extremely scratchy solo. As more devoted Manics fans knew, the group had actually dabbled with such sticky treats long before, their 1986 track 'Just Can't Be Happy' a gooey ode to unrequited love.

With 'Interiors (Song For Willem de Kooning)', Wire was back on more intellectual ground, his words a tribute to the Dutch-American artist de Kooning, who had continued to paint expressionist canvasses long after being diagnosed with Alzheimer's Disease. Following an initial dip in his abilities due to the illness, it seemed that the more de Kooning worked, the more his condition seemed to improve: "They're now saying that his art is the best treatment he can have for Alzheimer's," Nicky told *Vox*. "People say it's actually therapeutic for him."

Though the Manic Street Preachers had proved themselves a newly charged, highly contained and mightily impressive trio throughout *Everything Must Go*, they had both the dignity and presence of mind not to sever all ties with their past. Hence three compositions on the album featured lyrics written solely by Richey Edwards, while further "rough drafts" he left behind had been completed by Nicky Wire. Taking these 'co-writes' first, 'Elvis Impersonator: Blackpool Pier' challenged pre-existing notions of US supremacy in vintage Manics style: using the image of a corpulent Presley wannabe singing for his lunch on a seaside promenade, the message seemed to be that the American dream had become fat and bloated, its glory years now truly gone to seed. Worked on in the last studio sessions in which he participated, Richey had only written a short treatment of 'Elvis Impersonator...' which Sean didn't care for at the time. It was left to Wire to rescue it by adding an extra verse and fleshing out Edwards' original idea with a few thoughts of his own. "There weren't many lyrics anyway," he later conceded, "and I never spoke to Richey about what (his) general idea was." Opening with a luxuriant harp strummed to within an inch of its life, before revving up into a full-blown rock wig out, 'Elvis Impersonator', the first track on the record, was one of its more impressive, if challenging moments.

The second track that benefitted from both Edwards' and Wire's wordplay was 'The Girl Who Wanted To Be God', though again, Nicky had attached his lyrics to Richey's 'after the event'. Taking its title from a biography about Sylvia Plath, Wire freely admitted he wasn't sure what Edwards had being getting at, or indeed, whether his words were "autobiographical or not". Nonetheless, the end result was an uplifting, Sixties-tinged pop number that would have sat well in the back catalogue of Sandie Shaw, Dusty Springfield or Petula Clark, if of course, they had chosen to sing songs about troubled poets transcending human form.

Of the three numbers featuring stand-alone Richey lyrics, 'Removables' was by far the oldest, dating back to 1993. After several failed attempts to bring the song to life while recording in West London's Britannia Studios, the band took a break during which they were informed of Kurt Cobain's suicide. In honour of Nirvana's frontman, they began to play the track in a semi-acoustic setting, much like Cobain's cover of David Bowie's 'The Man Who Sold The World'. The idea worked and 'Removables' was later recorded in one take at Château de la Rouge Motte with James adding some electric guitar to spice up its chorus. Full of images of decay, stunted progress and the transitory nature of existence, 'Removables' was a sad reminder of Edwards' more bleak preoccupations.

'Small Black Flowers That Grow In The Sky' was equally disturbing in its subject matter, but truly brilliant in evoking the appalling conditions some animals suffered in zoos around the world. "Once you roared, now you just grunt, lame..." Inspired by a documentary Richey had seen on the BBC, Nicky Wire recalled the story behind the song to *NME*: "Richey called me up one night. We'd been watching the same TV programme. He said 'I've just seen this brilliant show'. It was about animals going mad in their cages. They end up shitting all over the walls... because they're so bored. Gorillas just smearing themselves in shit... leopards walking the same line a thousand times a day, up and down the same path. There's a terrible line in (the song): 'Harvest your ovaries, dead mothers crawl'. They'd be taking the eggs out of this leopard before it could have babies. Just horrendous, really."

The third and final Edwards lyric was fused to one of the Manic Street Preachers' finest ever tunes: 'Kevin Carter' was Richey's viewpoint of the life and death of the real life photographer named in the song's title. Carter had won a Pulitzer prize for his images of human suffering in famine areas such as Southern Sudan, but was later accused of capitalising on such tragedy for his own fame and profit. Nerves already shattered by his earlier experiences photographing Apartheid atrocities, and stung by the largely unfair criticism of his work, he turned his camera to wildlife instead. But it proved only a temporary diversion. Suffering from chronic insomnia, nightmarish 'flashbacks' and recurring money problems, Carter committed suicide in 1994. "Richey," Wire confirmed, "knew more about Kevin Carter's life story than anybody." Filled with images of vultures stalking dying children, discharging assault rifles and "tribal scars in Technicolor", Edwards had managed to perfectly encapsulate Carter's rise and fall in just 19 lines. Despite the distressing subject, it was a pleasure to hear James Dean Bradfield's voice once again negotiate Richey's waterfall of adjectives, verbs and clear disregard for anything approaching cadence or rhyme: "There was something about the melody that I really didn't want a vocal on it," Bradfield later said. "And as soon as I put the vocal on, I thought it sounded like shit." It really didn't. Topped off with a lambent trumpet solo from Sean Moore, 'Kevin Carter' was yet another highlight on a record already full of them.

Everything Must Go's final track, 'No Surface, All Feeling' also had a direct and affecting link to Richey Edwards. In tribute to their missing friend, the Manics had resurrected an old demo version of 'No Surface...' recorded at Surrey's House In The Woods studio in January 1995, to which Edwards contributed guitar. "It was just before he left," Nicky said. "James actually played it to Richey in the bedroom one night, but I don't think he ever heard it properly." The decision was subsequently made to use this version, with a couple of vocal touch ups and a new ending, to close the album. With Nicky's lyric mulling over the band's climb to notoriety, the need for future change and the telling admission "It may have worked, but at what price?", 'No Surface, All Feeling' proved a touching conclusion to *Everything Must Go*.

Justly proud of their efforts, the Manic Street Preachers had deliberately set out in search of new frontiers with *Everything Must Go*, but not wholly at the expense of their former incarnation. By using some of Richey Edwards' remaining lyrics, they had made a wise decision, celebrating his gifts and honouring the significance of his contribution to the band. But by also pushing forward with Nicky Wire as their primary wordsmith, they had also introduced a crucial note of optimism to their emotional palette. "Singing Nicky's lyrics," said Bradfield, "is a purifying experience for me, and they lend me a certain sense of humility and humanity. Richey's lyrics were a challenge and they were always confrontational to my nature. I just had to dive headlong into them." For James, the primary aim of *Everything Must Go* wasn't to maintain the Manics' status as cult outsiders, but place them closer to the centre of things where they could be of use. "To be universal," he told Q, "you've got to stain the consciousness of the people. You've got to dig out a truth that everybody knows but don't want to hear, then tell them in a manner that's so articulate, so aesthetically indignant, so beautiful, that they've got to accept it back in their lives again. That's what I want to do: touch something universal with your own language."

The success of *Everything Must Go* far exceeded Bradfield's aesthetic ambitions. Debuting at number two on the UK charts, it would stick around for a further 80 weeks, spawning three more Top 10 singles: 'Everything Must Go' (five), 'Kevin Carter' (nine) and 'Australia (seven). A million-plus best seller that also re-activated interest in the Manics' back catalogue (nearly 250,000 more copies of the group's first three albums were sold by the end of 1996), *Everything...* also received critical plaudits from almost every direction: "As LL Cool J once had it: don't call it a comeback," reasoned *Vox*'s Mark Sutherland. "The return of the

Manics verges on the imperial. Because *Everything Must Go* is not just the work of pretenders, but more that of (returning) natural monarchs. A superb rock group at the very height of their powers." *Melody Maker's* Stud Brothers heartily agreed that this was an album worth making a real fuss over: "The oddest thing is how excited it all sounds. Power chords, bursts of horn and needle sharp solos all contribute to an unlikely sense of triumphalism...we're glad they're still here, and with this (record), they all *are* still here." Q's Tom Doyle was also there to cheer the Manic Street Preachers home: "Twelve tracks then, of emotionally driven commercial rock is what we're left with and surely that's enough. The only message for the devoted comes with the reverb-laden, Spector inspired title track, where the rousing chorus finds Bradfield singing: 'And we hope you can forgive us, but everything must go.' In the light of everything, who could possibly bear a grudge?"

Nicky Wire was painfully aware that the disappearance of Richey Edwards had certainly aided the group's commercial cause. In fact, Edwards' vanishing and the circumstances around it seemed to have triggered a peculiar, but typically British response. The Manics, once derided for their out-of-date punk posturing, the vulgarity of their approach – *the sheer neediness of it all* – were now being properly embraced by both the intelligentsia and general public alike. Their recent plight, subsequent dignity and the artistic mettle they had shown meant that all previous slights, small grudges and wounding critical knives were put back in the drawer. Instead, Wire, Bradfield and Moore were now invited to sit at the grown ups' table – a reward for their troubles, a salve for their wounds. "This moment feels optimistic, but it's sweet and sour," Nicky said at the time. "Everyone feels sorry for us right now. I think it might be a honeymoon period. I feel sorry that it took Richey to go missing before some people would accept us. The only slight hang up, I suppose, (is) that I think he would have loved us becoming that big."

Both Sean Moore and James Dean Bradfield felt much the same when it came to Richey, with Moore actually wanting to reset the clock back to the beginning. "In a way," he said, "I wish that it could all have started with this album." For Bradfield, who had dreamt of precisely such success while busking for loose change in Cardiff City

Centre, there was an element of lost opportunity when it came to his absent friend. "I can't help thinking... 'Richey, if you'd just have held on a little bit longer, things might have been a lot different. Maybe then, you could have had all the things you wanted. You might have been happy...'"

Chapter Seventeen

As You Sow, So Shall You Reap

As sales for *Everything Must Go* confirmed, the Manic Street Preachers had re-invented themselves brilliantly following the loss of Richey Edwards. From their newly acquired 'everyman' image to the gentler, more optimistic sounds presented on their fourth album, they were a 'born again' phenomenon, the band it was "OK for everyone to like". Of course, this created its own set of challenges for previous Manics disciples who had to watch their 'Holy Bible' find its way into the home of new converts – ones who previously wouldn't have given it the time of day only two years before. No longer a cult, more a proper church, their beloved group had opened up its proverbial doors to all and were now the property of anyone who could afford to make a donation.

For some hardcore fans, there was simply no parting with the old time religion. By breaking the shackles of their raucous past, the Manics – so the argument went – had betrayed their roots and were now seeking only commercial glory. For other fervent supporters, simply carrying on without Richey was an act of unforgivable treachery, a soiling of 'the great work'. Worse, there were also accusations that they were exploiting Edwards' disappearance for their own grubby ends. Even if the band had asked for forgiveness on the title track of their new record, there was none to be had in certain quarters. Given that the three men in question were still coming to terms with their friend's departure while also trying to absorb recent victories, such condemnation was always going to be given short shrift. "We don't need to justify ourselves," Nicky told *Select*, "because we've done enough of that." As for charges that they had blunted their edge and sold out for cash, the Manics were a tad more diplomatic in their response: "Yes, we've become more optimistic, more positive," said Sean, "But saying that, I think some of the drama has gone, now that Richey isn't around."

It was always going to be difficult for a certain type of Manic Street Preachers fan to allow the band to move out of touching distance and find their place on a bigger stage. After all, even with the reasonable success obtained by *The Holy Bible*, the Manics had remained a concert hall draw rather than a stadium rock attraction: the type of group followers could see with their own eyes rather than binoculars. And in Richey, they had a very troubled, but also very human hero, a man who reflected their doubts and fears, and gave them a poetic voice. But it was always worth remembering that it had been Edwards himself who had preached the Manics' manifesto of global domination and multi-platinum sales. The only really irritating bit was that it took him vanishing from sight to set them on a course towards actually pulling it off.

Inevitably, responding to such inane enquiries and daft accusations when they had produced some of the most rounded and professional work of their career was bound to cause the Manics irritation. They already knew that Edwards' story had provoked interest in their work and granted them sympathy, opening doors into the heart of the British public that had been previously locked. But *Everything Must Go* had been about asserting their own authority and playing to their own strengths. It also had the effect of drawing the band closer together. This fact, coupled with the manner in which Richey had vanished left them doubting there would be a place for him in the group, should he return. "We were best mates," Wire confessed, "and while I couldn't bring myself to be friends with him any more, there's a part of me that will always think of him as my best mate. But if something goes wrong, be it your work, your art, love or a friendship, immediately all the good memories become overshadowed by something else, something fraudulent." Bradfield echoed Nicky's concerns, introducing an element of self defence to the equation: "I just couldn't be friends with him again," he told *NME*. "Just for the sake of us three. If it all went off again, just imagine how much it would fuck you up..."

For the moment, all such issues of closure would have to be placed aside as the Manics prepared themselves for a year long round of shows promoting *Everything Must Go*. And it has to be said, their first proper steps back into live performance were clever by anyone's standards, giving them the opportunity to tout their wares to a new, huge and potentially lucrative audience. In a fine scoop, the band had bagged a prestigious series of stadium-size appearances supporting the UK's biggest act of the time, Oasis.

While the Manic Street Preachers had been away dealing with issues of loss, attendant grief and sonic re-invention, the 'Britpop' movement had swept aside all in its path. Ending grunge's sour-faced stranglehold on British youth, groups such as Blur, Pulp and Supergrass had risen to see off all the plaid shirts, navel gazing and 'complaint rock' associated with the Seattle scene. Lighter, more optimistic and certainly more sardonic, these bands and the dozens that followed in their wake concentrated on the pleasures of being young rather than the gloom and uncertainty that sometimes came with that condition. The sound they offered was also an antidote to the fuzzed out, down-tuned guitars and primal screaming of Nirvana, Soundgarden and Pearl Jam. Instead, Britpop took its melodic cues from Sixties icons like The Beatles, Kinks and Small Faces – part music hall, part mod, part arty experimentalism – but always with a nod and a wink in place of a frown. By mid-1996, the UK was overrun with such acts: Sleeper, Shed Seven, The Bluetones, Dodgy, Cast, Echobelly, even Menswear; all good looking, sharp/casually dressed and each vying to make their mark on a domestically re-invigorated pop scene.

At the front of the pack was Oasis. Led by the two-pronged assault of Mancunian brothers Noel and Liam Gallagher, Oasis had fused a rhythm-heavy take on the Beatles' melodic strain with the attitude of the Stones and Sex Pistols to produce a razor sharp singularity. Unlike their nearest rivals, Blur, Oasis offered no art school cleverness. And unlike Pulp, they had little time for lionising their working-class roots with clever lyrical asides. Everything Oasis offered was about escape into the 'now': cigarettes, alcohol and class 'A' drugs. In short: live forever, consequences later. Perfectly capturing the zeitgeist of the UK's need for political, cultural and musical change at the time, Oasis was 'Cool Britannia''s house band and Nicky Wire thought they were the bee's knees: "I love Oasis. Three years ago, I realized that if every fucking band was like us, it would be an awful world. They're incredibly focused and hardworking and I love the idea that you could have genuine aspirations to be massive, yet still hold on to your integrity. Yes, have ideas for world domination, but feel natural with it. And don't forget, Liam is an integral part of the danger of the group and I admire Noel's stamina."

Unfortunately, the pairing of Wales' original 'rebel sons' and Britpop's ascendant shin-kickers sometimes didn't sit well within a stadium environment. Though the brutalities of their former regime had now been replaced with more melodic and incisive fare, the Manics were still a hard sell to Oasis' core audience. More interested in hearing about wonderwalls and sliding away than 'Roses In The Hospital' and 'Motorcycle Emptiness', James Dean Bradfield had to fight hard for all favours gained. Worse, there was little sympathy from certain quarters of the crowd when it came to the group's recent travails, with chants of "Where the fuck is Richey?" breaking out more than once.

That said, when Oasis returned to Manchester City's Maine Road Stadium for a triumphant homecoming in front of 35,000 fans on April 27, the Manics more than held their own. Delivering a brisk, assured 10 song set that drew on all points of their career, the band easily won themselves an encore, but as usual chose not to perform it. Unused to the Manics' little foibles, a small, but vociferous number of those gathered chose to hurl insults when it became clear that 'seconds' were not forthcoming. "We've always had a lot of trouble about not doing encores, to be honest," Nicky later told the *Irish Times*. "Over the years, people involved in the record company would say 'We've never had this from a group before. Did you hate the audience?' And we'd be coming off stage thinking it was one of the best gigs we've ever done. There have been occasions where a gig has been so rapturous that you do feel that slight inclination. You feel like giving more... but I think we've learned from (very early) experience." Wire was no doubt referring to a concert in mid-1991 when, finally acceding to management pressure, the band emerged from the wings after a protracted break only to find everyone had left the venue. "The encore," Nicky concluded, "is like a marketing tool. It's this idea that you're getting more value for money when really it's the same songs with a rest in-between. For us it just seems a bit false."

If the Manics continued to believe that encores represented little more than audience manipulation, other more genuinely emotional factors also held sway over their return to live duty. In fact, during a warm up show at Manchester's Hacienda Club the night before they played Maine Road, Nicky Wire became increasingly fixated with that part of the stage previously reserved for Richey Edwards. By the time the gig was over, he was inconsolable. "When we came offstage," Nicky recalled, "I virtually had a breakdown. I was just crying hysterically for three hours." Wire had fared little better when the Manics previously supported Oasis at Cardiff's International Arena, with both he and Bradfield seemingly unable to venture beyond their own allotted areas towards Edwards' old stamping ground. "It just takes a while to get used to..." James later said.

With support duties to Oasis temporarily behind them, the Manic Street Preachers struck out for a reunion with old fans – and many a new one – as they headlined their first UK dates in close to two years. Beginning their run at Glasgow Barrowlands on May 23, 1996 (the week *Everything Must Go* was released), the band wove through Middlesbrough, Wolverhampton, Manchester and London before arriving at Newport Centre for their own homecoming of sorts on May 31. In comparison with the lean presentation of earlier years, the Manics were now positively obese in both their stagecraft and theatrics. The beginning of each concert was marked by a majestic orchestral remix of 'A Design For Life', while an impressive slide show filled with slogans, images and the odd picture of Richey flashed above the audience's head on huge video screens. The lighting too, was a far cry from their humble beginnings, with bursts of red, green and white bathing Bradfield, Moore and Wire when the moment demanded it. However, there was always a place for old favourites as the group seldom, if ever failed to deliver 'Motown Junk', 'Motorcycle Emptiness' or 'You Love Us' before the proverbial curtain fell.

Further dates across Europe followed, including festival appearances in Holland, Ireland, Belgium, Germany and Sweden, after which they returned to England to back Oasis for two record-breaking shows at

Knebworth on 11/12 August. With over 125,000 in attendance on each day, the Knebworth dates represented both the zenith of Oasis' popularity and, with benefit of hindsight, the last days of the Britpop phenomenon. For Nicky, it was also his first chance to see another set of rising stars in the form of punk/big beat specialists, Prodigy. "I saw Prodigy for the first time at Knebworth supporting Oasis and thought they were absolutely amazing," he later confirmed, "especially (confronting) an Oasis audience... with a full-on, dance attack. That was pretty brave of them, that and the fact that they wear make-up, which always gets me going."

As for the Manics themselves, their performances at Knebworth were best described as 'solid', the group fighting against a wobbly PA system, packed beer tents and a "middle of nothing" late afternoon slot. For James, who allegedly hated the whole experience, the best thing about the Manics' brush with the summer sun was an opportunity to expose his chest to the elements: "It's always a bit frustrating to be playing the support slot. It's their gig, not ours. That said, it was nice to get some fresh air in my lungs." If nothing else the group could take heart from the news that 'Everything Must Go', the second single drawn from their new album, was still riding high in the UK Top 10 at the time of the Knebworth shows.

In September, the Manics were on the road with Oasis yet again, though this time, their destination was America. The band's very own 'Black Dog', all previous trips to the States – either actual or planned – had ended either in disappointment or disaster, so hopes were high that their latest jaunt might be different. Following Richey's disappearance and the band's subsequently aborted tour, Sony hadn't even bothered to release *The Holy Bible* in the US, and the Manics' profile across the Atlantic remained almost non-existent. However, their support slot with Oasis offered intriguing possibilities, with two white hot UK acts plying their wares to an audience eager to learn what all this Britpop fuss was about. As before it all ended in tears, though on this occasion, Bradfield, Wire and Moore could take no blame as things fell to pieces around them.

From the moment Oasis touched down on US soil, rumours began to circulate that the Brothers Gallagher were not getting on. As this was essentially normal behaviour between the two no alarms were raised – even when Liam failed to appear in Rosemount, Illinois for the group's opening performance on August 27, leaving Noel to sing instead. Sadly, things grew only worse as the tour progressed and by September 11, Oasis announced that Noel Gallagher was taking no further part in live shows and had flown home to England. All remaining dates were cancelled. Though Liam and Noel would patch things up within a week or so, this was no great consolation to the Manic Street Preachers, who appeared to have again been brought low by their US 'curse'.

There was some light at the end of the tunnel. The Manics had already played three of their own headlining dates – albeit at smaller venues throughout New York State – so the decision was made to soldier on with a series of club appearances across the country. Nonetheless, attendances at these 13 gigs rarely rose above 500 and the band succeeded in selling only a paltry 3,000 copies of their new opus, *Everything Must Go*. Still, the failure of yet another American jaunt, or Oasis' part in its downfall, didn't seem to worry Nicky Wire unduly. "It wouldn't actually bother me if I never went to (the States) again," he later told Q's Phil Sutcliffe. "I don't like the place, I don't like the people, I don't really want to go back there. The only good thing... was supporting Oasis, because it was when they were on the verge of going mental and we were quite sane."

In fact, when it came to the Manchester quintet, Wire remained full of compliments, even positing a theory as to why Oasis had attained a level of superstardom thus far denied the Manics: "Oasis made me a fan again. They've completely revitalised British music. We'd like to think it could have been us. Perhaps we didn't have the guile. We were too nasty, too confrontational. We waged war on the punters, the press, even on the concept of gigs. I'm still glad we did those things, though. They made us different. Most people thought we were pretentious wankers, which undoubtedly we were."

Though Nicky may have harboured the odd notion that the British public still thought of his band as "failed university lecturers in punk pantomime clothing", there was now strong evidence to the contrary. The home grown success of *Everything Must Go* and the attendant publicity surrounding it had sent ticket demand for the Manics' autumn tour through the roof, with as many as 40,000 seats sold before a note was even played. So long a cult act, they were now in serious danger of becoming one of the UK's most popular groups. This fact was underlined when they opened their latest round of live engagements at Livingston's Forum on October 5. As well as the usual proliferation of established fanatics, the crowd was awash with brand new converts. While these casually dressed, slightly older types might have been unsure of the words to 'La Tristesse Durera' and 'You Love Us', they were more than happy to sing along with 'Australia' and 'A Design For Life'. Change, as they say, was in the air.

Another essential modification to previous practice came with the Manics' choice of support bands for their tour. Instead of seeking out cutting edge noisemakers in the vein of The Wildhearts or politically informed rap collectives like Credit To The Nation, Wire and Co. elected to champion young Welsh groups. Hence, Catatonia, Super Furry Animals and the exceedingly young but exceptionally talented Stereophonics were all given their time in the spotlight. "When we started out," Wire explained to *Melody Maker*, "there was a lot of ridicule for just being Welsh... everything was derogatory. (Yet), there's always been a lot of creativity in Wales, though people thought (it) was Bonnie Tyler or Tom Jones. It's good that's changed."

This new attitude didn't stop with the hiring of support acts. Nicky had also taken to draping his onstage amplifier with the *Y Ddraig Goch* (or 'Red Dragon') – the official flag of Wales. When questioned about this recent volte face and reminded of the Manics' original eagerness to distance themselves from both the town and country of their birth, Wire was open to the charge but also eager to explain the band's current position. "Well, me and James do have big arguments about this. Sometimes I'll feel very guilty about not knowing any Welsh, not delving back more into (our) non-industrial history, but James is quite adamant that we're creating something new, so I go along with him on that. The Valleys' 'Welshness' is very new: it's like we're creating our own language. But I still do think we're a uniquely fucked-up race of people. No two ways about it." While it was heartening to hear an older, wiser Nicky speak positively about creating a new 'Welshness', one couldn't help but remember when his views were steeped in the acid of youth: "If you go to Wales and drink Babycham," he said in 1991, "you're guaranteed to get beaten up. Or you would, if the fuckers weren't too depressed to beat you up..."

There was precious little Welsh depression on display when the Manic Street Preachers rolled into Cardiff on December 12, 1996 for an appearance at the city's premier concert venue, the International Arena. Only nine months before, the band had opened there for Oasis. Now, they were the headliners in their own right, playing to a capacity crowd of 6,000 demented souls. Again, the Cardiff date was another clear example of their ascendancy into the ranks of the 'elite'. But, as the audience sang back the words to their recent Richey-penned Top 10 single, 'Kevin Carter', it also served as yet another reminder to the Manics of the road travelled in order to get there. That they were obviously still smarting from Edwards' loss was clear from one of the B-sides to 'Carter' – the forlorn, acoustically driven 'Sepia'. Written as a "Miss You" to their friend, 'Sepia' used images of "framed adolescence" and eternal melancholia to drive home its emotional point, but Wire's most affecting line had to be "Bleeding inside, I manage to keep it all in, I keep it all in..." Their war might be close to being won, but at least the group had the decency to remember those still missing in action.

Following an intense 27 date trek across Britain and Europe, the Manics finally came to a temporary halt in London before Christmas with three shows in three distinctly different settings. First up was Brixton Academy on December 14, which saw the trio (plus touring keyboard player, John Green) in excellent, if slightly frenetic form. The following night, they travelled west for a more intimate headlining gig at Shepherd's Bush Empire. Here, the group was joined onstage by the former girl of their dreams, Kylie Minogue, who added her lissom voice to 'Little Baby Nothing'. For some in the audience, this was role reversal at its very finest. When the young and unknown Manics had first approached the pop princess to sing on the track in 1991, Minogue was enjoying a run of hits via her association with producers Stock, Aitken & Waterman, and politely declined their offer. However, since she left SAW to strike out on her own in 1992, the hits had gradually dried up and Kylie was now in need of some serious chart action. Perhaps, cynics argued, Minogue's sudden interest in the recently successful Welsh band might have more to do with her future career prospects than love of their music. Whatever the case, the Australian singer (who actually claimed strong Welsh heritage) acquitted herself admirably and backstage talk was all about a future collaboration.

The Manics' final London appearance took place within the welcoming walls of the Forum in Kentish Town on December 16. Once again the group found their stage invaded, though this time it was a rock'n'roll ruffian rather than a diminutive pop princess who invited himself to the party. In a frankly surreal 10 minute performance, Oasis' Liam Gallagher sang little but stole the show. Beginning his contribution to the evening by staging a pretend fight with Nicky Wire, Gallagher then made several attempts to kiss the bassist before throwing his beer bottle into the air and disappearing whence he came. Even Sean Moore looked confused.

1996 was a year that saw the Manic Street Preachers progress from their former position as an emotionally wounded, but quietly confident cult act to arena hopping behemoths. With *Everything Must Go*, they had also found their way into over a million homes worldwide, providing a serious, reflective but mostly upbeat soundtrack for 'old guard' and 'new converts' alike. Of course, such achievements always came with a price: the Manics had lost some of their original following to accusations of betrayal, sell out and other forms of downright stupidity. But Wire, Bradfield and Moore had little cause for regret, and more, had observed the loss of their friend with a contained dignity that only the most sour-faced could pick fault with.

If the public had rewarded the Manics' many accomplishments by buying their record and attending their live shows in droves, then it was left to the critics and wider music industry to provide the trophies. This they did in startling fashion, heaping award after award upon the group. *Everything Must Go* picked up 'Writers' Best Album of 1996' from both *The Guardian* and *The Sunday Times*, while *The Daily Telegraph* and *Independent On Sunday* named it in their top picks for the year. The music press were also not shy in handing out the medals, with *NME*, *Melody Maker*, *Vox*, *Select* and *Music Week* all honouring the band with their 'Writers' Best Album' choice. Even the more hard-line metal magazines were in a giving mood, as *Kerrang* and *Metal Hammer* pinned 'Silver' and 'Top Ten Writers Albums' gongs to the Manics' chests.

It didn't stop there. In late January 1997, the group walked away from the *NME* Brat Awards with readers' nods for 'Best Single', 'Best Album' and 'Best Live Act', but not before shouting "This is for Richey!" from the stage. It was a line they heartily repeated when receiving two Brit Awards for 'Best Single' and 'Best Album' from presenter Zoë Ball some four weeks later. "I remember thinking 'What's Zoë Ball doing here, giving us an award?'" said Moore, "Then I thought 'What am I actually doing here?" Wire, on the other hand, took the opportunity to engage millions of viewers with his views on then sketchy government plans to eradicate comprehensive schools: "Comprehensives have produced everything," he railed, "the best bands, the best art, the best boxers..." Whether Nicky later sent a letter of apology on behalf of the group to the Headmaster of Oakdale Comprehensive School for several previous slights regarding their own education still remains uncertain.

As the months rolled on, so did the nominations. And though the Manics were pipped to the post by Pulp's *Different Class* for the exalted 1996 Mercury Music Prize, they did win something perhaps even more impressive: 'Best Contemporary Song' for 'A Design For Life' at the 42nd Ivor Novello Awards on May 29, 1997. An honour regarded in the highest esteem by songwriters, previous recipients of the 'Novello' included Sir Paul McCartney, David Bowie, Kate Bush, Queen, and somewhat ironically, John Lennon. Even if the Manics had once threatened to "Get their dicks out and piss on it," should they ever win one such award, the band were privately thrilled to be walking home with an accolade named in honour of Wales' first international entertainer.

Away from the champagne, laurel wreaths and rose strewn red carpets, the Manics continued on their campaign of beguiling the masses, spending a goodly proportion of mid-1997 on the road. A 10-date Irish/UK tour beginning at Dublin's Olympia Theatre on March 29 and ending with a high profile appearance at London's Royal Albert Hall on April 12 brought their cause to thousands more new fans. The band then turned their attentions to charity, joining Dodgy, Space and The Beautiful South at Anfield stadium on May 10 for 'Rock The Kop – The Hillsborough Justice Concert', where all proceeds raised went to supporting families of the 1989 Hillsborough football tragedy. Exactly a week later, James Dean Bradfield took the stage at Brixton Academy for a short solo set, this time in aid of the Missing Persons Helpline, the organisation that had done so much in helping Richey Edwards' family publicise his disappearance. The Manics then reconvened for one of their largest ever shows, selling out Manchester's 23,000 capacity Nynex arena on May 24. The performance, which covered material from all points in their career, was ably captured by music promo director Dick Carruthers and released as *Everything – Live*, the band's first commercially available video: "The Nynex gig," James later said, "is when we knew we'd *really* arrived."

With at least a hundred dates already behind them, one might have thought the Manic Street Preachers had little time to breathe between live commitments. But the group, or at least parts of it, had still managed to fit in a number of collaborations with other artists during this busy period. Bradfield for instance, was making cautious but positive noises about finding another band to mentor, having greatly enjoyed his co-production experiences with Dave Eringa on Northern Uproar's debut single, 'Rollercoaster'/'Rough Boys' in 1996. Wire was also extolling the benefits of extracurricular teamwork as he wallowed in positive reviews for 'Waiting For Today To Happen', a track he co-wrote with Ian Broudie for The Lightning Seeds' fourth album, *Dizzy Heights*. However, James and Nicky actually found working as a duo the most effective way to engage with other musicians. This point was first driven home by 'Lopez', a song composed alongside 808 State for the electronic dance outfit's greatest hits collection, *808.88.98*. Featuring lyrics by Wire and beautifully sung vocals from Bradfield, 'Lopez''s break beats and woozy atmospherics were a far cry from the Manics' own style, but that didn't stop the track entering the Top 20 when released as a single in 1997. In fact, James was so taken with his voyage into electronica, he repeated the experiment again soon after, taking on bass, vocal and production duties for Massive Attack's Eastern-sounding 'Inertia Creeps'. The number was later released on the trip-hopper's best selling 1998 album, *Mezzanine*.

Wire and Bradfield's other soiree into the collaborative process during 1997 was with Kylie Minogue. As revealed, Minogue was at something of a career impasse since shedding her 'girl next door' image in the early Nineties, and aside from the brilliant 'Confide In Me' and a wobbly Nick

Cave duet, 'Where The Wild Roses Grow', hits had been progressively harder to come by. Keen to re-establish her market position but also find some credibility in the process, Kylie had thrown the net out wide for songwriters to aid her cause. Ever the devoted fans, James and Nicky came running to help. The resulting two tracks, 'I Don't Need Anyone' and 'Some Kind Of Bliss' were as far away from Minogue's glory days of 'I Should Be So Lucky' and 'Better The Devil You Know' as it was possible to get. Sounding like Manics outtakes from *Everything Must Go*, minus any real urgency or sense of dramatics, Bradfield even had the cheek to drop in a couple of meandering guitar solos in the songs to further weaken their appeal. To her enduring credit, Kylie drew out a tune where she could but there was little saving either number. Inexplicably, 'Some Kind Of Bliss' was released as a single in September 1997, providing Minogue with her lowest ever chart position of number 22 in the UK. Though Bradfield and Wire had tried to expand the Australian singer's repertoire and provide new sonic possibilities, they readily acknowledged this was not their best work. "When James and I wrote a little ditty for Kylie, it was four days of misery," said Nicky. "It just seemed utterly pointless." Minogue, of course, would recover from the experience.

With high impact appearances at Newport Centre and the Reading and Feile Festivals in late August 1997, the Manic Street Preachers finally ended their on the road promotion of *Everything Must Go* and came to rest. But even if the band were done for the time being, their record company was not. In celebration of the Manics' ascent into the ranks of rock's premier league, and fully aware that any new product was at best a year or so away, Sony elected to re-release their first ever singles in deluxe CD format. Therefore, 'Stay Beautiful', 'Love's Sweet Exile', 'You Love Us', 'Slash N' Burn', 'Motorcycle Emptiness' and 'Little Baby Nothing' all fought their way back into the charts with varying degrees of success. Predictably 'Motorcycle Emptiness' fared best, reaching a semi-creditable 41, while 'Love's Sweet Exile' proved it had grown no better with advancing years by stalling at 55 (chart wise, the other four tracks all nestled between them). Though this was little more than a callous marketing exercise by Sony to extract maximum profit from the Manics' back catalogue, hearing the likes of 'You Love Us' and 'Slash N' Burn' on the radio again showed how far the group had come –

and indeed, what they had left behind. Packed with anger, energy and requisite servings of piss and vinegar, these recordings were a reminder to all of the naive, yet refreshing qualities the early Manics brought to the UK music scene. Derivative, certainly. Overwrought, without doubt. But there was also a pinpoint intensity to the work that hinted at future greatness.

And then there was the presence of Richey Edwards. Now almost three years gone, his lyrical contributions to songs such as 'Motorcycle Emptiness' and 'Stay Beautiful' had in the meantime taken on new avenues of meaning – the despair a little deeper, the quest for perfection a little more pronounced. Whether the Manics had, dare one say it, become more successful without his input or more optimistic in their worldview was hardly the point. Edwards had brought an aura of intellectual authority to the band that was simply irreplaceable, and they were the first to admit it: "In terms of taking on the world (or) changing people's lives," Nicky told *Q*, "we haven't regained that. And without Richey...perhaps we never will."

As the Manics closed the door on 1997, they could take comfort from the knowledge that in the last 18 months, the group had played to hundreds of thousands of fans, scored four Top 10 singles and made a platinum-selling album. They had also won a glut of awards from a variety of sources, and gained the grace and favour of their fellow artists who were now keen to collaborate rather than avoid them in studio corridors. They had befriended Britpoppers, been embraced by electronica and were even on first name terms with pop royalty. The band's next move, whatever that might be, would now guarantee them the ears of the British public and the interest of critics across the land. It was an enviable position to be in, almost a seat among the gods. Such matters, however, would have to wait.

For the time being, there were carpets to be cleaned.

Situationist chic. The Manics model the slogan-bearing clothes that became their early trademark. "You can ignore our songs," said Richey Edwards, "but when we walk down the street and see our song titles on our chest, you've got to think something..." *(Tom Sheehan)*

Nicky blows a kiss to fans when leaving Osaka Station, Japan on May 10, 1992. *(Paul Slattery)*

The band onstage at Club Citta, Kawasaki, Japan in May, 1992.
(Paul Slattery)

While filming the video for 'Motorcycle Emptiness', the Manics visit Yokohama's 'Big Wheel'.
(Paul Slattery)

Richey and unknown extra captured during filming at Tokyo's Pacific Hotel.
(Paul Slattery)

'Suicide Babies and the Beautiful Boy'. Nicky, Sean and Richey declare war on gender stereotypes while filming the video for 'You Love Us', 1992. *(Tom Sheehan)*

On stage chaos, backstage recovery. *(Paul Slattery)*

Apocalypse Now. The Manics abandoned the glamour of their past incarnation in favour of the military look to promote 1994's masterful *The Holy Bible*. Clockwise from the top: A hooded Nicky, Richey, James and Sean. *(Tom Sheehan)*

A frail Richey Edwards visits L'Empire Des Morts in Paris, November 1994. Nicky Wire: "At this point, Richey was marking every day out of ten, and he gave this day a very good mark... almost a perfect day." *(Tom Sheehan)*

Aftermath. Backstage at Mah Boonkrong Hall, Bangkok, April 1994. Richey captured moments after making a series of self-inflicted cuts across his upper chest. The small knife he used was a present from a fan. *(Kevin Cummins)*

The Manics meeting Cuban leader Fidel Castro in February, 2001. While hopes for the band's visit to Cuba were originally high, events took a different course leading James to later describe their experiences as 'Manic Street Folly'. *(Tom Sheehan)*

And then there were three. Following Richey Edwards' disappearance in February, 1995, the Manic Street Preachers chose to carry on as a trio, subsequently enjoying a new level of commercial success with their 1996 album, *Everything Must Go*. *(Tom Sheehan)*

Chapter Eighteen

Joy In Repetition

During 1997, the Manic Street Preachers signed a new deal with Sony's music publishing arm, ATV, reputedly worth £1 million. Having also sold close to two million albums worldwide and collected a lucrative stream of revenue from near endless touring plus merchandising sales, the band now found themselves in an extremely solvent financial position. Or, in layman's terms, rich.

For James Dean Bradfield, this meant buying rather than renting a plush bachelor flat in London's St. John's Wood, full malt rather than blended whiskies drunk freely in member's clubs and almost all the CDs and hardback books he desired. For Sean Moore, greater wealth enabled him to purchase more gadgets and newer technology, the smell of a freshly opened Walkman, mobile phone or computer game sending shivers of delight down his spine. For Nicky Wire, money equalled vacuum cleaners and lots of them. "I love seeing my Dyson suck up my dog Molly's black hair," he told *Esquire*. "I recently went home to Blackwood – just for one night – and it's sad, but the first thing I did was hoover. Cleanliness. I absolutely love it." Having suffered from an Obsessive Compulsive Disorder (OCD) all his life, cleanliness was next to godliness for Nicky and rumour had it that he owned three of James Dyson's innovative grey and yellow creations: one for the upstairs of his house, one for downstairs, and one more just in case the other two broke down. "I just love Dysons," he said, "they're a work of art."

As evidenced, since the disappearance of Richey Edwards, Nicky Wire had taken to his role as principal spokesman for the Manics with something approaching gusto. Unlike Richey, who could be relied on for a form of "cuddly nihilism" during interviews, Wire embodied a very different type of sound-bite king. Still refreshingly honest, but now much more aware of his responsibilities in representing the band, Nicky successfully walked the wire between what Victorians called 'an Entertainment' and the modern press termed a 'cultural commentator'. That said, as Bradfield closed his eyes – digging deep for the definitive response to questions – and Moore found something incredibly interesting in the middle distance to focus on, Wire was still capable of just going for it: "Cleaning's an OCD thing. When I come home and my wife, Rachel, obviously hasn't hoovered for the last four days – because she's not as into it as I am – I'm straight out with the vacuum cleaner. She goes out, takes the dog up the mountain, and I have a big clean."

However, behind all the talk of dust reduction, golf and the prospects of the Cardiff Devils ice hockey team, Nicky remained an intellectual at heart, and one who viewed the recent fall of the Conservatives to New Labour with relish, but no blind optimism: "I just thought the general election was brilliant TV. I loved it. But, maybe I'm too cynical. I never thought there'd be any radical change. Having said that, I never thought (Labour) would do what they did to education and (start) charging fees. Most other things they've done I kind of agree with, but that is despicable. I would probably never have gone to university if that had been the case." Additionally, unlike Noel Gallagher and others from the pop/rock community who accepted invitations to visit Prime Minister Tony Blair at his new Downing Street address, Wire remained sceptical of such posturing: "The whole 'Cool Britannia', Tony Blair thing is just a yawn. I can never understand how anyone would get caught up in it." Yet, he did concede that the cliché – 'Things can only get better' – contained a ring of truth: "Unfortunately, everything is just better, isn't it? You can't lie about it: being alive in Britain in 1998 is much better than it was in '88 or '90 or '91.. but there's no radicalism. The thing that makes me more angry than anything else," he concluded, "is the lack of understanding of history. People seem to have no grasp of it. That's the scariest thing... because everything's going so well, 50 years of social struggle could be swept aside. By New Labour. By averageness."

Of course, there were those who believed the Manic Street Preachers' recent work also represented a shift to the middle, or at least, a blunting of the knives. Though *Everything Must Go* had been a strong and mature return, in comparison with earlier works, there was a definite loss of the old radicalism one associated with the band. The sounds were softer, the lyrics more considered, the anger more contained. Inevitably such notions revolved around their formative image and proclamations, the continuing absence of Edwards and the sheer bile of the Manics' last album before his disappearance, *The Holy Bible*. Again, Nicky was keen to point out that this was the work of younger and very different men: "We're 29 now, and that can suck the urgency out of you," he told *Melody Maker*. "It's all right for a fan to want to freeze us there, still walking round in combats playing 'Die In The Summertime', but if we were frozen there, we'd all probably be dead."

As to charges that the Manics' newfound wealth had stolen them away from supporting former causes or found them jumping on the New Labour bandwagon, Wire fought back hard. "We gave quite a lot of money to the Socialist Labour Party. I just thought it was important to have that choice." He was also proud to recall the Manics' 1997 pre-show meeting with SLP leader and former president of the National Union of Mineworkers, Arthur Scargill, at Liverpool's Royal Court Theatre. "Meeting Arthur Scargill was one of the great moments of Manics history. We've got this really fantastic picture of us and Arthur... and he's (got his thumbs aloft). He was right into a speech within five minutes."

The political ideology and left wing views that the miners' strike had activated within the Manics more than a decade before were still clear, present and correct when the group finally released a brand new single on August 24, 1998. With words written by Nicky Wire, 'If You Tolerate This Your Children Will Be Next' took its inspiration from the Spanish Civil War and celebrated the idealism of global volunteers who flocked to Spain in 1936 to fight for the Republic against fascist military rebels. Wire's interest in the subject had been re-activated by reading George Orwell's 'Homage To Catalonia', the writer's personal account of his battle experiences alongside communists during the conflict (Orwell was shot through the throat by a sniper and almost killed while at the Spanish war front). Internally aligning the book to one of his favourite Clash songs, 'Spanish Bombs', which also praised the heroism of native Republicans and their 'International Brigade' volunteer colleagues, Nicky set to work on building a set of lyrics.

The end result was an impressive study of the past sacrifices men made to fight something they believed to be simply evil, while also issuing a warning to listeners that political apathy and disinterest provide no defence against such a threat happening again. "It's also about how generations today don't know how lucky they are," Nicky told Q. "The International Brigade went to fight with the Spanish against the fascists just because they wanted to fight fascism... this really naïve ideal. There's no way any generation now would just go and fight a war for an ideal." Featuring a line directly taken from an English volunteer who left for Spain saying "If I can shoot rabbits, then I can shoot fascists", the song's title was also liberated from a Spanish Republican poster from the time: an affecting photograph of a child killed by Nationalist bombs, the accompanying slogan read "If you tolerate this your children will be next..."

Married to a willowy, sorrowful tune with an ever-spiralling chorus, 'If You Tolerate...' was a distance away from any previous Manics single, its appeal subtle rather than overt. Equally the song's video, directed by Wiz – whose existing promo credits included 'Love's Sweet Exile' and 'A Design For Life' – took some getting used to. Presenting the group trapped among faceless children as part of a strange "totalitarian experiment", it was meant to pay homage to the cult 1997 science fiction film *Gattaca*, but more resembled an outtake from *Star Trek*. Worse, 'If You Tolerate...' was also going head to head with a new single release from fearsome pop bunnies Steps, who were equally intent on laying claim to the UK chart's top spot. If the Manics wanted their first ever number one, they were going a strange way about it. But at least it was good to know they now had former Happy Mondays frontman Shaun Ryder on their side. "The Manics are one of the best bands in the world," he wrote for *The Sport*, "and I really dig what this dude is singing about. He's getting fuckin' political on your arse and I'm a fuckin' political animal."

In the end, 'If You Tolerate...' was a gamble that paid off in spades. Selling over 176,000 copies within a week, the song finally put the Manic Street Preachers at the top of the UK charts. As with 'A Design For Life' two years before, their individual reactions were mixed. After glugging several glasses of champagne, Nicky reached for the phone. "I wanted to ring everyone and tell them I was number one," he later recalled, "but then I realised I didn't have any friends."

While Sean's response remained his own, James was a bundle of astonishment: "I didn't know how to react, so I just didn't react... (but) not to be a bridesmaid any more... it was nice to be taken off the shelf." For a moment at least, it appeared that Bradfield's proverbial wedding day celebrations might be spoiled as Doc Martin-wearing punk legends The Stranglers stepped forward with accusations of copyright infringement. According to Stranglers bassist Jean-Jacques Burnel, their publishing company had alerted the band to a strong resemblance between 'If You Tolerate...' and their own 1979 Top 20 hit, 'Duchess'. "I don't think they're ripping us off," said Burnell, "but my publisher does." Truthfully, there were incidental (and entirely accidental) similarities between the tunes but nothing to go to court over. The Stranglers eventually felt the same and no legal action was taken.

A fine track that put a strong, refreshing political statement in the number one spot for the first time in many a moon, 'If You Tolerate This...' was compelling evidence of the Manic Street Preachers' newfound commercial power to please without compromising on their integrity. "To have a song like that, with those sentiments, seep into popular consciousness, then go to number one... well, that was what we'd always wanted to achieve," James later confirmed. "That was always part of the original plan…the manifesto. God, that would have made Richey happy." Given the resolute success of 'If You Tolerate This...', attention now focussed on whether the band could equal or even surpass this achievement with their newest album.

Recorded in a series of fits and starts over a 10 month period, the Manics had visited seven locations in all to create their latest work. The story started as far back as August 1997 when they began cutting demos at Whitfield Studios near Goodge Street in London's West End. Though several tracks were laid down at Whitfield (including a duet and subsequent B-side, 'Black Holes For The Young', with Sophie Ellis Bextor), the group was unhappy with the results and moved on to their former stamping ground, Big Noise Studios in Cardiff. This time round, two producers were drafted in to oversee the process, with Mike 'Everything Must Go' Hedges and Dave 'Gold Against The Soul' Eringa more than happy to share a desk while at Big Noise. Moore captured a number of useable drum tracks on tape, which the Manics then took with them to France for the next stage of their journey. Returning to Château de la Rouge Motte, where they made their previous album, proved a wise decision. Happy with the environment and atmosphere, the trio and their producers worked well, and by the end of January 1998 the majority of the record was complete. However, it wasn't quite over yet. Flying back to Wales, they soldiered on at Rockfield Studios and Valley Farmhouse before again shooting down the motorway to London to finish the mixing process.

Sometimes, this 'Band of Gypsies', plane-hopping, multiple studio, all hands to the pump approach yielded fine results, with The Rolling Stones and Led Zeppelin having produced great work on the fly. But there was always the danger that too many locations coupled with too many opportunities might end with incoherent and muddled product. Nonetheless, Sean Moore seemed passive enough when recalling the saga behind the Manics' new disc. "When we were recording there was no pressure whatsoever," he said. "We spent a lot of time with the arrangements of the songs and the instrumentation. Throughout our history, right from *Generation Terrorists* through to *The Holy Bible*, we've always tried to use different instruments and different ways of recording, so hopefully this is a progression from the last album." Yet, he did concede that there was the odd worry as to how fans might take to their latest opus: "We're waiting to see if people will accept (things) as readily as 'A Design For Life' and whether this record will be immediate. *Everything Must Go* took a while for people to get into and we worry (this one) might take even longer."

The opportunity to find out came on September 19, 1998, when the Manic Street Preachers' fifth studio album, *This Is My Truth Tell Me Yours* was shipped to stores. A more progressive, experimental release than *Everything Must Go*, and full of unconventional instrumentation such as tampuras, omnichords, Wurlitzers and mellotrons, *This is My Truth...* was the sound of a band testing its perimeters, but with sometimes mixed results. In fact, the record's photograph sleeve neatly summed up the contents within: taken by Andy Bell on a beautifully sunny day at Black Rock Sands near Porthmadog, the picture showed James staring up into a clear blue sky, Sean studying the sand beneath his feet and Nicky looking headlong into camera. Three directions at once, with no consensus as to which path might be the right one to follow.

When the band got the music right, they did so fantastically well. Both 'Tsunami' and 'You Stole The Sun From My Heart' were great pop rock singles, a fact confirmed when they reached numbers five and 11 respectively on the UK charts in March and July of 1999. Sneaking up on the listener with a deceptively quiet, push/pull verse before letting fly with its infuriatingly catchy chorus, 'You Stole The Sun...' was vintage Manics – a proud successor to the likes of 'La Tristesse Durera' and 'From Despair To Where'. 'Tsunami' was a more peculiar concoction, using the exotic sounds of a sitar to lull the senses while the song's hook lay waiting to pounce only moments later. 'The Everlasting' was yet another single – making number 11 on December 12, 1998 – and yet another superior effort. All tremolo guitars, sad orchestration and restrained drumming, this was an anthem in the vein of U2's 'One' or The Verve's 'The Drugs Don't Work', and at one time at least, a potential contender for album title as well. "Yep," Wire later said, "I wanted people to be able to go to the shops and say 'Can I have the Everlasting Manic Street Preachers?'". 'Be Natural' too, was an interior-sounding gem, its circumspect nature and haunting qualities redolent of new, progressive rock-tinged superstars, Radiohead. "*OK Computer* (is) one of British music's healthiest ever achievements," said James, "(a) band who made the album they wanted to, and then sold more records than Michael Jackson." Yet, when the sounds failed to gel, the Manics could sound ponderous and overblown, with 'I'm Not Working', 'Black Dog On My Shoulder' and 'You're Tender And You're Tired' all disappearing in a cloud of their own self-importance. Perhaps Bradfield's newfound experiments with bizarre guitar tunings might have had something to do with it. "I wanted to get these strange harmonics in the chorus for 'You're Tender...'" he said. "If you try to play (it) in standard tuning, you'll have a heart attack."

On his first solo lyrical adventure without Richey Edwards, Nicky Wire provided all words used for *This Is My Truth Tell Me Yours*, even coming up with the record's title while attending an event to mark the 50th anniversary of the National Health Service on a wet Tredegar Mountain in early 1998. "I was standing there, just thinking 'There's no way any other member of a band in Britain would be doing this in the whole of the world'," he told *NME.* Through the speakers, Wire then heard an old tape recording of the voice of Aneurin Bevan, the Welsh politician so important to the founding of the NHS in 1948: "This is my truth," boomed Bevan's catchphrase, "tell me yours." It was epiphany time: "One of those moments when things connect and it's mega, it makes it all worthwhile." Though Nicky had initially suffered writers' block when it dawned on him that he was now sole lyricist in the band, the final results on *This Is My Truth...* proved strong and were drawn almost exclusively from his own views and interests. "Lyrically, (it's) just about my world – the world I exist in and the things that make me sad and happy. The things that make me get up in the morning and the things that make me go to bed."

The breadth of subjects covered by Wire was no less eclectic or potentially controversial than those Richey Edwards showed interest in or obsession with. In 'S.Y.M.M.' (or South Yorkshire Mass Murderer), Nicky bemoaned the death of principles while also attacking the subsequent injustices of the Hillsborough tragedy. 'Tsunami' meanwhile, placed a spotlight on the perplexing tale of Jennifer and June Gibbons, twins who ceased communication with the outside world while still children, before later gravitating towards crime. "They were twins that grew up in West Wales, but never spoke," Wire later told Q. "They ended up in Broadmoor with Peter Sutcliffe after committing arson. A strange, sad story."

'Black Dog On My Shoulder' was another dark-eyed lyric, focusing on the growth of depression throughout the Western world, while 'Ready For Drowning' simultaneously celebrated and castigated Welsh culture: "Ready For Drowning'," said Nicky, "is the most complete song I've ever written, I think." And one of the most complex. Pinging between real life conversations with local cab drivers eager to learn the whereabouts of his missing friend, villages deliberately flooded for profit and the effects of alcohol abuse on Welsh youth and celebrities, 'Ready

For Drowning' was a multi-dimensional treatise on an ageing country and its search for a new identity.

Wire seemed happiest when venturing into personal dilemmas and private feelings. 'You Stole The Sun From My Heart' crystallised for all to hear in song what Nicky had been saying in interviews for some time – that touring was as much a curse as a pleasure. "Sometimes, I could live without it," he later confessed. "I'm the one who wishes we could just go into the studio to record albums and release them." 'Born A Girl' too, was marginally confessional, playing with notions of male bondage in the face of feminine freedom. For a man known for his love of make-up, and whose latest foray into cross-dressing was a majestic see-through number worn proudly onstage at 1997's Reading Festival, Wire knew more than most about such things. "There's no doubt about it. I have in my time, loved dressing up in women's clothes. I can't say I'm desperate to be a woman, but sometimes I feel it would have been a bit easier if I'd been born one. My body shape is quite a lot like a woman. I've got extremely big hips. I've got a very small waist, but a really odd pelvic girdle. And let's be honest," he concluded, "a large percentage of our fans prefer to see me in a dress. There's no two ways about it."

The band's early history and Nicky's own particular brand of romanticism was duly covered on 'The Everlasting'. "James wanted it to sound like a hymn... 'The Old Rugged Cross'. (The song) deals with the eternal search for something we can never find." And with 'Nobody Loved You', Wire had crafted a moving tribute to Richey Edwards, recalling teenage shopping trips to Cardiff alongside his friend. "Give me some more of your carrier bags and let me dream of a new autumn light..."

Where lyric and melody fused together best on *This Is My Truth* was surely the hair-raising ballad 'My Little Empire'. Featuring an outstanding vocal performance from James Dean Bradfield and a restrained turn from the band, Wire's words contemplated the existential bliss he felt while at home, and how the overwhelming desire never to leave his own front door might one day be his undoing. "It's my favourite song on the record," Nicky told *Melody Maker*. "It's saying that the things that make me happy can be just as destructive as alcohol or drug addiction. Sometimes I think I lead such an introverted life, such a withdrawn life, with no social interaction, that perhaps it'll lead to disaster – but it's also what keeps me sane." Bradfield was also adamant that the song was centrepiece, lynchpin and highlight of the new album: "My Little Empire' explains how a lot of (our) songs are written," he said. "It explains the ideals and values that have constructed Nick's environment. I don't think there are many people who'd write a song like 'My Little Empire'. It's about the value of Nicky's style of authorship. And out of that song arises the album."

A good, if not necessarily great album that found the Manic Street Preachers again stretching their boundaries, if only to occasionally get lost in the effort, *This Is My Truth...* nonetheless consolidated their marketplace position as one of Great Britain's biggest acts. Debuting at number one with over 140,000 copies sold in the first week of release, the record stuck around the UK charts for over a year, its eventual worldwide sales exceeding three million. "I don't think the British (success) surprised us so much, because we'd worked so hard... non-stop for 10 years and if you aren't going to do it by then, you never will," Wire later admitted, "(But), definitely in Europe it was a big surprise. Places like Finland and Sweden... I never thought we'd do that, really. I don't know why, I just think we were quite a difficult band in translation, lyrically. And you know, then going to Japan and selling 100,000 records over there and stuff. Even the Germans liked us..."

Artistically, it was a somewhat different matter, with several critics either cautious in their praise or bemoaning the group's continuing shift away from their vitriolic past to a more centrist, adult-orientated sound: "The serenity of the melodies, coupled with the epic build ups – not to mention James Dean Bradfield's increasingly Mercuryesque voice – bring Queen to mind on several occasions," wrote *Mojo*'s Sylvie Simmons. "Lyrically though, it couldn't be more different. As well as Nicky Wire's more personal and provocative lyrics, there are songs (of) disaster (and) the flooding of Welsh villages. The Manics remain a fine, if smoothed down rock band." *Uncut*'s Stephen Dalton took a decidedly more gloves off approach: "The Manics have always demanded special treatment, even before they earned it...(and) the climate of protective reverence that surrounds them can be off-putting. Too many excuses have been made in the past for graceless MOR bluster and feeble, sixth form lyrics." However, Dalton's review did soften before concluding: "But for all (their) flaws and contradictions, *This Is My Truth...* still feels like a work of fierce intelligence and principle... the first Manics opus of our education-slashing Blairite era sounds more than ever like a hymn to old Labour values: moralistic, class-conscious and, in its own way, conservative. For a guitar band to bring such topics to rock's increasingly bare ideological table without making arses of themselves is justification enough for their existence."

Having bathed in the critical equivalent of asses' milk since *Everything Must Go*, the Manics were aware a counter attack regarding their continuing artistic worth might be on the cards. "It doesn't take a genius," Wire confirmed at the time. "The British media loves knocking you down when you get successful. It was something we were prepared for, to be honest, (and) we understood it. I think Blur have experienced it just the same as we have. If you hang around long enough and get successful enough, people tend to give you a critical going over." There was also the fact that the group were now almost a decade away from their Beatle-slaying, slogan bearing origins and time – as much as anything else – might be responsible for wearing away some of those missing sharp edges. "We're less nihilistic and more constructive now," Nicky told *Q*'s Stuart Maconie. "That just comes with age." James was equally keen to point out that the group's new record came from a more reflective, less aggressive standpoint, with Celtic longing replacing more familiar barbs of anger: "*This Is My Truth...* is full of homespun wisdom. It has a certain melancholy that comes from the hills, calling you up from the ground to join it." For Sean, however, the equation was perhaps more simple still: the Manics, like many approaching their Thirties, had grown up and grown out, and if fans were still expecting blood and thunder, they were in for something of a disappointment. "We've become old and bloated," he told *The Face*. "Maybe to the record company, (that's) a problem – myself, I don't care. I suppose it's like cars. As you get older... you start moving towards the Volvos, practical boring greyish sorts of cars."

If accusations were beginning to fly that the group was becoming irrelevant in the ever-youthful seas of pop and rock, it certainly didn't hurt their ticket sales. After a warm up date in Cork's Opera House, the

Manics supported new stadium fillers The Verve at Slane Castle in Dublin on August 29, 1998, earning them another encore they chose not to perform. Post concert, Nicky Wire found himself deep in conversation with then Northern Ireland Secretary Mo Mowlam, who was impressed to meet a musician more familiar with the finer points of devolved power sharing than Madonna's latest chart position. Following several more Irish concerts, the band then took on a series of 'back to basics' shows at intimate venues across the UK such as Margate Winter Gardens and Hereford Leisure Centre before beginning their first European tour as headliners.

While zigzagging from Stockholm and Brussels to Dusseldorf and Barcelona, the Manics also found time to pick up a 'Best Band In The World Today' trophy at *Q* magazine's annual award ceremony, held at London's Intercontinental Hotel on October 30. Though the honour was considerable, embarrassment reigned for Nicky who found himself posing for photographs alongside R.E.M's Michael Stipe, the subject of one of his less logical and more offensive outbursts at the Kilburn National several years before. For Wire, any such pratfalls were now firmly in the past. "I've (trained) myself to watch my mouth," he told *NME*. "I used to look forward to interviews, use them as an opportunity to make a point, but now they're an opportunity to fuck up. It's a shame, but that's why I don't open my gob so much – the armour has been dented, the invincibility gone. And you've always got to think of Richey's family. You can't just think about being in a band any more."

Perhaps unavoidably, the return of the Manic Street Preachers to public duty also resulted in a new sighting of Richey Edwards. This time, he was allegedly spotted in the Underground Bar, a small pub in the small town of Corralejo on the Canary island of Fuerteventura. In a report first published by Tenerife's *Island Sun* newspaper, a British-born barmaid named Tracey Jones said that she and several of her customers became aware of a thin man keeping to himself at the back of the tavern. When one patron shouted "You're Richey from the Manic Street Preachers!" he bolted for the door and "within seconds... was gone". Jones later confirmed: "We were sure it was just like Richey." Picked up by the *South Wales Echo,* the story soon spread to the UK nationals with *The Daily Telegraph* and several other broadsheets taking an interest.

Again, the Manics' manager, Martin Hall, found himself pressed into making a statement on behalf of the band: "It seems very strange that all these sightings are in bars at night in high-profile holiday resorts. As far as we know, Interpol were involved when he first went missing and I don't think there was an application for another passport, so I don't know how Richey could have left the country. We just pass these sightings on to the police and let them get on with it, but this is all very upsetting for his parents." As ever, nothing more came of the incident, though Edwards' parents continued to assert their belief that he was still alive but just not wanting to be found. Like his fellow band members, James Dean Bradfield had now squared part of the circle regarding Richey's disappearance, the desire to move on firmly superseding the emotional paralysis of 1995. But he continued to feel for Edwards' family: "The only time I think it would be good for Richey to come back is for his parents and sister. But for us, I don't feel there's an answer there in him coming back, to be honest. If he hasn't needed to for this long – whatever he's done or whatever he's doing – it must be best for him. That's the way I feel about it."

To mark the end of 1998, the Manics once again set off on the road, this time concentrating their efforts on the UK alone. As their single 'The Everlasting' hit number 11 in the charts, the group played some of their biggest ever shows, starting at Bournemouth's INT centre on December 10 before heading to Glasgow, Newcastle and two concerts at London's Wembley Arena. The tour ended with a three-night stand at Cardiff International Arena from December 20-22, Welsh rising stars Catatonia again providing worthy support. In line with pre-existing tradition, James took a solo acoustic stroll though Wham's 'Last Christmas' before the band re-joined him for a surprise burst of 'Revol' to mark Richey's 31st birthday. Some in attendance didn't actually recognise the song.

Though the Manics were approaching household name status, their tunes as likely to be whistled on building sites as played on obscure radio stations, it seemed to bring them little public joy. In an uncharacteristically drunken interview with *The Face*, Nicky admitted that he had never expected "success would avalanche into some kind of mediocrity", and it was privately rumoured that the group had been as artistically disappointed by *This Is My Truth...* as some of their critics.

Moore seemed to sum up the malaise behind the multi-platinum sales: "Basically we're an experiment gone wrong," he told Q. "Which, I suppose in a way, we are. We were going to do one album and split up, and as time's gone on we've become this five-album thirty-something everything-that-we-didn't-want-to-be (band). That's the thing. We feel, personally to ourselves, that we have kind of spoiled it. However much we still enjoy what we do and people still enjoy listening to us, there's always that thing in the back of your mind that you think, 'It didn't quite go right, did it?"'

But as the next 12 months came to show, it hadn't gone that wrong either.

Chapter Nineteen

A Sort Of Homecoming

As with *Everything Must Go*, the Manic Street Preachers had to duck low to avoid being hit by all the platitudes thrown at them for *This Is My Truth Tell Me Yours*. On January 25, 1999, the group picked up six trophies in all at the *NME* Premier Awards, including 'Best Band', 'Best Album', 'Best Single' and 'Best Video' for 'If You Tolerate This...'. To illustrate that Nicky Wire had finally won the hearts of the record buying public after several early attempts to alienate them completely, the bassist also took away 'Pop Personality's Brain That Should Be Kept For Posterity' and 'Pop Personality You Would Like Most For Prime Minister'. To keep his size 11 shoes firmly on the ground, *Melody Maker's* readers awarded Wire 'Fool Of The Year' and 'Unsexiest Man' in its annual poll, though he also received a nod for 'Man Of The Year' in honour of his other good works. Away from all the humour, Richey Edwards was voted 'Most Sadly Missed' person by the rock weekly's subscribers.

Another month and yet another honour. Repeating their success of two years before, the Manics took to the stage at the 1999 Brit Awards to receive industry nods for 'Best British Group' and 'Best Album'. This time comprehensive schools were off the agenda in their acceptance speech, though Wire displayed an impressive command of the skipping rope as he bounced up and down between jumps while James sang the band's thanks in mock opera tones. The theme of history repeating itself also followed them to the Mercury Prize, where they again failed to win, being beaten this time by Talvin Singh's mellifluous release, *OK*. Yet, if there was embarrassment amid all the plaudits, and a sense that they might have strayed far from their original attentions, the trio were in no hurry to give it all up in favour of obscurity: "I want to stay as big as we are," Bradfield told *NME*, "as long as we never become cowards, intellectually or artistically. We've been inept sometimes in the past, never quite walked it like we talked it, but we've never been cowards."

Nor greatly affected by stage fright, as it turned out. Seldom off the road for much of 1999, the Manics began their world-hopping itinerary in Australia, playing several dates at Sydney's RAS Showgrounds and Melbourne's Big Day Out, among others throughout January. For Wire, this was another victory of sorts, his fear of flying having precluded the band from venturing to the Antipodes until then. Keen to re-acquaint themselves with the Japanese fans, who pushed *This Is My Truth...* into their Top 10, the Manics then appeared at Osaka's Zepp arena and Toyko's Akasaka Blitz before returning to Europe for a comprehensive tour lasting until late March. Back on the road two months later for the summer season, the group plied their wares at Holland's Pink Pop gathering before everything literally threatened to go down the toilet at the 1999 Glastonbury festival.

In an apparent break with their socialist leanings, the Manics allegedly commandeered a Portaloo for their own private use backstage, placing a sign on it that read: "These facilities are reserved exclusively for the Manic Street Preachers. Please respect this. Thank you." Given that said toilets were like proverbial gold dust at the site, such an apparent abuse of power didn't long escape the notice of left-leaning folk journeyman Billy Bragg, who quickly alerted others to the slight. Soon, the insults were reportedly being traded between both camps: "That's a nice socialist gesture, lads..." said an aggrieved Bragg, while Nicky struck back a little harder: "I wouldn't let him piss in my toilet for all the money in the world. Get back to the army you dickhead, and stop stealing Woody Guthrie songs."

Within hours, the argument had quietened down and all four were on speaking terms again, but not before *The Sun* and several other tabloids had picked up on the story. Years later, Wire still saw the funny side of it all: "It made me feel quite good, actually. It was a typical sort of old-style Manics thing that showed how easily people are still wound up. So I just thought it was hilarious. If you'd seen the toilets at Glastonbury, you'd know what I mean. If we'd done that in 1992, I think the press would've probably loved it. I'd said and done a lot worse things than that. Because now you kind of feel like it's a bourgeoisie, giant rock band thing. But, you know, it was all good fun."

Away from the constant gigging, the Manics somehow found time to reactivate their interest in collaborative work. James Dean Bradfield had accepted an invitation from legendary Welshman Tom Jones to contribute to *Reload*, an album of cover versions and duets specifically chosen to again place the barrel-chested singer at the centre of the pop market. Joining the likes of The Pretenders, Van Morrison and fellow Welsh acts Catatonia and Stereophonics, Bradfield traded vocal licks with Jones on a fine rendition of Elvis Presley's old standard, 'I'm Left, You're Right, She's Gone'. The star turns and canny song choices on *Reload* worked a treat, putting Tom Jones back at the top of the UK charts for the first time in 30 years when the record was released on September 16, 1999. Earlier in the year, Bradfield had also lent his talents to a benefit concert in aid of Kosovo organised by Nicky's brother, Patrick Jones, at the Blackwood Miners' Institute. Sharing the stage with another old school Welsh celebrity, comedian and folk singer Max Boyce, Bradfield later donated one of the Manics' platinum discs with signed original artwork to the appeal. The Jones/Bradfield connection didn't end there. Now something of a cult artist in his own right, Patrick Jones had temporarily put aside writing plays to record *Commemoration And Amnesia*, a collection of poetry set to music. In a show of solidarity with his friend, James wrote accompanying tunes for two pieces – the title track and 'The Guerilla Tapestry'. Not to be outdone, Nicky also contributed to his sibling's project, airing many a thought on Welsh identity across the track 'Hiraeth', a phrase loosely translated as 'romantic longing or connection' to the land of Wales and its people.

Though they had tried to escape its connotations, rubbish its language and assassinate its character in their earliest incarnation, the Manic Street Preachers had never quite escaped the shadow of Wales. Nor had they been particularly convincing in their apparent dislike of the country either, the band's scathing attacks on Blackwood and it surrounding areas coming across more like punk-approved teenage petulance than genuine adult spite. This fact was only strengthened with the passage of time, as Nicky Wire began making several positive noises about his birthplace, and often telling the press he wished he could stay there forever. In 1993 he took positive action on this matter, returning to Blackwood for his marriage ceremony before settling down with his new bride in nearby Wattsville, just three or some miles up the road. Even Richey Edwards – possibly the most vitriolic of the quartet regarding Wales' worth – had considerably quietened his criticisms, buying a flat in Cardiff two years before disappearing into thin air on the Severn Bridge, a matter of miles from his childhood home.

Following their return to the spotlight, the Manics had become increasingly associated with Wales and Welshness, Nicky flying the Red Dragon on his amps and wearing it across his back when picking up the group's first Brit award in 1997. The band had also championed new Welsh talent by using the support slot on their tours to draw attention to the likes of Super Furry Animals, Catatonia and Stereophonics. In turn, those acts had taken their opportunity and run with it, all gaining artistic credibility and chart success as the Nineties drew to a close. At the same time, a growing sense of pride was evident in the young Welsh, now as keen to celebrate their heritage as their predecessors had been to denounce it. This forward momentum was no doubt driven by a national referendum in 1997, which led to certain powers being devolved from Whitehall and the creation of the National Assembly of Wales. As the country took possession of its budgets, and concentrated on attracting new industry, the horrors of the miners' strike and the mass unemployment that followed it seemed forever consigned to the past. Valley girls, valley boys, all wrapped up in the spirit of 'Cool Cymru'. And at the heart of this youthful revivalism were the Manics: prodigal sons once seemingly content to spit in the face of their birthright, they were now at the forefront of a new, internationally successful form of Welshness, flying its flag, giving it shape.

Even if it seemed a little implausible to foist the Manics upon the shoulders of Owain Glyndwr, William Price and Aneurin Bevan just yet, there was no denying that the band had recently done much to promote Wales' newfound cultural confidence. Opening doors for other acts to follow, speaking intelligently of the problems the country faced in interviews and song, the Manic Street Preachers had come – willingly or not – to a point where they *were* the poster boys for new Welshness. Or at least the Welsh Tourist Board (WTB) certainly thought so. In a turn of events one would have deemed almost impossible in 1991, the WTB had begun proudly using the Sonic Stealth Brothers' remix of 'A Design For Life' to promote Wales as a tourist destination, its soothing qualities a perfect advertisement for the green, green grass of home. "Yes, the first Manics album was full of polemical power," said Tourist Board official Robin Gwyn at the time, "but when you're 28, you have different concerns than you did at 18. So you tend to reassess what you think of certain issues. And (the group's) later output has certainly been useful in marketing Wales, because it's more amenable to a wider demographic."

The Manic Street Preachers' natural place in Wales' national ascendancy was rubber stamped when the band returned from another disappointingly short American tour to headline Cardiff's Wales Millennium Stadium on December 31, 1999. A huge, imposing venue that had only fully opened its doors to the public some 11 months before, the Millennium Stadium was the UK's largest indoor venue at the time, and capable of holding over 60,000 people. For Bradfield, the location, if not the stadium itself, brought back some familiar memories: "Right across the road from the Stadium was this old venue, The Square Club (now closed), which we played in 1989. The only people in the audience that night were Richey's sister and our manager. And now there we were, playing in front of 65,000 people... amazing." The event, nicknamed 'Manic Millennium' was opened by a poetry reading from Patrick Jones, before support acts Shack, Feeder and Super Furry Animals further warmed up the crowd. Shortly before the main attraction took the stage, a video of Welsh pop stars, icons and politicians was played, with the likes of Tom Jones, Shirley Bassey and Charlotte Church trading goodwill messages alongside Arthur Scargill, Max Boyce and John Cale. Preamble over, the lights then duly dimmed and the Manics nailed themselves to history.

On the night, they were quite magnificent. Nicky, all pink mini skirt, eyeliner and 'Culture Slut' top appeared transported by the occasion, while James and Sean held the company line with a procession of whirling dervish poses, slashing barre chords and precision drumming. Kicking off proceedings with new anthem in the making 'You Stole The Sun From My Heart', the group saw their way through 14 songs until midnight, when they took a brief pause to see in the new century. Then it was eight more tunes of the highest quality. To their credit, the Manics didn't just stick with the hits. Among the likes of 'Motorcycle Emptiness', 'Everything Must Go' and 'If You Tolerate This...', space was found for lesser known gems such as 'Faster', 'Of Walking Abortion' and 'Stay Beautiful'. In a moving tribute, Bradfield also dedicated his solo version of 'Small Black Flowers That Grow In The Sky' to an absent Richey Edwards: "The best and coolest companion of the decade..." Two or so hours after they began, the group ended proceedings with an inevitable 'A Design For Life', as James issued one of the great backhanded (and very Welsh) compliments of his career to the assembled throng: "Cardiff, the most beautiful place in the world, for tonight at least." At with that, and a bit of amp and instrument smashing from Nicky, they were gone.

A career-defining performance, attended by all the band's families – including Richey's parents and sister – the 'Manic Millennium' was the closest the group had come yet to fulfilling the terms of their original manifesto. That fact was not lost on Nicky Wire: "We sold 60,000 tickets on our own, without announcing who else was on the bill," he said after the event. "I still haven't got over it. James was up till 10 the next morning. I stayed up until five... through nervous excitement, really. We kind of said we'd do (this) 10 years ago and everyone laughed at us then." To ensure the event was ably captured for posterity, the band filmed their Cardiff appearance and released it on DVD under the rather apt title *Leaving The 2Oth Century* some months later.

For most groups, headlining an event the size and grandeur of Cardiff's Millennium Stadium in front of their home crowd would have been a fitting and spectacular end to a career. But the Manic Street Preachers, in no mood to stop, were after yet another small entry in the record books by stealing away with the first UK number one single of the new millennium. The track they chose to do it was 'The Masses Against The Classes', a raucous, overdriven mid-tempo stomper that borrowed as much from The Beatles' 'Twist And Shout' as it did from the Manics' own Beatles-baiting 'Motown Junk'. Beginning with the taped voice of rogue philosopher Noam Chomsky hacking into government's role in perpetuating a capitalist-driven housing market, 'The Masses...' ended with Bradfield howling a line from Albert Camus' famous absurdist novel, *The Outsider*: "A slave begins by demanding justice and ends by wanting to wear a crown."

In between all the vintage sloganeering, listeners were treated to a Nicky Wire lyric not entirely dissimilar to 'A Design For Life' in its simultaneous celebration and mourning of the working man's plight while James stirred things up musically with a dishevelled, but pleasing guitar solo. Like 'If You Tolerate This...' and *This Is My Truth...*, Wire had liberated the song's title from another politically-themed source, this time approximating 19th century Liberal Prime Minister William Gladstone's famous quote for the Manics' own purposes: "All the world over, I will back the masses against the classes." As these things went, 'Masses Against...' wasn't a bad attempt at re-activating the sounds of the band's agit-punk heyday, especially if one took into account its spare production values, courtesy of Dave Eringa. However, the song was no 'Faster', nor even on a par with 'Slash N' Burn'. That said, it was up against Boyzone for the top spot, so deserved a shot at the title on moral grounds alone.

The campaign for getting the Manics their second number one was a clever one. Eschewing obvious promotion angles, the band chose to do little advance publicity other than to confirm 'Masses Against...' was a 'stand alone' track that would not appear on their forthcoming album. Their record company also made clear that the single was to be deleted from wholesale supply on the day of its release, meaning that fans had an extremely compressed timescale in which to buy it. Two strong reasons then, to get down to the shops before it disappeared. Released on January 10, 2000 in a cover sleeve that featured the Cuban flag (minus its single white star), 'Masses Against...' was backed by a so-so cover of Chuck Berry's self-defining 'Rock And Roll Music' and a fine new composition, the moody 'Close My Eyes'. A week and 35,000 sales later, it was also top of the charts.

"We had a ball making 'Masses Against The Classes'," Nicky confirmed on hearing the good news. "We did it really quick, all three takes were just bashed out. Blur did (the 'stand alone' single with) 'Popscene', Oasis did it with 'Whatever' and The Beatles also did it. All the best bands did it, so we wanted to do it."

A grand end to one millennium and a capital start made to another, the Manic Street Preachers had few battles left to win following the one/two punch of Cardiff and 'Masses Against The Classes': "After the Cardiff gig," Wire later admitted, "we thought that we just couldn't do any better in terms of scale and size, so we started thinking about what we might do in a different way." Taking their victories where they found them, the band wisely left the front line to others throughout the year 2000 to pursue what "different" actually meant. The results were decidedly mixed.

Chapter Twenty

Know Your Limits

As the Manics temporarily left the public arena to contemplate the future, a terribly sad reminder of past events was published in *The Sunday Mirror on* February 20, 2000. In an effort to prompt her absent son's return or at least gain some information about his possible whereabouts, Sherry Edwards had written an open letter to Richey. Its contents were at times heartbreaking to read: "Dear Richard, we all love and miss you so much and you are never out of our thoughts. I worry about you constantly, not knowing where you are and how you are keeping. I am scared that your decision to disappear like that has made you feel that you can never come back. We all want to tell you that's not true. We don't care where you went or why you did it... to see you walk through our door or even hear your voice again would make me the happiest person in the world.... you are my precious son and I will never give up looking for you. All my love as always, Mum."

As the letter confirmed, though it had now been five years since Richey's disappearance the Edwards family were still suffering the effects of his loss, but remained hopeful he might return: "We have to face the possibility that he may be dead, but until we know for certain what has happened we will always stay hopeful that Richard is alive," Sherry Edwards told the newspaper. "Once you give up hope, you have reached the end. None of us really knows what happened to my son. He could be anywhere, doing anything, but each day is as torturous as the last." As before, while the *Sunday Mirror* piece again generated interest in the Edwards' cause, no firm leads were established.

With *This Is My Truth Tell Me Yours* selling over three million copies worldwide, one might have thought the Manic Street Preachers would be ecstatic with their musical lot. But as Nicky Wire admitted, the band had "gone off ourselves a bit" in the final stages of making the album, becoming uncharacteristically bored with the labours of recording. The remedy for this situation was 'Masses Against The Classes'. A stark return to first principles, it dispensed with their recent fondness for clever melodic structures and peculiar instrumentation in favour of a back-to-basics approach: raw guitars, shouty vocals, politics up front and centre, and all over in three minutes or thereabouts. To even their surprise the gamble had paid dividends, putting them back at number one with a song that would have sat well on *Generation Terrorists*. Moreover, the Manics had enjoyed themselves while cutting the single, the opportunity to commit their sound to tape in three minutes rather than three months a thrilling reminder of how things used to be before it all got very complicated indeed. "You know," Wire admitted, "I just think it was time to get bloody minded again."

Eager to capitalize on that feeling, the group played around with various ideas at Monmouthshire's Valley Studios in November 1999 during downtime before their historic Cardiff stadium gig. Yet work began in earnest during the summer of 2000 when the Manics flew to El Cortijo Studios in Southern Andalucia, Spain. A beautiful secluded location, deep within Ronda National Park but also close to the cities of Granada and Seville, El Cortijo's villa-like splendour boasted a swimming pool, several bedrooms and recording facilities offering views of the surrounding green hills. Evidently, if the group were keen to return to their roots, they were determined to do it with suntans. In a break with recent tradition, overrehearsing new material was actively discouraged, the trio limiting themselves to five takes per song before moving on to something else. "No rehearsing things to death," Wire later said. "We really wanted to retain the rough edges." In this way, the Manics kept their creative juices flowing, the onus on spontaneity rather than careful planning. For inspiration, Nicky returned to *The*

Holy Bible, hoping to channel some of the honesty and invention present in Richey Edwards' words. Filling endless sides of A4 with ideas, Wire finally began to feel he had made the breakthrough he was seeking. "Lyrically," he later told *NME*, "I caught up with Richey. I can now stand on my own two feet."

This relaxed, but equally clipped approach seemed to work for the group, though James' fondness for recording at odd hours began to wear on Nicky after a while: "He went to bed in American time zones. We'd be getting up at seven in the morning and James would just be going to sleep. It was like he was living in New York. I don't know, he just does these bizarre hours. There I'd be, heading off to bed early, and he'd be keeping me up with these bloody guitar chords." Despite such small glitches, within the space of just six weeks they had amassed 16 songs – all of which they felt were worthy of release. Though their devotion to capturing the moment had served them well, there was still the need to add some finishing touches in order to make the material shine. Their business concluded in Spain, the Manics and their producer – the now omnipresent Dave Eringa – returned to London's Abbey Road Studios to tweak, mix then master the final product. By January 2001, the album was ready for release and Wire was talking up its title: "It's called 'Know Your Enemy' and the 'Enemy' is what we had let ourselves become."

One of Nicky's recurrent interests when working on the words to the Manics' forthcoming record had been past and present events in Cuba. From a historical standpoint, Wire had been drawn to the infamous Bay of Pigs invasion of 1961, when the United States made an ill-advised and completely unsuccessful attempt to overthrow communist dictator Fidel Castro. Raising a small army of Cuban exiles living mostly in Miami, US military operatives had trained them in infantry and guerrilla tactics before aiding their assault on Cuba's Playa Giron ('Bay of Pigs') beach. Already aware of the supposedly secret plan, forces under the leadership of Castro took just three days to defeat the invading forces, leading to major embarrassment for America's new president, John F. Kennedy, and stronger ties between Cuba and the Eastern bloc. A more recent preoccupation for Nicky had been the plight of Elian Gonzalez, a six year old Cuban boy who left the country in a small aluminium boat with his mother and 12 others to seek asylum in the US. The vessel faltered and most of the passengers, including Elian's mother, were lost at sea. After floating in rubber tubes for hours, the young Gonzalez and two other survivors were rescued by fishermen and brought to live with family in Miami.

When Elian's father became aware of what happened, he demanded that his son be returned home. The subsequent custody battle involving US and Cuban authorities ballooned into something approaching an international incident before the child was finally returned to his native land in June 2000. Taken with Gonzalez's story, Wire fashioned the lyric 'Baby Elian', a withering analysis of US political opportunism in the face of simple human lives that Bradfield set to a contemplative, New Order-like melody.

Nicky's Cuban fascinations became reality when it was announced to the media that the Manic Street Preachers would mark their return to live performance with a special one-off concert at Havana's Karl Marx Theatre on February 17, 2001. This event would also mark the release of the group's new album. Even with a proven track record for stirring up controversy, this was new ground for the Manics, their planned appearance representing the first time a Western rock band would play in the communist republic of Cuba – a country reported to have outlawed such displays lest they provoke civil disorder. "We were just going out there to play a gig," Moore later said, "but in a strange way, it escalated into a diplomatic visit." He wasn't wrong.

Planning for the Manics' visit to Havana had actually begun months earlier, when manager Martin Hall visited the city to talk things through with the Cuban Ministry of Culture. Reportedly underlining the group's friendship with Arthur Scargill and continuing support of socialist principles, Hall received cautiously optimistic noises from Cuba's officials, though they wished to investigate the Manics' reputation a little further. "They were extremely helpful," Hall told *NME*. "We gave them some records and videos and they were totally up for it. Then they saw Nick in a dress and they were like, 'But he won't play wearing a dress, will he?' I said 'He's The Wire. He does what he does." It was the first indication that the band were now venturing into an entirely different political realm, but Nicky (who had thought up the idea for the visit) was more than willing to forgo the mini-skirts for the greater good.

After some more negotiation, the concert was agreed with permission even granted to film proceedings for a future DVD release.

Accompanied by several cameramen, a small army of journalists, one or two senior record company executives and their wily manager, the Manics arrived in Cuba some three days before their Havana appearance. During this period, the group met with cultural representatives, filmed sections for their documentary/concert film and held a round of press conferences and various interviews. For some writers present, the band venturing to Cuba was an obvious display of solidarity with a communist republic that had repeatedly fallen out with its American capitalist neighbour only 180 miles away. Wire wasn't in the mood to dodge such assertions. "Cuba has been a major influence on me," he said. "This is not a student Che Guevara (poster on the wall) thing. Cuba... is the last great symbol that really fights against the Americanisation of the world. It's the nearest thing on the planet to a true socialist state."

Perhaps, but there were other, less pleasant, rumours floating around about Cuba's domestic policy: frequent human rights abuses, 'behaviour modification' for homosexuals, extrajudicial executions, not to mention the thousands who risked their lives each year in perilous seagoing journeys to escape the country for the shores of the US. Again, Nicky was firing on all thrusters: "Do you really think I don't know about (such things)? Every sad *Lonely Planet* cunt... believes that every Cuban they see gazes at the Gulf of Mexico wishing they were on a boat. If that were true, there wouldn't be anyone here, would there?" While Wire defended the Manics' motivations for visiting Cuba, Bradfield fretted over their forthcoming performance, wondering out loud who might actually be attending: "I have no idea who's coming to the gig," he again confessed to *NME*. "It could be a load of international journalists and some government officials. It could be two Cuban kids and a dog... we just don't know."

The answer came on February 17, when some 15 minutes before show time at the Karl Marx Theatre, Cuba's Minister of Culture presented himself in the Manics' dressing room with the question: "Would you like to meet someone very, very important?" Answering nervously in the affirmative, the band – plus photographers, reporters and anyone else who could keep up – were ushered down several corridors before coming face to face with Fidel Castro, revolutionary, autocrat, fearless leader and 20th century icon; the scourge of America, the man who bested Kennedy, and by the looks of it, a dab hand at photo opportunities too. Though 74 years old at the time, Castro was still bushy of beard and full of life, introducing himself to Nicky and co. in a blaze of helicopter arms and firm handshakes. Addressing the trio in Spanish via an interpreter – Castro was fluent in English, but refused to speak the language for 'ideological' reasons – the President explained that due to a prior engagement, he had to leave at 10 p.m. sharp. But should the group start a little early, he could see their performance. In a well-publicised exchange, Wire pointed out that "It might be a bit noisy."

Without missing a beat, Castro shot straight back: "I will try and adapt my ears to the noise. It cannot be '*louder than war*', can it?" Within seconds, the Manics had been provided with the title of their DVD, and would now be running on 'Castro Time' until they left the country several days later.

The one thing the Manics agreed on regarding their Cuba experience was the Karl Marx gig was one of the highlights of their career. "The concert itself was absolutely brilliant," Bradfield later confirmed. "[There were] 5,000 people going for it without really knowing anything about us at all. It was like a Seventies gig. The Eagles or something. Everybody was standing in their seats, clapping, screaming. Just... mega." Performing against the backdrop of a huge Cuban flag, though Nicky still managed to fly the Welsh Red Dragon on his amp, the band played an excellent set to a baying crowd who paid just 17 pence each for the privilege. Drawing on five albums' worth of material, and throwing in several new songs for good measure, the Manics gave Cuba a taste of 'Motorcycle Emptiness', 'You Love Us' and 'A Design For Life' alongside forthcoming singles 'Found That Soul' and 'So Why So Sad'. Two tunes in particular drew large applause: a strident version of 'Kevin Carter' was further enhanced by the presence of local trumpeter Yazek, who lit a fuse to Sean's original melody line, while James' acoustic rendition of 'Baby Elian' was predictably cheered to the rafters. Even President Castro, who professed a fondness for the song's lyrics while talking to the group backstage, was moved to rise from his second floor seat and join in the clapping as Bradfield strummed the final chords. Ending the night with Chuck Berry's 'Rock And Roll Music', the Manics left the stage full of glee. "It was absolutely monumental," chirped Wire. "Some bands go to Downing Street to meet the PM. We go to Cuba and Castro turns up." Nicky should have taken it as a sign.

The following morning, the Manics again found themselves communing with the Cuban President as he asked them to attend the opening of a university with him. Yet more official engagements loomed. "Castro had said 'You must visit the country with me,'" James later confirmed, "And we said 'But we'll miss our flight'. He replied, 'We will hold the plane'". As the Ministry of Culture further extended its courtesies, Nicky and Sean were duly invited to meet Elian Gonzalez himself. While the honour was considerable, the band felt that things were slipping away from them and into the hands of Cuban press officers. "We didn't actually go there to meet Fidel Castro or meet Elian and go to his school," Sean reiterated. "We just went to Cuba to play a concert."

Bradfield was also beginning to feel the same way: "When Castro actually turned up, we were absolutely flabbergasted. Then, he just kept turning up and we felt a little bit inside the publicity machine. I loved the experience, though." Even Wire, the mastermind behind the Cuba visit and the most publically supportive of the country's principles had his doubts by the end: "We really enjoyed the first five days, but as for the last two days or so... we kind of felt like we were being corralled into something."

When the Manics finally left Cuba for home on February 21, they must have been dealing with mixed emotions. On the positive side, Castro had opened many doors for the band – even personally complimenting Nicky with the words "You must know a lot about Cuba" in reference to his lyrics for 'Baby Elian'. Sean too had many reasons to enjoy the trip, feeling comfortable among the people and the places he saw: "I'd have been happy to have stayed there for a couple of months." Yet, there was also the feeling that the experience had been partially soured by losing control to a propaganda machine far bigger than the one that surrounded a multi-platinum band. "In the end," reasoned Wire, "it became a mutual contract. He got what (he needed) out of it. We got a DVD. But Castro was very charming, very witty and very charismatic. I guess we wanted an adventure and went there with no preconceptions. We visited Cuba before making any statements, and it remains a country worth visiting."

As time went by, the band increasingly distanced themselves from the trip, sometimes almost grimacing at the memory. "We knew we'd draw praise and condemnation in equal measure and it was always going to be a very complicated experience," said James. "With benefit of hindsight, you could call it 'Manic Street Folly'". Nicky seemed even more disappointed, worried that by meeting with Castro, there were some that might feel that the group were condoning "all his bad policies over the years". However, when the mood struck him, Wire was still capable of tapping into his vintage 'Generation Terrorist' persona when it came to throwing sticks at Castro's mortal enemy: "Whatever you might think, the good thing about Cuba is it's still untouched. And it hasn't got any fat Americans in stupid shirts looking really ugly..."

Whether the Manics' Cuban folly was a publicity stunt gone awry, a two fingered salute to the US following years of being commercially ignored by that market or simply a brave attempt to reinvigorate their political principles didn't really matter at the time. Of greater concern was the imminent release of new product in the UK. In another novel marketing campaign, the group had elected to put out two singles, 'Found That Soul' and 'So Why So Sad', simultaneously on February 26 as a taster for their forthcoming album. In the case of 'Found That Soul', the Manics were still clearly indebted to the same muse that had helped shape 'Masses Against The Classes', the song a raucous, guitar driven slice of pop-punk that vaguely recalled Nirvana's classic 'On A Plain'. "Actually," said Wire, "we were after an Iggy & The Stooges vibe."

The video that accompanied the track was also an extremely straightforward affair. Made on a budget of just £5,000, the band were filmed in 'night vision' at London Zoo's Nocturnal House, a cast of bats and big-eyed sloths darting in and out of frame as Bradfield, Wire and Moore worked away in the dark. To add a little more artfulness, a host of Manics fans appeared reading their favourite books throughout the clip, with Graham Greene's *Brighton Rock*, Danny Sugerman's *The Days Of Guns N' Roses*... and Noam Chomsky's *The Common Good* all receiving some free promotion.

On the other hand, 'So Why So Sad' appeared to directly channel the spirit of the Beach Boys, its myriad vocal harmonies and twisting, carousel-like keyboard melody a clear homage to the work of Brian

Wilson. "'So Why...'s just about the idea of being disconnected or insulated from what's going on around you," Wire explained at the time. Unlike 'Found That Soul', no expense had been spared on the video for this song, as dozens of extras dressed as soldiers and holiday makers fought battles and drank cocktails on a sunny beach while the Manics looked on dejectedly from the luxury of a cliff-side house. The promo was meant to draw attention to how youth now takes its freedom for granted, enjoying themselves in the very locations where only 60 years before wars were being waged in pursuit of freedom. Again, it was all very artful, but unless one possessed a Masters' degree in European film studies, the clip was more likely to cause vigorous scratching of the head than create any great understanding of what the band were actually trying to say. By releasing both singles on the same day, the Manic Street Preachers ensured that neither track reached number one, their audience split right down the middle as to which one to buy first. In the end, only 200 sales actually separated the two with 'So Why So Sad' debuting on the charts at number eight while 'Found That Soul' trailed just a place behind. "If we'd just released one single, it would have probably got to number three," said Wire. "When you've had two huge albums already, it's impossible to sustain that level of popularity."

It seemed that sustaining quality might also have been something of an issue for the Manics as their sixth album, *Know Your Enemy*, proved when released on March 19, 2001. Drawing its title from a saying found within the Chinese military strategist Sun Tzu's ancient book, *The Art Of War*, *Know Your Enemy* was a sprawling, hit or miss affair, embracing several music styles but proving proficient in only two or three. When the band played hard – as with 'Found That Soul', 'Intravenous Agnostic', 'Dead Martyrs' and 'Freedom Of Speech Won't Feed My Children' – they were almost impossible to beat, the sheer sonic thump of these tracks as good as anything present on *The Holy Bible*. This fact was underlined by some top notch instrumental performances, with Moore and Wire finding new life among all the power chords while Bradfield extended his guitar vocabulary to include the sound of crashing cars, alien probes and DJs scratching their turntables into oblivion. One also couldn't fault the band's continued abilities in spotting a good tune, the likes of 'Ocean Spray' and 'Let Robeson Sing' both big on melody and strong in chorus. Yet, the misfires were many and varied. 'The Year Of Putrification' betrayed its stomach-wrenching title by sounding like a weak R.E.M. outtake, all jangly 12 strings and anaemic percussion. 'The Convalescent' was just as disappointing, fusing the power of The Clash to a meandering New Order song. 'My Guernica' proved little better, the Manics unsure whether they wanted to be Sonic Youth, Nirvana or *The Game* period Queen before just giving up altogether.

Then there was 'Miss Europa Disco Dancer' and 'Wattsville Blues'. In the case of the former, the Manic Street Preachers had found their inner 'Bee Gee', producing a sugar coated dance pastiche that ended with Wire lambasting the hollow nature of the club scene: "Brain dead motherfuckers..." Regrettably, the spoof was so brilliantly rendered, the only audience likely to engage with it were the very ones being insulted. No doubt, several years before the group could have presented 'Miss Europa...' to Kylie Minogue for consideration. But being a clever type, she would have probably handed it right back. With 'Wattsville Blues', Nicky actually stepped up to the microphone himself, making his album debut as a 'singer' (Wire's first lead vocal actually appeared on the witty 'Ballad Of The Bangkok Novotel', the B-side to 'Found That Soul'). An ode to never wanting to leave his new home town, and therefore little more than a thematic continuation of *This Is My Truth's...* 'My Little Empire', 'Wattsville Blues' was melodically weak as a kitten. Worse, unlike James Dean Bradfield, whose voice had matured into one of the finest of British rock music in recent years, Nicky Wire was no Bono or Freddie Mercury. Instead, he more resembled an asthmatic Lou Reed, without benefit of the New York miserablist's tonal character or withering delivery: "The way 'Wattsville Blues' and 'Miss Europa Disco Dancer' were written and constructed was completely new for us," James later said. Perhaps, but they were both best given a wide berth.

On the positive side, Wire's lyricism had continued to improve – becoming sharper in its targeting, more humanist in its outlook. And even if one didn't quite share his endless sneering at all things American, it had to be said he remained an impressive force when turning a spotlight upon the country's shortcomings. As already evidenced, 'Baby Elian' was a strong attempt to bring about an understanding of the cynical and opportunist forces making political capital from a very human drama. 'Let

Robeson Sing' was another gallant effort, recalling the black American concert singer, actor and civil rights activist Paul Robeson's eight-year struggle to have his passport reinstated by the US State Department.

Still on the American-bashing trail, 'Freedom Of Speech Won't Feed My Children' took issue with forcing US notions of liberty on countries best left to their own devices several years before it became fashionable to do so. It was certainly a lyric Nicky was keen to refer back to in 2005 as the Iraq war still smouldered on. "Unfortunately, it was four years before every fucker got interested in politics," he told *The Scotsman*. "It took everyone a war. Where have these people been the last four years? Forty years? American foreign policy's never changed. The track 'Freedom Of Speech Won't Feed My Children' on *Know Your Enemy* says everything we ever needed to say on that subject."

However, Wire also had a tendency at times to be oblique and intellectually impenetrable. 'My Guernica', for instance, was meant to draw attention to the possibilities art offered in making a political statement. But aside from its title – a reference to Picasso's famous painting depicting the atrocities of the Spanish Civil War – lines such as "The mirror man has seen defeat, hide away, be old and grey" made it difficult to follow Nicky's train of thought. It was the same with 'His Last Painting', a lyric that played with religious imagery and feelings of torment, but beyond that seemed reluctant to reveal its true meaning. Given that Wire had already acknowledged his close study of *The Holy Bible*'s wordplay while writing for *Know Your Enemy*, some critics were quick to draw (often negative) comparisons between him and Richey Edwards – inferring that Nicky was either trying too hard to be clever or just copying his absent friend. It was a charge that irritated him, provoking an onstage outburst at the Manchester Apollo later in 2001: "It's just because I'm more intelligent than you, that's all," he shouted to journalists covering the show, "and you want to fuck me, but you can't..."

Realistically, certain similarities between the two were hard to deny, with 'The Convalescent' featuring a couplet that could have come straight from the pen of Edwards: "Klaus Kinski with love off Werner Herzog... scream until the war is over, Srebrenica cousin of Treblinka." But where Wire essentially differed from Richey was in his continued sense of optimism and use of first person grammar to establish an emotional link with the listener. It was a technique that served him well in the opening stanza to 'So Why So Sad': "Things get clear when I feel free, whatever next comes easily, when gentle hands give life to me, when your eyes fill with tiny tears when I'm this still, you are my life..."

For the first time, Nicky Wire also had genuine competition when it came to writing lyrics for the Manic Street Preachers, as James Dean Bradfield broke a decade long silence with the gently affecting words to 'Ocean Spray'. Bradfield had written the song in memory of his mother, Sue, who had passed away in 1999 following a seven-year battle with cancer: "When you're very ill and you've had lots of operations," he later told *Q*, "they always make you drink lots of cranberry juice. It's one of the best things to keep infection away. My mother was in the hospital every day and she would say 'Can you get me some Ocean Spray?'... the fact that she was so obsessed with drinking it showed me how much spirit she had left, that she put so much faith in something so small, that drinking cranberry juice would keep her alive. It inspired me... in the face of something which is so devastating." A sincere recollection of a troubling time in his life, 'Ocean Spray' managed to convey both the intensity of emotion and sense of removal one feels when facing the death of a parent: "When bad events happen in your life," James acknowledged, "you feel disconnected from them. It's almost as if real life slows down."

As *Know Your Enemy* ended with a 'hidden' bonus track – an extremely faithful cover of McCarthy's jangly 'We Are Bourgeois Now' – it was clear enough that the Manics had made a real effort to challenge the constrictions of the sound that had recently brought them widespread fame. Obviously uncomfortable with the softer, immaculately produced hues present on *This Is My Truth...*, they had striven to create a tougher, less polished album, one that 'felt right' rather than just ticking the right boxes. "*Know Your Enemy* was about getting back to our roots," Wire later admitted. "Everyone eventually gets to the point where they want to understand why they started something in the first place, and we wanted to get our anger and passion back." Bradfield was equally dogged about the album's appeal, putting its contents up there with the very best of the band's previous work. "It's a much more instinctive record with a much harder edge and production (left) at a minimum. It could be our first album, it could be our last album, we think it's that good."

Nonetheless, while this attempt to re-establish their guiding principles had been extremely successful when the group played to their more aggressive strengths, it had faltered elsewhere. The sheer diversity of styles on show had made the record uneven in tone and difficult to engage with. Equally, with 16 tracks to get through – and not all of them good – *Know Your Enemy* was a bloating listening experience that could have done with some judicious trimming around the edges. This was not a point missed by the critics. "By the end of 1999, the Manics' success was distorting their core values," reasoned *Mojo*'s James McNair. "*Know Your Enemy* attempts a resolution... involving a stylistic volte face (with) much dirt under the fingernails. There are great songs here, but as Nicky Wire's 'Wattsville Blues' demonstrates, the odd filler too. Returning the stadium act to the garage was never going to be easy."

Q's John Aizlewood also acknowledged the uneven quality of *Know Your Enemy*, taking the Manics to task for the arrogance of their approach: "Even the most casual listener knows how songs (like) 'Dead Martyrs', 'His Last Painting' and 'My Guernica' might sound: horrible, shouty vocals, idiotic lyrics, no tune to speak of and an almighty soulless hole at the heart of it all." But Aizlewood was quick to praise the occasional diamond in the rough: "For every punk rock pastiche, there's something the genuine greats would be proud of. They're still talking about jacking in all in, and for much of *Know Your Enemy*, it sounds like they already have. Yet, when they turn things round, you rather hope they went on forever. Cull the arrogance, the laziness, the ill-considered ignorance the... sneering and they're wouldn't be a better album than *Know Your Enemy*, and not just of this year."

Despite its shortcomings, *Know Your Enemy* nevertheless debuted at number two on the charts when released in March 2001, once again confirming the Manics' commercial standing as one of the bigger rock acts in the UK. Healthy European interest also helped prove that the band's overseas audience were more than willing to follow them into some distinctly untrammelled terrain in pursuit of their listening rewards. Further, the album generated two more moderately successful singles – 'Ocean Spray' reached number 15 in the UK in June, while 'Let

Robeson Sing' made it to number 19 three months later. Yet, its eventual sales tally was nowhere near as high as the two records that preceded it, though at the time, this fact wouldn't have bothered Nicky Wire in the least. "We've made an album that's achieved what we wanted," he said. "I've been telling people this isn't just our best album ever. It's one of *the* best albums ever."

In subsequent years, *Know Your Enemy* has gained a reputation among some fans as the Manics' 'great lost disc', its experimental nature perceived as brave, the band's attempt to re-imagine their roots and push back their boundaries a cause for celebration rather than scorn. Perhaps it's best viewed as a clearing of the decks or a 'hole in the wall' allowing the group an escape from the uncomfortable responsibilities of being populist rock icons into a more comfortable and dignified setting. Right, wrong or somewhere in between, *Know Your Enemy* also proved itself to be the Manics' last proper album for over three years.

Chapter Twenty One

Slipping Into Fiction

As with every other Manic Street Preachers release, *Know Your Enemy* prompted a long and winding tour of the UK and Europe, the band flying and driving all over the place between March and September of 2001. This time, however, they mainly turned their back on arenas in favour of cosier venues, allowing fans to see the hair and skin flying in front of them rather than above their heads on a video screen. As the shows proved, it was a wise decision on Moore, Bradfield and Wire's part, the trio appearing relaxed and possibly relieved to return to halls rather than fields. Of the new material on show, single releases 'Found That Soul' 'Ocean Spray' and 'Let Robeson Sing' all went over well with crowds. But somewhat oddly, the Manics often chose to leave 'Intravenous Agnostic' – one of *Know Your Enemy's* better moments – out of the set in favour of the clodhopping delights of 'Miss Europa Disco Dancer' and Nicky's toe-curling 'Wattsville Blues'. Obviously out to amuse themselves as much as the audience, the group also occasionally re-activated their love of cover versions, giving Guns N' Roses' 'It's So Easy' and 'Paradise City' spirited run throughs on several dates.

Having performed shows in Copenhagen, Lisbon, Paris and Berlin as well as a thoroughly enjoyable two-night stopover at London's Brixton Academy, the Manics finally returned to the festival circuit during the summer of 2001, appearing at Holland's Pink Pop and Zeebrugge's Beachrock events. They then flew back to Great Britain for a one-off performance at Cardiff's International Arena before heading off to meet thousands more fans at the Reading Festival on August 25, with The Fun Lovin' Criminals providing able support. The group then temporarily concluded their live work with an intimate night's entertainment in aid of Amnesty International at London's small, but perfectly formed Scala theatre in King's Cross. The gig took place on September 12, only a day after the event now commonly known as '9/11', when New York's World Trade Center was destroyed in two plane attacks with the loss of nearly 3,000 lives. Like several bands at that time, the Manics subsequently cancelled a planned 14-date tour of European cities, including Amsterdam, Stockholm and Warsaw, due to begin on October 1. No official explanation was proffered by Hall Or Nothing at the time, but it was widely rumoured within musical circles that already nervous flyer Nicky Wire was in no mood to contemplate boarding an aircraft following the fall of the Twin Towers. The Manic Street Preachers did not play any more shows for nearly a year.

But as the group took a lengthy sabbatical from both recording and live performance, an important date loomed elsewhere on the calendar. On February 1, 2002 Richey Edwards had been missing for seven years. Under the terms of the British legal system, this timescale meant that Edwards' parents could now declare their son 'legally dead' and gain access to his estate. Still convinced that Richey was very much alive, Graham and Sherry Edwards politely declined to sign any paperwork and asked that the investigation into his disappearance continue. "We want our son back," said Graham, "not the money." Only a month later, the partial remains of a foot wearing a Diadora training shoe were discovered by a fisherman on the River Severn. The story was run by the *Daily Star* soon after, though they neglected to inform the Edwards family beforehand, prompting James Dean Bradfield to label the tabloid's reporters as "fucking cunts". As Richey favoured Converse trainers, both the Manics and Rachel Edwards thought it unlikely that the shoe or the remains it held were anything to do with him. Yet, an investigation was run by Diadora on the trainer's manufacture date while the police analysed the foot for DNA traces. It turned out that the shoe brand in question was only a year old – thus ruling Richey out of the equation. The remains were later identified as Damien Allen, a 24-year-old who had gone missing from hospital some months earlier. July 2003 brought another scare, when a skeleton was found in the Severn Estuary. When the teeth were cross-referenced against Edwards' dental records, it turned out not to be Richey. "If people knew how much these things hurt..." Wire said at the time.

The legal decisions faced by Richey Edwards' parents in 2002 were another reminder of how much time had passed since the events of February 1995, and the fact that despite so many sightings, hopeful leads and alarming discoveries, the mystery surrounding his disappearance was no nearer being solved. Though Edwards would now have been 35 years old, his image remained in stasis, frozen at the point when he abandoned his car near the Severn Bridge and strolled away for destinations thus far unknown. To his parents and sister he remained alive and omnipresent, and they would not give up hope of finding him. "As far as we are concerned," Graham Edwards confirmed to the *Mirror*, "Richey is still alive and we have always felt the same."

Yet, as Edwards' actions continued to beguile and his persona stayed hermetically sealed, life had moved on for his former bandmates who were now family men. In 2000, Sean Moore had finally married his teenage sweetheart, Rhian, in a reported 'surprise' ceremony. And while he had always said he had no plans for children, reasoning that "this world is a horrible place", Moore's wife gave birth to a baby girl, Matilda Poppy, at the end of February 2002. Nicky wasn't far behind in the parenting stakes, as he too became a father to Clara Enola Jones in the same year. Somewhat improbably, this movement towards domestic bliss would soon entice perennial bachelor and master of "the pullage", James Dean Bradfield. A man who had admitted that "I always get bored with the company of women really quickly," while describing his ideal date as actress/politician Glenda Jackson, Bradfield was only months away from meeting future wife Mylene Halsall. A PR agent some five years younger than him, Halsall performed the previously impossible task of getting James to say "I do" in July 2004 at a quiet service in Florence, Italy.

Nothing, however, marks the passage of time in musical terms more than a Greatest Hits album, and the Manics finally succumbed to the inevitable in October 2002 with the release of *Forever Delayed*. A 20-song package (with a separate DVD collecting the band's videos thus far), *Forever Delayed* was the culmination of over 10 years of chart activity, from the furious punk thump of 'Motown Junk' to *Know Your Enemy's* Beach Boys-worshipping 'So Why So Sad'. As was often the way of these things, the compilation also included two new tunes, the Sixties inflected ballad 'Door To The River' and the Radiohead meets Depeche Mode faux electronica of 'There By The Grace Of God'. "Forever's always been my favourite word," Wire said prior to the record arriving in shops. "There's a line in 'Roses In The Hospital' – 'Forever delayed' – and that's what I want(ed) to call the greatest hits: *Manic Street Preachers: Forever Delayed*. It's just so lovely and beautiful (with) so much depth in it."

Forever Delayed was preceded by the single release of 'There By The Grace Of God', which put the Manics back in the UK Top 10 at number six. The song also approximated a line "And all the drugs in the world can't save us from ourselves" from the unlikely source of Goth rock icon Marilyn Manson's controversial 'Coma White'. Obviously, Wire had quite an interest in Manson (AKA Brian Warner), having already referred to the pale-skinned one and his alleged onstage bottom wiping antics on *Know Your Enemy*'s 'The Convalescent': "And Brian Warner has a tasty little ass." Though *Forever Delayed* did well enough, reaching number four on the album charts, it also infuriated some fans of the group by concentrating only on the hits while omitting other key moments from the Manics' back catalogue. For long time devotees, the presence of 'Faster' alone from *The Holy Bible* and only a smattering of songs from the pre-*Everything Must Go* era was an obvious indication that the band had abandoned their principles and finally sold out.

Both Wire and Bradfield chose to deal with such charges of commercial profiteering in their own ways. "We just wanted to do it within the parameters of a greatest hits record," Nicky later said. "We didn't want to dilute it (by) picking our favourite album tracks and various things." For James, track selection was as much about quality control as anything else: "There's a lot of bands these days that don't even get past their second album, so trawling through years of hits was a little strange," he told *Planet Rock*'s Dave Fanning. "And some of the songs were shit. A song like 'Love's Sweet Exile', well, it's irredeemable. Equally, 'Suicide...'

is only on there because the Germans like it. It's like an old photo album. Sometimes the photos are embarrassing, but you've got to look at them." Logical and reasoned points all, but it didn't stop some previous supporters voicing their displeasure or even disavowing the Manics on various websites as the group themselves set off on a 26-date European tour in support of the disc during the autumn of 2002.

By July 2003, the dissenters had their way when the band finally relented to pressure from the old faithful and released *Lipstick Traces: A Secret History Of Manic Street Preachers*. A comprehensive 35-track career trawl of B-sides, cover versions and previously unavailable songs, *Lipstick Traces...* was like manna from heaven to the more discerning Manics fans. Featuring a leopard skin cover part designed by Nicky, the collection took its name from Greil Marcus' 1989 book *Lipstick Traces: A Secret History Of The Twentieth Century*. A fascinating read, Marcus had examined the historical connectivity and cultural shunts that eventually produced The Sex Pistols' 'age of anarchy', using movements such as Anabaptism, Dadaism and even the Knights of the Round Table to make his point. For Wire, there were obvious parallels to be drawn from Marcus' ideas to the Manics' own journey, their more obscure and lesser known works as important to the development of the group's philosophy and eventual success as any Top 10 hit.

And he was right. With very early material such as the Clash-influenced 'Sorrow 16', one could already hear echoes of what would be absorbed and rejected by the time the band recorded 1991's *Generation Terrrorists*. Similarly, 1993's 'Comfort Comes' was a dry run for what became 'Faster', Bradfield slowly pulling together the John McGeoch-like angular guitar chording that eventually informed the Manics' greatest moment. And with 1992's 'Donkeys', the B-side to 'Roses In The Hospital', one might have been listening to an *Everything Must Go* or *This Is My Truth* outtake. When not looking for clues as to how the Manics became the Manics, there was also great fun to be had from *Lipstick Traces...*. 'Mr. Carbohydrate', for instance, wittily recalled Nicky's staple diet of chips and predilection for hypochondria when on the road, while 'Valley Boy' transported Welsh working class values to an Amsterdam setting.

The myriad cover versions selected for inclusion on *Lipstick Traces* were equally worth a listen. Aside from obvious choices such as the band's hyperventilating take on Guns N' Roses' 'It's So Easy', Mike Batt and Art Garfunkel's sickly sweet, coma-inducing ode to dying rabbits, 'Bright Eyes', was given the Manics treatment. Acknowledging their roots, The Clash's 'Train In Vain' also turned up on the two-CD set, while Primal Scream's 'Velocity Girl' allowed Bradfield to return to his busking days at Cardiff City Centre. Fans were even provided with the opportunity to listen to James' see-sawing live rendition of Wham's 'Last Christmas' in the comfort of their own home, a concert favourite of many years finally making it onto disc for the first time.

As ever, Richey Edwards had not been forgotten as 'Judge Yr'self' appeared nearly a decade after the band first recorded it for possible use on the soundtrack of the 1995 film *Judge Dredd*. Ageing impeccably well, 'Judge Yr'self' was a tantalising glimpse of the direction the Manics might have pursued had Richey conquered his problems and chosen to stay. Chugging along like a harder-edged Nirvana, the song's lyrics explored the clashing of old and new gods, while also espousing the need to find one's own truth: "Blessed be the blades, blessed be the sighs, Dionysus against the crucified..."

A mightily impressive collection that actually did the trick of living up to its title, *Lipstick Traces: A Secret History...* entered the UK charts at number 11 on July 14, 2003 and was backed with a small number of festival appearances by the band, including Glastonbury and Manchester's Move event. Then, following a 'secret' gig at HMV's flagship store on London's Oxford Street on July 14, the Manics again disappeared for the best part of a year to work on their next record, "a concept album about death" provisionally titled 'Litany'. The very fact that Nicky Wire had even put the words "concept" and "album" together in the same sentence when referring to Manics product was enough to chill the blood.

The producer originally brought in to help realise the band's new vision was the legendary Tony Visconti, whose back catalogue of credits included pop and rock royalty such as Marc Bolan, David Bowie, Iggy Pop and Thin Lizzy, among many others. Decamping to Looking Glass Studios in Manhattan's 'Noho' district, initial expectations were high and the group plus Visconti recorded several songs in all, but only three – 'Cardiff Afterlife', 'Emily' and 'Solitude Sometimes Is' – actually ended up on the finished album. With their New York experiment behind them, the Manics returned to Wales and Cardiff's Stir Studios to continue work. This time round, old friend Greg Haver oversaw the lion's share of production duties with Tom Elmhirst offering additional support.

"Like many artists at their level, the Manics were already really motivated," Haver later remembered, "and the reason they like to work with people they know is there's a lot of intensity, a lot of piss taking and a lot of pain getting to the final product. But it's worth it." Working in a "virtual studio space" tracks were cut quickly, with band members often recording their contributions at different times of the day, rather than in the same room at the same time. This process was quite deliberate, the intention to create an air of 'separation' and detachment that would hopefully find its way onto the record. After a spell at Grouse Lodge Studios in West Meath, Ireland, final mixing took place at the Metropolis complex, not far from James' new house in Chiswick, West London.

The first result of the Manics' endeavours, the single 'For The Love Of Richard Nixon' boded well, helping quell fears that in their quest to produce a dreaded 'concept album', the group had transformed themselves into oil-scented, kaftan-wearing hippy types. In fact, quite the opposite seemed to be the case. Full of prodding electronic drum beats, swishy keyboards and a complete absence of Bradfield's trademark "slashing guitar", '...Richard Nixon' was a lush, dewy-eyed, synth-pop tribute to one of America's most complex presidents. "It's a metaphor for the fact you're always remembered in your life for one thing," Wire told *The Scotsman*'s Ian Watson. "Nixon's always going to be remembered for Watergate and being a crook. But he was a brilliant politician. He wasn't like George Bush. He wasn't a fucking idiot. He was the first American president to go to China, which was an amazing piece of foreign policy. Most people associate us with Richey going missing. Even your family sometimes associate you with one or two things which you can never escape. So the idea of the song is just digging a bit deeper." As '...Richard Nixon' debuted at a striking number two on the UK charts on October 14, 2004, it appeared the band might be really be onto something. But then came the album.

Having dropped the working title 'Litany' somewhere between New York, Wales and Ireland, the Manics Street Preachers' seventh studio effort was now called *Lifeblood,* though according to Nicky, it still retained its original conceit. "'If you strip it to its barest lyric," he said, "it's a concept album about suicide, really." On first inspection, things looked reasonably promising, the record sleeve's bold design – courtesy of photographer John Ross – depicting part of a woman's torso splashed in blood against a stark white background. An arresting, if somewhat disturbing image, several similar pictures were contained in the disc's accompanying booklet. As usual, there was also a printed quote to stimulate thought before one began listening, this time from the 16th century French philosopher and mathematician Rene Descartes: "Conquer yourself, conquer the world..." So far, so very Manics. But when it came to the songs of *Lifeblood* itself, profound disappointment reigned.

Coming on like a lost pop rock record from the mid-Eighties, *Lifeblood* had an all pervading air of melancholy to it, which, given Wire's lyrical pre-occupations and statements about "death" and "suicide", shouldn't really have come as any great surprise. However, said melancholy had more often than not transmuted itself into sounds of extreme dullness, with tunes sometimes so bland it was difficult to distinguish one from another. Consequently, the likes of 'Glasnost', 'Fragments', 'Solitude Sometimes Is' and 'Always/Never' floated by in a sticky fog of synthesisers and rich vocal harmonies. In fact, keyboards – whether synthetic or of the wire and wood variety – dominated proceedings throughout, Bradfield's usually strident guitar more content to nestle within the melody than pierce through all the 'Twinkle Twinkle Little Star' orchestration.

When James did come out of hiding, *Lifeblood*'s mood was temporarily lifted, the Abba-lite 'Song For Departure' greatly benefitting from an ill-tempered, Slash-influenced six string outburst. Equally, 'To Repel Ghosts' found the guitarist on top form, his reverb-affected musings giving the song a U2/Echo And The Bunnymen-like atmosphere that was difficult not to like. 'Emily' and 'Cardiff Afterlife' were also worthy of mention, recalling Eighties hits such as Black's maudlin but masterful 'Wonderful Life' and The Associates' evergreen 'Party Fears Two'. Yet for every '1985', where the Manics threatened to engage at the highest musical level, there was a song such as 'I Live To Fall Asleep' that brought it all tumbling down again.

Lyrically, Nicky Wire hadn't been kidding about *Lifeblood*'s mournful preoccupations. The song '1985' read like an eulogy to lost youth while consecutively scorning a time when the fate of Britain's miners fought for TV coverage with ice-skating champions Torville and Dean. But other than 'Emily', which paid tribute to pioneering suffragette Emily Pankhurst before crying out for contemporary equivalents, '1985' was one of very few songs that even touched on matters of state – Wire preferring this time around to concentrate on the personal rather than the political. "I'm just bored shitless writing about politics," he said. This change manifested itself in songs such as 'Solitude Sometimes Is', which yet again mined Nicky's obsession with shutting the door to keep the world away, and 'I Live To Fall Asleep', a lyric that drew parallels between his devotion to slumber and the eternal rest of suicide. "Sleep is beautiful for me," he said, "but I hate dreaming because it ruins 10 hours of bliss. I had a lot of bad dreams when Richey first disappeared. Not ugly dreams, but nagging things. Until we wrote 'A Design For Life', it was six months of misery." As with the music of *Lifeblood*, sometimes this shift in lyrical emphasis worked, with 'Glasnost' using a phrase more associated with the fall of communism to explore wider human feelings of openness and reconciliation. And sometimes it didn't, as 'Always/Never''s themes of self-flagellation and inner confusion steered perilously close to self-pity.

Where Wire's pursuit of more intimate associations did pay real dividends was on 'Cardiff Afterlife', an elegant lyric seeking to recover the reality of Richey Edwards as a friend and bandmate from the more public myth he now threatened to become. According to Nicky, the song was not about finding closure, but more a reclamation of the exceptionally gifted, occasionally infuriating but always very human being they all knew and loved: "I witnessed splendour, and evil no-one saw, and I felt kindness and vanity for sure..." And though Wire acceded that the future might always be "paralysed" from not knowing exactly what happened, he, like Edwards' family had not abandoned all sense of expectation: "With no grave," he said, "there's hope."

'Cardiff Afterlife' ended *Lifeblood* on an elegiac, yet still uplifting note, but not one that could drown out less impressive tracks that preceded it. Immaculately produced and musically well executed it might have been, but the album was still a largely vapid affair that lacked passion and intensity, two qualities the Manics could normally be relied upon to deliver in spades. Without doubt the weakest release of their career, this fact was drummed home when after debuting at number 13 in the UK charts on November 1, 2004, *Lifeblood* fell out of the charts never to return within the space of two weeks. In fact, it was very hard to find anyone with good words to say about it.

"It would have been unthinkable that nearly 15 years later the Manics would be looking back on the (Eighties) with the wistful nostalgia of *Lifeblood*," reasoned BBC's Lucy Doherty. "This record is soaked in it: the lyrics, production, instrumentation and sheer gloss all take you back, with the band admitting references to The Cure, New Order and even early U2. This isn't trendy Eighties retro though: James Dean Bradfield's vocals cry out with heartfelt longing for the past. On the opening track '1985', James repeats the mantra 'No going back' and despite the song breaking into bizarrely uplifting peals of sound, I'm left with a feeling of real loss." Yet even Doherty's enthusiasm began to wilt in the end: "*Lifeblood* may be imbued with a powerful melancholia, but it's not perfect. In recent years the Manic Street Preachers seem incapable of making an album that's not slightly disappointing. It's hard not to expect more from the band that made the magnificent *Holy Bible*."

An untimely reminder of when the Manics might have been at their very best came only four or so weeks after *Lifeblood*'s descent into relative obscurity, as *The Holy Bible: 10th Anniversary Edition* was released on December 6, 2004. A luxuriously packaged three disc set, *The Holy Bible: 10...* included a crystal clear remastering of the original album, and depending on one's point of view, the notorious or glorious (and as yet unreleased) US mix, which added a meaty bottom-end thump to the original material. Giving fans genuine value for money, the collection also included an 80-minute DVD of band interviews recounting their experiences in making the record, plus various live tracks, Radio One Sessions, demo recordings and concert footage. A fine testament to a pivotal moment in Manics history, someone at Sony even had the presence of mind to dig up James' infamous balaclava-wearing shenanigans on *Top Of The Pops* and include it among the contents.

Of course, it was hard not to play 'compare and contrast' with *The Holy Bible* and *Lifeblood*. One represented a needle-sharp statement of intent, its intellectual scope and instrumental sorcery having few equals in the course of Nineties rock, perhaps only Alice In Chains' *Dirt* and Nine Inch Nails' *The Downward Spiral* rivalling its hopeless descent into brilliance. *Lifeblood*, on the other hand, was the work of now seasoned veterans of the music wars, looking back at the things that made them who they were with a mixture of longing, occasional disdain and wistful melodies. "*Lifeblood*," Wire reasoned at the time, "is *The Holy Bible* for 35 year olds." Yet, as the band admitted on listening to tracks such as 'Faster' and 'P.C.P' all over again, they had never truly recaptured the essential balance present in their days with Richey Edwards. "Yes," said Nicky, "we're haunted by ghosts. We're haunted by the way we looked, the symmetry, the four of us, everything was perfect."

The melancholic atmosphere that hung thickly over the Manic Street Preachers' return to musical duty and the commercial failure of *Lifeblood* itself also transferred itself to the band's short 'Past-Present-Future' concert tour of December 2004, when for the first time in nearly a decade few shows sold out. More, the Manics later admitted that playing new, softer material such as 'For The Love Of Richard Nixon' and 'Solitude Sometimes Is' wasn't granting them as much pleasure as more energetic fare like 'You Love Us' or even 'You Stole The Sun From My Heart'. "Yeah," Bradfield later confirmed, "I did miss the physical aspect of playing an instinctive rock album. At some point you just want that physical release."

There were certain compensations to be had. Keen to promote *The Holy Bible*'s return to shops, the group took several of its songs out of mothballs, introducing 'Die In The Summertime', 'Yes' and 'P.C.P' to the likes of Wembley, Cardiff and Manchester Arenas. Another step forward to their live sound was the addition of Guy Massey on rhythm guitar. A studio engineer who had already worked with the Manics on both *Everything Must Go* and *Know Your Enemy*, Massey brought some extra clout to proceedings while also helping James shoulder some of the burden of covering all bases with just six strings. As the group had vowed never to replace Richey onstage, there were some mumblings of discontent from certain quarters, but as Wire explained, this was a sonic requirement and not a spiritual betrayal. "Good god, no. Guy's not replacing Richey. No-one's ever going to replace Richey. It's just a musical thing."

As if to actively disprove the theory the Manics were in serious decline the group's next single release from *Lifeblood*, 'Empty Souls', bucked the odds by crashing into the charts at number two on January 10, 2005, held off from becoming the UK's 1,000th number one hit by Elvis Presley. Another gloomy tune, though in possession of a fine, sonorous chorus, 'Empty Souls' had originally featured the line "collapsing like Twin Towers", in a sad reference to 9/11. But for the single version, Wire changed it to "collapsing like empty flowers" (due to a mixing oversight, however, James could still be heard singing the original line on the background vocal). The song was also an effective illustration of how much Bradfield's role as a composer had changed when making the Manics' latest album: "When I write something, usually everything's in my head straight away," he said. "For instance, with 'A Design For Life', I had a string part, and for 'If You Tolerate...', it was a synth. With 'Empty Souls', we rehearsed it with me playing the main riff on guitar. Then I realised it was going to sound better with piano. And that happened with quite a few songs on the album. Suddenly, another musician was covering my natural ground as a guitarist... I simply (knew) I had to re-design my guitar playing."

Despite its success, 'Empty Souls' proved to be the last single generated from *Lifeblood*, both band and record company mutually concluding demand for any further product from the album would be limited at best. This rapid distancing from their least successful work was also clear from the Manics' concluding shows of the 'Past-Present-Future' tour throughout April 2005, where only 'To Repel Ghosts', 'Cardiff Afterlife' and '1985' were occasionally let out of a now well-locked trunk. "For all of *Lifeblood*'s merits," Nicky later said, "it didn't put many smiles on people's faces." Bradfield was equally philosophical, citing temporary confusion as a major cause behind the record's failure: "We've been very careful... to not actually slag *Lifeblood* because we did find a different version of ourselves. Sometimes when you delineate and deconstruct, you find nothing, that's the scary process. But we did find something, (even if) we confused ourselves and our audience in the process."

Another point of confusion for the Manics faithful occurred at the band's final Hammersmith Apollo show on April 19, 2005. In a kindly gesture to fans for their continuing support, Moore, Bradfield and Wire had organised the pressing of 3,000 copies of a three track CD called *God Save The Manics* to be given away free at the concert. As one of the tracks, 'Picturesque', featured lyrics written by Richey Edwards, these CDs were quite the prize. However, due to some confusion among staff at the venue as to whether they were to be distributed pre or post gig, boxes full of the discs were left by the entrance, allowing some unscrupulous souls to reportedly grab them by the armful while others missed out. To their credit, the Manics later posted the CD's contents on their official website as a free download. Aside for the slight mishap, the group's Hammersmith appearance went exceedingly well, the band rolling back the years by playing the likes of 'Stay Beautiful' and 'Archives Of Pain', with even a rare live outing granted to 'ifwhiteamericatoldthetruthforonedayitsworldwouldfallapart'. And then among the festivities, James announced in an almost Ziggy Stardust-like moment that this would be their last performance for the next two years. After a pause, and a sharp intake of breath from around the auditorium, it was straight back to business before 'Motown Junk' brought an end to a difficult few months and paved the way for a very quiet few years.

Of course, the Manic Street Preachers had hinted at this type of action before. At the time of *Know Your Enemy*, for instance, they even made noises about packing it all in forever. Such talk had come and gone. But the negativity surrounding *Lifeblood* and its rapid disappearance into the commercial ether seemed to have really taken its toll on the band. More, for the first time the Manics appeared genuinely at sea – having temporarily lost their place in the rock'n'roll guide book they first read while teenagers in Blackwood.

"I don't know if we're relevant to people who love Franz Ferdinand and The Libertines," Nicky said. "I'm not sure. We might be relevant to Dido fans. I don't really care." But Wire, like Bradfield and Moore, actually cared very much. Having studied the ceremonies, sung along with the best loved hymns and even written a few themselves, the band were not quite ready to hand back the keys to the kingdom just yet. All they needed to do was figure out what their next move might be.

"Sometimes you've got to be brutal with yourself," Nicky mulled at the time, "and think, 'Do you want to make underrated masterpieces for the rest of your life and fizzle away or do you want to get that Technicolor moment back into the band?'"

After some consideration, the Manics prompted for the latter.

Chapter Twenty Two

What Immortal Hand Or Eye?

In commercial terms, the Manic Street Preachers' seventh studio offering, *Lifeblood,* had tanked. Giving the band their lowest chart placing in 12 years, the album announced its departure from the charts almost as soon as it arrived, the content confusing fans and antagonising critics. The reasons for such negativity were simple enough: *Lifeblood* hadn't been a great record. Not even a good one. Also, it was released at a time when British rock was undergoing another change of the guard with the emergence of groups like Coldplay and Keane who offered a more studied, some might even say anodyne, brand of soft rock that generated huge sales but found little favour with the more hawkish end of the music press. Those fans looking for something a bit meatier were catered for by the likes of Franz Ferdinand and former Manics support act Razorlight, while for those who liked their pop, punk and political satire bundled together in a neat little package, Green Day's *American Idiot* and The Libertines' self-titled second disc both had it covered, and The Strokes and Interpol held up the more artful end of things. After an almost four year absence in terms of brand new product, the Manics were always going to find it difficult to reclaim their rightful place at the proverbial dinner table when it was so crowded by hungry newcomers.

Of equal importance was the fact that the Manics themselves were getting older, as evidenced by the reflective, Eighties-indebted stylistic and lyrical content of *Lifeblood*. This was no longer a group of 'Generation Terrorists', but men with wives and families, their concerns very different from those facing the choice of which university to plump for or career to pursue. To his credit, Wire had confronted such issues of relevancy in an open and honest manner, wondering who exactly the Manics were appealing to. And like the band, their core following was now also in its thirties, a time when jobs, children and mortgages tended to take precedence over the dogged pursuit of finding a mint copy of 'La Tristesse Durera' with the dubious lost treasure 'Patrick Bateman' on the B-side. The group's self-enforced break then, seemed to make some sense. No longer young enough to offer cutting edge thrills, nor old enough to be re-embraced as rock's elder statesmen, the Manics now sat somewhere in the middle – and 'sitting it out' or re-thinking their strategy was a far more logical step than just walking away in a huff. "After *Lifeblood*," reasoned James Dean Bradfield, "we decided people deserved a rest from us..."

Yet, if the Manics were temporarily unsure how to proceed, or whether there was even an audience interested in their next move, at least one of those questions was soon enough answered. In July 2005, BBC's current affairs programme *Newsnight* announced the results of their 'Quintessential Viewer's Poll', a survey spanning themes such as favourite novel, work of art or record. To more than a little shock, *The Holy Bible* topped the 'Top Five Albums' list, ahead of the multi-million selling likes of Pink Floyd's *Dark Side Of The Moon* and Radiohead's *OK Computer*. "The biggest surprise was the triumph of *The Holy Bible* by the Manic Street Preachers, an album which I suspect most quintessential *Newsnight* employees have never heard," said *Newsnight* Editor Peter Barron at the time. "On the whole we're not big Manics fans, but I understand they like us." The placing of *The Holy Bible* in pole position was not only an enduring tribute to an inspiring album, but also confirmation that the group's devotees hadn't forgotten to vote with the click of a mouse when the occasion required it. Additionally, the feather-boa wearing, slogan-covered front rows of the Nineties had evidently taken the Manics' politico-intellectual crusades into adult life, preferring to keep up with what was going on in the world around them rather than vegetate in front of *EastEnders*. More sentimentally, *The Holy Bible*'s number one position was further testimony to the continued importance of Richey Edwards in the lives of many fans. Though absent a decade his work lingered on, its themes of psychological suffering, the mistakes of politicians and the atrocities of war ringing loud in the era of 'Care in the Community', Iraq and Afghanistan.

In keeping with their announcement at Hammersmith Apollo, the Manics did not perform any more concerts during 2005. Nor indeed, 2006. Instead, they more or less went to ground. There were occasional stirrings in the hedgerow, however. Just two months after receiving their *Newsnight* honour, the band re-surfaced momentarily to provide a track for *Help! A Day In The Life*, a record in aid of War Child, whose work in protecting children from the effects of conflict had now progressed to the Middle East. This was the second time they had worked with the charity – the first being 1995's 'Raindrops Keep Falling On My Head – and this time the Manics donated an original composition, 'Leviathan'. A brisk rock song with chugging guitars, big drums and a huge chorus, 'Leviathan' was clear indication Bradfield and Moore had utterly dispensed with the fey experimentalism of *Lifeblood* and were back to something approximating top form. Wire too had abandoned trying to commune with his inner teenager and fashioned a lyric that took its title, but not necessarily all its inspiration from Thomas Hobbes' groundbreaking 16th century political tome on social contract theory: "Reprobates and MPLA, Patty Hearst, oh, they're all the same... Leviathan, I am your son." Collecting artists as disparate as Gorillaz, Belle & Sebastian, Kaiser Chiefs and Maximo Park, *Help! A Day In The Life* briefly became the world's fastest selling download album.

Six months later the Manics were at it again, this time re-grouping to cover 'The Instrumental' for inclusion on *Still Unravished*, a tribute disc to the quirky Eighties indie act The June Brides. Oddly, another of the Welsh trio's adolescent heroes, The Jasmine Minks – whose 1984 album *...All Good Preachers Go To Heaven* may have contributed at least something to the Manics' eventual choice of name – also performed a version of 'The Instrumental' on the same record.

Though it may have appeared to the outside world that the Manics were essentially on gardening leave during much of this time, behind the scenes it was a markedly different story – at least for some. While Sean Moore had quite sensibly chosen to spend his vacation with family and various gadgets during the group's sabbatical, James Dean Bradfield and Nicky Wire couldn't keep themselves away from the studio, each tentatively cutting demos for a solo disc. Having already dipped their toes into the uncertain waters of the 'Concept Album', it shouldn't have come as any great surprise that two of the three were now planning another of rock music's classic fall back positions: when in doubt, go it alone. Nonetheless, as news finally surfaced that both Bradfield and Wire were to release stand alone efforts, it was also made clear that these records would in no way impact on the Manics' future. The band itself was very much an ongoing, if still silent concern: "We kept wanting to go back in the studio to do an album," James later confirmed, "but we really tried to stick to (our decision) for the first time."

Missing the steady hum of amplifiers and the pounding of sticks, Bradfield quickly made the decision to spend his days working up new material. To this end, he booked time in two recording facilities: Miloco Square Studios in London's Hoxton district and Stir Studios, off the Penarth Road in Cardiff. "They (didn't) sound like big rooms and I liked the idea of stuff being a bit more cloaked, more murky and Seventies-esque." Commuting between locations via train, James spent much of his journey from Paddington to Cardiff playing with song ideas inside his head, which he would then try out on arrival. Though initial sessions were sluggish due to the unfamiliarity of his situation, Bradfield soon warmed to the solo experience, covering guitar, bass and vocal duties while returning producer Greg Haver took care of the majority of drum work. For additional inspiration, James listened to doomed Welsh band Badfinger, six-string blues rock/fusion legend Jeff Beck and early Simple Minds while cutting tracks.

The resulting album, *The Great Western* – named in honour of the railway line that brought Bradfield between London to Wales – was a mature, sophisticated effort allowing the Manics frontman to again make friends with the windswept choruses that had made *Everything Must Go* such a success. Particular highlights included the majestic, but mournful 'Émigré', the cheerful, tongue-in-cheek 'Run Romeo Run' and first single 'That's No Way To Tell A Lie', which updated Thin Lizzy's chugging pop rock sound for the 21st century and placed James at number 18 in the UK charts. Other tunes of note included 'Bad Boys And Painkillers' for which Nicky Wire had provided a typically caustic lyric and a stupendous cover of Jacques Brel's 'To See A Friend In Tears'. Perhaps reticent to overplay the 'guitar hero' angle too much, Bradfield had reigned in the 'scorched earth' soloing of the Manics' early days in favour of a more rounded approach, with tracks as likely to be driven along by acoustic picking as wall to wall barre chords.

Lyrically, James also proved himself to be no slouch. 'Which Way To Kyffin' was a fitting and considered tribute to feelings inspired by the work of acclaimed Welsh fine artist Kyffin Williams, who sadly died in September 2006 only two months after *The Great Western* was released: "He sits and prays for the light to die, to show the life hidden from our eyes." Drawn to Williams' rain-lashed, darksome land and seascape paintings, Bradfield had actually contemplated driving to Anglesey in search of the man himself, but chose to capture his thoughts in song instead: "Like the chorus says, I was trying to paint myself a different life so you can be captured in the painting and don't have to leave it." Another fine tonal composition was 'An English Gentleman', written in honour of original Manics manager, Phillip Hall. For James, the song was a way of bringing to public light the down to earth, yet still swaggering qualities of the man who had placed his faith, and indeed, quite a bit of his fortune in launching the band's career: "Driving west to see who we are... You gave us more than we needed, friend..."

While making *The Great Western*, Bradfield had admitted to much chewing of nails when it came to lyric writing. Unlike Richey Edwards and Nicky Wire, who often approached their subject from a position of intellectual authority, James was still reaching for clarity when crafting the words themselves. "When I write a lyric, I'm writing it to try and understand the subject," he later told *NME*. However, trepidation had acceded to pleasure soon enough: "I just realised that I actually really enjoyed it a lot. Seeing 'words and music by James Dean Bradfield' written down actually made me feel happy. For once I lost a bit of my insecurity."

A strong, sublime effort, *The Great Western* finally clarified that while critics had spent as much time mulling over the thoughts of Edwards and Wire, it was Bradfield's tunes they were humming while doing so. Reaching number 22 in the UK charts on July 30, 2006, James supported the album with a short British tour, playing the occasional Manics tune such as 'Ocean Spray' and 'No Surface, All Feeling' while also indulging his love of The Clash with covers of 'The Card Cheat' and 'Clampdown'.

When it was revealed that Nicky Wire solo product was also imminent, expectations were not particularly high. Wire, after all, had spent many a year proclaiming his playing and song writing abilities to be limited at best, and that he was more interested in "looking cool, like Sid Vicious or Paul Simonon" than following the path of bass virtuosos such as Jaco Pastorius or Jeff Berlin. Further, as *Know Your Enemy*'s underwhelming 'Wattsville Blues' confirmed, Nicky was not blessed with the strongest of singing voices, his croaking tones perhaps more suited to a duet with The Fall's Mark E. Smith than The Who's Roger Daltrey. It was therefore wise to approach Wire's new album, *I Killed The Zeitgeist*, with a sense of mild caution when it was released in mid-September, 2006. Suffice to say, the tallest Manic Street Preacher had obviously been hiding his musical light under a bushel, for Nicky's efforts were an unexpected delight. A low-fi, but surprisingly melodic collection, *I Killed The Zeitgeist* numbered Krautrock, the Plastic Ono Band, Teenage Fanclub and even The Strokes among its influences. Moreover, Wire had also kept his songs short, brisk and to the point, with no opportunities given to unwanted instrumental dawdling. However, the most pleasing revelation was Nicky's voice: having worked hard on expanding his Lou Reed impersonation by adding a little of New Order vocalist Bernard Sumner's nasal bite, he was now in real danger of being able to carry a tune.

This improvement in Wire's vocal performance helped add much life to 'Stab Yr Heart', 'The Shining Path' and the title track itself, a winning slice of ragged punk dynamics that had been made available as a free download on the Manics' official website some months earlier. With 'Break My Heart Slowly', the first single released from the album (it reached number 74 in the UK), there was yet more evidence of Nicky's skills as a songwriter, the tune bubbling away nicely before hitting its doleful, but still catchy chorus. On the lyrical side of things,

Wire provided listeners with some distinguished if morally pessimistic wordplay: 'Withdraw/Retreat' for instance, appeared to be yet another written testimony from Nicky to the horrors of socialisation, a theme again touched upon in 'You Will Always Be My Home: "The people, they don't know what it means to be alone..." 'Kimono Boys' was all sly critique, its point of attack seemingly directed at the vacuous nature of the rock'n'roll lifestyle and reportedly drawing some inspiration from the troubled personal life of Libertine Pete Doherty. The track also featured the lead guitar talents of James Dean Bradfield, presumably returning the favour Wire did him in providing lyrics to 'Bad Boys And Painkillers', which mined a similar subject to 'Kimono Rock' itself.

'Bobby Untitled' found Nicky revisiting the story of Bobby Sands, and in so doing, also indirectly referencing an old friend. A provisional IRA volunteer jailed at Belfast's Maze Prison in 1981, Sands had led a protest of Irish republican prisoners against the removal of their 'Special Category Status' in the form of a hunger strike. Refusing all food Sands died after 66 days, his passing outraging Northern Ireland's Catholic community and acting as a trigger for new recruits interested in joining the IRA. As teenagers, the formative Manic Street Preachers were all aware of the media coverage surrounding the tragic extremes Bobby Sands had gone to for a cause he and others believed correct, but in the case of Richey Edwards, interest bordered on mild obsession. Fascinated by the level of political commitment and physical control exercised by Sands, Richey followed his circumstances avidly until death. With lines such as "If someone could hold you now, if fate could play a different hand," it was tempting to believe that Wire might have been addressing two souls rather than one with his words.

Aside from the title track, and 'Nicky Wires) Last' [sic] which both railed against the world and its failings with requisite venom and art punk energy, 'So Much For The Future' was surely *I Killed The Zeitgeist*'s most striking moment, summing up in three short minutes the philosophy behind the entire album. Best described as a 'hymn to nihilism', and containing the withering couplet "No fear of boredom, embrace it it's modern," the song ended in a quite magnificent collapse of white noise and discordant piano, crushing melody lines and rhythms as it went before fading to silence. "It's a perfect symbol of nihilism reaching its peak," Wire later said. "I think *I Killed The Zeitgeist* [as a whole]... was a conscious decision to be as nihilistic as I possibly could, because I wanted to come back to the Manics and reconnect... put myself where I was when I was 20 – when you still had idealism, when you still had the naïve belief that you could actually change something, your own life or the lives of others."

Recorded in the same Cardiff studio that James Dean Bradfield cut *The Great Western* and employing much the same work ethic – Wire handled almost all guitars, bass and vocals while the ever-present Greg Haver co-produced and played drums – *I Killed The Zeitgeist* garnered Nicky little commercial success. Debuting at a lowly number 130 on the charts, the album was gone again in a wisp. Nonetheless, critics were extremely supportive of his efforts, with the *NME* even going as far as to suggest it might be the best Manics-associated release since *Everything Must Go*. Like James, Nicky backed *I Killed The Zeitgeist*'s release with a small number of shows, the highlight of which had to be the Hay On Wye Festival, where a slightly 'tired and emotional' Wire hung on tight to a mostly empty wine bottle during a ramshackle but entertaining set.

While James Dean Bradfield and Nicky Wire's solo records had proved themselves to be enjoyable and allowed fans a glimpse 'behind the creative curtain', they could only be regarded as stop gaps before the two again focused their attentions on reactivating the Manics. Wire was the first to admit it: "It's just much more fun being in a band. Making a racket together. To me, vanity projects are great fun, but they're not really the main business of life." In this view, Nicky was joined by Sean Moore, who when asked what he had learned from his colleagues' recent experiences, needed few words to clarify his position: "It taught me not to do one."

The return of the Manic Street Preachers to public life began in earnest on December 8, 2006 as the band finally broke a year and a half silence to perform a 45 minute set at XFM's 'Winter Wonderland' in Manchester Arena for the charity *Shelter*. Given the occasion and compressed time frame, the Manics' performance had to be tight, hits-focussed and unashamedly populist, and despite sounding a little under-rehearsed to begin with, that's precisely what they delivered. Opening their set with the familiar wallop of 'You Love Us', the group played their way through all the usual suspects including 'Motorcycle Emptiness' and 'If You Tolerate This...' before screeching to a halt with 'Motown Junk' and 'A Design For Life'. But they were also confident enough to introduce two new songs, both of which provided first proof that the Manics' forthcoming album might be very good indeed. With 'I'm A Patsy', the onus was on power chords, industrial strength choruses and clever wordplay, all the things in fact, one associated with the band's glory days. 'Autumnsong' was equally impressive, sounding as if the essence of The Beatles and Guns N' Roses had been distilled into a single song. "A mix of *Generation Terrorists* and *Everything Must Go*, that's what we're after," Nicky had told the *NME*. Based on this evidence, the Manics might very well have found it.

Preparations for the band's eighth studio album had actually begun as far back as the late autumn of 2005, when the Manics met up in Cardiff to test out new ideas. "We went to a crappy little rehearsal studio," said Nicky, "no manager, no producer, just ourselves making music. If something didn't excite us, we simply dropped it." Convinced that the last five years were a wilderness period where they had mislaid their "true nature", Wire, Bradfield and Moore went in search of it all over again, trying to recapture the quintessence of their sound: "Basically," Wire continued, "we'd lost that Sex Pistols 'Fabulous Disaster' thing and we wanted to get it back." For James, this process of reclamation meant temporarily dispensing with all vestiges of their recent past, including any extraneous instruments. "We had a keyboard player with us since 1996, (and that was) great in a lot of ways, but... maybe it made us lose sight of when we used to practise together in our living room," he later told *Uncut*. This stripped down approach meant that guitars and drums rather than Omnichords and synthesisers were the order of the day. "If you looked at our lead-off singles since 2001," said Bradfield, "hardly any of them had any kind of punk rock influence in them. 'The Love Of Richard Nixon' actually sounded like Pat Metheny. We just thought, 'Fuck, let's just go for it.'"

Given these initial sessions had gone well, the temptation to charge straight into the studio and begin recording was exceedingly high. Nonetheless, the band had already made a promise to both themselves and their audience that a break was in order, and both Bradfield and Wire were committed to promoting solo projects. Therefore, actual recording was delayed until March 2006, when the Manics plus producers Dave Eringa and Greg Haver again flew to Ireland's Grouse Lodge Studios in pursuit of lost greatness. "I'm not saying it was a real return to roots," Bradfield later confirmed, "but it was a return to using your first idea, rather than chasing the second or third one, like on *Lifeblood*. Sometimes it's nice to just disengage your brain."

As always, the majority of the group listened to old albums for inspiration. In James' case, this meant digging out The Skids, Aerosmith, Mott The Hoople and The Jeff Beck Group's ever potent Sixties releases *Truth* and *Beckola*. "Those were the kind of records I always used to practise to," he told journalist Robin Turner on the group's website. "They were the kind of people who were never ashamed to play a solo." Wire, meanwhile, concentrated on the likes of The Clash's *Give 'Em Enough Rope*, Hole's *Celebrity Skin*, various Alice Cooper records and The Who's 1973 classic *Quadrophenia*. "That record was a big lyrical influence," he said, "the way Pete Townshend reconnected with his audience. (Before that) he was convinced he had completely bamboozled Who fans to the point that people didn't understand what the band were about, which is I think, what *Lifeblood* did with our fans." Ever the reductionist, Sean Moore was more interested in re-connecting with the realities of his original contribution to the band's sound than the influences that helped shape it. "I was just thinking about what I'd have done when we were first in the band, just keeping it really simple... I just tried to be me when I was 21 again."

Following additional recording slots at Cardiff's Stir Studios and East London's Strongroom, the Manics found themselves with some 30 songs on tape. They then began the brutal job of whittling these down to a concise 10 track collection, a process Nicky Wire likened to "reducing ourselves to a pile of rubble" at the time. But when final mastering took place under the guidance of Howie Weinberg at New York's Masterworks complex, the band were left with just 38 minutes of music and an equal amount of high hopes and troubling fears: "If this one doesn't make our audience happy, then perhaps we should call it a day," Wire reasoned. "But luckily, I think we might have pulled it off..."

The case for the plaintiff was proved beyond all reasonable doubt in April, 2007 with the release of the Manics' first official single in over two years. Entitled 'Your Love Is Not Enough', the song was undoubtedly the group's best work since *Everything Must Go* and a breath of fresh air in comparison with the drab ordinariness of *Lifeblood*. 'Your Love Is Not Enough' also featured the inestimable talents of The Cardigans' Nina Persson, who had agreed to duet with James over the tune's keening rock melody. "'Your Love...' was written as a duet from the off," Nicky later confirmed, "and it was a conversation in my head between me and Richey, trying to figure out what makes a country or a person gain some kind of contentment – is it love, democracy, hate, war, whatever." Wire also made clear that when he was putting together the song's call and response libretto, Persson was the only person he had in mind. "I'm a huge fan of her lyrics, I think the last two Cardigans albums are fucking amazing and she's written all the words. I genuinely believe there's some sort of spiritual connection, something happened with it – you know, it just did." For Nina herself, the opportunity to work with the Manics required little or no thought at all: "I only work with the people I want to and when I got the request, I said 'Yes' more or less immediately."

The mechanics of capturing Persson's contribution to the track were slightly more complex, with James Dean Bradfield travelling to the States to meet with the singer in a Manhattan studio. "We finished the record in Grouse Lodge and on that day Nick and Sean flew home to Wales and I flew to New York to get her vocal," he recalled. "Just watching somebody else sing one of our songs, there was something kind of valedictory about it. I was amazed that she managed to get her head around some of our phrasing. She just completely did it in the first take, doing the old Frank Sinatra 'muso' thing of singing right behind the beat... Nina had obviously taken her time to think about it, and watching her sing, I wanted her to be in the band for more than one song. It was amazing, she's very talented, very cool."

The rest of the band only met The Cardigans' frontwoman when making a video for the single some months later. "She turned up completely on her own, had her own make-up, no trouble," said Nicky, "and then at the end... you just saw her disappearing on her own into the night with a can of Grolsch!" During downtime in filming the promo, Persson passed her time with one of her favourite hobbies: knitting. "Yeah, that was really sweet," Wire laughed. An already fine song greatly enlivened by the presence of one of pop's more distinctive vocalists, 'Your Love Is Not Enough' hopped to number two in the UK charts on April 30, paving the way for the Manics' new album, *Send Away The Tigers* just a week later.

The title of the band's eighth studio release took its perplexing title from legendary Sixties British comedian and noted depressive and alcoholic Tony Hancock, who used the phrase 'Send away the tigers' to describe how he felt when on a drinking binge. A long time fan of Hancock's sour musings on life, Wire used to tune in to repeats of his radio shows with Richey Edwards while at university: "Yeah, Richey was a big fan too. (We) used to listen to *Hancock's Half Hour* at Swansea University." Committing suicide in 1968 after a spell of depression brought on by a downturn in his career and further TV failures in Australia, Tony Hancock left behind a sad note saying "Things went wrong too many times". As already evidenced, this quote struck a chord with Edwards, who quoted it more than once in press interviews.

As with almost all of Wire's lyrics, *Send Away The Tigers* had secondary and tertiary meanings, the phrase also referencing a controversial incident during the Iraq war in 2003 when a battle between invading forces and the Republican guard resulted in a number of animals escaping from Baghdad zoo. When the fighting concluded, American soldiers used the compound for the site of a party, resulting in one of their number trying to pet a still caged Bengal tiger. When the animal finally turned on the man, severely mauling his arm, one of his colleagues shot it. For Nicky, there were obvious associations between Tony Hancock's doomed attempts to free himself from bad professional choices and the soldiers' irresponsible actions when supposedly liberating a country. Wire also managed to connect UK Prime Minister Tony Blair's decision to sanction the Iraq invasion and Hancock's choice to sack his writing team – an action that ultimately destroyed his career. "These decisions haunt (you) forever," Nicky later said.

Once one got beyond the complexities of the album's title, the rewards were a joy to behold. Unlike *Lifeblood*, where confusion often reigned and the Manics sounded tired of themselves, *Send Away The Tigers* was crisp and full of life – melodies soaring rather than choking in a swamp of excessive instrumentation. This stripped back, frills-free musical approach seemed to agree especially with Sean Moore, whose stick work on 'Underdogs', 'Indian Summer' and 'Rendition' was a master class in understated percussion. Bradfield was also on top form, his vocal delivery never clearer, his guitars seldom more fiery. And with 'Winterlovers', Nicky Wire ended nearly two decades of sending up his own talents by playing a short, but very pleasing bass solo. Determined to re-assert their songwriting credentials, the Manics had ensured *Send Away The Tigers* was an album full of potential anthems. In addition to the title track and the infuriatingly catchy 'Your Love Is Not Enough', 'Autumnsong' and 'I'm A Patsy' sounded even more heroic on record than they did when first debuted live at Manchester Arena in December 2006. However, this choice to pursue 'the huge chorus' was theatrically overplayed on 'Winterlovers', which, with its choir of shouted "Na Na Na"'s, threatened to push the song into Bon Jovi territory. Still, it was a small complaint that fell away when faced with other pleasing moments such as the Clash-like rockabilly stylings of 'Imperial Bodybags' and the ever- ascending 'The Second Great Depression'.

When it came to writing lyrics to accompany *Send Away The Tigers'* big-boned approach, Nicky Wire had far from let down the side, his subject matter as varied as the songs were melodic. Re-embracing politics as strong source material, 'Rendition' found Wire pointing an accusatory finger at a US policy that allowed CIA operatives to extradite terrorist suspects to parts of the world where strong-arm interrogation techniques were still allowed. 'Imperial Bodybags', on the other hand, took pity on the tragedy of British and American families who saw their dead sons and daughters returning from a senseless war in the cadaver pouches of the title: "Disposable children wrapped in home-made flags, imperial body bags..."

'I'm A Patsy' was also partially motivated by political themes. As with 'Send Away The Tigers' Nicky had liberated the title from another more famous phrase, this time spoken by Lee Harvey Oswald, the man accused of assassinating US President John Kennedy in November 1963. When questioned as to his involvement in Kennedy's murder, Oswald had answered "I'm just a patsy", implying that he was a small cog in a much larger conspiracy. Taken with Oswald's words and the meaning behind them, Wire extended 'I'm A Patsy' into a wider examination of the role the stooge plays in affairs of the heart.

When Nicky stepped away from matters of state, his lyricism was equally effective. With 'Indian Summer', the Manics' scribe found himself swimming back into the same waters that had floated 'A Design For Life', his words extolling the virtues of comradeship and hope as an antidote to despondency and scepticism. 'Autumnsong' was even more intimate, as Wire recalled his feelings of first love as a teenager: "I needed a lot of regressive therapy for that." 'Underdogs' was also a love song of sorts, but one dedicated to the band's longstanding, sometimes frustrated, but always faithful supporters: "This one's for the freaks, you're so beautiful..." The tune, which had been made available as a free download on the Manics' website some weeks before *Send Away The Tigers*' release was emblematic of the group's desire to again regain the respect of their fan base after years of navel-gazing. "The album," Nicky later admitted, "was about us really trying to reconnect with our audience." As the record came to an end, one more possible mistake was excised with a 'hidden' cover of John Lennon's 'Working Class Hero'. After 17 years thinking about it, the group finally signalled that they were perhaps less than happy that Lennon's days had ended so senselessly after all.

Housed in an upbeat sleeve that presented two teenagers in fancy dress walking toward a camera held by photographer Valerie Phillips, *Send Away The Tigers* was a fine antidote to years of underwhelming performances. Presenting the Manics as re-invigorated, musically relevant and eager to please, the album was justly rewarded with a number two placing in the UK charts when released on May 7, 2007, falling just 690 copies short of the much coveted top spot. "God, that was frustrating," Wire later remembered.

With two further Top 30 singles with 'Autumnsong' (number 10 on July 23) and 'Indian Summer' (number 22 on October 1), *Send Away The Tigers* also garnered the band some of the best reviews of their career. "We know the Manics to be a passionate, intelligent rock band," reasoned *Uncut*'s John Robinson, "and here, a great leap forward is made. Over a lean 38 minutes they actually show us, rather than simply telling us. The (group have) reconnected with their finest tuneful moments, and created some great anthemic rock." For *NME*, the story was very much the same: "In many ways, *Send Away The Tigers* is the quintessential Manics album… It's the triumphant comeback of the year."

Though the group had once again reasserted their position as one of Britain's more important and enduring rock acts, there was still some trepidation on their part about returning to the stage after a near two-year absence. After all, ticket sales for the *Lifeblood* tour had been distinctly sluggish, and as already evidenced, their original fan base was now heading into its forties – an age more traditionally associated with visits to the theatre than the concert hall. The Manics needn't have worried, as demand for their 27-date UK tour was high from both old school supporters and a new wave of admirers drawn to the trio following the just success of 'Your Love Is Not Enough'. In advance of these gigs, Wire had promised the Manics would proudly honour their salad days onstage, with sets drawing on all points of a near two-decade career.

They kept their word and during an opening night performance lasting over two hours at the Cambridge Corn Exchange on May 8 the Manics reanimated the likes of 'Born To End' and 'Slash N' Burn', dug up lost classics such as 'Faster' and 'Roses In The Hospital' while also making room for up-to-date anthems 'Your Love...' and 'Autumnsong'. Another worthy addition to the set came with James' spare, acoustic treatment of *The Holy Bible's* savage 'Yes'. Standing centre stage clad in a red T-shirt, Bradfield appeared temporarily transported while singing Richey Edwards' caustic ode to the hypocrisies and indignities surrounding prostitution: "He's a boy, you want a girl so tear off his cock, tie his hair in bunches, fuck him, call him Rita if you want..." Of equal surprise was the fact that it was sometimes difficult to hear James above a crowd shouting these words right back at him: "'Yes' is the greatest lyric I've ever sung," he later confirmed.

As the tour rolled on, there were occasional difficulties to negotiate. Nicky for instance, who had taken to wearing a patch honouring progressive rock titans Rush on his Navy jacket, came a cropper over his broader dress sense at a bad tempered gig in Preston. Temporarily abandoning his new suited and booted image for the thrills offered by a miniskirt, some drunken types rewarded his choice by throwing their pint glasses at him, resulting in a badly cut leg. The injury joined an already torn calf muscle. Bradfield also found himself in the wars, sustaining a twisted knee after a particularly vigorous bout of onstage exercise. Nonetheless, the band's UK trek continued with a homecoming concert in Wales and an emotional return to London's Astoria Theatre, a venue where Richey had played his last gig with the group on December 21, 1994 and a place the Manics had avoided until now. Bradfield marked the occasion by dedicating 'Faster' to the "Genius of Mr. Edwards".

Another more potentially hazardous return came on August 13, 2007 when the Manic Street Preachers found themselves back among the not so very fresh fields of Glastonbury. Always a hit or miss affair for the band, previous highlights had included a very drunk Richey Edwards reeling around the stage in 1994 and a badly timed, but exceedingly funny reference to "bypasses" and "shitholes" from Nicky Wire. The Manics also had to endure what James Dean Bradfield had taken to calling "Crappergate", when the group's private Portaloo had threatened to destabilise socialism itself. "We've had a chequered history with this festival," James told *NME* with some understatement before their show, "... and I'm feeling scared." As with the tour itself, such worries proved unfounded, with the band turning in an assured performance of new and old tunes, before being joined onstage by a brown cardigan-wearing Nina Persson for a lively rendition of 'Your Love Is Not Enough'.

The *Send Away The Tigers* tour progressed throughout much of 2007, seeing the Manics roll across Sweden, Germany and Turkey on the festival circuit, before taking a short break in advance of several pre-Christmas shows that included a well-received gig at Cardiff International Arena on December 6. For Nicky Wire, who had recently moved from Wattsville to Newport after his home address was made public by the press, playing so close to home allowed him the luxury of seeing more of his new son, Stanley McCarthy. After a day's break to catch up with family and change nappies, the band concluded their near eight months on the road with further appearances at Birmingham's NIA and a two night stop off at London's Brixton Academy before a final gig at the Brighton Centre on December 14. Obviously in a festive mood, the Manics ended the year by posting the lyrically acerbic, though musically jolly 'Ghost Of Christmas' on their website. Essentially a composite of Wizzard's 'I Wish It Could Be Christmas Every Day' and Slade's 'Merry Christmas

Everybody' plus brass stabs and a fast moving guitar solo, 'Ghosts...' was the happiest sounding release of their musical life.

Of course, the Manic Street Preachers had every reason to be joyful. *Send Away The Tigers'* inspired songwriting and stout commercial performance had marked the end of six years of uncertainty and frustrating artistic choices, reuniting the band with their collective muse and core audience. Acting as a reset device, the album had washed away memories of *Lifeblood*, and in so doing, cleansed the Manics of any previous sins in the public eye. In short, hard work and a return to core principles had brought back the love of fans and critics alike. The latter was first confirmed when esteemed rock magazine *Q* awarded the band 'Best Track' for 'Your Love Is Not Enough' at the end of 2007. Not to be outdone, *NME* presented the Manics with their 'Godlike Genius' award on February 28, 2008 at a star-filled ceremony in the Indigo Theatre within London's cavernous O2 building.

Of all the honours foisted upon the group over the years, this was perhaps one of the most important. As teenagers in Blackwood, they had pored over every page of the publication, not always agreeing with the contents, but always returning for more the following week. "*NME* is what I grew up with," Wire told the paper, "and for all its faults, it still means a lot to me." Over the Manics' near two decades in the spotlight, *NME* had followed the band's ups and downs with almost microscopic intensity. Alongside *Melody Maker*, it had essentially launched the quartet's assault on the masses, captured 4Real, lauded their eventual triumph with *The Holy Bible* and supported their dignified return with *Everything Must Go*. In recent years, however, relations with the Manics had grown more fractious, the rock weekly taking issue with sub-standard product and questioning the group's continued relevance. But even during the lean times, Bradfield had kept faith: "Even when they were criticising us... hated us, I still kept reading." Evidently, staff at *NME* had also kept listening.

The Manic Street Preachers were presented with their *NME* award by Britain's only undefeated boxing champion – the still very Welsh Joe Calzaghe – following a barrage of video tributes from the likes of New Order's Peter Hook and rock pundits Zane Lowe and Jo Whiley. Though a filmed contribution from now untouchable pop goddess

Kylie Minogue refused to work due to a glitch, Steve Lamacq's recorded testimony brought back memories of a time when the group were still a four piece and had drawn blood to prove their credibility. "Richey's not here today," Wire said as he accepted the honour on behalf of the band, "but we fucking love him to bits, he was one of the greatest boys I ever knew..." As the Manics played a post-awards set at the O2 Arena that saw them walk onstage to the sound of leopard-skin wearing bagpipers, duet with Catatonia's Cerys Matthews on 'Your Love Is Not Enough' and end their night covered in glitter singing 'A Design For Life', it was difficult to guess what might be next for them.

Commercially re-established, artistically re-invigorated and critically re-embraced, their return from the wilderness was now complete. "We just learned to accept our true nature," admitted James Dean Bradfield, "just admit what we are... a punk rock'n'roll band." With few battles left to fight, the Manics chose to honour one final debt by dusting off an old journal and letting its words live again.

Chapter Twenty Three

Return Of The Beautiful Boy

The early spring of 2008 saw the Manic Street Preachers back in the charts, though this time via an exceedingly circuitous route. In love with new soul/pop chanteuse Rihanna's recent R&B hit 'Umbrella,' the band had recorded their own version of the track for inclusion on *NME Awards 2008*, a CD given away free with the music paper on February 27. Pleased with the results, the Manics then made 'Umbrella' available via iTunes as a download one week later, though they did not intend it to be viewed as a proper single release. However, as it was technically chart eligible, 'Umbrella' found its way to number 47 in the UK, further prompting an 'Acoustic' and 'Grand Slam' remix of the number that, with the original, were soon gathered together under the title 'Umbrella EP'. "That song is fucking genius," Wire said at the time.

'Umbrella' may well have charted considerably higher had the Manics still been on the road at the time, but following their *NME* honour, the group had gone to ground in search of new ideas. In a display of typical complexity, Wire, Bradfield and Moore had reacted to their ascent to 'God-like' status with a mixture of humility and confusion, the fact that they were again critically lauded causing them to feel something must be wrong. "It's a Welsh thing," offered Nicky. In fact, during early rehearsals, the band found themselves completely turning away from the winning anthems present on *Send Away The Tigers* in favour of stark, angular sounds not unlike those that ended up forming the backbone of *The Holy Bible*. Though Bradfield occasionally tempered such enthusiasms by peppering the sessions with some acoustic guitar, emphasis remained firmly placed on the scratching rather than the soothing.

With several ideas committed to tape, the Manics returned to the road following a circuit of festivals throughout the UK and Europe during the summer of 2008. Long time fans of Nirvana, the group took pride in supporting Dave Grohl's Foo Fighters at City of Manchester Stadium on June 2 in front of a crowd of 57,000, before setting off for Germany, Poland, Ireland and Russia, among others.

Their European responsibilities behind them, they then flew back to England for their fifth appearance at the Reading Festival on August 23. Opening proceedings with James' shout of "Hello, do you want to go 'Faster'?", the Manics offered their supporters a brisk and varied set that included a strong cover of Nirvana's 'Pennyroyal Tea' and a storming version of 'La Tristesse Durera' dedicated to Richey Edwards. The group – now permanently augmented onstage by additional guitarist and keyboard player – concluded their slot with the familiar double header of 'Motown Junk' (introduced with a snippet from The Supremes' 'Baby Love') and 'A Design For Life'. "We're a bunch of grumpy bastards a lot of the time so this is just what we needed," Bradfield said before walking offstage and onto the Leeds Festival the very next day.

Three weeks later, the band found themselves doing the honouring rather than being honoured when they played a short set at the 'Forever Heavenly Festival', held in London's Royal Albert Hall. A celebration of Heavenly Records' "18 years at the top" as an independent record company, the weekend event featured performances by the label's recent successes including Beth Orton, Magic Numbers and Doves, for whom the Manics had agreed to open on September 14. A strange, but exciting evening that saw the group perform the six songs they had originally recorded while at Jeff Barrett's small, but highly influential label, Wire was more than a little amused as they rattled through 'Starlover' for only the second time in two decades. "You can tell that me and Richey were 19 when we wrote those lyrics," he laughed onstage. "You have to make a fool of yourself when you're young." As one listened to the song's sub-Rolling Stones chorus "Starlover, you're just a souvenir," it was difficult not to agree with him, though Edwards' line "Leper cult disciples of a still born Christ" retained its ability to raise an eyebrow regardless of how many years had passed.

With benefit of hindsight, there were signs that the Manic Street Preachers might have been looking to their past to inform their future during 2008. The admissions regarding new harder-edged, more abrasive material had been one such symbol; increased references to days gone by and the performance of older material at their gigs being two further possibilities. But the announcement posted on the group's website on November 4 still carried with it a sense of mild astonishment. According to Nicky Wire, the Manics were currently in the studio recording their ninth album, its title either to be *I Know I Believe In Nothing But It Is My Nothing* or *Journal For Plague Lovers*. Working with them on the record was none other than Steve Albini, famed for his recordings with Helmet, The Pixies, The Breeders, PJ Harvey and most notably, Nirvana's final album, *In Utero*. In line with Albini's preferred methods, songs were being cut live to tape using old style analogue techniques rather than employing digital technology, a process Wire referred to as "No safety nets... daunting, but invigorating."

The disc, Wire confirmed, would be released in 2009 and all lyrics used for the project had been written by Richey Edwards. The shock, as they say, had struck. Manics fans had known for 14 years that Richey had presented his fellow band members with a set of completed or at least part completed lyrics in the weeks before his disappearance. There were even rumours that more writings had been discovered among his effects at the Embassy Hotel in Bayswater. But aside from confirmation from Wire a decade before that there may be as many as 60 pieces in all, exact details had remained elusive. And so it would be for a little while longer, for sadder news was on the way.

Only 19 days after Nicky Wire confirmed that the Manic Street Preachers had finally begun putting music to the words Richey had left behind, journalists broke the news that Graham and Sherry Edwards had been granted the court's permission to legally declare their son 'presumed dead'. In their role of administrators, the Probate Registry of Wales would produce documentation to the effect that Richey had passed away "on or since" February 1, 1995 though the family's solicitor, David Ellis, made clear that 'presumed dead' was "not the same as an acceptance that (Richey) is dead". Further, Ellis clarified that the Edwards' decision was driven by an "acceptance" that it was time to put Richey's affairs in order. As a consequence of these actions, his parents would inherit his estate, which was reportedly worth £455,990. Having lived with the aftermath of their son's disappearance for so long, the Edwards family respectfully asked that their privacy be respected from now on.

The Manics maintained a dignified silence regarding the choice that Richey's parents had made, a stance no doubt helped by the fact that they were abroad at the time. Aside from a brief statement from Terri Hall on their behalf confirming that they were "happy to go with" the Edwards' wishes, and the sorrowful admission that "We all hope that Richey comes back one day... but it is no longer a realistic hope and if this offers some kind of closure, (they) would be content with that", nothing else was said. However, in the coming months both Wire and Bradfield would talk, albeit briefly, about their feelings: "It had no bearing, consciously or subconsciously," James later confirmed to Q. Nicky was of a like mind, though there was an admission that media summations of Richey's 'passing' were difficult to read: "It had no relevance other than legal. The only thing I found hard was the obituaries. It was the best press he'd ever had."

Indeed it was. Having held their proverbial tongues for so long regarding Richey's fate, the broadsheets, tabloids and rock press were now free to speak their minds, subsequently running a series of features, tributes and obituaries to the Manics' original talisman. Some of these were accurate and pleasing to read, others less so. But almost all sought to present Edwards as "one of the tormented", a supremely gifted, yet troubled soul who had retained his mystery even beyond legal definitions of death. "A handsome, gaunt man," wrote *The Guardian*, "Richey Edwards embodied similar qualities to the 18th-century poet Thomas Chatterton or, more recently, the rock singer Pete Doherty." For *The Daily Telegraph*, Richey was no less than "The lost figure of rock, the industry's equivalent of Lord Lucan." Elsewhere, *The Independent* reasoned

Richey to have been "A vital component of the Manic Street Preachers as its polemicist and co-lyricist... to the band's fans he was to assume the status of a British Kurt Cobain." Poet. Prophet. Lost boy. Fallen angel. Even the less honorific summations seemingly obsessed with cuts, abrasions, anorexia and alcoholism conceded that Edwards had "a quality and intelligence" seldom found in the watery fields of rock music. Amid such rarefied opinions, it was hard to remember the man behind the myth. Ultimately, it fell to the Manics to provide Richey Edwards with the most appropriate, fitting and lasting tribute he could expect, and even they had some trouble coming to terms with that responsibility.

When Edwards had originally handed the group his journal of writings in the form of an A4 Ryman ring binder file "with a picture of Bugs Bunny on the front" just three or so weeks before he went missing, the Manics had no reason to believe this might be any 'final offering'. "Because Richey had been so prolific at that point," Wire told Channel Four, "... there didn't seem to be any great significance to it. But he obviously wanted the lyrics to be used. You don't put that much work into a journal if you don't want it to be used. (With hindsight), not realising was probably quite stupid of us."

Following Edwards' disappearance, five of the more complete lyrics contained within the file had appeared on *Everything Must Go*. However, the emotional fall out of subsequent events and the band's change of direction made it harder than ever to return to the material that Richey had left behind.

Nicky had admitted to picking through the journal on various occasions, its combination of words, collages, Jack Kerouac and J.G. Ballard quotes making him feel it might even be worthy of publication as a book, but the idea remained undeveloped. Later comments from the Manics' bassist about the poetic, sometimes "ranting" and "way too personal" nature of some of the contents might have also cast light as to why he chose not to pursue this option. Bradfield had also often taken his photocopied version of Edwards' ideas out of the drawer, though he admitted in 2002 that "I put the stuff away again, thinking 'There's some great lyrics here, but I don't know if they could ever make an album'." The sheer weight of taking such a project forward, it seemed, was just too much. Six years later, things finally changed.

Following the success of *Send Away The Tigers*, Bradfield had hit a creative impasse of sorts. Not wanting to "contend with the thought of competing with ourselves or anyone else", he became reticent to write any commercially-themed songs at all, putting aside potential hit singles in favour of "the darker stuff". Feeling incomplete, and strangely torn by the group's recent triumphs, James mulled over what direction to take before hitting on an idea: "It became obvious to me that the way forward was putting music to Richey's lyrics." Yet, Bradfield felt uncertain how his bandmates would take to such a proposal when they were currently enjoying their greatest success in nearly a decade. Worried by the dilemma, but sure he was right, he spoke with Wire and Moore. Both agreed with the suggestion almost immediately.

For Nicky, such an important project required its own particular "wish list". Obviously, Richey's lyrics took care of wish number one. But Wire also remembered that in the months before Edwards went missing, he and his friend obsessed over the songs and sound of Nirvana's *In Utero*. A tape of the album had even been found in the stereo of the Silver Cavalier Richey abandoned near the Severn Bridge. To truly capture the atmosphere and intent of the words he had left behind, Wire felt it important that the Manics procure the services of *In Utero*'s producer, Steve Albini. "At that point," said Nicky, "we were well-rehearsed and disciplined, we had the concept in our heads and the words were the guiding light, so (Steve) was one of the final parts in the link." But securing the talents of one of the world's most in demand, meticulous and allegedly misanthropic studio craftsmen might prove difficult. Thankfully Albini, who knew little of the Manics' previous work or "baggage", found space in his diary, agreeing to oversee the recording process while old hand Dave Eringa produced the results.

The final piece in the puzzle was artist Jenny Saville, who had provided the haunting cover for 1994's *The Holy Bible*. Though a now well established and exceedingly busy figure within the British art scene, Saville was more than happy to work with the group again, providing them with a striking image that would stir up more than a little controversy. "We were lucky this time as she let us use another piece of art for the sleeve," Wire later said. "I guess you could say she's a beautiful person."

Having cut original demos for the project at their newly purchased Faster Recording Studios in Cardiff (the band had bought Stir Studios and appropriately re-named it in 2008), the Manics plus Albini and Eringa entered Monmouth's Rockfield complex in October to begin production work. As he had previously done with Nirvana Albini set a brisk pace, dispensing with established digital methods such as Pro-tools, in favour of cutting live performances straight to tape. For Wire, watching the man who had supervised the recording of 'Heart Shaped Box' and 'All Apologies' work on his own material was always going to be a distinct pleasure – even if rumours of his sometimes difficult nature had preceded him: "You know, I didn't expect to become long-time friends, but I really enjoyed Steve's company. We ended up doing 80% of the record with him."

November brought a short break in proceedings as the Manics honoured several overseas commitments. But while on a long-haul flight to Hong Kong, Nicky seemed to undergo something of an existential crisis. Racked with doubt regarding the validity of what they had undertaken, he spent 11 hours badgering Bradfield with variations on one sentence: "Let's burn the tapes." For James, Wire's dilemma was one he had wrestled with over and over again: "By that point, Nicky couldn't judge whether we were doing Richey's words justice – whether this was the right thing to do. And I also felt a massive responsibility to do Richey justice. It was like being a curator and (the lyrics) were an ancient antiquity. (The journal) was before laptops and Richey used to carry an Olivetti typewriter around."

Though the 'essential rightness' behind making *Journal For Plague Lovers* had hung like a proverbial millstone around the Manics' collective neck at times, they returned to recording after their Far East dates with renewed vigour. In fact, the locked down, if 'none more metal', environment of Rockfield Studios seemed to aid their cause. Leaving any questions outside the door, the band approached Richey's lyrics without tears or overt displays of emotion, determined to create songs strong enough to carry all the rich complexities present in his wordplay. "In a way," Nicky reasoned, "(The journal) was the purest form of writing I think he ever achieved because there's no other force other than him and his creativity… he'd not written these lyrics to get hits." Wherever possible, the group tried to honour Edwards' work by not tampering with what he had written. In the case of haiku-influenced short verses, this was possible. However, where he had produced more opaque prose over several sides of paper, Wire and Bradfield had little alternative but to edit some of the contents in order to bring out the best ideas. A horrible task, but necessary if James were to have any chance of singing the lyrics without risk to his vocal chords. "Just rising to the bloody minded challenge of it," he said. "Lists of words, full stops after full stops. It reminded me of some of my experiences on *The Holy Bible.*" While Steve Albini had to leave for America a little earlier than anticipated, the Manic Street Preachers and Dave Eringa worked on, eventually finishing the record in February 2009. And according to Nicky, they had discharged their responsibilities admirably. "Richey was a true original, a true star," he told *Q*. "And this album is like a tombstone. No, an obelisk."

Released on May 18, 2009, *Journal For Plague Lovers* thankfully lived up to Nicky Wire's Stanley Kubrick-referencing hyperbole. However, though the album contained the same number of tracks and with Jenny Saville's cover portrait of a young girl's blotched face – her eyes confused, her expression vacant – the same arresting imagery, this was no black-eyed sequel to *The Holy Bible*. Instead, the Manics had crafted a musical landscape to suit Richey Edwards' lyrical preoccupations after the firestorms of 1994 had faded into the quieter, more resigned behaviours exhibited before his disappearance. "Richey's lyrics are different to *The Holy Bible*," Nicky told *NME* at the time. "There is a sense of more calm. It's like he's been through the process of doubting everything and questioning everything. And the conclusions he's reached, they're not particularly happy, but they are... rational."

Hence the music of *Journal For Plague Lovers*, while still caustic and razor sharp at times, did not display the same overwhelming intensity of *The Holy Bible,* the Manics more content to create occasional pandemonium than lasting carnage. That said, tracks like 'Peeled Apples', 'She Bathed Herself In A Bath Of Bleach' and 'Pretension/Repulsion' certainly drew inspiration from the same sonic sources the band had turned to in 1994, recalling the work of Nirvana, Killing Joke and Magazine. Additionally, 'Marlon J.D.' could easily have been a ... *Bible* outtake while 'All Is Vanity' resembled a companion piece to 'Mausoleum'. Yet, tunes such as 'Jackie

Collins Existential Question Time', 'Journal For Plague Lovers' itself and 'Me And Stephen Hawking' all displayed a lighter musical touch, referencing the likes of The Skids' 'Circus Games', The Pixies and early Eighties Rush. "Actually, the guitars on '... Stephen Hawking' are a tribute to The Minutemen," James later said.

Elsewhere, the tone was even more reflective, with the gentler hues of 'This Joke Sport Severed' actually reminiscent of the alternative folk/ country performers Wilco and the sadly missed Elliott Smith. There were also moments of genuine, albeit heartrending, tranquillity. 'Facing Page: Top Left' for instance, was an acoustically themed first cousin to 'Small Black Flowers That Grow In The Sky', while 'Doors Closing Slowly''s opening verses lulled the ear before waves of dissonance finally took hold. Seldom exceeding three minutes in length, brilliantly recorded and produced by Steve Albini and Dave Eringa, and immaculately performed by the Manics, the songs of *Journal For Plague Lovers* were a genuine treat. But their true worth could only be revealed in how well they accompanied the lyrics of Richey Edwards.

As ever before, the obsessions, preoccupations and passions Edwards had committed to paper in the months leading up to his disappearance were often breathtaking in their complexity: a collision of ideas so intricately rendered and riddled with potential meanings one was left genuinely tired after viewing them. According to Wire, Richey had been reading six books a week while writing the journal he left behind, a way of passing time during the night in the face of continued insomnia. This was evident in the lyrics of ... *Plague Lovers* as random observations circled in close proximity to penetrating insights. Sometimes, the results defied traditional analysis, or fell away into incomprehension, but there was no doubting Edwards' determination to capture the source of his fascinations. "I just love the insane ambition of Richey's intellect," Nicky later confirmed.

Even after Wire had trimmed back some of the contents, apportioning definitive meanings to Richey's lyrics on ... *Plague Lovers* without access to the man himself was difficult if not impossible, a fact the band were only too willing to concede. "Sometimes the record is like listening to Richey speaking in tongues," said Bradfield. But certain themes appeared clear or at least extremely familiar. With 'Peeled Apples', Edwards had referenced his earlier interest in geometrical forms within nature, the creation of seamless circles, babies' eyes and infinite figures still a source of endless fascination for him. "Richey was obsessed with the perfect circle," Nicky told *NME*'s Emily Mackay. "Van Gogh's figure eight, all that stuff. It was kind of a recurring thing that he never got to grips with."

Meanwhile, 'Marlon J.D.' again touched on Edwards' concerns regarding the perils of vanity and his particular absorption with Hollywood's original Method acting king, Marlon Brando. Borrowing a line or two from Brando's 1967 movie *Reflections In A Golden Eye* to make his point, Richey underlined the actor's wilful abandonment of his own attractiveness in favour of the comforts of obesity and dissolute living. As for the reference 'J.D.' in the song's title, theories still abound, though it may have referred to Brando's role as a juvenile delinquent in *The Wild One* or perhaps another Edwards influence, J.D. Salinger, the author/recluse responsible for *Catcher In The Rye*. The theme of distorted beauty was also present on 'Pretension/Repulsion', which mentioned *Une Odalisque*, a painting by the 19th century French artist Jean Ingres depicting a female nude with oddly extended proportions. The canvas drew heavy criticism from critics when first displayed in 1814. Strangely – on perhaps in keeping with Richey's joy of confounding expectation – the more obviously titled 'All Is Beauty' only touched briefly on the inevitability of physical decay before veering off to extol the benefits of old school Communist Bloc authoritarianism.

On occasion, Edwards also indulged his gift for satire, combining high and low art for comedic effect. With 'Jackie Collins Existential Question Time', he cast himself in the role of a TV presenter asking an invisible audience to solve absurd moral dilemmas before inexplicably referencing a spoof badge worn by Seventies punks: "Mummy, what's a Sex Pistol?" 'Me And Stephen Hawking' was equally bizarre, Richey's words placing cult Eighties wrestler and veritable man mountain Giant Haystacks in Bombay while also drawing possible analogies between the wheelchair bound physicist and himself: "Oh the joy, me and Stephen Hawking, we laugh, we missed the sex revolution when we failed the physical." On 'Virginia State Epileptic Colony', sly satire turned to cold cynicism, with Edwards lambasting the US government for allowing a Virginia hospital to involuntarily sterilise some 4,000 'mentally unfit' patients between 1920 and 1972 "for the protection and health of the state."

Richey's own experience of institutional life may also have informed the lyrics to 'Journal For Plague Lovers', its subject matter reflecting on the potential threat of losing one's own personality while undergoing treatment for psychiatric illness. The distressing results of emotional disorder were undoubtedly present on 'She Bathed Herself In A Bath Of Bleach', which told the story of a girl so desperate to please her lover, she was willing to burn her own skin. "There were some people he met... in treatment," Bradfield told *NME*, "and I think he just digested... (their) experiences." A harrowing tale reminiscent of *The Holy Bible*'s '4st 7lb', 'She Bathed...' was one of the album's more shocking, but undoubted highlights.

The lyrics to *Journal For Plague Lovers*' remaining songs confirmed the calmer, almost resigned plateau that Nicky Wire referred to when referencing Richey Edwards' writings during his last months with the band. However, Wire was also strikingly correct that Edwards' more tranquil wordplay did not translate itself to joy. 'This Joke Sport Severed' found him seemingly abandon all hopes of lasting intimacy, while 'Facing Page: Top Left' also discarded the pursuit of perfection, its subtext alluding to how seeming cures to mental anguish could be as hazardous to the psyche as the pain they sought to subdue: "Central dissolves. Exceed doses. Subscribed. Cleansed. Boring." For James, this was one of the most demanding songs to perform. "I don't know," he said. "It was just incredibly hard to sing." 'Doors Closing Slowly' was another bleak testament to Edwards' skills as a lyricist, its overt religious imagery and sense of everlasting torment shocking to hear: "Silence is not sacrifice, crucifixion is the easy life..." Wire later described 'Doors...' as "A song of resignation... of no possibilities left."

Plague Lovers...' last track, 'William's Last Words', was also its most affecting. Described by Bradfield as "almost like... a Gerald Manley Hopkins poem or something," '... Last Words' had taken up over a side of Richey's journal, and read like a piece of prose. "Most of the words in the journal (resemble) lyrics," Wire told Channel Four, "but 'William's Last Words' was a page and a half of A4 paper, so the editing process was quite severe, and I felt quite contradicted by that." Reprinted in full within the sleeve notes, '... Last Words' was full of Forties-style language and references, and seemed on face value to present a performer saying goodbye to an audience or friends. In this respect, it resembled a lost page from the script of *The Entertainer*, a stage play and subsequent 1960 film starring Laurence Olivier as Archie Rice, an ageing comedian coming to the end of his career. "I know Richey loved *The Entertainer*," Wire conceded, "and it could be a giant analogy (to that)." However, given the sense of finality expressed in '... Last Words' it was hard not to draw parallels between Edwards' prose and his subsequent actions. "I don't really know if it's autobiographical," Nicky reasoned. "There are obviously analogies to Richey's situation. But it also seems like he's writing about a character. With the edit though, the words become so loaded with meaning. It's hard for me to sum up."

The obviously emotive nature of '...Last Words' presented the additional challenge of how Edwards' thoughts might best be set to music. Worried its impact might be ruined if recorded as a ballad, James was also concerned his sonorous vocal style might push the song towards overt sentimentality: "I worried I'd over-sing it." The solution was to have Nicky Wire take on the responsibility of lead vocalist. And it worked. By using Wire's sighing, half-spoken tones, 'William's Last Words' took on a tranquil, almost leafy air, Richey's original sentiments safely drifting away on a raft of acoustic guitars and understated orchestration. "There is a rational man speaking here," Nicky later said. "The decisions he's come to might be quite grim, but he has come to them rationally. He's been through the process of just doing everything, (yet) he seems to have found his own way of dealing with it. There's also a serenity there, I think. Whether it's autobiographical, who knows. But it seems (like) an apex of calmness had descended on the beautiful boy."

As the hidden track, 'Bag Lady', faded from speakers one would have to be churlish not to concede that with *Journal For Plague Lovers*, the Manic Street Preachers had provided a superb and fitting tribute to their lost friend. Avoiding the perils of reproducing *The Holy Bible*, they had instead crafted songs to ably fit the tone and tempo of Richey Edwards' words, providing an appropriate musical platform upon which they could be heard: "When I opened the journal... this 'Pandora's Box', I fell in love with him all over again as a lyricist," said Wire. "In a way,

Plague Lovers... is a tribute album to someone we love, dearly respect and all those other clichés."

Entering the UK charts at a highly respectable number three, *Journal For Plague Lovers* was heartily embraced by Manics supporters who had waited years to hear Edwards' gifts again. The album was also accorded blanket acclaim by critics acknowledging both the difficulties faced by the group in taking on the project and their successful execution of same. "It's a risky tactic," wrote *Uncut*'s Sam Richards. "Imagine if New Order announced they'd uncovered a new stash of Ian Curtis' lyrics and were planning to record *Unknown Pleasures Two*. (Yet), this is a brave, compelling record that stands shoulder to shoulder with the Manics' best. Even if they struggle to make another album as good as this without Richey's lyrics, *Journal...* provides a satisfying sense of closure." The *NME* went even further with their praise: "In years to come, this decade will be characterised as one of cheap and cowardly irony and obfuscation. (But) in the realm of alternative rock, Manic Street Preachers will be regarded as notable for successfully balancing sincerity and intelligence, regardless of what value those commodities hold at present. *Journal For Plague Lovers* is an outstanding album in its own right and is not *The Holy Bible*. But then again, what is?"

As the music press and broadsheets tried to invent new superlatives to describe the Manics' achievement, a bum note was struck elsewhere. In a frankly bizarre display of censorship, Jenny Saville's striking cover art for *...Plague Lovers* found itself wrapped up in a plain slipcase as four of the UK's major supermarket chains refused to stock the disc unless the offending image of a child's red-blotched face was covered. "You can have lovely shiny buttocks and guns everywhere in the supermarket on covers of magazines and CDs," protested Bradfield at the time, "but you show a piece of art and people just freak out." In its defence Sainsbury's music buyer, Nicola Williamson, said: "We felt that some customers might consider this particular album cover to be inappropriate if it were prominently displayed on the shelf." Though it may have ultimately affected their sales, it was nonetheless enjoyable to see the band again mired in controversy after years of more gentile behaviour.

As with nearly all their major releases, the Manics set off on a UK tour in support of *Journal For Plague Lovers*, opening at Glasgow's Barrowlands on May 25. From the start, the concerts proved difficult for Nicky who was nursing a prolapsed disc that threatened to go into spasm every night. However, if the condition caused him to be slightly less animated than usual or occasionally darkened his mood, it didn't affect the quality of music played on stage. Dispensing with established protocols, the band had split their set into two distinct parts. For the first half of proceedings, they played *...Plague Lovers* in its entirety, an intense and exciting idea that not only honoured the memory of Richey Edwards, but also allowed fans the visceral pleasure of hearing the album in a live environment. After a 10 minute break, the Manics reconvened for part two, presenting a more traditionally based list of songs plus the occasional curio. Though Wire felt the group might "live to regret" the decision to perform such a show, overall reaction from their supporters was extremely positive, the mix of the old, entirely new and somewhere in between a striking change to previous years.

Following dates at Llandudno's Cymru Arena, London's Roundhouse, Dublin's Olympia and Belfast's Ulster Hall, the Manics took a night off to receive *Mojo*'s 'Maverick Award' on June 12. A fitting tribute to acknowledge a career of often non-conformist choices and more than a few displays of eccentric bravery, the award was presented to them by Guns N' Roses' original bassist and current Velvet Revolver Duff McKagan. Having spent much of the late Eighties in thrall to *Appetite For Destruction*, this was also a chance for the band to meet one of their genuine heroes. A matter of 24 hours later, they were back onstage, this time appearing at Denmark's Broen Festival, before more gigs beckoned in Poland, Serbia and Scotland's T in the Park on July 11. Unfortunately, ill health struck Nicky Wire again, a bout of severe gastroenteritis forcing the Manics to pull out of a scheduled appearance at Japan's Nano-Mugen Festival. But he was more than sufficiently recovered by September 21, when after a break of nearly 10 years, the Manic Street Preachers finally returned to America and Canada for a 12-date tour.

Since their first visit to the States in 1992, much had been made by the music press of the band's consistent failure to break the US market. Bad luck and bad timing had obviously played their part. Early controversies, bear baiting album titles and lack of record company support were three more possible reasons. Public pronouncements regarding their dislike of the country and openly hostile lyrics won't have helped their cause either. But whether it was their unashamedly political image, Cuban alliances or the fact that the Americans simply didn't 'get' them, the Manics had always drawn a losing hand stateside. That said, they continued to enjoy an exceedingly small, but madly devoted fan base across the Atlantic, and for those who had kept faith, 2009's US jaunt was one of the few opportunities to witness the group in action.

As ever, the Manics' lack of profile across the Atlantic meant they appeared at intimate clubs rather than cavernous arenas. Dispensing with their two-part British show format, the band played a more varied set in venues such as Los Angeles' Avalon Club, Denver's Bluebird Theatre and Chicago's Metro before arriving at New York on October 7 – the city where they arguably enjoyed their highest profile. Unlike previous gigs, which saw attendances rarely rise above 300, Manhattan's Webster Hall had room for 1,500 at least, and the band's performance was well-attended. Now content to simply enjoy themselves rather than sow the seeds of global domination, the Manics provided a fine night's entertainment for the East Village onlookers, see-sawing between new gems such as 'Peeled Apples' and 'Jackie Collins Existential Question Time' and classic fare like 'La Tristesse Durera' and 'You Love Us'. *NME* described the event as "a band finally at peace with their past, and relishing the chance to give something special to the American fans who thought they might never get a chance to see the band again."

Just before the Manics began reacquainting themselves with their select, but ever faithful audience across the Atlantic, the group had issued an album of ... *Plague Lovers* remixes on September 15. A clever conceit that found British Sea Power, St. Etienne, Underworld and The Horrors putting their own personal touch to 'William's Last Words' and 'Doors Closing Slowly' among others, *Plague Lovers: The Remix Album* continued the Manics' tradition of encouraging other artists to re-interpret their material in sometimes odd, but mostly pleasing ways. This lasting affection for the collaborative process was again in evidence on October 23, when James Dean Bradfield and his guitar returned to London's Roundhouse to join genuine Welsh legend Shirley Bassey on stage for a sterling rendition of 'The Girl From Tiger Bay'. The track, which the Manics had written for Bassey's new all star disc *The*

Performance – joining other contributions/appearances from Pet Shop Boys, KT Tunstall and John '007' Barry – was a real treat, with James' yearning vocal perfectly complementing Shirley's much celebrated roar. Alongside Wire, Bradfield had also contributed to Patrick Jones' latest spoken word CD, *Tongues For A Stammering Time*, earlier in the year. Another challenging collection from Nicky's brother, *Tongues...* featured the additional talents of Billy Bragg, proving once and for all that time not only heals all wounds, but also unblocks most toilets...

In real terms, 2009 was the year that saw the Manic Street Preachers reclaim their place as one of the most important bands of their generation. *Journal For Plague Lovers* had been a compelling, noble work that offered a "dignified salute to an absent friend" while potentially introducing Richey Edwards' voice to a new generation. A typically brave choice, rewarded by strong sales and critical praise, the album had overturned nearly 14 years of rumour and intrigue with 13 tracks of lasting artistic excellence. More, it had also restored an essential equilibrium the band thought lost to time.

"The actual symmetry of the four of us," said Wire, "... *Plague Lovers* felt like we'd restored the balance." Their task achieved, the Manics again drew the curtains around themselves to start planning for the future.

Chapter Twenty Four

Nailed To History

2010 has so far brought little news of the Manic Street Preachers. Aside from the odd website post and confirmed festival appearance, the band have been resolutely out of the public eye, content to continue work on their 10th studio album, provisionally titled *It's Not War, It's The End Of Love.* According to Nicky Wire, the record will be "about the smaller things in life. Lyrically, I want it to be about the tiny things... that give joy, because amongst all the debris all that is left are the tiny things." In the past Nicky has been known to change his mind, so it all might turn out very differently. But as time has come to show, he has more than earned that right...

In June 2009 with the Manics in attendance, a plaque was unveiled on the wall of Cardiff's new £15 million public library. It read: "Libraries gave us power," the first line of the group's most popular song, 'A Design For Life'. At the ceremony, Wire, Bradfield and Moore were treated to a rendition of the tune by the Cardiff Arms Park Male Voice Choir, a moment Nicky described as "spine tingling". Twenty years before, such a scene would have been simply inconceivable. Yet, now it seems entirely fitting. In fact, against all expectation the Manic Street Preachers are firmly in danger of becoming national treasures: "But like most national treasures," James reasoned, "you always run the risk that at some point or another, people will turn against you."

Despite Bradfield's reservations, the Manic Street Preachers are unlikely ever to face the guillotine. In the course of a two decade career, they have shirked off their manifesto-waving origins to become a group respected for the sincerity of their approach and the honesty of their convictions. Not the attributes one would normally associate with most rock'n'roll bands, but given their contribution to the genre – and indeed beyond it – a fine tribute nonetheless. "We've always occupied our own space," Wire once reasoned. "We've never been part of any fashion, any trend, not Britpop, not Nu Rave, not Seattle. We exist within our own atmosphere and we stand for something that stands alone. That's why we have longevity."

At times, however, following the Manics' progress has been infuriating. The sloganeering, bear-baiting, endless contradictions and lapses in concentration have often acted as barriers to their cause, testing one's patience and causing much gritting of teeth. But these very irritations are also an essential part of their charm, aiding their knack of turning every seeming calamity into something potentially magnificent. "There's still some romance to us," said Bradfield. "We're comfortable with our own nature, we don't try and deconstruct ourselves to fit in with the present musical landscape. We're still a punk rock'n'roll band."

As the Manics would be the first to admit, at the heart of their story – past, present, future, was, is, will be – stands Richey Edwards. Now 15 years gone, the complexity of his character and fiercely intelligent lyricism continue to beguile, a fact strongly evidenced by *The Holy Bible*'s ever-growing reputation and the critical plaudits recently foisted upon *Journal For Plague Lovers*. Of course, it would also be a distinct pleasure to hear his opinions of recent times, from the rise of New Labour to the fall of the banks. But that opportunity is now surely gone, no matter how much one might cling to small hopes. Still, his work remains: ever fascinating, or as Nicky Wire might have it, everlasting.

That there will always be a place for the Manic Street Preachers, should they so wish it, seems assured. Though they failed in the pursuit of their original manifesto, their importance continues to grow, the band's musical integrity and capacity for reinvention acting as a template for other groups to follow. However, their example should not just be confined to music. As Wire has often proudly said, one of their great achievements has been to inspire people to read books they might never have read and engage with subjects they might have previously ignored. Study. Learn. Think. "Libraries gave us power" indeed.

A fine band who started their career as Generation Terrorists by berating their birthplace only to find themselves at the centre of its culture 20 years later, the Manics have proved the clichés right and come a long way. Deserving of their praise and sometimes their criticism too, they have defied expectations, survived tragedy, and by persisting, ultimately triumphed. Given the group's ability to adjust their perspective, modify their sound or simply confound expectation, it seems ridiculous to even speculate where the future will take them. But as Richey Edwards once said: "The future. That's a big nasty word, isn't it?"

Manic Street Preachers. Born to boredom. Nailed to history.

Acknowledgements

In the course of researching this book, I consulted the following television/radio networks, programmes, magazines, newspapers and (now ceased) publications. In some cases, I extracted previously published interview material. For this, I remain grateful to: *NME, Melody Maker, Q, Mojo, Kerrang!, The Face, Record Collector, Sounds, Smash Hits, The Guardian, The Times, The Daily Telegraph, The Independent, The Sun*, the BBC (including a special thanks to BBC Wales), *Vox, Uncut, Esquire, Hot Press, Select, Deadline, Lime Lizard, Volume*, MTV, Channel Four, VH1, *Rapido, Viva Zwei, The Beat, CD UK, Much Music, Observer Music Monthly, The Quietus, Planet Rock* and *Snub TV*.

For providing additional source material, I'd like to offer my thanks and appreciation to the following individuals: Chris Heath, Adam Sweeting, Caitlin Moran, Jon Savage, John Niven, Emma Forrest, Nick Wise, Michael Heatley, Jabba, Vivian Campbell, Sylvie Simmons, Gary Crowley, Paul King, Sarah Cox, Steve Double, Emily Mackay, The Stud Brothers, Tom Hibbert, Ian Watson, Barbara Ellen, Simon Price, Martin Aston, Simon Price, Nils Neuman, Ted Kessler, John Niven, Andy Richardson, Peter Paphides, Tony Horkins, Tom Doyle, Richard Lowe, Taylor Parkes, Eduardo Sardinha, Phil Sutcliffe, Stuart Bailie, Steve Doherty, Greg Shilling, Cliff Jones, Niall Doherty, Stuart Maconie, Lucy O'Doherty, Sylvia Patterson, Amy Raphael, Dermot O'Leary, Martin Clarke, Jon Aizlewood, James McNair, Sam Richards, John Doran, and Dave Fanning.

I also must say kind thanks to the following websites, which alerted me to several published interviews and facts of which I had no prior knowledge: Manic Street Preachers, MANICS.NL, Removables, This

Is Yesterday, The Love Of..., The Last Of Richey Edwards?, Vision Blurred, Black Garden and The Runout Groove. Equally, I'd like to offer genuine appreciation to those who posted various Manics clips on You Tube. Another quick debt to be repaid: God bless the AA for getting me to Blackwood in one piece.

Now, some personal doffing of the cap. To Chris Charlesworth – once again, thanks for your support, continued patience and good humour. To Ben and Cathy: well, well. Congratulations, you two and all the best for the future. Where's my drink, by the way? To Rakesh and Demi: always a pleasure, thanks for the hospitality and you're welcome here any time. To Mr. Constantine: another year, another 15,000 cigarettes; pass on my good wishes to Chas, Gemma and Alan, who started the joke and must still be laughing.

As ever, to Messrs. Cutler, Kelly, Joseph, Robinson and Stewart – thank you, gentlemen, I'll see you in The Queens or on the terraces. And last but surely not least, my heartfelt thanks to Trish, for getting me through two jobs in one piece, making me laugh and keeping me sane. You're right, I am a lucky boy...

While writing this book, it became very clear how much support charities such as Missing People provide to families and friends when a loved one disappears. Obviously, such a charity needs all the donations it can get. If you wish to donate to Missing People, here's the phone number and e-mail address: 020 8392 4521 and supporters@missingpeople.org.uk.

To the Manics: my enduring thanks and appreciation.

To Richey Edwards: thank you.

Discography

Singles
7", 10", 12", Cassettes, CDs and Downloads
(All UK releases unless otherwise stated)

Suicide Alley/Tennessee (I Get Low)
SBS 002 7" August 1989

New Art Riot/Strip It Down/Last Exit On Yesterday/Teenage 20/20
Damaged Goods YUBB 4 12" (1,000 copies with black & white label, 1,000 copies with various coloured labels) June 1990

New Art Riot/Strip It Down/Last Exit On Yesterday/Teenage 20/20
Damaged Goods YUBB 004 P 12" (3,000 copies on pink vinyl) 1990

New Art Riot/Strip It Down/Last Exit On Yesterday/Teenage 20/20
Damaged Goods YUBB 4 CD December 1991 (Re-issued July 1993 and September 1996)

Motown Junk/Sorrow 16/We Her Majesty's Prisoners
Heavenly HVN8 12 12" January 1991

Motown Junk/Sorrow 16/We Her Majesty's Prisoners
Heavenly HVN8 CD CD January 1991

You Love Us/Spectators Of Suicide
Heavenly HVN10 7" May 1991

You Love Us/Spectators Of Suicide/Starlover/Strip It Down (Live)
Heavenly HVN 10 12 12" May 1991

You Love Us/Spectators Of Suicide/Starlover/Strip It Down (Live)
Heavenly HVN 10 CD CD May 1991

Feminine Is Beautiful/New Art Riot/Repeat After Me
Caff CAFF 15 7" July 1991

Stay Beautiful/R.P. McMurphy
Columbia 657337 7 7" July 1991

Stay Beautiful/R.P. McMurphy/Soul Contamination
Columbia 657337 6 12" July 1991

Stay Beautiful/R.P. McMurphy/Soul Contamination
Columbia 657337 8 12" (Poster sleeve) July 1991

Stay Beautiful/R.P. McMurphy/Soul Contamination
Columbia 657337 2 CD July 1991

Stay Beautiful/R.P. McMurphy/Soul Contamination
Epic MANIC1 CD CD Re-issue September 1997

Love's Sweet Exile/Repeat
Columbia 657582 7 7" November 1991

Repeat (UK)/Love's Sweet Exile/Democracy Coma
Columbia 657582 6 12" November 1991

Repeat/Democracy Coma/Love's Sweet Exile/Stay Beautiful (Live)
Columbia 657582 8 12" (Limited edition) November 1991

Love's Sweet Exile/Repeat (UK)/Democracy Coma
Columbia 657582 2 CD November 1991

Love's Sweet Exile/Repeat (UK)/Democracy Coma
Epic MANIC2 CD CD Re-issue September 1997

You Love Us/A Vision Of Dead Desire
Columbia 657724 7 7" January 1992

You Love Us/A Vision Of Dead Desire/It's So Easy (Live)
Columbia 657724 6 12" (Limited edition) January 1992

You Love Us/A Vision Of Dead Desire/We Her Majesty's Prisoners/
It's So Easy (Live)
Columbia 657724 2 CD January 1992

You Love Us/A Vision Of Dead Desire/We Her Majesty's Prisoners/
It's So Easy (Live)
Epic MANIC3 CD CD Re-issue September 1997

Slash 'N' Burn/Motown Junk
Columbia 657873 7 7" March 1992

Slash 'N' Burn/Motown Junk
Columbia 657873 4 Cassette March 1992

Slash 'N' Burn/Motown Junk/Ain't Goin' Down
Columbia 657873 6 12" March 1992

Slash 'N' Burn/Motown Junk/Sorrow 16/Ain't Goin' Down
Columbia 657873 0 CD March 1992

Slash 'N' Burn/Sorrow 16/Ain't Goin' Down
Epic MANIC4 CD CD Re-issue September 1997

Motorcycle Emptiness/Bored Out Of My Mind
Columbia 658083 7 7" June 1992

Motorcycle Emptiness/Bored Out Of My Mind
Columbia 658083 4 Cassette June 1992

Motorcycle Emptiness/Bored Out Of My Mind/Under My Wheels (Live)
Columbia 658083 6 12" (Picture disc) June 1992

Motorcycle Emptiness/Bored Out Of My Mind/Crucifix Kiss (Live)/
Under My Wheels (Live)
Columbia 658083 9 CD June 1992

Motorcycle Emptiness/Bored Out Of My Mind/Crucifix Kiss (Live)/
Under My Wheels (Live)
Epic MANIC5 CD CD Re-issue September 1997

Theme From M★A★S★H (Suicide Is Painless)/Fatima Mansions: Everything I Do (I Do It For You)
Columbia 658382 7 7" September 1992

Theme From M★A★S★H (Suicide Is Painless)/Fatima Mansions: Everything I Do (I Do It For You)
Columbia 658382 4 Cassette September 1992

Theme From M★A★S★H (Suicide Is Painless)/Fatima Mansions: Everything I Do (I Do It For You)/Sleeping With The NME
Columbia 658382 6 12" September 1992

Theme From M★A★S★H (Suicide Is Painless)/Fatima Mansions: Everything I Do (I Do It For You)/Sleeping With The NME
Columbia 658382 2 CD September 1992

Little Baby Nothing (7" version)/Never Want Again/Suicide Alley
Columbia 658796 7 7" November 1992

Little Baby Nothing (7" version)/Never Want Again/Suicide Alley
Columbia 658796 4 Cassette January 1993

Little Baby Nothing (7" version)/Never Want Again/Dead Yankee Drawl/Suicide Alley
Columbia 658796 2 CD1 January 1993

Little Baby Nothing (7" version)/R.P. McMurphy (Live)/Tennessee (Live)/You Love Us (Live)
Columbia 658796 5 CD2 January 1993

Little Baby Nothing/Dead Yankee Drawl/Suicide Alley/Never Want Again
Epic MANIC6 CD CD Re-issue September 1997

From Despair To Where/Hibernation
Columbia 659337 4 Cassette June 1993

From Despair To Where/Hibernation/Spectators Of Suicide (Heavenly Version)
Columbia 659337 6 12" June 1993

From Despair To Where/Hibernation/Spectators Of Suicide (Heavenly Version)/Starlover (Heavenly Version)
Columbia 659337 2 CD June 1993

La Tristesse Durera (Scream To A Sigh)/Patrick Bateman
Columbia 659477 4 Cassette July 1993

La Tristesse Durera (Scream To A Sigh)/Patrick Bateman/Repeat (Live)/Tennessee
Columbia 659477 6 12" July 1993

La Tristesse Durera (Scream To A Sigh)/Patrick Bateman/What's My Name (Live)/Slash N' Burn (Live)
Columbia 659477 2 CD July 1993

Roses In The Hospital/Us Against You/Donkeys
Columbia 659727 7 7" October 1993

Roses In The Hospital/Us Against You/Donkeys
Columbia 659727 4 Cassette October 1993

Roses In The Hospital/OG Psychovocal Mix/OG Psychomental Mix/51 Funk Salute Mix/Filet-O-Gang Mix/ECG Mix/Album Version
Columbia 659727 6 12" October 1993

Roses In The Hospital/Us Against You/Donkeys/Wrote For Luck
Columbia 659727 2 CD October 1993

Life Becoming A Landslide/Comfort Comes
Columbia 660070 4 Cassette January 1994

Life Becoming A Landslide/Comfort Comes/Are Mothers Saints?
Columbia 660070 6 12" January 1994

Life Becoming A Landslide/Comfort Comes/Are Mothers Saints/Charles Windsor
Columbia 660070 2 CD January 1994

Faster/P.C.P.
Columbia 660447 4 Cassette May 1994

Faster/P.C.P./Sculpture Of Man
Columbia 660447 0 10" May 1994

Faster/P.C.P./Sculpture Of Man/New Art Riot (In E Minor)
Columbia 660447 2 CD May 1994

Revol/Too Cold Here
Columbia 660686 4 Cassette August 1994

Revol/Too Cold Here/You Love Us (Heavenly Version)/Life Becoming A Landslide (Live)
Columbia 660686 0 10" August 1994

Revol/Drug Drug Druggy (Live)/Roses In The Hospital (Live)/ You Love Us (Live)
Columbia 660686 5 CD August 1994

She Is Suffering (Edit)/Love Torn Us Under
Columbia 660895 4 Cassette September 1994

She Is Suffering/The Drowners (Live)/Stay With Me (Live)
Columbia 660895 0 10" September 1994

She Is Suffering (Edit)/She Is Suffering (Acoustic Version)
Columbia 660972 1 CD September 1994

She Is Suffering/Love Torn Us Under/The Drowners (Live)/Stay With Me (Live)
Columbia 660895 2 CD1 September 1994

She Is Suffering (Edit)/La Tristessa Durera (Scream To A Sigh) Vocal Mix/ La Tristessa Durera (Scream To A Sigh) Dub Mix/Faster Dub Mix
Columbia 660895 5 CD2 September 1994

A Design For Life/Bright Eyes (Live)
Columbia 663070 4 Cassette April 1996

A Design For Life/Mr. Carbohydrate/Dead Passive/Dead Trees & Traffic Islands
Columbia 663070 2 CD1 April 1996

A Design For Life/A Design For Life (Stealth Sonic Orchestra Version)/ A Design For Life (Stealth Sonic Orchestra Instrumental Version)/Faster (Vocal Mix)
Columbia 663070 5 CD2 April 1996

Everything Must Go/Raindrops Keep Falling On My Head (Live Acoustic Version)
Sony 663468 4 Cassette July 1996

Everything Must Go/Black Garden/Hanging On/No One Knows What It's Like To Be Me
Sony 663468 2 CD1 July 1996

Everything Must Go/ Everything Must Go (Chemical Brothers Remix)/ Everything Must Go (Stealth Sonic Orchestra Remix)/ Everything Must Go (Stealth Sonic Orchestra Version)
Sony 663468 5 CD2 July 1996

Kevin Carter/Everything Must Go (Acoustic)
Epic 663775 4 Cassette September 1996

Kevin Carter/Horses Under Starlight/Sepia/First Republic
Epic 663775 2 CD1 September 1996

Kevin Carter/Kevin Carter Busts Loose (Jon Carter Remix/Kevin Carter (Stealth Sonic Orchestra Remix)/ Kevin Carter (Stealth Sonic Orchestra Version)
Epic 663775 5 CD2 September 1996

Australia/A Design For Life (Live)
Epic 664044 4 Cassette December 1996

Australia (Edit)/Velocity Girl/Take The Skinheads Bowling/I Can't Take My Eyes Off You (Acoustic)
Epic 664044 2 CD1 December 1996

Australia (Edit)/Australia (Lionrock Remix)/Motorcycle Emptiness (Stealth Sonic Orchestra Remix)/Australia (Stealth Sonic Orchestra Version)
Epic 664044 5 CD2 December 1996

If You Tolerate This Your Children Will Be Next/Kevin Carter (Live)
Epic 666345 4 Cassette August 1998

If You Tolerate This Your Children Will Be Next/Prologue To History/Montana Autumn 78
Epic 666345 2 CD1 August 1998

If You Tolerate This Your Children Will Be Next/ If You Tolerate This Your Children Will Be Next (Massive Attack Remix)/ If You Tolerate This Your Children Will Be Next (David Holmes Remix)
Epic 666345 5 CD2 August 1998

The Everlasting/Small Black Flowers That Grow In The Sky (Live)
Epic 666686 4 Cassette November 1998

The Everlasting/Black Holes For The Young (Featuring Sophie Ellis-Bextor)/Valley Boy
Epic 666686 2 CD1 November 1998

The Everlasting/The Everlasting (Deadly Avengers Psalm 315 Remix)/ The Everlasting (Stealth Sonic Orchestra Remix)
Epic 666686 5 CD2 November 1998

You Stole The Sun From My Heart/If You Tolerate This Your Children Will Be Next (Live)
Epic 666953 4 Cassette March 1999

You Stole The Sun From My Heart/Socialist Serenade/Train In Vain (Live)
Epic 666953 2 CD1 Cassette March 1999

You Stole The Sun From My Heart/You Stole The Sun From My Heart (David Holmes Remix)/You Stole The Sun From My Heart (Mogwai Remix)
Epic 666953 5 CD2 March 1999

Masses Against The Classes/Close My Eyes/Rock And Roll Music
Epic 668530 1 10" January 2000

Masses Against The Classes/Close My Eyes/Rock And Roll Music
Epic 668530 2 CD January 2000

Found That Soul/The Masses Against The Classes (Live)
Epic 670833 7 7" February 2001

Found That Soul/Locust Valley/Ballad Of The Bangkok Novotel
Epic 670833 2 CD February 2001

So Why So Sad/You Stole The Sun From My Heart (Live)
Epic 670832 4 Cassette February 2001

So Why So Sad/So Why So Sad (The Avalanches Remix)/Pedestal
Epic 670832 2 CD February 2001

Ocean Spray/Little Trolls/Ocean Spray (Ellis Island Sound Remix)
Epic 671253 4 Cassette June 2001

Ocean Spray/Groundhog Days/Just A Kid/Ocean Spray (Video)
Epic 671253 2 CD1 June 2001

Ocean Spray (Version)/Ocean Spray (Live)/Ocean Spray (Kinobe Remix)/Ocean Spray (Medicine Remix)/Ocean Spray (Video Havana)
Epic 671253 5 CD2 June 2001

Let Robeson Sing/Fear Of Motion/Let Robeson Sing (Ian Brown Remix)/Let Robeson Sing (Felix Da Housecat Remix)
Epic 671773 6 12" September 2001

Let Robeson Sing/Masking Tape/Didn't My Lord Deliver Daniel (Traditional)/Let Robeson Sing (Video)
Epic 671773 5 CD1 September 2001

Let Robeson Sing/Let Robeson Sing (Ian Brown Remix)/Let Robeson Sing (Felix Da Housecat Remix)/Let Robeson Sing (Havana Live)/Let Robeson Sing (Havana Video)
Epic 671773 5 CD2 September 2001

There By The Grace Of God/Automatik Teknicolour/It's All Gone/There By The Grace Of God (Video)
Epic 673166 2 CD1 October 2002

There By The Grace Of God/Unstoppable Salvation/Happy Ending
Epic 673166 5 CD2 October 2002

There By The Grace Of God (Video)/There By The Grace Of God (St. Etienne Remix)/There By The Grace Of God (Starecase Remix)/ Multimedia
Epic 673166 7 DVD October 2002

The Love Of Richard Nixon/Everyone Knows/Nobody Cares
Epic 675342 1 CD1 October 2004

The Love Of Richard Nixon/Everything Will Be/Askew Road/ The Love Of Richard Nixon (Video)
Epic 675342 2 CD2 October 2004

The Love Of Richard Nixon (Video)/Quarantine (In My Place Of) Short Film/Voodoo Polaroids
Epic 675342 9 DVD October 2004

Empty Souls (Version)/All Alone Here
Epic 675610 1 CD1 January 2005

Empty Souls (Version)/No Jubilees/Litany/Empty Souls (Video)
Epic 675610 2 CD2 January 2005

Empty Souls (Video)/Dying Breeds (Short Film)/Failure Bound
Epic 675610 9 DVD January 2005

Underdogs
Columbia MSP 03 7" (One side only) and Download March 2007

Your Love Alone Is Not Enough/Fearless Punk Ballad
Columbia 8869707561 7 7" April 2007

Your Love Alone Is Not Enough/Boxes & Lists
Columbia 8869707560 2 CD1 April 2007

Your Love Alone Is Not Enough/Love Letter To The Future/Welcome To The Dead Zone/Little Girl Lost/(Video)
Columbia 8869707561 2 CD2 April 2007

Your Love Alone Is Not Enough/Your Love Alone Is Not Enough (James Solo Acoustic)/Your Love Alone Is Not Enough (Nina Solo Acoustic)
Columbia (Download) April 2007

Autumnsong/The Vorticists
Columbia 8869711829 7 7" July 2007

Autumnsong/Red Sleeping Beauty
Columbia 8869711830 2 CD1 July 2007

Autumnsong/The Long Goodbye/Morning Comrades/1404
Columbia 8869711829 2 CD2 July 2007

Autumnsong/La Tristesse Durera (Scream To A Sigh) Live/ Autumnsong (Acoustic Version)/Autumnsong/Autumnsong
Columbia (Download) July 2007

Indian Summer/You Know It's Going To Hurt
Columbia 8869715934 7 7" October 2007

Indian Summer/Anorexic Rodin
Columbia 8869715933 2 CD1 October 2007

Indian Summer/Heyday Of The Blood/Foggy Eyes/Lady Lazarus
Columbia 8869715932 2 CD2 October 2007

Indian Summer/Indian Summer (Demo)
Columbia (Download) October 2007

Umbrella/Umbrella (Acoustic)/Umbrella (Grand Slam Mix)
Download March 2008

Albums
(All UK Releases unless stated otherwise. The majority of titles are available for download)

Generation Terrorists
Slash N' Burn/Nat West-Barclays-Midland-Lloyds/Born To End/ Motorcycle Emptiness/You Love Us/Love's Sweet Exile/Little Baby Nothing/ Repeat (Stars And Stripes)/Tennessee/Another Invented Disease/ Stay Beautiful/So Dead/Repeat (UK)/Spectators Of Suicide/Damn Dog/ Crucifix Kiss/Methadone Pretty/Condemned To Rock 'n' Roll
Columbia 471060 1/4 Double LP and Cassette February 1992

Columbia 471060 9 Picture Disc Double LP June 1992
Columbia 471060 2 CD February 1992
Columbia 471060 0 CD Picture CD June 1992

Gold Against The Soul
Sleepflower/From Despair To Where/La Tristesse Durera (Scream To A Sigh)/Yourself/Life Becoming A Landslide/Drug Drug Druggy/Roses In The Hospital/Nostalgic Pushead/Symphony Of Tourette/Gold Against The Soul
Columbia 4740649 1/4 LP and Cassette June 1993
Columbia 4740649 1 LP Picture Disc June 1993
Columbia 4740649 2 CD June 1993

The Holy Bible
Yes/Ifwhiteamericatoldthetruthforonedayitsworldwouldfallapart/Of Walking Abortion/She Is Suffering/Archives Of Pain/Revol/4st 7lb/Mausoleum/Faster/This Is Yesterday/Die In The Summertime/The Intense Humming Of Evil/P.C.P.
Epic 477421 1/4 LP and Cassette August 1994
Epic 477421 9 LP Picture Disc August 1994
Epic 477421 2 CD August 1994

The Holy Bible (10th Anniversary Edition)
Disc One:
Yes/Ifwhiteamericatoldthetruthforonedayitsworldwouldfallapart/Of Walking Abortion/She Is Suffering/Archives Of Pain/Revol/4st 7lb/Mausoleum/Faster/This Is Yesterday/Die In The Summertime/Intense Humming Of Evil/P.C.P./Intense Humming Of Evil (Live)/4st 7lb (Live)/Yes (Live)/Of Walking Abortion (Live)
Disc Two: (US Mix, Demos and Radio 1 Session)
Yes (US mix)/Ifwhiteamericatoldthetruthforonedayitsworldwouldfallapart (US mix)/Of Walking Abortion (US mix)/She Is Suffering (US mix)/ Archives Of Pain (US mix)/Revol (US mix)/4st 7lb (US mix)/Mausoleum (US mix)/Faster (US mix)/This Is Yesterday (US mix)/Die In The Summertime (US mix)/Intense Humming Of Evil (US mix)/P.C.P. (US mix)/ Die In The Summertime (Demo)/Mausoleum (Demo)/

Of Walking Abortion (Radio 1 Evening Session)/She Is Suffering (Radio 1 Evening Session)/Yes (Radio 1 Evening Session)
Disc Three: The Holy Bible DVD
Faster (Top Of The Pops/ Faster (Butt Naked)/ PCP (Butt Naked)/She Is Suffering (Butt Naked)/4st 7lb (MTV Most Wanted)/She Is Suffering (MTV Most Wanted)/Faster (Glastonbury Festival 1994)/P.C.P. (Glastonbury Festival 1994)/Yes (Glastonbury Festival 1994)/Revol (Reading Festival 1994)/Faster (US video)/Judge Yr'self (Video)/Yes (New Film)/Band Interview (30 mins)
Epic 518872 3 CD/DVD December 2004

Everything Must Go
Elvis Impersonator: Blackpool Pier/A Design For Life/ Kevin Carter/Enola/ Alone/ Everything Must Go/Small Black Flowers That Grow In The Sky/ The Girl Who Wanted To Be God/Removables/Australia/Interiors (Song For Willem De Kooning)/Further Away/No Surface All Feeling
Sony 483930 1/4 LP and Cassette May 1996
Sony 483930 2 CD May 1996

Everything Must Go (10th Anniversary Deluxe Edition)
Disc One:
Elvis Impersonator: Blackpool Pier/A Design For Life/Kevin Carter/ Enola/Alone/Everything Must Go/Small Black Flowers That Grow In The Sky/The Girl Who Wanted To Be God/Removables/Australia/ Interiors (Song For Willem De Kooning)/Further Away/No Surface All Feeling/Enola/Alone (Live)/Kevin Carter (Live)/Interiors (Song For Willem De Kooning) (Live)/Elvis Impersonator: Blackpool Pier (Live)/ Everything Must Go (Live)/A Design For Life (Live)/A Design For Life (Stealth Sonic Orchestra Remix)
Disc Two: Unreleased Material, Demos and Rarities
Dixie (Previously Unreleased)/No Surface All Feeling (Demo)/Further Away (Demo)/Small Black Flowers That Grow In The Sky (Demo)/ No One Knows What It's Like To Be Me (Demo/Australia (Acoustic Demo)/ No Surface All Feeling (Acoustic Demo)/Interiors (Song For Willem De Kooning) (Acoustic Demo)/The Girl Who Wanted To Be God (Acoustic Demo)/A Design For Life (First Rehearsal)/Kevin

Carter (First Rehearsal)/Mr Carbohydrate/Dead Trees And Traffic Islands/Dead Passive/Black Garden/Hanging On/No One Knows What It's Like To Be Me/Horses Under Starlight/Sepia/ First Republic/ Australia (Stephen Hague Production)/The Girl Who Wanted To Be God (Stephen Hague Production)/Glory Glory (Previously Unreleased)
Disc Three: DVD including Documentary, Live Appearances and Promos
Making Of Everything Must Go (45min Documentary)/Small Black Flowers That Grow In The Sky (Later With Jools Holland)/Australia (Later With Jools Holland)/A Design For Life (TFI Friday)/No Surface All Feeling (live at Reading)/Everything Must Go (Saturday Live)/A Design For Life (The Brits)/Enola/Alone (Manchester NYNEX Arena)/ Small Black Flowers That Grow In The Sky (Manchester NYNEX Arena)/The Girl Who Wanted To Be God (Manchester NYNEX Arena)/ Further Away (Video)/Home Movie (15min Documentary)/A Design For Life (Video)/Everything Must Go (Video)/Kevin Carter (Video)/ Australia (Video)
Epic 483930 3 CD November 2006

This Is My Truth Tell Me Yours
The Everlasting/ If You Tolerate This Then Your Children Will Be Next/ You Stole The Sun From My Heart/Ready For Drowning/Tsunami/ My Little Empire/ I'm Not Working/You're Tender And You're Tired/ Born A Girl/Be Natural/Black Dog On My Shoulder/Nobody Loved You/S.Y.M.M.
Epic 491703 1/4 LP and Cassette September 1998
Epic 491703 6 CD September 1998

Know Your Enemy
Found That Soul/Ocean Spray/Intravenous Agnostic/So Why So Sad/ Let Robeson Sing/Year Of Purification/Wattsville Blues/Miss Europa Disco Dancer/Dead Martyrs/His Last Painting/My Guernica/The Convalescent/Royal Correspondent/Epicentre/Baby Elian/Freedom Of Speech Won't Feed My Children
Epic 501880 1/4 LP and Cassette March 2002
Epic 501880 2 CD March 2002

Lifeblood
1985/The Love Of Richard Nixon/Empty Souls/A Song For Departure/I Live To Fall Asleep/To Repel Ghosts/Emily/Glasnost/Always/Never/Solitude Sometimes Is/Fragments/Cardiff Afterlife
Sony 518885 1 LP November 2004
Sony 518885 2 CD November 2004

Send Away The Tigers
Send Away The Tigers/Underdogs/Your Love Alone Is Not Enough/Indian Summer/Second Great Depression/Rendition/Autumnsong/I'm Just A Patsy/Imperial Bodybags/Winterlovers
Columbia 8869707563 1 LP May 2007
Columbia 8869707563 2 CD May 2007

Journal For Plague Lovers
Peeled Apples/Jackie Collins Existential Question Time/Me And Stephen Hawking/This Joke Sport Severed/Journal For Plague Lovers/She Bathed Herself In A Bath Of Bleach/Facing Page Top Left/Marlon JD/Doors Closing Slowly/All Is Vanity/Pretension/Repulsion/Virginia State Epileptic Colony/William's Last Words
Columbia 8869752059 1 LP May 2009

Journal For Plague Lovers
Peeled Apples/Jackie Collins Existential Question Time/Me And Stephen Hawking/This Joke Sport Severed/Journal For Plague Lovers/She Bathed Herself In A Bath Of Bleach/Facing Page Top Left/Marlon JD/Doors Closing Slowly/All Is Vanity/Pretension/Repulsion/Virginia State Epileptic Colony/William's Last Words/Bag Lady (hidden track)
Columbia 886975205 9 2 CD1 May 2009

Journal For Plague Lovers: Special Limited Edition
Peeled Apples/Jackie Collins Existential Question Time/Me And Stephen Hawking/This Joke Sport Severed/Journal For Plague Lovers/She Bathed Herself In A Bath Of Bleach/Facing Page Top Left/Marlon JD/Doors Closing Slowly/All Is Vanity/Pretension/Repulsion/Virginia State Epileptic Colony/William's Last Words/Bag Lady (hidden track)

A bonus disc, containing all original demos for the songs featured on *Journal...* comes with this Limited Edition. Additionally, it is packaged with a 36 page booklet containing Richey Edwards' original lyrics, artwork and collages.
Columbia 8869752059 2 CD2 May 2009
For completists, an EP, featuring remixes of various *...Plague Lovers* tracks by The Horrors, Underworld, Fuck Buttons and Underworld is available for download.

Compilations and Collections
(All UK releases unless otherwise stated)

Forever Delayed
A Design For Life/Motorcycle Emptiness/If You Tolerate This Your Children Will Be Next/La Tristesse Durera (Scream To A Sigh)/There By The Grace Of God/You Love Us/Australia/You Stole The Sun From My Heart/Kevin Carter/Tsunami/The Masses Against The Classes/From Despair To Where/Door To The River/Everything Must Go/Faster/Little Baby Nothing/Theme From M★A★S★H (Suicide Is Painless)/So Why So Sad/The Everlasting/Motown Junk
Sony 509551 9 CD October 2002

Forever Delayed: Special Edition
A Design For Life/Motorcycle Emptiness/If You Tolerate This Your Children Will Be Next/La Tristesse Durera (Scream To A Sigh)/There By The Grace Of God/You Love Us/Australia/You Stole The Sun From My Heart/Kevin Carter/Tsunami/Masses Against The Classes/From Despair To Where/Door To The River/Everything Must Go/Faster/Little Baby Nothing/Theme From M★A★S★H (Suicide Is Painless)/So Why So Sad/The Everlasting/Motown Junk
Bonus Disc: Remixes
La Tristesse Durera (Scream to a Sigh)(The Chemical Brothers Remix)/If You Tolerate This Your Children Will Be Next (David Holmes Remix)/Tsunami (Cornelius Remix)/So Why So Sad (The Avalanches Remix)/Faster (The Chemical Brothers Remix)/If You Tolerate This Your Children Will Be Next (Massive Attack Remix)/Kevin Carter

(Jon Carter Remix)/You Stole the Sun from My Heart (David Holmes Remix)/Tsunami (Stereolab Remix)/Let Robeson Sing (Ian Brown Remix)/The Everlasting (Stealth Sonic Orchestra Vocal Remix)/You Stole the Sun from My Heart (Mogwai Remix)/A Design for Life (Stealth Sonic Orchestra Remix)/Ocean Spray (Kinobe Remix)
Sony 509551 9 (5095519000) CD October 2002

Lipstick Traces: A Secret History Of Manic Street Preachers
Disc One:
Prologue To History/4 Ever Delayed/Sorrow 16/Judge Yr'self/Socialist Serenade/Donkeys/Comfort Comes/Mr Carbohydrate/Dead Trees And Traffic Islands/Horses Under Starlight/Sepia/Sculpture Of Man/Spectators Of Suicide/Democracy Coma/Strip It Down (Live)/Bored Out Of My Mind/Just A Kid/Close My Eyes/Valley Boy/We Her Majesty's Prisoners
Disc Two:
We Are All Bourgeois Now/Rock And Roll Music/It's So Easy (Live)/ Take The Skinheads Bowling/Been A Son/Out Of Time/Raindrops Keep Falling On My Head (Warchild version)/Bright Eyes (Live)/Train In Vain (Live)/Wrote For Luck/What's My Name (Live)/Velocity Girl/Can't Take My Eyes Off You/Didn't My Lord Deliver Daniel/Last Christmas (Live)
Sony 512 386 2 CD July 2003

Solo Singles and Albums

James Dean Bradfield

That's No Way to Tell a Lie/Lost Again
Columbia 82876861587 4 7" July 2006

That's No Way To Tell A Lie/Don't Look Back
Columbia 82876861592 8 CD1 July 2006

That's No Way To Tell A Lie/Kodachrome Ghosts/I Never Wanted Sunshine/That's No Way To Tell a Lie (Video)
Columbia 82876861582 9 CD2 July 2006

An English Gentleman/Victory And Defeat On The Kendon Hill
Columbia 8869700318 7 7" September 2006

An English Gentleman/Silver Birch Bonfire Blues
Columbia 8869700543 7 7" September 2006

An English Gentleman/Days Slip Away/Summer Wind/An English Gentleman (Video)
Columbia 8869700318 2 CD September 2006

The Great Western
That's No Way To Tell A Lie/An English Gentleman/Bad Boys And Painkillers/On Saturday Morning We Will Rule The World/Run Romeo Run/Still A Long Way To Go/Émigré/To See A Friend In Tears/Say Hello To The Pope/The Wrong Beginning/Which Way To Kyffin
Columbia 8287685727 2 CD July 2006

Nicky Wire
Break My Heart Slowly/Casual/Glam
Red Ink Enola ENOLAT 001 7" September 2006

Break My Heart Slowly/Derek Jarman's Garden
Red Ink Enola ENOLAD 001 CD September 2006

I Killed The Zeitgeist
I Killed The Zeitgeist/Break My Heart Slowly/Withdraw / Retreat/Goodbye Suicide/The Shining Path/Bobby Untitled/You Will Always Be My Home/So Much For The Future/Stab YR Heart/Kimino Rock/Sehnsucht (Neu Song)/(Nicky Wire's) Last/Everything Fades/Ocean Rain (Hidden Track)
Red Ink Enola LC15010 CD September 2006

Videos and DVDs
(All UK releases unless stated otherwise)

Everything Live
Introduction: A Design For Life (Stealth Sonic Orchestra Mix)/Everything Must Go/Faster/Kevin Carter/La Tristesse Durera (Scream To A Sigh)/Roses In The Hospital/Elvis Impersonator: Blackpool Pier/Motown Junk/Motorcycle Emptiness/No Surface All Feeling/This Is Yesterday/Australia/A Design For Life/You Love Us

Directed by Dick Carruthers, *Everything Live* features edited highlights of the Manics' performance at Manchester NYNEX on May 24, 1997. Also containing interviews and documentary footage, it was originally released on VHS but has never been upgraded to DVD for the UK market. However, a Japanese DVD version is available from the usual outlets.
SMV 2007592 VHS September 1997

Leaving The 20th Century: Manic Street Preachers Cardiff Millennium Stadium 1999/2000
Introduction/You Stole the Sun from My Heart/Faster/Everything Must Go/Tsunami/The Masses Against the Classes/The Everlasting/Kevin Carter/La Tristesse Durera (Scream To A Sigh)/Rock And Roll Music/Ready For Drowning/Of Walking Abortion/No Surface All Feeling/Motown Junk/Motorcycle Emptiness/Can't Take My Eyes Off You/Small Black Flowers That Grow In The Sky/Australia/Elvis Impersonator: Blackpool Pier/You Love Us/Stay Beautiful/If You Tolerate This Your Children Will Be Next/A Design For Life/Closing credits
DVD extras include interview footage, performances of 'If You Tolerate This Your Children Will Be Next' and 'Ready For Drowning' recorded at Château De La Rouge Motte, France, lyrics in both English & French and a full discography.
SMV 201126 9 DVD April 2000

Louder Than War: Manic Street Preachers Live In Cuba
Found That Soul/Motorcycle Emptiness/Kevin Carter/Ocean Spray/If You Tolerate This Your Children Will Be Next/Let Robeson Sing/The Year Of Purification/Baby Elian/Miss Europa Disco Dancer/Wattsville Blues/You Love Us/Motown Junk/Australia/Rock And Roll Music
Bonus live tracks on the DVD include 'So Why So Sad', 'A Design For Life', 'The Masses Against the Classes', 'You Stole The Sun From My Heart', 'Raindrops Keep Falling On My Head' and 'Freedom Of Speech Won't Feed My Children'. A Cuba documentary, tour diary, interviews, a photo gallery, discography and 'easter eggs' are also included on the disc.
Epic 201471 9 DVD 2001

Forever Delayed: Manic Street Preachers – The Greatest Hits DVD
Motown Junk/You Love Us (Heavenly Recordings Version)/You Love Us (Sony Music Version)/Stay Beautiful/Love's Sweet Exile/Slash 'N' Burn/Motorcycle Emptiness/Little Baby Nothing/Theme From M.A.S.H. (Suicide Is Painless)/From Despair to Where/La Tristesse Durera (Scream To A Sigh)/Roses In The Hospital/Life Becoming A Landslide/Faster/Revol/She Is Suffering/A Design For Life/Everything Must Go/Kevin Carter/Australia/If You Tolerate This Your Children Will Be Next/The Everlasting/You Stole The Sun From My Heart/ Tsunami/The Masses Against The Classes/Found That Soul/So Why So Sad/Ocean Spray/Let Robeson Sing/There By the Grace of God
Bonus Remixes and Extras:
La Tristesse Durera (Scream To A Sigh)(The Chemical Brothers Remix)/ If You Tolerate This Your Children Will Be Next (David Holmes Remix)/Tsunami (Cornelius Remix)/So Why So Sad (The Avalanches Remix)/Faster (The Chemical Brothers Remix)/If You Tolerate This Your Children Will Be Next (Massive Attack Remix)/Kevin Carter (Jon Carter Remix)/You Stole The Sun From My Heart (David Holmes Remix)/Tsunami (Stereolab Remix)/Let Robeson Sing (Ian Brown Remix)/The Everlasting (Stealth Sonic Orchestra Vocal Remix)/You Stole The Sun From My Heart (Mogwai Remix)/A Design For Life (Stealth Sonic Orchestra Remix)/Ocean Spray (Kinobe Remix)/Mitch Ikeda Photo Gallery and Discography
Epic 201776 9 DVD November 2002